DISCOURSE ON
AFRICANA STUDIES

DISCOURSE ON AFRICANA STUDIES

JAMES TURNER AND PARADIGMS OF KNOWLEDGE

Edited by

SCOT BROWN

DIASPORIC AFRICA PRESS, INC.
NEW YORK

This book is a publication of

DIASPORIC AFRICA PRESS

NEW YORK | WWW.DAFRICAPRESS.COM

Copyright © Diasporic Africa Press 2016

Library of Congress Control Number: 2014938289

ISBN-13 978-1-937306-21-2 (pbk.: alk paper)

Credit: The editor and publisher gratefully acknowledge the permission granted to reproduce the copyright material in this book, including permission to publish photos belonging to Dr. James Turner and the John Henrik Clarke Africana Library at the Africana Studies and Research Center. Every effort has been made to trace copyright holders and to obtain their permission for the use of copyright material. The publisher apologizes for any errors or omissions and would be grateful if notified of any corrections that should be incorporated in future reprints or editions of this book.

Front Cover: James Turner in the John Henrik Clarke Africana Library, March 1990. Photograph by Charles Harrington, Cornell University Photography. Division of Rare and Manuscript Collections, Cornell University Library.

CONTENTS

ACKNOWLEDGEMENTS

Thanks to Dr. James and Janice Turner for giving us a legacy to move Africana Studies forward. Many people helped to make this project happen. Regrettably, space does not allow for listing all of them. Kwasi Konadu, executive director of Diasporic Africa Press, is a visionary scholar and publisher—without his brilliance, dedication and generosity this book would not have been realized. My mentor, Dr. Robert Harris—also a longtime colleague of Dr. Turner—provided critical feedback and insight. Thanks to Brian Sales for planting the seeds for this work back in the early 1990s. Family, mentors, friends, elders and colleagues were so very helpful: James and Maxine Brown, Nikki Brown and Kimberly Brown; Eric Acree, Ernie Allen Jr., Ned Alpers, Delores Aldridge, Carol Anderson, Christine Barksdale, Tony Bolden, John Bracey, Greg Carr, Bettye Collier-Thomas, James Conyers, Margo Crawford, Leroy Davis, Sarita Davis, V.P. Franklin, Jonathan Gayles, Ken Glover, Cheryl Harris, Eldred Harris, Errol Henderson, Robert Hill, Lawrence Jackson, Leonard Jeffries, Charles Jones, Sundiata Cha-Jua, Robin Kelley, Shelby Lewis, Thabiti Lewis, James Mtume, Kalonji Olusegun, Sharon Powers, Sonia Ramsey, Kendahl Radcliffe, Kalamu ya Salaam, Daryl Scott, James Stewart, Brenda Stevenson, Nikki Taylor, Akinyele Umoja, Dr. Margaret Washington and Fanon Che Wilkins. Special thanks to the research assistants who worked on this project during its formative stages: Sung Choi, Jessica Harris and Tiffany Jones.

I am extremely grateful to all the authors of chapters and quotations for this volume: Leslie Alexander, Jared Ball, Monique Bedasse, Anthony Browne, Rosa Clemente, Kimberlé Crenshaw, Ron Daniels, Jonathan Fenderson, LaTasha B. Levy, Dylan Rodríguez, Agyei Tyehimba, Baye Adolfo Wilson. Their work in this book and—more importantly, in the struggle for Black consciousness, social justice and liberation—embody the spirit of Dr. Turner's Africana mission.

Finally, special thanks to those persons and scholarly institutions who supported this project with generous contributions of funds and resources: Allesandro Duranti, Mark Sawyer and Scott Waugh; the Ralph J. Bunche Center for African American Studies (UCLA), the Center for the Study of Race, Ethnicity and Politics (UCLA), the James Weldon Johnson Institute for the Study of Race and Difference (Emory University), and the National Council for Black Studies.

Scot Brown

FOREWORD: REFLECTIONS ON THE LIFE AND LEGACY OF DR. JAMES TURNER

RON DANIELS

Four decades ago at the height of the Black consciousness and Black Power movements, the National Council for Black Studies was founded as a mechanism to ensure the character and quality of Black Studies programs that were being created at colleges and universities across the nation in response to the demands of Black students. As a direct outgrowth of the movement for dignity, justice, equality, and empowerment of Black people, the vision and mission of Black Studies was "education for liberation." Therefore, a central focus of Black Studies was to address the "mis-education" of students of African descent by providing a critical understanding of their history and culture, an African-centered framework for examining the world, and the knowledge and tools to become change agents for an oppressed people. One of the visionary architects and leaders of this movement was a gifted young scholar-activist, Dr. James Turner, founder and director emeritus of the highly acclaimed Africana Studies and Research Center at Cornell University.

One of the highlights of the 35th Annual Conference of the National Council for Black Studies in 2011 was a Plenary Session honoring Dr. Turner, chaired by Dr. Alan Colon of Dillard University. The session was entitled "James Turner, Africana Studies and the Making of the Discipline." I was honored to join (former students) Dr. Scot Brown (UCLA), Professor Kimberlé Crenshaw (UCLA/Columbia), and longtime friends and colleagues Dr. Delores Aldridge (Emory University) and Dr. James Stewart (Penn State University) in paying tribute to the life and legacy of this pioneer of the Black Studies movement and one of the most formidable intellectuals (activist-oriented theorist) of the last half century. At a time when Black/Africana Studies programs are being challenged, demoted, or absorbed, it was an opportune occasion to reflect on the legacy of a scholar-activist whose ideas and praxis provided crucial underpinnings for the discipline.

My remarks on this auspicious occasion were offered through the prism of my relationship as a close advisor, confidant, friend, brother, and comrade in the struggle for more than four decades. Virtually every major decision about my life's work as a scholar-activist and organizer has been made with the advice and counsel of Dr. James Turner, a brother who relentlessly and uncompromisingly utilized his enormous talents for the uplift of African people. In that vein, I recall a conversation about the "state of the race" we had some years ago during a visit to Cornell in which he suggested that what we need are more brothers and sisters who will be "of the race and for the race." He noted that we now have an unprecedented number of Black people with a wide range of skills, talent, and resources, but far too many lack the consciousness and commitment to use what they have to advance our people. For as long as I have known Dr. Turner, he has been not simply of the race but unapologetically for the race.

Dr. James Turner in his office at the Africana Studies and Research Center, 2015.

Dr. Turner's racial and social consciousness was forged early in life. The son of what he describes as a "laboring class" family, he grew up in the housing projects in lower Manhattan, New York. The experience of growing up in a close-knit family struggling to subsist and improve their quality of life left an indelible impression on him, not the least of which was a deep and abiding respect for the strength and resiliency of Black poor and working people and the importance of community. Though the Turners' abode was "downtown," James Turner was but a subway ride away from Harlem, the capital of Black America—here he would avail himself of the opportunity to observe the multidimensional culture of the post-

Renaissance period and listen to street-corner orators excoriating white supremacy and calling for the "redemption of the Negro people of the world." One such lecturer was Minister Malcolm X, whose incisive analysis and compelling orations would have a lasting impact on a young mind thirsty for knowledge. Equally important, Turner would have the privilege of being mentored by some of the great "race men" of the era, including the incomparable Dr. John Henrik Clarke.

I cite this background and these experiences because they would shape Turner's sense of purpose in life and his vision of education for the sons and daughters of Africa in the Americas, particularly what was taught in the academies of higher learning. Early on Turner decided that no matter what his station in life, he must be committed to "return to the source," to be immersed in the Black freedom struggle to liberate the masses of Black people from racial degradation, political repression, and economic exploitation. From this stance, it was only logical that he would view the demand for Black Studies as an extension of the Black freedom struggle.

When Black students at Cornell seized Willard Straight Hall in April 1969 as part of a movement to protest conditions on campus, they demanded the creation of a Black Studies institute to make the curriculum more relevant to the interests of Africans in America. When the administration acceded, Black students, who had heard Turner articulate his vision of education for liberation at a conference at Howard University, selected him to develop the Africana Studies and Research Center at Cornell. From that vantage point, Dr. Turner aggressively and skillfully began the task of erecting an institution that would mirror the concept of education for liberation and thereby become a model for similar programs and departments that were springing up across the country.

The first charge was to make clear to students, faculty, and the administration that Black Studies was not simply a short-term add-on to the curriculum as a concession to protest but would be an emerging discipline with a focus on innovative teaching, stellar research, and outstanding scholarship. The objective was to produce critical-thinking scholar-activists equipped with the knowledge, consciousness, and commitment to be of service to the Black community at some level. True to his vision of the academy connected to the community, Dr. Turner worked tirelessly to make the Africana Studies and Research Center (AS&RC) a resource for Black students on campus (whether they were enrolled in AS&RC classes or not), the Black community in the city of Ithaca, Black America, and the Pan-African world. Faculty, students, and staff from the AS&RC were often engaged in providing support for community development initiatives in Ithaca and on the front lines with residents when issues or struggles of vital concern to the community emerged. Under Dr. Turner's leadership, the AS&RC became a place/space where leading scholars, activists, and organizers gathered to informally analyze the state of the "movement" and discuss strategies for impacting the Black community. At a more formal level, for years the AS&RC convened the annual State of Black America Conferences, where students and community leaders from across the nation would come to take stock of the state of the Black condition in America and the world and to debate how best to advance the interests and aspirations of Black people.

In addition, Dr. Turner consistently strategized to find ways of utilizing the resources of the AS&RC to support various struggles in Black America and the Pan-African world, most often by bringing leaders of various movements to Cornell to deliver lectures or conduct workshops or by sponsoring significant events in various locations around the country. When Minister Louis Farrakhan was contemplating rebuilding the shattered Nation of Islam (NOI), on more than one occasion Dr. Turner invited him to lecture at Cornell. The lectures also provided an opportunity for Minister Farrakhan and Dr. Turner to share ideas about rebuilding the NOI into a progressive, non-sexist, non-personality-centered organization. The Harambee Singers of Atlanta, who needed support sustaining the Pan-African Work Center, were also frequent performers at Cornell.

Dr. Turner consciously sought to make the AS&RC an intellectual haven for movement activists/freedom fighters, a place for them to acquire additional data and information to inform their work, refine their skills, and retool to better engage the struggle on the front lines. Taking note of the fact that James Forman—who served as executive secretary of the Student Nonviolent Coordinating Committee (SNCC) during the historic Mississippi Freedom Summer of 1964—was virtually a forgotten figure to the younger generation, Dr. Turner arranged for him to matriculate at Cornell, where he secured a graduate degree in Africana Studies. Forman went on to receive his doctorate at the Union Graduate School. His stint at the AS&RC revived his stature as a venerable freedom fighter. When Cynthia McKinney lost her seat in Congress after a malicious campaign, there was a space at the AS&RC to share her knowledge and experience with students. When a battle-scarred Ron Daniels needed respite from the tensions and conflicts of the movement, I was able to bring my academic credentials and lived experiences to teach classes in Black Social and Political Thought and the Political Economy of Black America. In one of the most rewarding experiences of my life, I was able to interact with amazing students like

Kimberlé Crenshaw. And, like Minister Farrakhan, I was able to take advantage of time spent at Cornell to receive invaluable counsel and support from Dr. Turner.

Because of his pioneering role in founding the Black Studies movement and selfless utilization of the human and material resources of the AS&RC for community development efforts, Dr. Turner is one of the most trusted scholar-activists in the movement. As such he was called upon to chair and coordinate the North American Delegation to the Sixth Pan-African Congress in Dar es Salaam, Tanzania, in 1974. This was no easy task because of the range of brilliant minds, prominent movement leaders, and divergent ideological views among the participants. Under these circumstances, there was consensus that the leader for such a challenging task was Dr. James Turner. In that same spirit, as chair of the National Malcolm X Commemoration Commission, he was able to marshal the energy, enthusiasm, and experience of community-based organizations and leaders across the country to make 1990 "The Year of Malcolm X" a milestone success.

Dr. Turner is not only a trusted leader; he is widely recognized as one of the most brilliant analysts and lecturers of our time. Few scholar-activists can break down complex ideas and convey them to an audience with incisive insights and understandable language like Dr. Turner. He is a master at the podium, a progressive, African-centered analyst, advocate, and activist who uses his roots in family and community to connect with, inform, and inspire sisters and brothers from all walks of life to be "of the race and for the race." If you want clarity on an issue affecting people of African descent in the United States or the Pan-African world, movement folks know to call on Dr. James Turner.

As I remarked during the tribute to Dr. Turner at the NCBS Annual Conference, his legacy is enshrined in the multitude of students who have studied with him, the community struggles that have been empowered by his advice and support, the activists who have counted on and benefited from his counsel, and the institutions that bear the mark of the AS&RC as a sterling model of education for liberation.

PREFACE

SCOT BROWN

Discourse on Africana Studies: James Turner and Paradigms of Knowledge is both a reader and an introspective tribute, comprised of writings by James Turner and commentary from several of his former students. The book strives to underscore critical connections between multiple dimensions of Turner's legacy (as scholar, activist, institution-builder, teacher, and mentor), while also aiming to contribute to the growing historicized literature on the Black Studies movement of the late 1960s and early 1970s. In recent years, a number of monographs and studies have crafted synthetic overviews and case studies of the Black Studies movement and its transformative intervention on college campuses, school districts, and in communities throughout the United States.[1] Invariably, critical dialogue generated by these works calls for the production of new research on specific leaders, rank-and-file activists, teachers, organizations, and particular sites in this vast social movement. The contributors to this book hope to influence this early phase in Black/Africana Studies historiography and provide a resource for discourse on the future of the discipline.

This project is closely tied to my own intellectual journey, having studied at the Africana Studies and Research Center in its master's program. My first impression of Dr. Turner in 1990 came from watching a video recording of a lecture given at the Afrikan Poetry Theatre, a grassroots cultural center in Queens, New York. The video for sale was sitting on a shelf of VHS tapes at the Kitabu Kingdom bookstore in Rochester, New York. Kitabu owners, Gerald and Terry Chaka, were strong supporters of African-centered education and scholarship. They allowed patrons to preview or listen to taped lectures. Turner's talk on the systemic structure of racism was a cogent and piercing analysis—grounded in Black Nationalist theory yet delivered with an accessible clarity akin to that of a Malcolm X speech. The tape sat beside lectures and books by John Henrik Clarke, Maulana Karenga, Haki Madhubuti, Frances Cress Welsing, Marimba Ani, Molefi Asante, Na'im Akbar, Oba T'Shaka, Vivian Gordon, and Yosef Ben-Jochannan. Black Nationalist and African-centered scholars found popular interest in their works during the 1980s and 1990s. Incidentally, nearly all the authors mentioned above at the bookstore had spent significant time as lecturers and invited speakers at the Africana Studies and Research Center. I entered the Africana master's program in 1991, and remained closely connected to it thereafter while pursing doctoral studies in history at Cornell University under the direction of Dr. Robert Harris. By the early 1990s, the Africana Studies and Research Center had gone through an important stage in its institutional maturation—the succession of leadership—with Harris serving as its second director to be subsequently followed by political scientist Dr. Locksley Edmondson. Turner remained, though, an inspiring intellectual force, holding numerous panel discussions and forums examining the epistemology of Black/Africana Studies as an academic discipline and presenting African-centered analyses of contemporary political issues.

James Turner and former students (from left to right) Kwasi Konadu, Leslie Alexander, Scot Brown, and Benjamin Nurse, May 1999.

Intense discussions and debate led by faculty, students, and invited speakers took place at least on a weekly basis at the Africana Studies and Research Center, usually in a conference room dedicated to Hoyt Fuller.

Collectively, we were involved in a meditation on the future of Africana Studies while confronting a political context that differed significantly from the period in which the Black Studies movement had surged decades earlier. We debated the primacy of gender, race, culture, and class in our respective visions for Africana Studies, Black liberation, and human freedom. In this setting, an Africana graduate comrade and fellow student of Maulana Karenga's cultural nationalist *Kawaida* theory, Brian Sales, had compiled and bound a few volumes of writings by Black Studies pioneers. Sales felt that Turner's works were particularly underappreciated since most of them had been published by Black independent journals, such as *Negro Digest/Black World, Black Scholar*, and the *Black Collegian*.

Familiarity with Turner's scholarship notwithstanding, an encounter with his analysis of race, Black political thought, and current events was unavoidable on campus: resounding in classrooms, residential halls, seminars, conferences, and rallies. In fact, there are scores of former students who have gone on as professionals, artists, intellectuals, and activists who cite Turner's teaching and mentorship as the basis for their political consciousness and commitment to social change. In fact, a detailed accounting of Turner's impact as teacher alone could consume an entire book-length study in its own right and make for an important follow-up to this project. *Discourse on Africana Studies*, however, is primarily focused on James Turner's scholarship. His works are organized and presented in four major foci and subject matter: Black Nationalism; Black/Africana Studies; Pan-Africanism; and the Politics of Race.

Turner's grounding, like that of many other founding program directors and department chairs, was the product of personal relationships with an older generation of intellectuals. The introductory chapter in Part I, "From Tradition to Discipline," hones in on these intergenerational connections and draws inspiration from historians John Henrik Clarke, Jacob Carruthers, and Sonya Ramsey in the use of intellectual biography as a method for mapping out the long activist-scholar tradition in relation to the Black Studies movement of the 1960s.[2]

Dylan Rodríguez opens Part II with an eye on the influence of Black Nationalism on other emancipatory social movements and schools of thought, noting a broad indebtedness to nationalist ontology—chiefly its emphasis on self-determination and autonomy. But what does "autonomy" mean within the parameters of academic institutions formed and sustained by concentrations of private wealth and state bureaucratic power? Turner grappled with this question over the course of many years. In the introduction to Part III, Jonathan Fenderson examines Turner's perspectives on the question of disciplinary autonomy and institutional self-determination.

In the foreword to this volume, Ron Daniels points out that Turner's leadership helped to provide material and political support for anti-colonial struggles in Africa and other freedom movements in the Diaspora. In Part IV, LaTasha B. Levy also delves into the international dimensions of Turner's Africana leadership and vision—particularly his service as chair of the North American Delegation to the Sixth Pan-African Congress in 1974, anti-colonial and anti-apartheid liberation support, and advocacy for universal education in African nations. Anthony P. Browne, in the introduction to Part V, situates Turner's studies on race in the context of a rich Black social science research tradition, centered on exposing the deep structural foundations of racial stratification and socioeconomic inequality. The section closes with the transcription of a speech given by Kimberlé Crenshaw at the Africana Studies and Research Center on the fiftieth anniversary of the *Brown v. Board of Education* decision. Crenshaw detailed the impact of Turner and the Africana Studies and Research Center on her development as a contributor to the "critical race theory" school of thought as well as the concept of "intersectional" analysis of oppression and subjugation.

The collective voices herein constitute only a small portion of students who have been trained and inspired by Dr. Turner over the course of forty-plus years of unwavering service to the struggle for education and liberation.

PART I

TOWARD AFRICANA STUDIES

James Turner on his way to a meeting about Cornell University divesting from businesses that operated in apartheid South Africa, ca. 1980s.

FROM TRADITION TO DISCIPLINE: JAMES TURNER AND THE MAKING OF AFRICANA STUDIES

SCOT BROWN

It is our intention to do more than just give psychic refurbishment to Blacks who have suffered the ravages of racism. We must give them a purpose for service, focusing not just on individual achievement but on creative, productive work that benefits the whole black community.

—*James Turner (1969)*

Historical memory of 1960s activism continues to evoke images of a generation of young leaders, intellectuals, and organizers boldly mobilizing to bring forth dramatic changes to the order of the day. In the late 1960s, James Turner joined with a bevy of young leaders determined to build educational structures aimed at assisting a struggle for transformative change in both the collective consciousness and social conditions of Black communities. His journey is not unlike those undertaken by many other founding leaders of newly established Black Studies programs and departments in the late 1960s and 1970s.

This introduction to Turner's intellectual history and activism is divided into three main categories: (I) Black Public Spheres and a Black Studies Tradition; (II) Black Studies as a Movement; and (III) Institution-Building: The Africana Studies and Research Center.

I. BLACK PUBLIC SPHERES AND A BLACK STUDIES TRADITION

New York City

James Turner's political education in New York City (especially Harlem, Queens, and Brooklyn) laid the basis for his undergraduate and graduate education. His experience in New York's Black public sphere is the product of a vibrant Black intellectual tradition born of local communities with rich sources of knowledge production and circulation. His parents, Willie and Frieda Turner, migrated along with a number of other family members to New York City from the Carolinas in the 1930s. Experiences in the rural South and entrée into the northern working class reinforced their conviction that Black employment stability was best secured through cultivated expertise in a skilled trade. Born in Brooklyn in 1940 and raised in Manhattan, Turner grew up preparing himself for a career in the garment trades. He consequently attended the High School of Fashion Industries. After graduating in 1957, he went on to work at Ripley's Clothing Store.

After work hours, Turner's worldview broadened as he became immersed in New York's jazz scene. Nightclubs such as the Village Vanguard provided opportunities to express his own imprimatur on late 1950s style, sporting collegiate-styled blazers and slacks—undoubtedly informed by an insider's knowledge of the fashion industry. The look, venues, sounds, and sensibilities associated with this scene, as Turner recalled, were "seen as part of being...sophisticated" or what was considered "real copasetic." The sounds of Miles Davis, Sonny Rollins, and Max Roach led him to the Record Shack on 125th Street in Harlem, downstairs from Daddy Grace's United House of Prayer for All People. This store allowed patrons to listen and review records before purchasing them.

Modal jazz tracks at the Record Shack were accented by resounding nationalist voices echoing from the front of Lewis Michaux's National Memorial African Bookstore just up the street. Colorful paintings of African heads of state and sloganeering banners decorated the façade of the building: "House of Common Sense and Home of Proper Propaganda," "World History Book Outlet," and "Repatriation Headquarters: Back to Africa Movement Recruiting, Register Right Here!"[1] Crowds routinely gathered around the entrance, making it a stage for public debate, organizing, and mobilization.[2] Throughout the twentieth century, outdoor and indoor spaces throughout Harlem have doubled as sites of cultural and political education.[3]

Amiri Baraka speaking at Goldwin Smith auditorium, Cornell University, ca. 1970s.

Harlem's public sphere in the late 1950s and early 1960s was a bridge that brought together seasoned veterans of the freedom struggle (e.g., Richard B. Moore, Carlos Cooks, and John Henrik Clarke) with newer voices such as Malcolm X, Sonia Sanchez, Larry Neal, and Amiri Baraka. Just a block away from Michaux's store stood the Frederick Douglass bookstore run by Richard B. Moore—a socialist and nationalist organizer whose imprint on Harlem extended back to the latter 1910s and 1920s, as a member of the Universal Negro Improvement Association and the African Blood Brotherhood. Moore was a respected elder and chair of an organization called the "Committee to Tell the Truth about the Name Negro and Its Evil Uses" around the time when Turner met him. Moore would answer Turner's interest in Black history by assigning an extensive reading list that included the writings of Frederick Douglass, W.E.B. Du Bois, Herbert Aptheker, and many texts on African history. Pan-Africanist historian John Henrik Clarke was also involved with the Committee. Turner describes Clarke as an "omnipresent" intellectual force in Harlem during the 1950s and 1960s. Turner was occasionally invited to Clarke's home in Striver's Row, where the historian regularly hosted scholars, literati, and activists including Langston Hughes, Romare Bearden, Larry Neal, and Lorraine Hansberry.

Turner also took note of Clarke's close friend and advisee, Nation of Islam minister Malcolm X, whose speeches drew large crowds to 125th Street. Malcolm's charismatic call for Black uplift was grounded in a deep sympathy for the plight of the poor. The minister was unwavering in his virulent condemnation of American society for creating oppressive conditions responsible for persistent Black poverty and, by extension, negative social behaviors—for example, delinquency, violence, drug abuse, and reverence for white standards of beauty. Malcolm's call to interrogate the systemic causes of social-economic crises in the Black community reverberated with ideas Turner embraced later on as an academic.

Social Work and Columbia University

After leaving Ripley's Clothing Store, Turner began working for the Mobilization for Youth program in 1961 at Columbia University's School of Social Work, coding data on New York youth participation in gangs. There, in the academy, he explored social theories and arguments consistent with some of the voices of Black freedom on 125th Street. Richard Cloward and Lloyd Ohlin led a school of thought in urban sociology at Columbia that shared aspects of the indictment of racism and socioeconomic inequality articulated by Malcolm X. Youth delinquency among communities of color, Cloward and Ohlin argued, was not an expression of social or cultural pathology, but the result of an alternative opportunity structure created by young people who were systemically excluded from mainstream structures of mobility—for example, quality education, housing, access to jobs, resources, and so forth.[4] This view made sense to Turner and spoke to his own previous experiences as member of a neighborhood gang or "street club" during his high school years, known as the Sportsmen. Under the pseudonym "Oren"—a reconfiguration of his nickname Reno—Turner's insights on life in the gang were captured, albeit sensationally, in Harrison Salisbury's book *The Shook-Up Generation.*[5]

By 1962, while working as a researcher at Columbia, Turner began to consider the notion of attending college himself. Theory and practice also converged with a job he acquired at the New York Youth Board counseling gang members and working closely with social workers Cecil Gross (Bendrise Toleh) and Vince Godwin (Kalonji Olusegun). Olusegun described the Youth Board as "a quasi-government agency formed to combat the gang violence...with social workers assigned to each known gang in the city."[6] Turner was responsible for assisting members of the Corona Chaplins, located in Queens. His primary duties were to help resolve conflicts with rival gangs and to counsel individuals with their own personal and legal problems. The position seemed ideal, but Turner soon discovered that he would eventually need a college degree in order to remain in the job on a full-time basis.

After a long-term courtship, Turner married Janice Pinkney, who was already enrolled at City College while working at P.S. 122 Junior High School as a teaching assistant. The Turners explored the possibility of going away together to attend college, along with their son, Hassan. The two of them confronted the ugly reality of racial apartheid in the United States when perusing the pages of *Lovejoy's Complete Guide to American Colleges and Universities*, in which certain schools were classified as "White Only." Though Jim Crow pushed them away from certain schools and even the South as a region, the Turners were drawn to another distinction mentioned in the institutional highlights of the *Complete Guide*—housing facilities for "married" students. After having been accepted to a number of schools that provided living quarters for families, the Turners decided on Central Michigan University, given its financial aid assistance, housing policies, and relative proximity to New York City. Fittingly, the school also had strong programs in education, sociology, social psychology, and urban politics.

II. BLACK STUDIES AS A MOVEMENT

From Central Michigan to Northwestern

With the acceptance letter in hand in the spring of 1963, Turner continued his regular route from the Queens office of the Youth Board, over to Harlem, and then to Columbia University. Malcolm X continued to be a forceful nationalist presence and inspiration in Turner's life. Turner's supervisor Kalonji Olusegun joined him at rallies featuring the minister at Mount Morris Park (Marcus Garvey Park). Bendrise Toleh, another social worker with the Youth Board, regularly joined Turner at the Nation of Islam's restaurant, where both had many opportunities to converse with Malcolm X and prominent members of the New York/Queens mosque. In the late summer of 1963, James and Janice Turner visited the restaurant and informed Malcolm of their plans to pursue undergraduate studies at Central Michigan University. He congratulated the Turners, advising them to return to Harlem after graduation to serve the needs of their community. The minister then generously arranged for his brother Philbert to pick the Turners up from the Greyhound bus depot in Lansing, Michigan, and host the couple at his home while they awaited the transfer bus to arrive for the remainder of their trip to Mount Pleasant. The Turners continued to correspond with Malcolm X throughout his suspension from the Nation of Islam and the formation of the Organization of Afro-American Unity, right up to the weeks prior to his tragic assassination.

While James moved quickly through Central Michigan's BA program in Sociology and Political Economy, Janice went on to complete a master's degree in Counseling Psychology and Education. The two of them did so while raising a young son. Well on his way to graduating with honors, Turner was encouraged to consider graduate school. In 1966 he decided on Northwestern University given its fellowship resources, strong African Studies program and archival holdings—especially the Melville J. Herskovits Library of African Studies. While in Evanston, Illinois, Janice worked as the director of the local Head Start program while James pursued a master's in Sociology with a focus on social mobility and stratification, and a certificate of specialization in African Studies.

Turner took courses in the African Studies Center with a sense of ideological purpose driven in part by inspiration from Malcolm X's quest for transnational solidarity and cooperation between the African American freedom struggle and nation-building efforts in Africa. Malcolm's call for stronger political ties between Blacks in the United States and Africa influenced the curriculum reform agenda of student and community agitators for Black Studies at Northwestern University and campuses across the United States. Black Studies advocates pushed for the inclusion of the study of Africa beyond the scope of mainstream African Studies. The education Turner received from independent scholars in Harlem (especially Richard Moore and John Henrik Clarke) drove home an implicit critique of African Studies as the province of Area Studies and a Cold War political agenda. This dissatisfaction with African Studies in the academy—a field dominated by white scholars and teachers—would foretell Turner's specific vision for Africana Studies in the academy.

Turner enrolled in an African history course along with John Bracey, a fellow graduate student with a kindred interest in radical politics. Bracey introduced Turner to Max Stanford (Muhammad Ahmad) of the Revolutionary Action Movement (RAM) and General Gordon Baker of the League of Revolutionary Black Workers and the Dodge Revolutionary Union movement—each of whom closely linked Black Nationalism to Marxian conceptions of class struggle and revolutionary change. Bracey, a graduate of Roosevelt University and student of St. Clair Drake, was already a major scholar of Black Nationalism and African American history, and also introduced Turner to Black Chicago. The Windy City's South Side rivaled Harlem with its networks of Black independent scholars, cultural workers, activists, organizations, and community-wide political ethos. These community networks proved to be important support for the ensuing battle for Black Studies at Northwestern.

Northwestern University

At Northwestern, Turner began a long career as a leader in the Black Studies movement. The years 1967 through 1970 were critical for the development of his distinctively activist conception of Black Studies. Northwestern has its own story as one among hundreds of college campuses and high schools thrust into a series of national and global events that led to the student-driven call for Black Studies. The call was part of a period ripe for change.

Prior to the eruption of Black student protests at Northwestern in 1968, Students for a Democratic Society established a chapter on the campus in 1965 and went on to organize antiwar teach-ins and demonstrations throughout the duration of the Vietnam War.[7] A wave of Black student activism took off alongside a surge in the number of African Americans admitted to predominantly white colleges. Increases in the number of Black students at Northwestern and other schools occurred in conjunction with ever-growing Black Nationalist and anti-imperialist sensibilities on campus—as exemplified symbolically in the popular slogan "Black Power" and the increased frequency of antiwar protests. From 1965 to 1967, the number of incoming Black freshmen rose from 7 to 70. By the spring of 1968, there were nearly 160 Black students among an undergraduate and graduate population of roughly 9,000.[8] Black student responses to administrative paternalism and racism on campus were indicative of an ideological turn toward Black Nationalism and the politics of self-determination.

These years were also a high point of Black Nationalist and Pan-African coalition building. National Black Power Conferences took place in 1967 and 1968 along with a host of major gatherings also inspired by a resurgent nationalist sentiment. Groups of Black students from all over the United States attended these conferences and situated their respective struggles on campus within the framework of a national dialogue on Black Power.

Howard University

Critics of the Vietnam War called attention to the disproportionately high number of casualties among Blacks in the armed forces and the irony of military service in the midst of an unfinished freedom struggle at home. In this regard, Nation of Islam member and heavyweight boxing champion Muhammad Ali—stripped of his title due to his opposition to the war—frequented college campuses as a lecturer, urging students to support Black empowerment in conjunction with opposition to the Vietnam War. Ali's "Black Is Best" speech, delivered before thousands at Howard University in 1967, situated his antiwar stance as part of an ascendant Black consciousness. Invited by the campus Black Power Committee, led by Howard sociologist Nathan Hare and a cadre of student activists, Ali spoke to the rising Howard student revolt that would ultimately prove to be a watershed for both the Black Studies movement and the professional trajectory of James Turner. By the time of Ali's Howard visit, protests against administrative authoritarianism and the overall lack of student power had merged with a struggle for curriculum reform, and the development of closer ties with the District of Columbia's African American community.[9] While these issues arose at a historically Black university, they were in harmony with key issues advanced by Black Studies advocates in predominantly white institutions as well.

Howard University had been an instrumental force in dismantling legal segregation in the United States. However, many students in the late 1960s felt the administration did not provide adequate support for the civil disobedience thrust of the freedom struggle or for the populist call for Black Power and self-determination. The administration collided with the activist-minded students and faculty on campus. Sociologist Nathan Hare worked to channel student discontent into a coherent vision for Howard to become a "Black university," with curricula and institutional policies directed toward community empowerment. Hare's poignant criticism of the administration's policy directives spawned his dismissal from the Howard faculty. Undaunted, Hare continued to work as a transformative leader in Black Studies—joining the faculty at San Francisco State University where he chaired the first department of Black Studies and cofounded the seminal Black Studies journal, *The Black Scholar*.[10]

Hare's ouster was a provocative example of an entrenched administrative authoritarianism at Howard, fueling further student outrage. Dozens of students also faced the prospect of expulsion for participating in protests in March 1968. In response, a group of students waged a sit-in at the administration building on campus. The standoff ended with a compromise between the students and representatives of Howard's board of trustees. The endgame did not yield an official adoption of the vision for a "Black university," but it accorded students more participatory power in governance and university affairs and a series of measures aimed at addressing the call for Black Studies in the curriculum.

James Turner as keynote speaker at the first African Heritage Studies Association conference, Howard University, ca. 1970 .

Howard students were in lockstep with Black students at high schools and college campuses all over the United States. In 1968, James Turner emerged as a graduate student leader in the rising Black Studies movement protests at Northwestern. The Black undergraduates at Northwestern formed their version of a Black students union called "For Members Only," led by Kathryn Ogletree. The graduate students followed suit, establishing the Afro-American Student Union, led by Turner. Confronted with racism on campus and in the Evanston municipality, these two organizations created a set of demands to the university expressly conveying their own sense of Black Studies as a cornerstone of anti-racist public policy. The "Black Student Statement and Petition to Northwestern University Administrators," delivered on April 22, 1968, implored Northwestern to (1) condemn racism as a matter of official university policy, (2) dramatically increase Black admissions, (3) recruit Black students from working-class and poor communities, (4) provide a Black cultural theme housing unit for students, (5) offer Black Studies courses, and (6) incorporate Black student input in the selection of faculty members to teach these classes.[11] The Northwestern statement contained propositions in line with general student power interests as well as demands for Black Studies.

On May 3, 1968, more than a hundred students of For Members Only and the Afro-American Student Union stormed into the bursar's office and occupied it. The occupation successfully moved the administration to negotiate and eventually accept the bulk of demands outlined in the "Black Student Statement."[12] Turner, one of the main spokespersons and protest organizers, declared the outcome "a complete victory."[13] As was the case at many colleges and secondary schools, the Black Studies department at Northwestern materialized because of sustained student and community activism. A clear pattern repeated itself, binding together diverse campuses throughout the United States: (1) Black students, scholars, and community activists articulate a transformative vision for change, (2) they deploy direct action protest methods to realize this vision, and (3) the institution responds with a series of reforms—with varying degrees of commitment to the progressive vision of education presented by the Black Studies movement. The events at Northwestern thrust Turner into the spotlight as an advocate for Black Power and Black consciousness.

By the latter 1960s, Chicago's local Black Studies movement had entered a national debate on Black self-determination in public school systems.[14] Turner participated in the June 1968 meeting of the National Association of Afro-American Educators held in Chicago, which brought together locally based educators and activists as well as those from other cities, including Donald Smith, Albert Vann, William Grier, Barbara Sizemore, Harold Cruse, and Lerone Bennett.[15]

The interplay between local and national Black Power efforts had direct consequences for the high school Black Studies movement throughout Chicago as leaders from different schools came together to develop a shared reform agenda and cooperative protest measures. In the summer of 1968, a contingent of Chicago high school student leaders attended a workshop on education at the Black Power Conference in Philadelphia chaired by Nathan Hare. The session applied the principles of community control to the education sphere, urging participants to "[m]ove immediately to effect total Black control of hiring, firing, retention, and promotion of all Black school personnel."[16]

Toward a Black University

As James Turner became more involved in Chicago-area public school struggles, the national scope of the movement steadily grew, inspiring a series of mass gatherings aimed at coordinating a shared direction for Black Studies throughout the country. The five-day conference, "Toward a Black University," held in November 1968 at Howard University, could be deemed a minor concession on the part of the administration in the wake of the protests earlier that year—especially when viewed against the backdrop of the enormous vision of Nathan Hare and student organizers. The conference added to the development of common leadership and curricular issues in the Black Studies movement. Described by the *Negro Digest* as "the most comprehensive group of Black thinkers ever to focus on this single issue," the event brought together a diverse array of educators, activists, artists and scholars, including Sterling Brown, Stokely Carmichael (Kwame Ture), Harold Cruse, Ossie Davis, LeRoi Jones (Amiri Baraka), Maulana Karenga, Don L. Lee (Haki Madhubuti), Acklyn Lynch, Rhody McCoy, Larry Neal, Alvin Poussaint, Max Roach, Sonia Sanchez, Andress Taylor, and many others.[17]

James Turner and Kwame Ture, chairperson of the Student Nonviolent Coordinating Committee and the All-African People's Revolutionary Party, speaking at the Africana Studies and Research Center.

Even more important was the cross-regional coordination among lesser-known faculty, activists, and students. Nearly two thousand people from all over the United States assembled in Washington, DC, for the event, many of whom were representatives of Black student groups that were in the throes of protest demands for a Black Studies department. Turner's future trajectory was shaped by this historic gathering in late 1968. Already seasoned as a student leader in the recently "victorious" movement at Northwestern, Turner, as part of the delegation from Evanston, was a featured speaker in one of the more than seventy-five workshops and strategy sessions at Howard. There, he networked with students from the Afro-American Society at Cornell University who were fighting for Black Studies on their campus. Members of the delegation from this Ivy League school were well-organized and had won major leadership powers in staffing the directorship of a forthcoming Black Studies center on campus.[18] At the time of the Howard conference, the Cornell delegation, as Turner recalled, "had a very clear agreement with the university and the Afro-American Studies committee of faculty and students, that Black students would play a central role in the selection process.... [N]o candidate could be selected or appointed if the students didn't approve."[19] Through the remainder of 1968 and early 1969, Turner maintained contact with the Cornell students, who pushed for his candidacy as director.

African Studies

Beyond college campuses, the Black Studies movement contested time-honored concentrations of white privilege and control in academic and professional organizations. Turner joined a group of scholars interested in reframing and centering African history and politics in Black Studies curricula. The task necessitated a fight for control over key instruments in the production of knowledge. The demand for courses in African history continued an older tradition of scholar activism directed toward correcting racist characterizations of Africans—and by extension their descendants—as intellectually and culturally backward. Though students led the battle to transform schools and universities into allied institutional spaces directed toward raising Black consciousness, scholarly and professional groups were likewise mobilized to affect power relations in their respective fields and occupations. During the latter months of 1968 and through 1969, Turner joined an uprising of Black scholars in the African Studies Association (ASA), while building ties with student activists at Cornell and other institutions.. In the aftermath of the tenth annual ASA conference in 1967, a group of Black members formally responded to the association's tendency to reinforce the dominance of white academics in the development of policy positions, scholarship, and dispensation of research funds. The Black caucus of the ASA was formed by the time of the next meeting in Los Angeles in 1968.[20] Michael Searles, one of the caucus coordinators, understood the symmetry between these developments and concomitant trends toward Black self-determination in professional, social, and political spheres of activity. He noted, "the year which had elapsed since the tenth meeting of the ASA stimulated in Black people the necessity to evaluate all facets of their existence." "This same necessity," he observed, "had produced black caucuses at many church, labor unions, and various educational institutions."[21]

Deploying the concept of "relevancy," the Black caucus position paper—delivered at the 1968 ASA executive board meeting—shared the lexicon of the Black Studies movement. "The African Studies Association," it declared, "is called upon by the Black caucus to immediately direct its energies toward rendering itself more *relevant* and competent to deal with the challenging times and conditions of Black people, in Africa, in the United States and other parts of the Black world."[22] This argument stoked Turner's long-held view that strengthening African American connections with Africa and the Black Diaspora are indispensable to the development of a revolutionary Black consciousness. The leadership of the ASA, to the contrary, was content with dismissing the Black Power/Black Studies movement and its companion interest in African affairs. This disposition was firmly rooted in both the African Studies professional association and field of African Studies. The ASA furthermore resisted the caucus call for increased access to leadership positions on its twelve-member executive board. The steadfast racial exclusion from leadership, coupled with a policy inclination toward disaggregating the study of Africa from the politics of the Black freedom struggle, created the conditions for a revolt within the ASA.[23]

The representation of Black scholars in African Studies became an issue for Black Studies advocates on the Northwestern campus as well. The African Studies Center there, like the ASA, had a pattern of excluding Black scholars from its weekly lecture series. "Here we have African Studies and they don't have any Black people," Turner remembered thinking. "[T]hey're controlling all of the instruction of our heritage."[24] The students raised these issues with the Center's director, Gwendolyn Carter, resulting in the eventual participation of Black Africanists such as Hollis Lynch, Elliott Skinner, and Turner's mentor, John Henrik Clarke. As a student leader, Turner grew to work very closely with Clarke as a co-strategist in actualizing the Black Studies mandate for self-determination in the production of knowledge of African history, politics, and culture. Turner joined with a group of young ASA dissenters led by Clarke who came together to form the African Heritage Studies Association (AHSA) in December 1968 in New York.[25]

In the months to follow, AHSA members along with the ASA Black caucus contingent more forcefully confronted ASA's slow responses to racial exclusion. The issue came to a head at the 1969 ASA conference in Montreal when the group deployed disruption protest tactics: constantly interrupting panels and plenary sessions. "We," Turner recalled, "went and pulled the microphone plugs out and said, this meeting is over—we declare this conference over, shut down."[26] The ASA was immediately thrust into an internal debate and critical assessment of its own racial politics, captured best in a series of articles published in the association's journal *Africa Today*. Essays by ASA's leading members conceded that the Association had serious problems with racial inclusion and could no longer ignore the importance of the Black Power movement.[27] Also, articles therein by John Henrik Clarke, Sterling Stuckey, James Turner, Rukudzo Murapa, and others sympathetic to the AHSA position—though driven by a critique of the ASA—went beyond the polemics of grievance and advanced an alternative view of African history, culture, and politics.[28] Collectively, these works captured key epistemological distinctions between Black/Africana Studies and mainstream African Studies, emphasizing (1) pioneering research on Africa by Black scholars (including W.E.B. Du Bois, Carter G. Woodson, Drusilla Dunjee Houston, William Leo Hansberry, and Edward Wilmot Blyden); (2) African historical contributions to world civilization; (3) cultural continuities between Africans and Blacks in the Diaspora; and (4) shared political interests (e.g., symmetries between African decolonization and the politics of self-determination).

III. INSTITUTION-BUILDING: THE AFRICANA STUDIES AND RESEARCH CENTER

Self-Determination and the Africana Vision

The occasion for Turner to institutionalize his own Black Studies vision grew demonstratively with the Cornell board of trustees' approval of an Afro-American Studies program in early April 1969. The accomplishment was the result of significant increases in the Black student population at

Cornell, especially after a Committee on Special Education Projects was formed in 1965. In 1963, the campus had less than twenty African American students, which expanded tenfold in five years.[29] Mirroring Turner's own experience at Northwestern, Blacks at Cornell faced an onslaught of racist incidents on campus and in the classroom. The Afro-American Society (AAS), formed in 1966, aired Black student grievances and proposed agenda items for anti-racist reforms at Cornell—and the establishment of a Black Studies program was a cornerstone demand.

Members of the AAS, having met James Turner at the 1968 conference at Howard University, selected him as the candidate for the directorship of Afro-American Studies while going through negotiations with the Cornell administration from the winter of 1968 through early 1969. The trustees approved funding for an "Afro-American Studies Center" during an academic year filled with organized student resistance to racist university policies and acts of violence targeting Blacks on campus and Ithaca's Black community. On April 19, just one day after a cross was set ablaze in front of the Wari House Cooperative (a Black women's residential hall), more than one hundred Black students along with ten or so Black Ithaca residents occupied the Willard Straight Hall student center, expelling employees and guests housed there during parents' weekend.[30] Just a few hours later into the morning, an unsuccessful attempt by white fraternity members to retake the building by force moved the protesters to acquire firearms for their own protection.[31] For hours into the night and the following day, the specter of an ensuing gun battle or bloody police raid on the Cornell campus paralyzed the university, and thus intensified negotiations between the administration and leaders of the AAS. The student occupiers demanded the nullification of previous disciplinary measures taken against a group of AAS members who had participated in previous protests, as well as amnesty for those involved in the Willard Straight takeover. After coming to an agreement, the administration met these demands. Late in the afternoon of April 20, the students, led by AAS leaders Ed Whitefield and Eric Evans, left the building holding guns—signaling the end of the takeover.[32] An Associated Press photographer won a Pulitzer Prize for his photo of Black students at Cornell, with rifles in hand, making a grand exit. The image became a part of the iconography of the late 1960s, emblematic of a commitment to the right of self-defense and collective courage.

The aftermath of the takeover accorded significant momentum to this quest for an "autonomous" Black Studies institution. Just a few months earlier, the AAS detailed its vision for the center with an emphasis on self-determination. "If Blacks," the AAS statement declared, "do not define the

type of program set up within an institution that will be relevant to them,
it will be worthless." This conviction informed the AAS's bold proposal
for a Black Studies unit: "Our aim is the creation of a Black College of
Black students and scholars within a White University which will deal with
the problems of Black America."[33] Cornell president James Perkins did not
support the proposal for a Black college but did concede to a number of
the specific measures in the AAS plan: curricular control, the allocation of
a building as the exclusive domain of the center, and continued Black student participation in the selection of its director.[34]

In the early summer of 1969, Perkins resigned while under fire from
critics who characterized his response as a weak capitulation to student
demands. His replacement, Dale Corson, swiftly acted on plans to fulfill
portions of the AAS demands for the Afro-American Studies Center. The
students earned a major victory when James Turner joined the faculty as
director of the Afro-American Studies Center in June 1969. Though not a
college in its own right, the Center was set up with the capacity to serve
students from diverse colleges within the university and with control over
the selection and promotion of its own faculty.

Having experience as a student activist, Turner understood the often
fleeting commitments to Black Studies on the part of universities and
colleges in search of expedient responses to student unrest.[35] These circumstances called for an articulation of the intellectual dimensions of this new
discipline while he was in the midst of building the administrative base
for the Africana Studies and Research Center. In an early public lecture
at Cornell in the fall of 1969, Turner countered trends in social science
and policy that described patterns in African American families—especially
single-parent households—as evidence of social pathology or cultural de-
ficiencies. He argued that Black social problems were rooted in political
and economic conditions, rather than cultural norms. "Institutions, he
admonished, "must change to meet the needs of the family."[36]

Black Studies, as Turner envisioned it, would render educational space
an ally in the effort to overturn socioeconomic and political obstacles to
freedom and opportunity in Black communities. "Black Studies," he contended, "must be viewed as part of a larger plan to arm as many as possible
with the knowledge to help black people." The Black Studies intervention
carried with it a grand redefinition of the very purpose of higher education
and its relationship to the production of social hierarchies and the distribution of power. Turner spoke directly to these implications, declaring that
Black Studies, at its best, would inspire an "examination of how the uni-

versity functions as a social instrument." "The university," he concluded, "must become an active agent of social transformation."[37]

The Africana Studies and Research Center

From the outset of its establishment in 1969, the Africana Studies and Research Center has been an agent of progressive leadership at Cornell and in the institutionalization of Black Studies. The very physical plant of the center as a stand-alone building—housed with an affiliated library (currently named the John Henrik Clarke Africana Library)—affirmed the Black student movement's commitment to "autonomy" as an aspirational principle. The distance from structures on campus that housed traditionally dominant academic departments was, and remains, emblematic of a commitment to reconfiguring the geography of knowledge production in the building of a new discipline.

World-renowned historian John Henrik Clarke teaching at the Africana Studies and Research Center, ca. 1970s. The Africana library was named in his honor.

Turner embraced "Africana" as a theoretical framework for a specific approach to Black Studies. Carter G. Woodson and W.E.B. Du Bois evoked the term earlier in the twentieth century as a reference to the history and cultures of continental Africans and people of African ancestry around the world.[38] In this spirit, Turner uses "Africana" to emphasize the interconnections between and within multiple geographies and peoples throughout the Black world. The classes offered at the center have been consistently reflective of this expansive vision and in a broad range of fields, such as African American history, African languages, Caribbean politics, and African literature and art history. The Africana Studies and Research Center, born of student activism and visionary leadership, thus became a place where interdisciplinary and transnational approaches to examining the Black experience stood as basic premises for its daily operations.

From Turner's vantage point, the focus on relationships between African peoples worldwide incurred a responsibility of active participation in the international politics of Black liberation. Turner positioned the center as a resource to support nation-building efforts and liberation movements in resistance to colonialism and apartheid. In keeping with this Africana vision, Turner accepted leadership roles in several political and cultural organizations: the African Heritage Studies Association, the African Liberation Support Committee, the National Coalition of Blacks for Reparations in America, the International Congress of Africanists, the North American delegation to the Sixth Pan-African Congress, TransAfrica, and the Malcolm X Commemoration Commission.

Within the Africana Center, Turner viewed having a core faculty as indispensable to the fulfillment of its political commitments and long-term survival. Having faculty professionally invested in the center itself—rather than outside departments—was essential to the fulfillment of the "truth-to-power" and movement-centered epistemology of Africana Studies. "Black studies professors," he contended, "must be free to pursue truth and publish the results without fear."[39] This structure contrasted with a rash of Black Studies programs hastily assembled on campuses (and in turn easily disassembled) as determined by the ebb and flow of student and community protests.[40] The goal of building independent departments was reinforced by positions taken on the part of the professional organization for the new discipline, the National Council for Black Studies (NCBS), founded in the mid-1970s. Turner was a part of the initial meetings that led to the formation of the NCBS.

James Turner and Jacquelyn L. Haskins, assistant to the director, reviewing curricula for the Africana Studies and Research Center, ca. 1970s.

Turner's participation in the effort to acquire more autonomy in Black Studies—at both the departmental and disciplinary levels—necessitated, in turn, a steady devotion to administrative work. While in the midst of grappling with the day-to-day challenges of leading the center, and institutionalizing Africana Studies during this early phase, Turner completed doctoral studies in 1975, at the Union Graduate School. His dissertation, examining structural racism and Black Nationalism, anticipated a range of ideas explored further in latter publications.[41] The Africana center, in any case, was also a space committed to the affirmation of independent scholars and artists whose works and contributions were neither determined nor certified by the academy. Newly established Black Studies departments in their formative years often shaped their institutional identity around this expansive view of the role of the arts in higher education. In line with this trend, numerous artists and intellectuals spent significant time at the Africana Center as teachers and scholars in residence—Haki Madhubuti, Eleanor Traylor, Gwendolyn Brooks, James Baldwin, Shirley Graham Du Bois, Sinclair Bourne, Julian Mayfield, Mari Evans, Sonia Sanchez, Toni Cade Bambara, Hoyt Fuller, Ekwueme Michael Thelwell, Cleveland Sellers, James Forman, Chestyn Everett, Walter Rodney, John Henrik Clarke, Ayi Kwei Armah, and Yosef Ben-Jochannan. Support and time at the Africana Center often took place during crucial, and sometimes difficult, periods in the lives of those committed to art and scholarship rooted in a commitment to radical politics.

*Poet and activist Sonia Sanchez, Gwendolyn Brooks, State of Illinois
poet laureate and Pulitzer Prize winner, and James Turner at the
Africana Studies and Research Center, ca. 1970s.*

Networks

The Africana Studies and Research Center functioned as a movement resource and incubator of activist values in cooperation with parallel institutions aimed at enhancing the quality of life for students and the Black community of Ithaca at large. The protests at Cornell in 1969 found a resolute base of support from Ithaca's Black community. The city is home to the long-established South Side Community Center founded in 1938 by Black women activists. South Side helped coordinate the Africana Center's outreach to Ithaca's public schools and has been a consistent vehicle for galvanizing local support for student organizing and the center.[42]

Black residential communities on campus were also crucial to the network that sustained the Africana Center. The Wari House Cooperative, mentioned earlier, was a housing unit founded in 1968 to establish a supportive environment for Black women on campus. Wari has been a consistent wellspring of student volunteers who have assisted in community service programs at South Side. The Ujamaa Residential College has been the most important part of the Africana Center's support network. Students interested in Black culture and politics lived in Ujamaa, and many were exposed to regular lectures from activists, community leaders, and artists. Ujamaa was founded in 1972 as an "experimental college in cooperative living" based on the African socialist ideal explicated by political philosopher Mwalimu Julius Nyerere, the first president of Tanzania. Ujamaa developed into a full-blown residential college, remaining a model for the infusion of Black Studies with student residential life.[43] Within its meeting halls, students and residential staff of Ujamaa actualized practical dimensions of the Africana Studies concept. Regular group discussions and direct interactions with visiting lecturers at programs such as Unity Hour (a weekly event) situated Ujamaa as a campus hub for political consciousness, debate, and community-service planning. For decades, Ujamaa has been a partner and key anchor for the Africana Studies mission.

Activist Scholarship: From Tradition to Discipline

The idea of Ujamaa evokes notions of cooperation and community. In many ways, James Turner was the beneficiary of this principle in operative form. He was mentored by a community of independent scholars and leaders. His grounding within these intellectual networks inspired a particular vision for Black Studies and its practical expression in the form of the Africana Studies and Research Center. Not unlike the biographies of other founding leaders of Black Studies departments and programs, his journey reveals the intersection of an older Black intellectual tradition with social movements of the 1960s. Turner's scholarship responded to a need to explicate the historical, ideological, and epistemological foundations of Africana Studies as a distinctive approach to new knowledge production.

PART II

BLACK NATIONALISM

As young students in the 1990s, we had been taught to be ashamed of slavery and our heritage as descendants of slaves. But through James Turner, we learned to think differently about ourselves and our people. Rather than shrinking from the horrors of slavery, we began to embrace the legacy of resistance against slavery as a celebratory moment, one that birthed the Black Nationalism of future generations. Personally, it has birthed my passionate exploration of Black identity and political consciousness in the nineteenth century in an effort to understand the historical and contemporary Black experience. Generations of scholars and students are indebted to James Turner for his visionary analysis and his uncompromising commitment to the model of scholar-activism that we strive to embody.

—*Leslie Alexander*

James Turner and Julian Mayfield, renowned Harlem Renaissance writer, director, and activist, ca. 1970s.

INTRODUCTION: JAMES TURNER AND THE PEDAGOGICAL INTENSITIES/ INTIMACIES OF BLACK NATIONALISM

DYLAN RODRÍGUEZ

I am one among many who has been indelibly formed by the liberatory urgency and collectivist political desires of Black radicalism, generally, and Professor James Turner's uncompromising and impactful pedagogy, specifically. For those of us who have been his students, there is an unshakable intensity embedded within the complex meanings, dynamic internal contradictions, and living historical possibilities of Black Nationalism that is inseparable from Turner's nuanced and incisive sociopolitical framings of this trajectory of the Black liberation struggle. Perhaps having even greater gravity, however, are the intimacies we share with Turner as part of an always still-emerging community of militancy and struggle, often striving for practical unity while struggling to constructively engage in political debate and internal (i.e., both interpersonal and intra-communal) critique.

A creative alchemy of militancy/intensity/intimacy remains one of the defining imprints of Turner's venerable presence within the broader scope of Black radicalism, and it suggests a conception of Black Nationalism that defies static typologies and incomplete critical inventories. Historian Robin D. G. Kelley writes of the commonsense narratives of post-1960s Black social movements that "black nationalism tends to be cast in terms of riots and 'buy black' campaigns rather than black activists' support for anticolonial movements and Third World solidarity."[1] Professor Turner's willingness to both share with and invite others into this alchemy—a willingness that has frequently extended to those who are neither "Black" nor conventionally "nationalist"—points toward yet another of the critical strains within the Black Radical tradition, which Kelley elaborates through the creative trajectories of surrealism: "Any revolution must begin with thought, with how we imagine a New World, with how we reconstruct our social and individual relationships, with unleashing our desire and building a new future on the basis of love and creativity rather than rationality."[2]

Following Kelley's rejoinder, and in the spirit of illuminating the dynamic and creative dimensions of Black Nationalist praxis as they surface in Turner's unfolding political-intellectual and scholarly legacy, I continue this introduction with a situated reflection on the constructive (and perhaps unexpected) vulnerability that his pedagogical work has fostered as part of the Black Nationalist legacy. I encounter Professor Turner, in this pedagogical context, as a teacher who extrapolates the heart of progressive, radical, and revolutionary Black Nationalism—a love of and utopian desire for Black community and self-defined humanity—into a political pedagogy that centers the Black liberationist genealogy as an *instructive* matrix, accessible to those willing to engage in its complex, dangerous, and beautiful alchemies.

The final time I sat in Professor Turner's office as an undergraduate student at the Africana Studies and Research Center was sometime in early May 1995. Anxious over the burden, privilege, and responsibility of attempting to carry forward what was then an equally earnest and naive—but no less militant—sense of scholarly commitment and activist urgency (I was to begin the PhD program in Ethnic Studies at the University of California, Berkeley, in the fall), I asked Professor Turner how he had been able to survive—and *flourish*—as an embodied intellectual pillar of Black liberation within a generally hostile and deeply white supremacist institution for so many years. (We should never forget that the emergence of Africana Studies at Cornell was not only catalyzed by a disciplined, armed takeover of Willard Straight Hall by Black students in April 1969, but that this genesis moment was further galvanized by the arson of the Center's original building exactly one year later.) His response—generously voiced as the advice he knew I required—has never left me, though I must admit that to this day I continue to revisit and rethink the meaning of his terms.

Professor Turner revealed that *to survive* requires being surrounded by people who fundamentally support one's *way of existence* as part of a collective practice of remaking life in the face of systemic repression and oppressive institutional circumstances; in my interpretation, this dimension of his thinking suggests a refusal of the dichotomy between "individual" and "community," and instead posits the necessity of a mutual subsuming of each term to a symbiotic commonality. In other words, if one of the central logics of white supremacy is a historical anti-blackness that simultaneously disarticulates the material and metaphysical conditions of healthy Black community, while rendering (formally/juridically) impossible the notion of Black people as autonomous and self-defined "individuals" ("citizens," human beings, etc.), then one of the primary urgencies confronting any freedom-making practice is an insistent embodiment/performance of *both forms of Black life*. In Professor Turner's pedagogical articulation of Black Nationalism, this is fundamental to the case to be made for Black survival, if it is not to be the kind of survival that is defined by protracted suffering under the life terms of global white supremacy.

Professor Turner continued by saying that *to flourish* under these conditions requires an ongoing revision of the delicate relationship between the work of internal/intra-communal critique/debate and the contingent political practices of "unity" (to be distinguished from "coalition" and "solidarity") that are frequently and urgently required under circumstances of acute collective and individual endangerment. Responding to the isolating, individualizing, and cynical professional-intellectual structures that characterize the most insidiously (self-)destructive aspects of the university and "academy," his words resonated the productive—in fact, radically *life-affirming*—capacities of a particular kind of political-intellectual community: one as deeply devoted to collective struggle as internal criticism when times are most urgent, and when circumstances (and hostile forces) create acute vulnerabilities for (some if not all) members of that community and those with whom it identifies. I understood this to mean that for radical intellectuals whose scholarly and institutional work intends to facilitate the abolition of oppressive and genocidal systems, the *stakes of intellectual and political critique* are extraordinarily intense—that, at times, lives turn on their critical outcomes.

Finally, as Professor Turner has always asserted so incisively, he reminded me that *mere survival is not sufficient* to embody the dire and desperate labor of creating one's humanity, building a dignified collective history, imagining while discovering the always-changing meaning of freedom, or defeating the insidious institutional dehumanizations fostered by a white supremacist social form and civilizational epoch. Resonating the most intimate dimensions of Black Nationalist politicality, Turner's private words continue to speak a social truth that is at the heart of Black liberation struggle and Black radicalism *writ large*: that prior to any rote political agenda that claims to represent the best of/for an oppressed people, there is a *precondition of militancy* that must animate the collective political desire and historical imagination. Further, according to Turner, this militancy is not merely a commitment to principled collective struggle in the context of socialized white hostility, but is a politically focused praxis that must confront "the irreducible racial contradiction which is a major component in the edifice of the American social system."

In its most generous and radical interpretation into the present, this precondition of militancy not only entails a refusal to compromise dignity, honor, and self-definition to the cultural and sociopolitical structures that continue to affiliate Black existence with the nadir of racial chattel and genocide, but also suggests a multiplication of the *kinds of Black subjects* whose militancy must be valued or prioritized—including imprisoned, feminist/womanist, gay/lesbian, transgender, youth, and undocumented migrant subjects. In other words, when the analytical premise of an "irreducible racial contradiction" is centered within a robust conception of Black radicalism (including but not limited to the critical rearticulations of Black Nationalist sentiment that frequently manifest within collective Black departures from white-dominant feminist and queer social movements), the sites of this fundamental social antagonism necessarily multiply to encompass the *specificities* of systemic anti-Black violence as they affect variable Black social identities.

It is within the stream of these pedagogical statements and methods that I wish to echo one of the least understood and most underappreciated tendencies within the long, complex, and overlapping traditions of Black Nationalism and Black radicalism: the endemic, unyielding, principled, and obstinate *generosity* of Black liberation (and progressive-to-revolutionary Black Nationalist) praxis as an invitation to historically colonized, racially denigrated, and imperially displaced peoples to revolt against global white supremacy, and to thrill in the processes of remaking while struggling for those slippery things we conveniently name "freedom" and "humanity." This, in part, is how James Turner has personified the heart of Black Nationalism.

THE HEART OF BLACK NATIONALISM

One of the most critically productive—and often mischaracterized—dimensions of the Black Nationalist genealogy is its insistence on a form of political militancy that is founded on a rewriting of the dominant institutional terms of "community" and "family." While these concepts of social organization remain overdetermined by their hegemonic deployments as disciplinary and normative gender/sexuality/class apparatuses, the most progressive tendencies within Black Nationalism have often attempted to infuse these notions with imaginings of Black togetherness that rearticulate the social form and political expression of kinship, affective bonds, interpersonal loyalties, geographic attachment, childbearing/child-rearing, parenting, (heterosexual) coupling, collective mourning, and domesticity. Accompanying the theoretical rigor and historical density of Turner's writing on Black Nationalism is an evident commitment to precisely this expression of the militancy/intimacy/intensity nexus.

James Turner is a significant practitioner of Black community. While this book reveals how his thinking, teaching, rhetorical presentation, and strategic approach to Black community have changed both subtly and contextually over the course of his political and intellectual career, the gravity and principled necessity of the *commitment itself* remains remarkably, and admirably, consistent. Such a commitment has been especially crucial during a historical period that has witnessed the formation of multiple conservative-to-liberal hostilities against material and ideological/spiritual expressions of progressive and radical Black community, from the War on Drugs and the rise of the prison industrial complex (the anti-Black logic of which is tantamount to massive social liquidation),[3] to hegemonic appropriations of "multiculturalism" (including "beyond the Black/White binary") and "post-racial/post–Civil Rights" political discourses/movements (which often imply the obsolescence or encourage the dissolution of Black political affinities).

If we are to learn anything from Professor Turner's lifework, it is this: to participate in the political desire of Black togetherness, a desire that is positioned at the heart of the (always still-emerging) imagination of the self-determining Black historical subject, is to profess and live a deep, historical love for Black people in the context of a racial global condition that is viciously, persistently, systemically anti-Black. It is this love of Blackness—as both a response to degradation and institutionalized dehumanization and a radically open-ended rewriting of the countless fatal vulnerabilities of Black global existence—that constitutes one of Black Nationalism's most durable and flexible legacies.

The force of this tenaciously political love practice can be seen to have had a *global* influence on the racially colonized wretched of the earth, from (at least) the early nineteenth century onward, including and exceeding the hallmark moment of the Haitian Revolution. Anticipating the psychosocial taxonomy of Black Nationalism elaborated by James Turner three decades later, C.L.R. James portrays the incipient nation-building impetus of a collective *Black affect* in revolutionary San Domingo as a condition of permanent insurgency against the deepest cultural-political infiltrations of white supremacist colonialism:

> At bottom the popular movement had acquired an immense self-confidence. The former slaves had defeated white colonists, Spaniards and British, and now they were free. They were aware of French politics, for it concerned them closely. Black men who had been slaves were deputies in the French Parliament, black men who had been slaves negotiated with the French and foreign governments. Black men who had been slaves filled the highest po-

sitions in the colony.... *There was no need to be ashamed of being a black.*
The revolution had awakened them, had given them the possibility of
achievement, confidence and pride. *That psychological weakness, that feeling
of inferiority with which the imperialists poison colonial peoples everywhere,
these were gone.*[4]

Resonating with James's depiction of this history-altering, conditionally
revolutionary insurgency of Black identity and collective identification,
Turner's theorization of Black Nationalist praxis in the early 1970s similarly
reframes the political grounds, practical concerns, and philosophical basis
of political struggle and "self-determination" for racially oppressed people.
To read James Turner in this historical moment, the analytic and political
practices of Black Nationalism are less centrally concerned with the
parochial measures of defining the parameters of the (imagined and proces-
sual) "nation" than they are with the idea of mounting and mobilizing a
collective *historicity*. Complicating this insurgent/revolutionary historicity,
however, is its ideological condition of coherence: since the rise of Western
(white supremacist) modernity, the legibility of such collective historical
subjectivities has been overdetermined by the strictures and presumptions
of some form of "national" membership or affiliation—precisely the kind
of affinity that was purposefully and systemically undermined (if not oblit-
erated) by the global formation of a genocidal racial chattel slavery. This
is why, in the case of Turner's conceptualization of Black Nationalism, it
is the particularity and necessary *oppositionality* of Black historicity that
distinguishes the Black Nationalist project from other (hegemonic) nationalisms. Turner writes:

> [S]uch a movement of ideas represents an effort to transcend the immediate
> conditions of an undesirable relationship by a process of reflection, which
> creates a different (and opposing) constellation of symbols and assumptions.
> Black nationalism is thus at once an ideological movement of both social-
> psychological and political portent.
>
> The theme of disgrace and subjugation is the point of departure of the whole
> ideological expression of black nationalism, which derives from the political
> and cultural uprooting of black people in general through colonial conquest
> and enslavement....This sentiment of belonging no longer to oneself but
> to another goes together with an awareness of being black, which becomes
> translated in social terms into a caste and class consciousness.

In both C.L.R. James's historical meditation on Black San Domingo and Turner's intellectual inventory of Black Nationalist praxis, it is crucial to note the apparent contradiction between the socially eruptive—and undoubtedly transformative—articulation of Black revolutionary/history-making subjectivity and the androcentric disposition through which this world-altering position is voiced, formed, and tentatively institutionalized. While I will revisit this and other internal tensions within the Black Nationalist genealogy in the next section, it is worth gesturing here toward the structural and rhetorical impact that post-conquest, white supremacist, and patriarchal formulations of "nation" have had on the epistemological and intellectual *departures* that multiple global liberation movements, including Black Nationalism, have incited.

In the case of San Domingo's Black nation-building project, the departure from white European colonialist dominance was at once sudden and incomplete—sudden in the sense that it decisively displaced the white man as the erosive material and metaphysical center of the island's ecology and political cosmology, and incomplete in its replication of the male-centered terms of "democracy, equality, and fraternity" appropriated and rearticulated from the French Revolution. In the case of Turner's writing, the period of the late 1960s and early 1970s marked a critical phase of the Black freedom struggle in which the repressive focus of the state and white society at large seemed inordinately fixated on the symbolic denigration and emasculation, as well as the accelerated social-political neutralization, of politically activated, organized, militant (and presumptively straight) Black men. In the historical contexts both authors are writing from/about, the terms of Black militancy reflect the masculinist aggressions of a racist/colonialist state, while displacing the specificities of racial-gender violence as they differently encompass Black women and girls. This contradiction is neither unique to nor exaggerated within the genealogy of Black Nationalism (or Black radicalism more broadly), although part of the prevailing political and historical common sense portrays radical Black men as acutely or uniquely sexist, misogynist, and patriarchal. Rather, one can see these gender and sexual contradictions running through the progressive and reformist elements of the Black freedom struggle (including the Civil Rights movement), as well as in anti-colonialist nationalisms *writ large*. Thus, if progressive-to-revolutionary Black Nationalisms have refracted the disciplinary gender and sexual normativities of the social formations from which they have emerged, how might we approach an anthology such as this one through a nuanced and contextualized critical-activist *reading practice*?

Here I would suggest a conception of Black Nationalism as simultaneously a refraction of the hegemonic productions of "gender" and
"sexuality" within white supremacist patriarchy and (for Black radical and
Black Nationalist women in particular) an *opening* into a practical gender-
egalitarianism that Angela Y. Davis has articulated as part of the historical
legacy of Black resistance to racial slavery and its multifaceted gendered vi-
olences. Responding to the male-focused scholarly studies of slavery that
remained prevalent at the time of publication of her widely read book
Women, Race & Class (1981), Davis writes:

> The salient theme emerging from domestic life in the slave quarters is one of
> sexual equality. The labor that slaves performed for their own sake and not
> for the aggrandizement of their masters was carried out on terms of equali-
> ty. Within the confines of their family and community life, therefore, Black
> people managed to accomplish a magnificent feat. They transformed that
> negative equality which emanated from the equal oppression they suffered
> as slaves into a positive quality: the egalitarianism characterizing their social
> relations.[5]

What remains somewhat under-theorized—and certainly underappreciated—within this trajectory of Black politicality is how key facets of Black
Nationalist political thought remain present and persistent within those
streams of the Black liberation struggle that might otherwise dis-identify
with "nationalism" as such. In other words, we might ask whether and how
some of the defining characteristics of the Black Nationalist *social and historical imagination* resurface throughout Black (radical) political thought
and may in fact organize some of the principal political desires, counter-
hegemonic (that is, anti–white supremacist, anti-heteronormative, anti-
patriarchal) practices, and collectivist rhetorics of Black freedom praxis in
all of its contemporary complexities, including Black radical feminisms,
Black queer radicalisms, and counter-nationalist Black socialist and communist formations. If we are to thoroughly engage the historical reach and
impact of what I am referencing here as the heart of Black Nationalism, it
is likely that we will discover that the categorical distinctions and critical
oppositions between Black Nationalist praxis and non-nationalist-oriented
Black radicalisms might not be as definitive as previously thought.

INTERNAL CONTRADICTIONS:
HETERONORMATIVITY, PATRIARCHY, ETC.

James Turner's earliest writings reveal how one of the primary (and ultimately productive) contradictions of 1960s and 1970s Black Nationalism—its period-specific androcentrism and heteronormativity—is *internally* undermined by one of the primary principles of the Black Nationalist political desire: "the exclusive right," Turner writes, "of members of the group to define, establish, and maintain their own group boundaries." While this position might be read as authorizing a unilateral push for the exclusion and marginalization of deviant others from a parochial and narrow understanding of Black community—a tendency that would reflect the avaricious exclusivity and chauvinism of the Western nation-state as it has been conceived through genocidal enslavement and conquest—it is also possible to interpret this articulation of Black Nationalism as an assertion of the necessity for constant, dynamic *re*definition and transformation of "group boundaries." That is, this principle of group self-definition and self-defense should not be *conflated with* the oppressive exclusionary and repressive tendencies of dominant national (racial) groups, especially when such conceptions of Black community directly invoke the contingencies of the Black freedom struggle as the periodic invigoration and mobilization of Black communities *at war* with systems of anti-Black violence and degradation. Further, this position reminds us that contrary to liberal mythologies of multiculturalist national togetherness and "post–Civil Rights" or "post-racial/racist" national belonging, there is a fundamental urgency to eschewing the fraudulent invitations to identify with the American national/global project, and to instead perform the political labor of analyzing and defining those "group boundaries" that crystallize at the precipices of domination, dehumanization, and (proto-)genocide.

Still, as with all liberation struggles grounded in an ideological and political imagination of community ("national" or otherwise), Turner's work invokes and infers multiple critical tensions within Black Nationalist praxis. These contradictions and tensions are by no means unique to the spectrum of Black Nationalist thought, but are in fact evident throughout the multiple streams of the Black liberationist/freedom struggle, from conservative assimilationism to reformist integrationism to revolutionary internationalism and beyond. It is through this critical framing that I wish to reread the male-naturalized and heteronormative conception of revolutionary politicality that seems clear within this moment of Black

Nationalist thought, and which also surfaces throughout the history of twentieth-century insurgent and anti-colonialist nationalisms.

A vast Black feminist scholarship and radical Black women's activism has elaborated how the organizational and ideological privileging of male political agency has often translated into patriarchal and misogynist practices within otherwise progressive and radical Black liberationist communities and organizations.[6] Yet it is also the case that insurgent Black Nationalist political formations—which can and should be seen as no more or no less flawed and internally contradictory than their conservative, liberal, and reformist counterparts—have influenced, enabled, and produced a spectrum of Black women's radicalism that overturns totalizing narratives of Black Nationalist patriarchy. This political contradiction—between Black Nationalism's patriarchal tendencies and its (often simultaneous) inspiration and enabling of radical Black women's (feminist and proto-feminist) political militancy and mobilization—constitutes an archive of Black women's liberationist praxis in which the "interlocking oppressions" of racism and sexism create a sometimes symbiotic, sometimes antagonistic relationship between Black Nationalist political desire and Black feminist critical intervention.[7]

James Turner and Dr. Gloria Joseph, feminist scholar and among one of the first professors at the Africana Studies and Research Center.

The recent publication of *The War Within*—a compilation of writings by and about former Black Panther, Black Liberation Army leader, and

U.S. political prisoner Safiya Bukhari—creates a significant entry into this archive, while also offering a political bridge to such widely read radical Black women's texts as Assata Shakur's *Assata* and Angela Y. Davis's *Autobiography*. One of the characterizing features of Bukhari's text is its refusal to permanently delineate or narrate the Black (women's) revolutionary imagination in a manner that cleanly distinguishes between feminist, nationalist, socialist, communist, or even militant reformist political-ideological practices. Bukhari's "Coming of Age: A Black Revolutionary" (1979)—written in the immediate aftermath of her political work in the Black Panther Party and leadership in the Black Liberation Army and during the middle years of her nine-year political imprisonment—frames her collected meditations on Black liberation as such:

> Genuine women's liberation for Black women, however, will only come about with the liberation of Black people as a whole; that is, when for the first time since our forefathers were snatched from the African continent and brought to America as slave labor, we can be a family, and from that family build a community and a nation.
>
> The powers-that-be were disconcerted when Black mothers, wives, and daughters and Black women in general stood by and, in many cases, fought beside their men when they were captured, shot, or victimized by the police and other agents of the government. They were frightened of the potential of Black women to wreak havoc when these women began to enter the prisons and jails in efforts to liberate their men. They were spurred into action when they were confronted with the fact that Black women were educating their children from the cradle up about the real enemies of Black people and about what must be done to eliminate this ever-present threat to the lives of Black people.[8]

Following Bukhari's terms of struggle, this still-emerging archive of contemporary Black queer and Black women's radicalism complexly (and sometimes unexpectedly) *articulates with* some of the formative political desires and social dreams of Black Nationalism. That is, if we are to apprehend Black Nationalism not as a singular or monolithic political platform or sectarian ideological position, but rather as a dynamic and internally diverse political ideology, imagination of community, collective identity, and freedom desire, then we might also learn from the profound *rearticulations of "nation"* that various forms of Black radicalism have posited. That is, contrary to hegemonic, conservative, and reactionary concepts of nation (or nation-state), which prioritize the repressive militarized policing of geographic and political-cultural boundaries, and/or focus definitions of national membership (citizenship) on the capacity to internally discipline "national character" while externally repulsing (real and projected) "invasions" of the national body, the progressive-to-revolutionary conceptions of Black Nationalism center the concept of *global* (*Black*) *liberation* as the premise of both Black "national" community and oppressed peoples' freedom *writ large*. Turner writes in "Black Nationalism: The Inevitable Response":

> Thus the American Black struggle is part of the world-wide struggle for anticipatory and inclusive identities on the part of peasants, workers, and youth. Black Nationalism is precisely about anticipatory and more inclusive identity, and self-determination.

This gesture toward "world-wide struggle" as the grounding force for insurgent nationalism, Turner seems to argue, necessarily invites a *rewriting and reconvening* of Black "identity" itself—a process that in turn fosters a political identification with Blackness that is "anticipatory and more inclusive." I would elaborate this position to suggest that, in its most progressive and radical renditions, Black Nationalist praxis *opens itself* to radical Black critique, including and especially Black feminist and Black queer departures and interventions.[9]

Put succinctly, Turner's writing encourages a nuanced understanding of how post-1970s Black social and political thought, and Black radicalism more generally, sustain persistent and productive *congruencies* with central facets of Black Nationalism, even as multiple strains of Black liberation praxis foreground key *incongruencies* with Black Nationalism as some of their central points of ideological and political departure. The landmark political-intellectual work of the Combahee River Collective during the 1970s signifies this complex political relationality with Black Nationalism.

> Above all else, our politics initially sprang from the shared belief that Black women are inherently valuable, that our liberation is a necessity not as an adjunct to somebody else's but because of our need as human persons for autonomy....We realize that the only people who care enough about us to work consistently for our liberation is us.[10]

The epistemological and philosophical schema of the Combahee River Collective's "A Black Feminist Statement" delineates a Black feminist communion that critically departs from the gender-conservative (and gender-reactionary) tendencies of Black Nationalism at the same time that it rearticulates the condition of collective and global Black militancy that characterizes the most progressive to revolutionary Black Nationalist trajectories:

> Black feminist politics also have an obvious connection to movements for Black liberation, particularly those of the 1960s and 1970s. Many of us were active in those movements (civil rights, Black nationalism, the Black Panthers), and all of our lives were greatly affected and changed by their ideology, their goals, and the tactics used to achieve their goals. It was our experience and disillusionment within these liberation movements, as well as experience on the periphery of the white male left, that led to the need to develop a politics that was antiracist, unlike those of white women, and antisexist, unlike those of Black and white men.[11]

Importantly, the statement continues, "Our development must also be tied to the contemporary economic and political position of Black people."[12] Further theorizing their critical (and *racially* irreconcilable) antagonism with their white feminist and white lesbian separatist counterparts, the Collective asserts a central radical Black feminist political contingency: the urgency and necessity of Black community as a critical labor, and as a *political objective in and of itself.*

> [W]e reject the stance of lesbian separatism because it is not a viable political analysis or strategy for us. It leaves out far too much and far too many people, particularly Black men, women, and children. We have a great deal of criticism and loathing for what men have been socialized to be in this society: what they support, how they act, and how they oppress. But we do not have the misguided notion that it is their maleness, per se...that makes them what they are.[13]

While much has been written—and much more remains to be discussed—about the centrality of Black queer and Black feminist thought to the internal transformations and critical redirections of Black radicalism (and of radicalism more broadly), I would suggest that the political complexities and fluidities of Black Nationalist thought and praxis exceed any categorical separation or political opposition between "nationalists" and Black radical critics of nationalism. Bukhari appears to encourage such a conceptualization when she recounts the dynamic gender politics of the Black Panther Party:

> The simple fact that the Black Panther Party had the courage to address the question of women's liberation in the first place was a monumental step

forward. In a time when the other nationalist organizations were defining women as barefoot, pregnant, and in the kitchen, women in the Black Panther Party were working right alongside men, being assigned sections to organize just like the men, and receiving the same training as the men. Further, the decisions about what a person did within the ranks of the Party were determined not by gender but by ability.

In its brief seven-year history women had been involved on every level in the Party [e.g., Audrea Jones, founder of Boston chapter; Brenda Hyson, head of Brooklyn office; Kathleen Cleaver, member of Central Committee; and Sister Rivera, leader of Mount Vernon, New York, office]. On the other hand, there were problems: men who brought their sexist attitudes into the organization. Some of the men refused to take direction from women. We had a framework established to deal with that. But many times the framework was not used because of liberalism, cowardice, and fear.[14]

Reading Turner and James alongside Bukhari, Davis, and the Combahee River Collective, it is possible to suggest a theoretical and historical framing of Black Nationalism that accounts for its (immanent) critical trajectories as well as its complex relation to other contemporaneous and emergent Black politicalities. Perhaps rather than representing Black Nationalism as a compartmentalized or isolated tendency within the Black freedom struggle, it can be historicized and theorized as one political-ideological (and psychosocial) *center of gravity/influence* within the larger schema of Black radicalism. It is in this context that James Turner's work will sustain a permanent influence.

"INTEGRATION IS DEAD"

James Turner and Bettye Collier-Thomas illuminate one of the primary theoretical recognitions enabling global anti-racist and anti-colonialist political formations in the latter twentieth century when they assert "that consciousness is a primordial force in behavior, that oppression, when it is successful, effectively reorders the consciousness of the oppressed." This claim resonates throughout the diasporic reaches of the Black liberation struggle and also shapes the revolutionary anti-colonialist struggles of multiple populations at the historic height of mass movements to overthrow global white supremacist and racist colonialism. One of the most frequently cited passages from Frantz Fanon's *The Wretched of the Earth* similarly emphasizes the cultural and psychic substructures of racial colonialism:

> When we consider the resources deployed to achieve the cultural alienation so typical of the colonial period, we realize that nothing was left to chance and that the final aim of colonization was to convince the indigenous population it would save them from darkness. The result was to hammer into the heads of the indigenous population that if the colonist were to leave they would regress into barbarism, degradation, and bestiality.... The colonial mother is protecting the child from itself, from its ego, its physiology, its biology, and its ontological misfortune.[15]

To follow the political logic delineated by Turner, Collier-Thomas, and Fanon, it becomes clear that anti-Black/white supremacist nation-building and the cultural genocide waged by racial colonialism do not merely institutionalize the cultural alienation and consciousness-disordering of the oppressed in a periodic or temporary manner. Rather, this is an *epochal* condition crystallized by the systemic continuities between the epistemic, ontological, and gratuitous violence/terror of racist dominance, which positions anti-blackness as its paradigmatic modality.[16] Here, the praxis of Black Nationalism can be understood as a field of activist political theorization that has differently engaged the question of whether and how an *epochally* alienated and psychically displaced people might be able to create, recover, rebuild, or otherwise rejuvenate a collective memory in the living present of racial chattel slavery, the Middle Passage, and Africa's racial colonization. The specificity of this intellectual labor—the necessity of its attending to the aspects of global Black experience that are *incomparable*—is central to what constitutes Black Nationalist thought as a complex and dynamic insurgency.

A vibrant scholarship has examined how the progressive and revolutionary Black Nationalisms and other Black radicalisms of the late twentieth-century United States were inspired and materially enabled by the emergence of anti-colonialist and anti–white supremacist nationalisms around the world.[17] This work indicates that Black radical politicalities have *always* been global in their thinking, and that Black Nationalism is one crucial strain within this radical Black globality wherein the position of Blacks as an oppressed nationality, and/or a national object of racial genocide, is most eloquently and rigorously articulated.[18] In addition to this historical recognition, James Turner's writing provides a theoretical platform through which to further address how the political and ideological innovations of U.S.-based Black Nationalisms have also created an intellectual, cultural, and symbolic matrix that has broadly influenced Black diasporic and global anti-racist/anti-colonialist movements *beyond the United States.* Black Nationalism, in other words, has not only been enabled and informed *by* global radical and revolutionary struggles; it has also actively exerted political influence *on* those global liberation movements.

Finally, this collection reminds us of the intimate relation between the conditions of Black liberation and the utopic conception of all oppressed people's freedom. To approach the complexity of this relation is to grasp at the possibilities of a Black revolution that "starts from the very first day with the basic claims of the colonized," and which yields a liberationist process that "is unconditional, absolute, total, and seamless."[19] It is to embrace the wonder of a *complete* social disarticulation that creates the fragile possibility of lived, practiced, created, and constantly critically transformed liberation. I conclude, then, with a gesture toward one of the central contributions of Black Nationalism to the global radical and revolutionary imagination: that to embrace Black Nationalism's radical heart, and its most revolutionary political desire, is to become intertwined with the immanent abolition of hegemonic nation-states as we have come to know them.

BLACK NATIONALISM: THE INEVITABLE RESPONSE[20]

JAMES TURNER

The political history of Africans in America is characterized by two predominating themes: attempts to oppress us and our determination to resist and free ourselves. We have believed freedom to mean different things at different times and in different places. We thought it was emancipation from being a slave; or sit-ins for equal use of public services and facilities; or a crusading bus ride through the South for social integration; or voter's registration so Black people could vote for the white politicians who were controlling the government. All of these thoughts about freedom were basic to the assumptions we accepted about the nature of American society, which were, in fact, derived from white America's description of itself. But being a flexible people and not one to hang on to false goals, each time we arrived at a stage and saw that freedom was not there, the movement pushed onward. The venerable scholar and political analyst C.L.R. James remarked recently that the African struggle in the Americas "has the richest political heritage, in terms of continuance over time, consistency of growth and development through stages."

Speaking about the failure of assumptions and the dialectic of the Black movement, C.T. Vivian, an ardent participant in, and maker of, the recent fifteen-year civil rights phase in the history of the struggle, writes: "The first and perhaps most fundamental assumption with which we began was that integration would be the route to Black freedom. *And this was an inherent part of all our other assumptions.* The concept of integration won our allegiance because it fit our understanding of how the people of a culture *should* relate to one another. It fit our understanding of the values which *should* determine the institutions and priorities of a society. It did not, however, fit American reality. And the measure by which we misjudged that reality is precisely the measure of the yawning gulf between Blacks and whites." He continues,

...Altogether, they show how completely the Black subculture accepted the pronouncements of the dominant majority. But in our actions we proved each of these pronouncements false. And, as this happened, we came closer to a definition of American which would allow us to operate effectively. But until this happened, we were impotent. As long as we believed what the nation said about itself, we chose strategies which were bound to fail. The fall of these assumptions changed most of our strategies and many of our tactics....Individual whites of goodwill are as powerless against this system as we, the excluded. Yet it was not until we saw the structures in which these men lived and worked reject their voices that we learned that individuals, Black or white, cannot effect change in America. The structures of the nation respond only to amassed power, not to verbal or moral appeals.

...History might have taught us this lesson if we had listened....But this was something we came to learn through our own struggle and failure....America would not give us our rights just because we pointed out that it was the correct thing to do. Rights, after all, are potential power. We were looking at justice and equality before the law as moral, ethical, and human questions. Those we faced saw more accurately that these were the coordinates of eventual power....This was too high a price for America to pay for a mere moral principal....What we had to learn was that when white America gave it was for its good, not ours.

...Almost everything we learned in the Movement makes integration impossible as a goal for the Black community today....So integration is dead....Integration is dead, but Black people did not kill it. They could not because they were never in a position to do so. The Black minority has never had control of the concept or definition of integration.

In the integration model, the majority power is always the broker of the terms....For this reason, the integration model has always had a built-in obsolescence....Separatism has taken the place of integration as the strategy and tactic of the Movement.[21]

The shift in the Movement toward Nationalism is a coming that was perhaps inevitable. This turn in the Movement rejects integration, because of its irreducible racial contradiction which is a major component in the edifice of the American social system. Black Nationalism is a strategy of survival, and a philosophy of social reality in as much as it recognizes the essential racial dichotomy in American economic organization and its political process, and the fundamental racial separatism in the structure of social institutions and culture in the United States. Commenting in a speech entitled "Beyond the Dilemma," Dr. Kenneth Clark crystallizes the racial conditions:

> The pathology of the ghetto is now clear and recognized—the statistics of infant mortality, disease, rat infestation, broken plumbing, littered streets, consumer exploitation, riot-burned buildings that have not been replaced, inefficient schools, a discriminatory system of police and court procedures.

The litany of pain and despair is the same in every dark ghetto and, despite the anti-poverty programs, Title I funds, Model Cities, and so on, the ghetto is still dark and still desperate.

...Segregated schools, and the tyranny and the barbarity of American ghettos, are the institutionalized inescapable immorality of American racism...the knowledge that segregated schools inflicted permanent damage upon [Black] children (and violated their constitutional rights as well) was not enough to compel the American people to plan and implement a massive and effective program for desegregation of our public schools....The history of racism has prepared many, if not the majority, of Americans psychologically to accept injury to—or the outright expendability of [Black] children.[22]

Unlike the civil rights movement, which focused on the struggle for legal equality and integration, Black Nationalism addresses itself to the cultural and psychological malaise of the oppression Blacks have had to endure. Nationalism has taken many forms among Africans in America. Some of the most recent varieties are religio-nationalism, represented by the Nation of Islam; cultural nationalism of Ron Karenga and Amiri Baraka; Marxist revolutionary nationalism of the Black Panther Party; economic nationalism of the Black Capitalism Advocates; political nationalism of the Republic of New Africa; and Pan-African nationalism of Brother Malcolm X.[23] As a political orientation the basic proposition shared by all variants of Black Nationalism (though advocating different social blueprints at times) is that all things created and occupied by Blacks should be controlled by Black people, and that the purpose of every effort should be toward achieving self-determination (variously defined) and a relatively self-sufficient Black community.

As the civil rights movement gave way to the struggle for Black Power, there was a revival of Black Nationalism, which is now expanding into a revolutionary ideology proclaiming that the approximately 25 to 30 million African people in America constitute an underdeveloped nation.[24]

Dr. C.J. Munford, Black political scientist, explains the Black Nationalist concept of nation:

There is absolutely no reciprocity of purpose, expectancy, and self-definitions between whites and American Blacks, despite the fact that they inhabit the same geopolitical space. Social reciprocity must be based on mutually beneficial economic relations and a recognized equality of humanity. Nothing of the kind prevails between Black and white. The only bonds are the historic ones of slavery and dehumanization and the current confrontation and conflict....

Like other colonized people who have risen to demand freedom, the Black colony in the United States constitutes a nation. It is different from other emergent nations only in that it consists of forcibly transplanted colonial subjects who have acquired cohesive identity in the course of centuries of struggle against enslavement, cultural alienation, and the spiritual cannibalism of white racism. This common history which the Black people of America share is manifested in a concrete national culture with a peculiar 'spiritual complexion,' or psychological temperament. Though the Black nation expresses its thoughts, emotions, and aspirations in the same tongue as American whites, the different conditions of existence, the long trail of exploitation and dehumanization at the hands of American white colonial overlords, and heroic resistance have, from generation to generation, welded the bonds of a national experience as different from that of white existence as day is from night. And what differentiates nations from one another are dissimilar conditions of life.[25]

Perceived from this perspective, liberation can only come when Black people achieve territorial integrity, plus economic cohesion, and full ascension of their culture, their dignity, and their nationhood, based on political control and social security.

This emerging ideology represents a new awareness of the radical implications of Black Nationalism (the political implications of which, until now, had usually been rather conservative.) Of necessity, many Black radical movements have been involved in a cultural revolution—a man cannot begin to be involved in the revolutionary process until he looks at himself (and thereby at others) with new feelings and new ideas. The Black cultural revolution is thus an important process: It has led to an affirmation of self, an affirmation of Blackness. For as Julius Lester writes:

Culture in a revolutionary context must be an instrument of communication, which serves to raise political awareness...as well as serving to further intensify the commitment of the people to revolution.[26]

From a different perspective, Christopher Lasch similarly points out that

the radical implications of Black Nationalism can only emerge once the cultural battle has been carried into the sphere of politics, at which point it becomes clear that Black Nationalism as a political program demands the radical decentralization of American institutions and perhaps also the social-

ization of these institutions....Indeed, one of the potentially revolutionary
aspects of Black Nationalism is its capacity to demonstrate that cultural and
political questions are always related.[27]

Thus, economic and social oppression of Blacks cannot be separated from
the spiritual and psychological chaos in their lives due to subjugation by
American racism.

However, reflecting cultural, ideological, and moral bias, most sociological studies of Black Nationalism have been more descriptive than analytical, more concerned with outlining characteristics of Black Nationalist organizations and their members than with defining the subjective meaning
of the movement. Thus, these studies have ignored the central significance
of Black Nationalism: the emergence of Black group-consciousness, self-
assertion, and cultural identity.

Consensus models and other conservative variants of order theory define racial strife in pathological terms.[28] Black Nationalism, therefore,
has been generally interpreted as not only socially deviant, but socially
dysfunctional. Pluralism, like egalitarianism, is only entertained within a
consensual framework. Pervading the literature on minority problems is
the belief that society, especially American society, is united by consensus
on basic values. This is largely a consequence of Gunnar Myrdal's influential interpretation of the "race question" in terms of social will, the
notion that society has a common will and a common culture. Hence, the
predictable and popular assumption that assimilation into the "superior"
white society is the Black man's only solution.[29]

But while consensus models accept the core values of the dominant
groups as functional for society, some of these values may in fact be inimical to particular groups, who are thus increasingly led to question the
legitimacy of the social system. Proper study of Black Nationalism, on the
other hand, employs a conflict perspective: When an aggregate comes to
realize itself as a group, a movement will evolve, defining the boundaries of
the group and its terms for relations with other groups. Thus, Black Nationalism can be objectively defined as:

1. The desire of Black people to determine their own destiny
   through formation, preservation, and control of their own
   political, social, economic, and cultural institutions.

2. The determination of Black people to unite as a group, as a people in common community, opposing white supremacy by striving for independence from white control.

3. The resistance of Black people to subordinate status and the demand for political freedom, social justice, and economic equality.

4. The development of ethnic self-interest, racial pride, group consciousness, and opposition to and rejection of the dominant ideas of white-defined society perceived to be incompatible with this objective.

5. The re-evaluation of self and of the Black man's relationship with the social system in general.

THE GENESIS OF BLACK NATIONALISM

Black Nationalism is not new to the American scene. It has been one of the two main trends among Black people in America, even antedating the integration trend. It reached its highest level in this country with its rise of the Garvey movement, the greatest Afro-American mass movement in history, and is a force of widespread influence in contemporary Black society.

The drive toward Black Nationalism has been more than just an occasional silent fit of anger or expression of despair. For the past two centuries, individuals and organizations have emerged periodically to urge Black men to seek solutions other than integration, to use a system of defining their problems different from that prescribed by the dominant white group. Black Nationalism has sought to establish and express group identity and collective consciousness through conversion of the "Negro" as a socially defined category into a socially determined group of *Black* people.

As early as 1787, the freed slaves of Newport, Rhode Island, formed the Free African Society to promote group cohesion and repatriation to Africa. African societies were formed in other parts of the northeast section of the United States, uniting their members on the basis of their African-ness and previous condition of forced servitude, as well as the commonly experienced threat of violence.

In 1815, Paul Cuffee of Boston, a well-to-do entrepreneur, piloted himself and a group of other ex-slaves across the Atlantic to Sierra Leone in West Africa. In 1820 appeared *Walker's Appeal to the Colored Citizens of the*

World, by David Walker, which was followed slightly more than a decade later by Henry Highland Garnet's "Address to the Slaves of the United States," and his *Call to Rebellion* in 1843. In 1852, Martin R. Delany, Harvard-educated physician, writer, editor, and theoretician, published his book, *The Condition, Elevation, Emigration and Destiny of the Colored People of the United States Politically Considered*, which was a statement of Black Zionist doctrine. Dr. Delany proposed an expedition to the eastern coast of Africa for purpose of eventual settlement there.

It is worthwhile to quote a few passages from this book, because the sentiments it conveys persist:

> Every people should be the originators of their own designs, the projectors of their own schemes, and the creators of the events that lead to their destiny—the consummation of their desires.

> We have native hearts and virtues, just as other nations, which in their pristine purity are noble, potent, and worthy of example. We are a nation within a nation....But we have been, by our oppressors, despoiled of our purity, and corrupted in our native characteristics...leaving us in character, really a 'broken people.' Being distinguished by complexion, we are still singled out—although having merged in the habits and customs of our oppressors—as a distinct nation of people....[30]

Faced with the social fact that "Blackness and dignity remain incompatible in American culture,"[31] Black Nationalism has sought to crystallize ambiguous and troubled race feelings into a definite racial consciousness to create a corporate self-awareness and collective response on shared values.

Hence, the basis for understanding Black Nationalism lies in acknowledging of the historical by-products of the slave system. The African and his descendants were conquered, enslaved, demeaned, and then converted to accept of their low status. Black men were told that they had no history, no culture, and no civilization; and for them it was often economically rewarding and socially advantageous to repeat this litany. Some individuals, however, began to realize that this was nonsense and sought to dissipate this lack of self-pride. There has arisen an awareness of cultural dispossession that rivals concern for problems of material deprivation: From this context Black Nationalism arises, looking inward to historical and social traditions in order to overcome low status and prestige, and constructing a new vision predicated upon collective traits of social distinction.

Black Nationalism as a refutation of slavery's racial ideology and segregation is a direct challenge to white supremacy. For slavery and segregated rule were not only a political and economic affair; they also imposed a specific social framework on the Black man's experience both of the world and of himself. Political and economic domination constantly underscored racial and cultural differences between Black and white men. In turn, Black Nationalism, by confronting white domination with its own form of racial protest and zealous partisanship of the Black race, has done more than draw together sentiments and attitudes of the collective Black reaction. It has embodied them in a heightened form that moves toward a racial ideology:

> Anti-white sensibilities among black nationalists operate to supply a unifying ideology which transcends the experience of any single individual. In point of fact, however, black nationalism is much more a than response to white outrages (although it is of course that, too)....Black nationalism is a sophisticated and pervasive political ideology based on a generalized understanding of the history of the black man in the United States.[32]

Undoubtedly, such an inclusive ideology directed at the dominant group in society polarizes feelings and induces conflict between the two groups. But this external conflict also establishes group boundaries, promotes group identity, and strengthens group cohesion.[33]

An ideology, when it becomes explicit, is a kind of thinking aloud on the part of society or a group within it. It is a direct response to the actual conditions of life and has a social function, either as a defensive system of beliefs and ideas that support and justify an established social structure, or as a rational project for the creation of a new order. The latter type of ideology, even when it includes a certain degree of idealism, also implies a reasoned program of collective action.

Black Nationalism thus springs from the desire to reverse an intolerable situation; its adherents view the basis of social life as competition between groups for social and economic power. It challenges the legitimacy of the system of white domination imposed on Black men, whose experience of dispersal, humiliation, and subjugation generates social conflict. Against this background it is not difficult to understand that a development like Marcus Garvey's "Back-to-Africa" movement was not simply atavistic expression; it was presented not as an escape from America, but as a way to confront and overcome the social realities of racism, a positive rather than negative gesture. Garvey appreciated the psychological needs of his adherents, realizing that freedom from contempt is inextricably linked with political freedom.[34] Garvey's re-evaluation of Africa had the precise function of abolishing the world order created in the minds of Black men by white men; for Garvey saw that the Black man is doomed as long as he takes his ideals from the white man, sealing his internal feeling of inferiority and self-contempt.

Two points stand out clearly in the progressive development of Black Nationalism. First, it has been a movement of reaction against white cultural domination concomitant with political domination. Secondly, without the pressure and conflict generated by segregation, without the historical and social factors which dominate the situation of the Black man in America—that is, without the racial factor—the forms of reaction to cultural contact would have had a completely different character. For the cultural position of the Black man in America possesses its own specific characteristics: the Black man lives in a symbiotic relationship with the white man, held in subordinate position by the caste system. Furthermore, the Black man is governed by the white dominant group, especially in the areas of religion and social morality. The wish for independent expression finds a ready springboard in those elements of Black subculture which segregation helped define and structure.

Thus an ironic aspect of Black popular movement is the way in which white ideas act as catalysts of nationalist feelings. Christian egalitarian teaching, for example, helps show Black converts the fundamental contradiction of white domination and the avowed humanitarian principles of Western culture, thereby underscoring the hiatus between objective practice and declared values of white men. The powerful emotional disaffection for the white man that inspires Black Nationalism is born of judging the white man against his own principles.

As social historian Lerone Bennett has observed, there has been a process of gradual estrangement from the unilaterally subjective mainstream tradition in America since Reconstruction. Since that time, Black men have become real to themselves, acting so as to make themselves real to others as well:

> Parallel with the growth in racial consciousness was a rise in Negro nationalism which should not be confused with specific nationalist movements. The key elements in the nationalist syndrome were: (1) a common sense of oppression, (2) pride in the achievement of Negroes, (3) extreme sensitivity to racial disparagement, (4) a belief in the manifest destiny of Negroes, (5) a feeling of identity with the nonwhite peoples of the world.[35]

Thus the American Black struggle is part of the worldwide struggle for anticipatory and inclusive identities on the part of peasants, workers, and youth. Black Nationalism is precisely about anticipatory and more inclusive identity, and self-determination.[36] Self-determination always relates to two essential factors—power and control; power to protect vital self-interest, and control over immediate social and geographical space occupied by a people (or group). Thus, Black Nationalism refers to the necessity for African people in America to exercise sovereignty over their lives and community.

THE SOCIOLOGY OF
BLACK NATIONALISM[37]

JAMES TURNER

The 1960s witnessed an upsurge of Black nationalism. Scholars and masses alike articulated this ideology and sought to define it theoretically, and to create new strategies for its application. James Turner has emerged as one of the most articulate spokesmen of the Black nationalist theoretical perspective. Turner's attempt in this essay to systematize a theory of Black nationalism and to relate it to sociology represents the task that many Black social scientists have undertaken to give practical and intellectual legitimacy to those emergent areas which are facilitating the redefinition of Black life and culture.

The movement of black nationalist ideas is dominated by the collective consciousness of its adherents as members of a minority group, which is subordinated to another and more powerful group within the total political and social order. The ideological preoccupations of black nationalism revolve around this central problem: the black man's predicament of having been forced by historical circumstances into a state of dependence upon white society, which is considered the master society and the dominant culture. The essential theme of black nationalism can be seen as a counter-movement away from subordination to independence; and from alienation, through refutation, to the ultimate goal of self-affirmation. In this respect, such a movement of ideas represents an effort to transcend the immediate conditions of an undesirable relationship by a process of reflection, which creates a different (and opposing) constellation of symbols and assumptions. Black nationalism is thus at once an ideological movement of both social-psychological and political portent.

The theme of disgrace and subjugation is the point of departure for the whole ideological expression of black nationalism, which derives from the political and cultural uprooting of a black population through colonial conquest and enslavement. The overwhelming sentiment that dominates in this connection is the belief that the group is being denied a "true" and unadulterated experience of its humanity as a result of being forced into a social system whose cultural values preclude an honorable accommodation. The black nationalist recognizes himself as belonging to an out-group, as an alien in the white society which controls the total universe in which he moves. This sentiment of belonging no longer to oneself but to another goes together with an awareness of being black, which becomes translated in social terms into a caste and class consciousness. The association between race and servitude is a constant theme in Afro-American literature. The economic exploitation and social discrimination which defines persons of African descent as a social category gives many of its members an avid sense of race consciousness as a consequence of mutual humiliation.

Becoming a black nationalist seems to involve a realization that persons of African descent are treated categorically by the dominant group. Subsequently, there develops the firm conviction that Afro-Americans must become transmuted into a conscious and cohesive group. The rationale is that a group giving a unitary response can more effectively and honorably confront oppression. Race, color, and mutual resistance to the dominant group (and its imposed assumptions about the minority) become vehicles for realizing conversion from category to group. Loyalty to group cultural attributes and commitment to collective goals allow the group to adhere. Black nationalists argue for the exclusive right of group members to define, establish, and maintain their own group boundaries.

The black man's principal role and meaning in Western history has been as an economic tool.[38] This is what Aimé Césaire, paraphrasing Marx, has called "the reduction of the black-man into an object."[39] However, the chief preoccupation of black nationalists is with the black people first as a "race," and secondarily as a class. They are concerned with the collective image of the Black man in American society and his human status in the world. They are concerned about a white racial ideology, which defined the Black man as inferior—and the consequent social relationship between Black and white men which acquired the moral values summarized by Bloke Modisane:

> White is right, and to be black is to be despised, dehumanized...classed among the beasts, hounded and persecuted, discriminated against, segregated and oppressed by government and by man's greed. White is the positive standard, black the negative.[40]

The cultural and political ascendancy of white men over black men, combined with the active denigration of black men, has thus had the effect of vitiating the latter's self-esteem, with profound psychological consequences that involve shame and self-hatred.[41] Black men throughout the world suffered this negation as human beings. This is the external reality with which the ideology of black nationalism is concerned.

Historically, contact between black and white peoples has been seriously influenced by certain cultural premises that predicated the groups' social relations. Slavery and the colonial enterprise were nationalized as a civilizing mission aimed at transforming the Black man through education and subsequent assimilation of the ideals of Western civilization. In most cases, the transformation required black men to dissociate from the basic social patterns of their original ethnic and cultural environment. This predicament—of cultural infusion via systematic social restriction and isolation—has been variously referred to as the "dilemma of the marginal man," the "pathology of the uprooted man," and by R.E. Park, the "cultural hybrid," a result of culture contact and acculturation, but also of systematic social segregation and denial of human consideration.[42]

Black nationalism becomes, as a result, testimony to the injustices of segregated rule and an expression of the black man's resistance and resentment. In this respect, one of the most striking social-psychological innovations of black nationalism has to do with the reversal of color association within a dominant and pervasive white-ideal cultural context. A reversal of white, Western symbols implies as well as reversal of the concepts associated with them. Thus, black nationalism is a refusal of those white values which are regarded as oppressive constraints.

It can be noted that, in general, the theme of revolt in the ideology of black nationalism represents a reinforcement of the antagonism created by the caste situation between the white dominant group and the black subordinate minority. Black nationalism's refutation of white political and cultural domination represents an attempt to sever the bonds that tie the black man to white definitions.

> ...The American Negro can no longer, nor will he be ever again, controlled by white America's image of him.[43]

It is an attempt at toppling what some young Black intellectuals call "the dictatorship of definition." The corollary to this claim for freedom from white determination of Black identity is a search for new values. Revolt involves not only a confrontation with an oppressive and undesirable social status, but is also an act of self-affirmation and a cogent expression of identity. The following passage is illustrative of this point:

> Our concern for black power addresses itself directly to this problem, the necessity to reclaim our history and our identity from the cultural terrorism and depreciation of self-justifying white guilt. To do this we shall have to struggle for the right to create our own terms through which to define our-

selves. This is the first necessity of a free people, and the first right that any oppressor must suspend.[44]

The quest for new values thus leads the black nationalist to the belief that self-definition and self-determination are one and the same, and his new self-perception must of necessity be predicated upon terms that diverge from white, Western values.

A group of black women expressed this same concern in asking, "Is *Ebony* Killing the Black Woman?" in the title of their article:

Ebony magazine stands today as a classic illustration of middle class negro [small *n* is indicative of general scorn for the term as well as the behavior of the class of people being referred to] attempts to assimilate themselves into the mainstream of white american [small *a* is for symbolic de-emphasis] life. *Ebony* has been a highly successful magazine because it has mirrored the values and standards of the larger, dominant white society....*Ebony* has sought to perpetuate the fallacy and old cliché, 'If it's white it's all right.' The latest in this long line of insults and abuses was the cover story of the February [1966] issue. Under an article entitled, 'Are Negro Girls Getting Prettier,' *Ebony* cleverly selected a carefully screened group of girls to represent what they claim is positive proof, that 'negro' girls are indeed getting prettier. The great injustice here is that girls chosen by *Ebony* did not nearly reflect a full cross-section of all black folks.

The psychological effect—on our people—of a publication such as *Ebony*, with its skin bleaching cream and straight hair ads, is demoralizing and tends to reinforce the already evident inferiority and self-hatred complexes of the black community. As a race we have been taught by whites that black is ugly; for example to be 'blacklisted,' 'blackmailed' or 'blackballed'—everyday phrases—denotes exclusion or alienation. By the same token, the symbols used to extol the virtues of honesty, purity and truth are always white....Thus we come to realize the majority of the masses are moved to act or react by the symbolism of the language they speak. The ideas, thoughts and deeds the oppressor wants us to see and react to, are those ideas which strengthen, defend or assert the goals of the established order. When a supposedly black magazine comes forth with the same ideology as the oppressor, it indicates the extent to which the oppressor has used his symbols, through culture, to psychologically enslave black people. It also indicates how successful the oppressor has been....Every race has its own standards of beauty. Every race maintains a loyalty to its cultural and historical roots. Why then would a publication such as *Ebony* want us to lose our inherent standards of beauty, and substitute in its place a European Criteria [*sic*]?[45]

The issue of identity is inescapable, and pride in race is playing a crucial part in the new identity; it no doubt will lead—as it already has done—to a considerable degree of racial self-consciousness. Many black men and women are not struggling to become free simply in order to disappear. This is contrary to the liberal argument "that the race problem can be solved in this country only by total integration and complete assimilation and eventual miscegenation," but there are Afro-Americans who do not want to disappear and desire to preserve specifically Afro-American values and cultural traits. Such sentiments are expressed by a female student in Robert Penn Warren's book:

> ...The auditorium had been packed—mostly Negroes, but with a scattering of white people. A young girl with pale skin, dressed like any coed anywhere, in clothes for a public occasion, is on the rostrum. She is...speaking with a peculiar vibrance in a strange irregular rhythm, out of some inner excitement, some furious, taut élan, saying[:] '—and I tell you I have discovered a great truth. I have discovered a great joy. I have discovered that I am black. I am black! You out there—oh, yes, you may have black faces, but your hearts are white, your minds are white, you have been white-washed!'[46]

This exclamation of a sense of new "discovered" identity is a conscious experience of "an increased unity of the physical and mental, moral and sensual selves, and a oneness in the way one experiences oneself and the way others seem to experience us."[47]

Most research and analysis of race relations during the past three decades seems to accept the liberal assumption of historian Kenneth M. Stamp that "Negroes are, after all, only white men with black skins, nothing more, nothing less." But black men in America are not simply carbon duplicates of white men; to contend that they are is misleading. Differences in skin color, hair texture, and physical features are fact. But the issues are not whether differences exist, but what they mean socially:

> Identified as a Negro, treated as Negro, provided with Negro interests, forced, whether he wills or not, to live in Negro communities, to think, love, buy and breathe as a Negro, the Negro comes in time to see himself as a Negro....He comes, in time, to invent himself and to image creatively his face.[48]

The Afro-American subculture maintains a subterranean and private world of rituals, symbols, and motifs. Rupert Emerson and Martin Kilson make the following observations in their discussion of black nationalism:

> ...The Black Muslims still represent, at the level of the Negro's subterranean world, a force of ultimate significance. This is found in its influence upon the new stage in the Negro's self-definition. This stage, moreover, has been reinforced by the rise of more rational black nationalist concepts than those represented by the Black Muslims, and all of them have been affected by Black Muslims, and all of them have been affected by the debut of African nationalism on the international scene....There are, however, many other groups of this sort, and they are likely to have a more sustained influence upon the Negro's new thrust for self-realization...than the Black Muslims. Unlike the Black Muslims, these organizations are secular in orientation, intellectually capable of coping with the modern world; and they reject naïve political goals....[49]

According to St. Clair Drake, "Increased identification of educated Negroes with some aspects of the Negro subculture and with the cultural renaissance taking place in Africa may become the norm."[50] It is not unusual to find people in the larger urban ghettos, who were previously wary about identifying themselves with Africa, now proudly proclaiming their blackness and developing interest in African politics, art, poetry, and literature. Among the educated, and not so educated, discussions of Negritude are becoming commonplace. Among many young people there is a certain reverence for the memory and image of such men as Patrice Lumumba, Kwame Nkrumah, Jomo Kenyatta, and Malcolm X, to name a few. These men are looked up to as black heroes and role models. It is interesting to note, in this regard, that the late Medgar Evers—slain NAACP civil rights field director for the state of Mississippi—had named one of his sons Kenyatta. Ordinary black men and women who a short time ago were processing their hair and using hair-straighteners and skin bleaches are now wearing the new "Afro" and "natural" hairstyles, as well as African-style clothing. A few are even taking African names and learning to speak an African language.

Erik H. Erikson explains such social-psychological phenomena as the development of a conscious identity: "Identity here is one aspect of the struggle for ethnic survival; one person's or group's identity may be relative to another's; and identity awareness may have to do with matters of an inner emancipation from a more dominant identity, such as the 'compact majority.'"[51] Writer John O. Killens comments on the function and value of the new identity: "One of the main tasks of Black Consciousness is to affirm the beauty of our blackness, to see beauty in black skin and thick lips and broad nostrils and kinky hair; to rid our vocabulary of 'good hair' and 'high yaller' and our medicine cabinets of bleaching creams. To de-niggerize ourselves is a key task of Black Consciousness."[52] [Others have likewise noted:]

> Thus the black artist who embarks upon a search for new standards and values for his salvation must, among other things, discard the tools presented to him by the social order which has proved to be the number one enemy to his sensibility and conscience....If he is committed to his people [he] looks elsewhere for new standards and values, for new identification and allies.[53]

The fundamental question that black nationalism raises is whether integration is really desired or, more specifically, whether Afro-Americans "should" want integration. "In the whole history of revolts and revolutions, 'integration' has never been the main slogan of a revolution. The oppressed's fight is to free himself from his oppressor, not to integrate with him."[54] Black nationalist ideology molds a new image of the dominant group. The essential concern becomes "not free from what, but free for what?" There is a radical conception in process which has Black men redefining themselves and, of necessity, re-evaluating "the white man." The objective of the process is to wrest the black man's image from white control; its concrete meaning is that white men should no longer tell black men who they are and where they should want to go. The proposition that obtains from such a conception is that black men must no longer be bound by the "white man's" definitions. This is a clear response to the control of communications media by the dominant white group[:]

> In the past, some Negroes attempted to define themselves by becoming counter-contrast conceptions, by becoming, in short, opposite Negroes, opposite, that is, to what white men said Negroes were.[55]

In its crudest and simplest form black nationalism is the assertion that black is good. At its most intellectually sophisticated level of development, it is the affirmation of the validity of traditions and values of black people derived from their peculiar heritage and creativity. This process has been described by one sociologist "as the backfire of the dynamics of American assimilation which gave rise to an increased sensitivity, on the part of black people, in reacting to the institutionalized nature of bigotry. Also, a subsequent development of a more positive regard for black culture and community, and a determination to reconstitute the basic processes of United States life as they affect black people." He further contends that "the most pervasive trend for today's young black intellectuals is their vigor and degree of self-consciousness about being black."[56]

Black nationalism seeks to achieve the diminution of "the white man"—that is the demise of the idea that because of a certain color of skin one man (or group of men) is ordained to determine the lives of other men because of their darker skin color. The basis for understanding black nationalism is in acknowledging the historical by-products of the slave system[:]

> The tragedy bequeathed by racist beliefs and practices has in modern times been experienced by no other people, save for the Jews who fell into Hitler's hand, so deeply as by the Negro Americans.[57]

The African and his descendants were conquered, enslaved, demeaned and then converted to accepting their low status. Black men were told that they had no history, no culture, no civilization; and it was, for them, often economically rewarding and socially advantageous to repeat this litany. Some individuals began to realize that the idea was nonsense and sought to dissipate its inherent lack of self-pride. From this refutation comes an awareness of cultural dispossession, which becomes as equal a concern as the problems of material dispossession. Out of this context black nationalism arises. There develops a pattern of looking inward to historical and social traditions in order to overcome low status and low prestige. Attempts are made to construct a new "vision" predicated upon collective traits of social distinction. This vision, because of the "artificial" character of its development and cultural equivocation, is not merely ambiguous or difficult, but is ambivalent and often looks irrational.

That black nationalism is based on a vehement racial consciousness can be imputed to white domination and its consequent racism. In the final analysis, black nationalism can be reduced to a challenge to white supremacy—a refutation of the racial ideology behind slavery and segregation. In order to understand certain aspects of black nationalism and its peculiarities, it is important to consider the fact that slavery and segregated rule was not only a political and economic affair, but that it also imposed a specific social framework for the black man's experience both of the world and of "himself." The fact of political domination created contact between black and white men under conditions that constantly underscored racial and cultural differences. Black nationalism, by confronting white domination with its own racial protest and zealous partisanship of the "black race," does more than draw together sentiments and attitudes that go into a collective black reaction, but embodies them in a heightened form that in fact moves very distinctly towards a racial ideology. [On this, Frank Kofsky wrote:]

> ...Anti-white sensibilities among black nationalists operate to supply a unifying ideology which transcends the experience of any single individual.

In point of fact, however, black nationalism is much more than a response to white outrages (although it is of course that too). In the hands of such a gifted exponent as Malcolm, black nationalism is a sophisticated and pervasive political ideology based on a generalized understanding of the history of the black man in the United States.[58]

Malcolm X explains himself: "When we Muslims had talked about 'the devil white man,' he had been relatively abstract, someone we Muslims rarely come into contact with..."[59] A frequently repeated statement in many of his speeches was that

> [u]nless we call one white man, by name, a 'devil,' we are not speaking of any 'individual' white man. We are speaking of the 'collective' white man's historical record. We are speaking of the collective white man's cruelties, and evil, and greed, that have seen him 'act' like a devil toward the non-white man. Any intelligent, honest, objective person cannot fail to realize that his white man's slave trade, and his subsequent devilish actions, are directly responsible for not only the presence of this black man in America, but also for the condition in which we find this black man here....[60]

Undoubtedly, such a broadly general and inclusive ideology directed at the dominant group serves the function of polarizing feelings and inducing conflict in the relationship between the two groups. Lewis Coser suggests that such external conflict establishes group boundaries and gives identity to the group and strengthens its internal cohesion.[61]

A prominent ex–civil rights leader and former activist explains th[e] experience [of social strain and tension generated by white domination:]

> The evil of slavery—and to some degree Negroes are still enslaved—is in the way it permitted white men to handle Negroes: their bodies, their action, their opportunities, their very minds and thoughts. To the depths of their souls, Negroes feel handled, dealt with, ordered about, manipulated by white men. I cannot over-emphasize the tenacity and intensity of this feeling among Negroes and I believe any fair-minded person pondering the history of the Negro's enforced posture in a world of white power would concede the justice of the feeling.[62]

The black man's worth was low, indeed, not only in the eyes of his white overlord, but as consequence, also in his own eyes. He was on the lowest rung of the racial hierarchy which Western civilization had established. As Aimé Césaire, the West Indian writer and initial conceiver of Negritude, observed, "At the top, the white man—the being, in the full sense of the term—at the bottom, the black man...the thing, as much as to say a nothing."[63] The black man retained an awareness of his racial differences and was forced to organize his life on a racial basis[....] In short, black nationalism is inspired by a wish for freedom from both domination and contempt.

James Farmer writes about the shift in emphasis from integration, which had been largely rooted in the black middle class, to emphasis on race and nationalism, which has been the traditional appeal to the black masses. He gives considerable insight as to the movement's motives:

> Almost imperceptibly the demand for desegregation had shaded into a demand for black dispersal and assimilation. We were told, and for a while told ourselves, all Negro separation was inherently inferior, and some of us began to think that Negroes couldn't be fully human in the presence of other Negroes. Well, we have since come to learn that all separation need not be inferior in all cases and in all places.

> ...We have learned that what is needed is not 'invisibility' but a valid and legitimate visibility....We have found the cult of color-blindness not only quaintly irrelevant but seriously flawed. For we learned that America couldn't simply be color-blind. It would only become color-blind when we gave up our color. The white man, who presumably has no color, would have to give up only his prejudices, but we would have to give up our identities. Thus we would usher in the Great Day with an act of self-denial and self-abasement. We would achieve equality by conceding racism's charge: that our skins are an affliction; that our history is one long humiliation; that we are empty of distinctive traditions and any legitimate source of pride.[64]

He recalls a meeting to reconcile a serious strife between "nationalists" and "integrationists" in CORE chapters in the San Francisco Bay Area:

> One fellow, a Negro, immediately said, 'Brother, Farmer, we've got to dig being black.' He kept repeating it over and over again, and I knew exactly what he meant. He meant that blackness of the skin had been accepted as a deformity by Negroes, that it had to cease being that, and had to become a source of pride, and so did all the culture and memories that went with it....Some form of nationalism is necessary, even healthy, though the willfully color-blind refuse to acknowledge this....The doctrinaire color-blind often fail to

perceive that it is 'ideally' necessary for the black man to be proudly black today....We have come to realize that we must live here and now rather than in eternity.

...The system of segregation was mounted and perpetuated for the purpose of keeping the black man down; that it was and is a conspiracy to instill in the Negro and the white a sense of Negro inferiority.

...In a free society many Negroes will choose to live and work separately, although not in total isolation. They will cultivate the pride in themselves which comes in part from their effort to make this a free land....In helping themselves they will come to love themselves. And because they love themselves, they will be determined to help themselves.

...We will accept, in other words, Malcolm X's insight that segregation will become separation only with a separate effort of Negro heart and soul rejecting the notion of some of the older civil rights organizations—that desegregation and integration 'in itself' will accomplish miracles.

Perhaps 'independence' is a better term than separation. We shall become independent men.[65]

[...] It is apparent that as the black power movement gains more strength, becomes more aggressive, defines its objective in terms of specifically Afro-American interests, and not on white liberal terms, and is controlled by an increasingly politicized Afro-American element, it will appear more threatening and separatist to the dominant group. It would be a mistake, however, to dismiss such development as a futile and sectarian obsession with self—a kind of black narcissism. In the larger context of Afro-American experience, it represents, for many, the ultimate and perhaps most stable sense of self-awareness.

In their search for identity, the adherents of black nationalism have to accept and fully explore their particular situation. But, while preoccupied with a sectional and limited interest, they are inspired by a universal human need for fulfillment[....]

RACE, CLASS, NATIONALITY AND COLOR: THE AFRICAN AMERICAN SEARCH FOR IDENTITY[66]

BETTYE COLLIER-THOMAS AND JAMES TURNER

The great problem of the hour appears to be, by what name shall we be known? Are we colored folks as many of our white friends rather patronizingly dub us? Shall we confess to being Colored Americana? Must we accept the clumsy polysyllabic Afro-American, or shall we plead guilty to being plain, common every day NEGROES?[67]

—Editor F. Z. S. Peregrino, *The Star of Zion*

Thruout [sic] the colored press of the country there is an oft expressed wish to reject the term "Negro" as indefinite and contemptuous and "colored" as nondescript, suggesting instead "African," of African descent, and "black."[68]

—*The Afro-American Ledger*

The recent movement to have the term African American used as the race designation for people of African descent in America is part of a continuum whose roots trace to the early nineteenth century. In 1828 a reader condemned *Freedom's Journal*, the first Black newspaper published in America, for using Negro, the most persistent and debated nomenclature.[69] Concurrent with the supporters of Negro, other terms were launched, some of which prevailed for a time. Beginning with African, historically, terms such as Negro, Colored, Anglo-African, Afro-American, Africo-American, Aframerican, Hamite, and Ethiopian are representative of some of the many appellations which sought legitimacy. From the 1830s to the middle of the 1890s, Colored American and the more commonly used derivation Colored were the most popular terms. At the beginning of the twentieth century, Negro gained considerable support as a generic term, becoming by 1920 the most commonly used expression for race designation. Increasing dissatisfaction with the term Negro, most noted in the late 1930s, culminates with the Black power movement of the 1960s. During the 1960s, Black and Afro-American emerged as key terms for race designation, frequently used interchangeably. In 1988, African American was posited as the most appropriate and comprehensive race designation. This unsettling and persistent struggle to find a suitable name continues to be rooted in issues related to race, color, and nationality, and was central to the effort to define a group identity.[70]

For almost two hundred years the question of identity has been a troubling issue, that characterizes the peculiar psychological dimensions of the Black experience in America. This issue has caused troubling psychological ramifications for African descendants from their inception in America as a dominated people to the present.[71] Slavery denied Africans their original identity, leaving them with a sense that they were lacking a fundamental wholeness as human beings. Africans were confronted, not only with a condition of loss of freedom, but with the repudiation of the very legitimacy of their culture and human identification. The institution of slavery promoted efforts to deny Africans a legitimate foundation for the very nature of their being, in a sense to case them from being to nothingness. The ultimate human degradation is nothingness. The fate of the African was compounded by the imposition of labels and stigmas with which enslavers attempted to present Africans as caricatures of humanity. As if having to endure forced exile were not enough, Africans were further victimized by the European claim that they were sub-humans, without notable references to history and culture. Consequently, the classic quest of asking, "Who am I?" became a tragic refrain of pain that echoes in the Black voice throughout the ages to the present.

The pursuit of a group identity was further complicated by the slave experience, which permitted the persistent violations of Africans' human rights, which exposed them to an unprecedented incidence of rape and other sexual violations of every imaginable variation. As a result of almost two centuries of sexual exploitation of African women, offspring of varying physical coloration with diversified features were produced. Among free Blacks, light and dark mulattoes were prevalent in cities such as Boston, Washington, Philadelphia, Atlanta, Savannah, Charleston, St. Louis, and New Orleans. Representing a different physical type from that of their African antecedents, they were set apart by their color, and sometimes their class. This formed the basis for creating an intragroup color consciousness, and a related system of classification of physical types, which has had significant sociological ramifications in the life of African descendants.[72]

In plantation society, frequently the distribution of status, work assignments, and quite often legal benefits and privileges derived from color designations. In some cases, the value of the slave, as property, increased if the admixture produced a person of unique beauty. For comely female slaves it could mean a life of concubinage, as they were frequently bought for that purpose. In the slave economy color complexion was a sign of market value, thus providing a concrete and material base in economic valuation, and a principal of social division among human beings. The equation of color with increased sale price applied to males as well as females. The racial ideology of the planter assumed that certain occupations and crafts, particularly those related to functions of the household and service to the body of the master, were preferably associated with certain color ranges. This notion of hue and division of labor was a general principle that applied to both genders of the slave population.

The issue of color as a social value emerged as a cultural symbol that has complicated "race designation"; and as an ideology, it enhanced the symbiotic connection between slave and master. Color valuation intersected with racial concepts of superiority and inferiority, as well as views of cultural aesthetics. The "colorophobia" of the dominant culture was internalized in the socialization process of the slave population, with unfortunate consequences for the stability of internal race relations. Color configurations served as criteria and qualification for caste membership in social organization, and beginning in the antebellum period, and as a basis for the creation of colored societies, social clubs, familial relations (i.e., marriage choices), and in some instances, whole communities. As a result, intracolor conflicts have created the most disruptive problems in the racial history of people of African descent.[73]

Color has been, and still is, often referred to as an associated variable of class in African American society. Consequently, its vexation is equaled by the difficulty that Black people have in honestly discussing this concern. The issue of color, rooted in the sociology of racial slavery, has thereby complicated the discourse on race designation. The plantation's legacy launched color as a functioning social value that pervades the cultural life of slave descendants. Emerging from plantation society is a segmented system of social organization in the Black community that is readily based on color standards. This is the consequence of internalizing the imposed conditions of slavery.

Plantation societies in the Western hemisphere were most often stratified by color. These patterns were most distinct and formal in the Caribbean, where reference to browns and blacks are still quite evident today. Though it can be reasonably argued that this pattern was subtler in North American slavocracies, it nonetheless is an insidious force that has dramatically influenced the cultural psychology of those exposed to color definitions. This "value" of color, as a social standard, becomes reified in folk life. Not only does it affect the obvious conceptions of beauty, but equally so perceptions of intelligence, leadership capabilities, and prominence. This type of racial thinking—and its related practice of conscious color selection among middle and upper class sectors of the community—becomes self-generative to the extent that people with lighter complexions are more likely to have disproportionately higher material standards of life, i.e., education, upward mobility, property ownership, and wealth. The syndrome reproduces itself over generations.[74]

The historical data supports the observation that all too often the offspring of miscegenation on the plantation were more likely to be manumitted, be given property and some money, and have provisions made for their education, all of which accrued to them a distinct social advantage over others, even after the abolition of slavery. This meant that the light-complexioned sector of the slave population were in a better position to assume leadership in the economic, social, and political life of black America. The tragic dimension of these unfortunate circumstances was that some, if not all, of these people began to demonstrate in their attitude and behavior a belief in their inherent superiority over others. These beliefs became embodied in the popular culture, and are promoted in colloquial language, social proscriptions, beauty culture, and standards for membership in "society" and in the media. The refrain, "If you're light, you're all right; if you're brown, stick around; if you're Black, get back," is a telling commentary on this problem. A review of the literature on race designation clearly shows the deep-seated ambivalence about color, racial identity, and nationality among people of African descent. Colorphobia has a direct implication upon the choice of terms that groups of people have felt were either appropriate or inappropriate for them.

Issues of race and color bore a direct relationship to questions of nationality. Black people arriving in 1619 on the shores of Jamestown knew that they were Africans and referred to themselves as such, although their enslavers referred to them as Negroes. For most of the seventeenth century, African descendants clung tenaciously to the knowledge of African lineage and later referenced themselves in relationship to Africa. As miscegenation advanced and manumissions became more prevalent, there grew up a class of free persons that preferred terms such as "Free People of Color" and "Colored." Organizations founded during the late seventeenth and early eighteenth centuries often included either African or Colored in their titles. The frequency of appending African to organizational titles and of using it for race designation declined with the growth of the free Black population. Increasingly, by the middle 1830s the term African incurred disfavor with some free Blacks, who felt that in "blood and nativity" they were "Colored" Americans. Their choice of the term "Colored" was influenced by their opposition to the program of the American Colonization Society, which actively promoted the return of free Blacks to Africa. And for some free persons, the term African, like Negro, was associated with the slave status. To distance themselves from the slave experience, they excluded African as a name of choice.[75]

While African and Coloured were the favored words of reference among antebellum African descendants, Negro was used primarily by slaveholders and the white press. The use of the term Negro appears to date back to the beginning of the African slave trade. In 1442, Anton Gonslaves, lieutenant of Prince Henry the Navigator, used the Portuguese term Negro to describe captive natives from the coast of Guinea, who were black in color. These "Negroes" were taken to Cuba as slaves and later were brought to America, where the term Negro was later used to replace "Blackamoor" and "Ethiopian," English words for Black people. In the eighteenth century, Johann Blumenbach, an early anthropologist [and] founder of the study of man as a science, classified the human race into five species, one of which he called Negro. For many Blacks, Blumenbach's definition of the Negro was not comprehensive enough to incorporate the American of African descent through whose veins now coursed the blood of native Americans and Europeans. In simplistic terms, white Americans defined a Negro as any person who had the smallest portion of African ancestry. In the twentieth century individual states developed statutes which defined in detail how many Black antecedents were necessary to designate a person as a Negro.[76]

In the nineteenth century, some Americans of African descent, who had an evident trace of white blood, rejected the term Negro, arguing either that it was associated with slavery, or that it referred exclusively to persons whose skin was Black. In 1855, Mary Ann Shadd Cary, editor of the *Provincial Freeman*, responding to objections to the use of Negro, stated that the term was not comprehensive enough. Cary, stressing her preference for Colored, argued that Negro, like white, couldn't include "varieties of the same class, as, for example, the Indian and the European, the African, and the Colored American of almost entire European ancestry." Cary preferred Colored because it related to people of color worldwide, including Black, white, brown, red, yellow, and their varieties.[77] The term Colored was widely used throughout the West Indies to designate persons who were part African and part Caucasian, whatever their complexion, but it never applied as in America to full-blooded Africans, nor was the term Negro ever applied to any but pure Blacks.[78]

After the Civil War, former slaves wishing to forge a new identity changed their surnames and sought a new race designation that would more appropriately give recognition to their aspiring nationality as Americans, and bestow upon them a racial pride.[79] For many, "African" symbolized a distant past and separated them from their newly bestowed citizenship. Celebrating their inclusion into the American body politic, some wanted to be known simply as Americans, removing all vestiges of their former status as slaves. Thus, while the search for a new race designation ensued, Colored continued as the popular term of choice, and African and Negro were eschewed. In 1870 members of the African Methodist Episcopal Church debated whether or not the word African should be removed from the denominational title. The issue was enjoined on the pages of the *Christian Recorder*, the denominational periodical. Supporting the retention of African, one reader, writing under the [pen name] "Ham," argued that the Fifteenth Amendment granted Black men the vote, but it did "not make Black men white, nor white men Black; neither does it make the Englishman, the Irishman, the German, nor the African an American in the strict sense of the word." Pointing out that the Irish, French, German, and English all boasted of their ancestry, Ham questioned whether Africans were ashamed of theirs.[80]

The argument over race designation continued throughout the 1870s and 1880s. By 1890, "Negro" was perceived less as a term of social degradation and used more as a word related to black skin color. The discussion of what the race designation should be escalated in this period. Proponents for Negro and Afro-American, the newly spawned term, waged a vociferous battle for support. Arguments were introduced supporting Negro as a generic term for the race, which could incorporate race and color. The debate of the 1890s was dramatically waged in the pulpit, on the rostrum and in the press. It came at a time of increased "colorphobia" in the Black community.[81] As the lines were drawn between light- and dark-skinned Blacks, persons having light skins were depicted as being obsessed with being white, duplicitous in their dealings with the race and ambivalent in their fealty.[82]

The most visible defenders of the term Afro-American, Everett J. Waring, an attorney, and T. Thomas Fortune, editor of the *New York Age*, were very light-skinned and had come from fairly privileged backgrounds. Waring was descended from a long line of free Blacks, who became noted for their achievements in education, law, and the arts. In 1888, Waring became the first Black lawyer to practice before the Maryland state bar. Describing himself as "the author, inventor, coiner (as you please) of the word," War-

ing explained that the term Afro-American should not be confused with
African American, Africo-American, or Afric American, words popularized
around 1867. Carefully pointing out that none of these terms ever came
into general use, he asserted that his word, Afro-American, was universally used. According to Waring, he "coined" Afro-American in 1878 while
teaching in the public schools of Columbus, Ohio. He explained that he
used the term *coined* to offset the arguments of classical scholars that he
destroyed the root of the word African. Explaining the choice of "Afro,"
Waring stated, "I am aware that Afric is the root of the word. Had I derived my word, I would have violated well known rules of etymology, if I
destroyed the root, Afric. But scholars know there are no rules governing
the coinage of words."[83]

John Edward Bruce, a very outspoken journalist, and avid promoter
of the word Negro, challenged Waring's authorship of the term Afro-
American.[84] According to Bruce, the term was first used in April 1836 by
a white writer in the *Anti-Slavery Record*, in an article entitled "The Moral
Character of the Afro-Americans."[85] Bruce's challenge of authorship gained
no adherents; for most Black leaders, the issue was whether or not the term
was appropriate and would it prevail.

Because of his forceful advocacy for Afro-American, Fortune was sin-
gled out by Bruce as the "champion of the 'mixed people' or 'Afro-
Americans.'"[86] The argument over race designation that ensued between
Bruce and Fortune ostensibly began with the 1897 publication of an article
in the *New York Sun*, entitled "The Color Line." In this article, Fortune
made reference to Dr. Edward Wilmot Blyden's lectures during his travel in
the South. Bruce alleged that Fortune misrepresented Blyden's intent and
purpose in discussing the relationship between the "Blacks and the mulattoes." Bruce accused Fortune of misquoting Blyden in order to exalt the
Afro-American, "to which class Dr. Blyden and a majority of the Negroes
of America do not belong." The discussion appeared to revolve around a
statement made by Blyden in response to the Reverend Dr. Pollard, the
minister of St. Mark's Church in Charleston, South Carolina. The Reverend Pollard in a speech before the Laboring Men's Association declared
that he "had the shrewdness of his Anglo-Saxon nature and the endurance
of his Negro nature." He deplored the fact that the contemporary discussions of race placed him outside of the Black and white race, however much
he identified with the "Negro." Pollard concluded that the race problem
could be resolved only through the united efforts of African descendants
of all shades and colors. At this point, Blyden interrupted Pollard, asking
"how he managed with his church which was notorious for its colorpho-

bia." It appeared that Blyden's comments were construed as being offensive by Fortune and some mulattoes.[87] Bruce used this incident to publicize color discrimination within the race, which appeared to have escalated during [...] the late 1880s and in the 1890s.[88]

Although concerns for intragroup color discrimination and race designation are key themes in African American history, with few exceptions they have been overlooked by scholars. Reasons for this neglect are rather complex. National and international racism, as directed at people of color, has been the major agenda. Many African Americans feel that giving credence to color discrimination within the race will divert attention from the larger issue of societal racism. However, there are few areas of the African American experience in which intragroup color discrimination has not had an impact. Indeed, it is an issue that goes to the heart of the African American identity crisis, which is prevalent at every point in history. In the 1890s "colorphobia," as African American leaders termed it, was a major concern. Having light or dark skin could have an impact on one's ability to advance socially, politically, and economically within Black and white America.

It is not easy to define the influence of color in the lives of African Americans, but it is essential that we explore its ramifications. Color was a race, class, and gender issue. In terms of race, color has been a major societal issue—defined in terms of Black or white, Negro or Caucasian—that overshadows many other aspects of one's life. It has been more of a gender issue, and to some extent a class issue, within the Black community. Its effects have reached more deeply into the lives of Black females than those of males. Color, particularly the gradations of skin color, physical features, and hair texture, is a part of the heritage of slavery. Miscegenation helped create a people who range from white in complexion to any shade of tan, brown, and black one can imagine. Light-skinned females with white features of every class, formally or informally educated, had greater opportunities to advance economically and socially; yet color and class were frequently interrelated. Mulattoes frequently had earlier and more opportunities to be educated and establish an economic base. Since the traditional American values attached to education, family, occupation, money, social position, and organizational connections were key factors in determining one's class, more light-skinned Blacks tended to belong to a higher socio-economic group. Light-skinned females were preferred for certain jobs. They were also viewed as being more desirable by some Black and white males.[89]

For at least two decades before the arrival of Marcus Garvey, John Bruce was the chief advocate of the term Negro. Linking nationality and color, he continued to promote Negro as the proper designation for the race. Bolstering his argument with census statistics, in 1898 Bruce pointed out that in 1890 there were 7,470,040 people classed as Negroes, 6,337,980 of which were pure Blacks or of African descent. Mulattoes, or persons of mixed heritage, constituted 1,132,060. Given these numbers, Bruce asserted that the majority of the race, being dark-skinned, preferred Negro. For Bruce, the term Negro defined the ethnological status of the race, not Negroid. Bruce pointed out that Negroid, the term coined by Johann Blumenbach, implied an admixture, as did Afro-American.[90]

Linking the issue of color discrimination and race designation, Bruce argued that the promotion of the term Afro-American was a political move launched by light-skinned Blacks.[91] This is another example of how people who are self-conscious of color and complexion are motivated to choose one term or the other. In the case of the light-complected persons such as Fortune and those he represented, their objection to the term Negro was based on their interpretation that it referred to "blackness" of complexion. Because they were uneasy about their apparent heritage of racial mixture, they preferred Afro-American, which they felt more accurately reflected their clear African ancestry and indicated some white parentage, which was a consequence of the American experience. Whereas in the case of dark-complected persons, the term Negro was considered much more appropriate, in that it gave reference to an honorable African origin to which they felt all members of the race should be proud heirs.

In order to appreciate the politics of race designation, as it has evolved through the various periods of African American history, it is critically important to understand the shifting preference in terminology within the context of the sociopolitical connotations at different stages of the discourse. In the nineteenth century "Negro" is heralded as a reference to Africa and blackness, whereas in the twentieth century the meanings are reversed and Afro-American assumes a more direct assertion of identification with African lineage, without regard to shades and complexions. Throughout the debate, however, there are large sections of the community who consider Negro to be too closely related to racially pejorative phrases like "nigger" and "negress" to be acceptable as a nomenclature of dignity for the race.[92] How and why people felt the way they did about various terms was largely influenced by the common perception of their characteristic meanings at particular times in American culture. But the most persistent contention revolved around the ambivalence related to complexion. However, this internal discussion is at all times mediated by the standards of racial categorization imposed externally by the dominant white society and Black people's reaction to it.

The discussion about choice of terms acceptable for race designation was a highly charged political debate. Especially in the nineteenth century, many people in the Black community, primarily ones with more education, were gravely concerned about their insecure political status in America. They realized that there were powerful and influential sectors of the white elite that argued for the removal of all African-descended persons as aliens in American society. Therefore, the concern was that if they continued to permit themselves to be referred to as African, the dominant community would be encouraged to view them as outsiders in the American body politic. Until the Civil War, persons of African descent had no legal base on which to reference Black people as citizens in America. In the latter part of the nineteenth century, the opposition to the term African was almost singularly based upon a reference to the right of citizenship in America, especially after the passage of the Thirteenth, Fourteenth, and Fifteenth Amendments.

In the early twentieth century, Negro is widely embraced as the generic term for Black people worldwide. By 1915 support for Negro as a universal term emanated from three distinct sources. There were those who argued that Negro was anthropologically and ethnologically correct. Others reasoned that Negro was the most commonly used term, and finally some felt the term was legally correct, since most states legislated that anyone with a trace of "Negro blood" was Negro.[93]

The Harlem Renaissance—proclaiming the "New Negro," the prominence of the Garvey Movement, and its celebration of Africa—reinforced Negro as a term of independent nationality, as well as an appropriate name for race designation. In 1926, Amy Jacques Garvey claimed that Marcus Garvey was responsible for dignifying the term Negro. She stated that "today the world writes Negro with a capital 'N,' quotes his expressions, and takes him seriously, while the race devotes its energy to building a nation in Africa, and takes pride in its wonderful physique and beautiful black skin."[94] The Garveyites argued that "Negro is an Honorable Name." They contended that the term was objectionable to some Black people because of "the immediate and tragic past with which it is associated. To say Negro today is to recall slavery, persecution, disfranchisement, lynching, etc." They concluded that a change in name would not eliminate the problem, since the need was to make the term "Negro" represent "something besides contentment and conservatism, both in religion and politics."[95] By the second decade of the twentieth century the question of racial designation and definition of nationality became wedded to the term Negro.

The nationality question is yet another dimension of the discourse on race designation. While the issue of nationality is a consistent theme of African American political thought, it nonetheless emerges at this period with greater articulation to race designation. During this time, those who were strongly partial to the term Negro felt that it stressed a historical reference to a place of geographical origin. It was their perception that the advocates of "Colored" and "Afro-American" were trying to obviate their natural association with Africa as the root of the race. While in one respect their reference to Negro concentrated on skin color, they also were concerned that the term Negro emphasized a direct association with Africa as place of historical beginning for the race. As such, they were claiming Africa as definition of nationality as used in the American context, such as Irish, Italian, Chinese, Polish, German, Japanese, Mexican, and so forth. Therefore, Negro provided an appropriate prefix that established [a] definition of nationality for Black people in the customary American pluralistic tradition. Furthermore, this established the base for consideration of African-descended people as an ethnic group, as opposed to simply a racial or color category. In American culture, the central problem of racism in this regard was and is the tendency of white Americans to perceive and define people of African descent singularly in racial and color terms, ignoring the ethnic characteristics that they recognized in other Americans, largely those coming from Europe. Indeed, it logically proceeded from the assumption of African inferiority—that they were without ethnic characteristics because they were incapable of culture, and therefore had no national (historical) origin of significance. Assertions to this effect are profuse in American literature, by scholars as well as popular commentators.

At the turn of the [twentieth] century the term Negro was effectively rooted in American jurisprudence as the term of legal definition that distinguishe[d] people of African descent from those of European identity. State legislatures throughout the country provide[d] legislative edicts regulating all persons in American society who have traceable African parentage. This effectively circumvent[ed] the arguments of significant social distinctions based on miscegenation. While there were variations in different state codes, they nonetheless established a national pattern of determining racial identity for a person as a Negro based on traceable African descent. In Kentucky, Maryland, North Carolina, Mississippi, Tennessee, and Texas, the statutes asserted that "a person of color" was one who descended from a Negro to the third generation, inclusive, though one ancestor in each generation may have been white. In Alabama, "a person of color" was one who had as much as one-eighth Black ancestry. In Virginia, a Negro was defined as one having at least one-sixteenth Black ancestry. In Oklahoma, anyone referred to as Negro or being in the Negro or colored race was considered to be of African descent. In Arkansas, "persons of color" included all who had a visible and distinct admixture of African blood.[96]

In the 1920s, the *Amsterdam News* reported that the term Negro no longer simply meant black, that it in fact incorporated race and color. Social and civic organizations began concerted campaigns to have Negro established as the prevailing terminology. The *New York News* asserted that the NAACP, the Urban League, and Tuskegee and Hampton Institutes were actively campaigning for the exclusive use of Negro as the race designation.[97] This observation was basically correct. Though the term Colored continued to be used fairly widely for at least the next two decades, it was nonetheless supplanted by the growing popularity of the term Negro, which became the prevailing nomenclature for the race. From the late 1930s through the 1950s, the question of Negro as an appropriate race designation was frequently discussed. In the 1960s it was seriously challenged.[98]

The common usage of the term Negro was supported by the convergence of two quite different social movements prominent in the Black community. On the one hand, there was the Black nationalist and Pan-Africanist ideology of the Garvey Movement that claimed Negro as a universal terminology, referring to all peoples of the Black race emanating from Africa. The Garveyites, like their nineteenth-century counterparts, were quite specific in their usage of the term as referring to people of African origin and those of dark complexion who were commonly perceived in society as being members of the Black race. For them, usage of the term Negro also provided a vehicle for international linkage and unity among the Black people of the world. Marcus Garvey was quite pointed in his use of the term and the definition he ascribed to it.[99]

Responding to an article in the *New York World*, attributing a statement to the famed anthropologist Dr. Franz Boas, a Columbia University professor who claimed that people in Northern Africa were not to be classified as "Negroes, because they were not of that race," Garvey said:

> Whenever a black man, whether the Moroccan, Algerian, Senegalese, or what not, accomplishes anything of importance he is no longer a Negro. The question, therefore, suggests itself, 'Who and what is a Negro?' The answer is, 'A Negro is a person of dark complexion or race....' These people understand that their destiny is linked up with all other men of color throughout

the world…that the hundreds of millions of darker people are looking
toward one common union and destiny through the efforts of universal cooperation….[100]

For Garvey it was the elasticity of the term that especially made it functional, for he accepted the racial categorization of the American and European
colonists, who asserted that anyone with traceable African ancestry was socially and legally defined as Negro.[101]

The NAACP and the Urban League were leading forces in the movement
for integration in America, although they came to their agreement on the
term Negro from a slightly different objective. While they too accepted the
broad definition of Negro as inclusive of all persons of African descent,
regardless of shades of complexion, they were primarily concerned with
dignifying the term and emphasizing its specific peculiarity as an American
phenomenon. To them, the term Negro is less universal in its connotation
as it is distinctive in reference to the American racial experience. They
would argue that the Negro's rightful claim to being an American was
based on the fact, in their view, that the Negro ethnologically and phenotypically was a unique product of American culture.

Nonetheless, these divergent social currents in African American political thought converge in promoting the term Negro to dominant usage
during the period 1930 to 1960. In the latter two decades of this period,
consolidation in the usage of this term focused in a nationwide campaign
by intellectuals, the Black press, civil rights organizations and civic associations for the capitalization of the term "Negro."[102] However the 1960s was
to begin another interesting and dramatic shift in the historical evolution
in the continuing discourse on racial designation.

The quest for self-affirming identity became a hallmark of the 1960s
liberation struggle that captured the minds and hearts of Black people into
the 1980s. The rise of the Black consciousness/Black power movement re-
new[ed] the debate over appropriate race designation and expand[ed] its
conceptual dimensions. The politics of identity, so characteristic of this period, juxtapose[d] "Negro" and "Black" as paradigms of political attitude
and consciousness.[103] Though, as was true in the earlier part of the previous stage with Negro, the term Black is asserted during this period as
most likely to achieve effective unity within the race and dispel pejorative
stereotypes associated with color and complexion. It is important to note
here the continuity in motive: the search for a unifying term that will at
the same time exorcise divisive values of color and class. H. Rap Brown, as
President of SNCC, captured the tenor of the new term in the debate with

his exhortation that "Every Negro is a potential Black man." The Nation of Islam poignantly emphasized the growing ambivalence toward the term Negro during this time with their usage of the phrase, "the so-called Negro."[104]

The issue of color and race designation converged in the early 1960s in ways that would be considered historically peculiar. We have already indicated that the issue of color has been consistent and that the issue of race designation is recurrent at certain periods in history. Issues of race, color, and nationality converge in the 1960s in new ways to create a dynamic force in Black political perspective. It was as if there were an accumulation of the political legacies of African Americans. Emerging from and superseding the civil rights movement was the Black consciousness/Black power movement. Many African American historians contend that it is more appropriate to refer to this period as the Black liberation struggle. Civil rights in this context may be conceived of as one dimension of the Black liberation struggle.[105] Civil rights is the struggle for inclusion and democratic rights in the civil society, whereas liberation suggests a more comprehensive agenda that involves objectives of political empowerment, cultural redemption, cultural integrity, economic development, self-reliance, and self-determination. In the 1960s, the advocates of Black power projected these ideas in varying combinations, capturing the imagination of Black people on a mass scale.

The idea of a new consciousness, i.e., Black consciousness, was considered essential to the advancement of the movement. Artists and intellectuals, as cultural workers, advocated the necessity for reclaiming and affirming Africanity and particularly cultural heritage. It was posited that such an objective would enhance the quality of cultural life in the Black community and would institutionalize values of self-respect and solidarity.[106] Furthermore, such a stance would constitute resistance to Eurocentric hegemony over society's critical ideas. The point advanced was that in order for Black people to fight effectively in the political arena, they would have to rescue the sense of their being from the presuppositions and impositions of white dominance. Phrases commonly repeated by activists during this period were that "Black people would have to change themselves in order to change society," and, "You have to love yourself, in order to truly love another and for others to respect you." The underlying notion is that consciousness is a primordial force in behavior—that oppression, when it is successful, effectively reorders the consciousness of the oppressed. Malcolm X was frequently known to exclaim that the oppressed cannot have the same consciousness as the oppressor in order to be free.[107]

It was in this context that "Negro" received special attention. The political activist of this period felt that Negro was a term associated with enslavement and domination; that it was a term of imposition that purposely defined Black people as *object* as opposed to *subject*; that it produced a perspective that disengaged Black people from their African origin and historical place, and therefore, it represented rootlessness and alienation.[108] The late Richard B. Moore frequently proclaimed that "there is no Negro land in the world," and that "Negro" lacks historical specificity. As a term, its lineage derived from slavery. Therefore, in the political parlance of the day, Negro became synonymous with denial of historical location and political consciousness.[109] The "so-called Negro," as the exponents of the Nation of Islam would say, was ahistorical if not unhistorical in reference, and associated with social obsequiousness. The Negro was projected as socially obedient and insufficiently rebellious, if not anti-revolutionary. Consequently, Negro became a metaphor for socio-cultural oppression. Political activists referred to Negro as a caricature for reactionary political behaviors. Therefore, the term was rejected. And among Black consciousness advocates, Negro was used as a term of derision and an example of their loss of historical being as a people.

Malcolm X played a pivotal role in the repudiation of the term Negro. As a minister in the Nation of Islam, he cast aspersions on the term, broadly emphasizing the organization's reference to the "so -called Negro." After leaving the Nation of Islam he organized the Organization of Afro-American Unity. Malcolm's embracement of the term Afro-American promoted its acceptance among persons in the Black power/Black consciousness movement. In his speeches at this time he use[d] the phrase, "We are an African people," to emphasize the relationship of Black people in America to Africa.[110]

It was in this manner that a movement toward a new terminology for a new identity was inspired. Concern was also expressed over the ways in which African Americans, as a people, had internalized forms of their oppression. Particular emphasis was placed on ways in which the hierarchy of color/complexion had gained currency and value in the social psychology of Black folk. To address this problem, intellectuals and political activists argued the criticality of a term that would jettison the bonds of racist ideas and produce an internal sense of liberation. Almost simultaneously two terms emerged, Afro-American and Black. For many persons it was also important that the new race designation make specific reference to Africa. In a natural progression, both terms were accepted and used frequently used interchangeably.

The term Black was seized upon as a generic reference for all complexions of the folk. It was felt that since blackness had been the primary reference for devaluation of Africans as a people, and held a lower rank in the color scale, that if it could be rehabilitated and established as the normative center for African American identity it would logically induce unity across the color spectrum. Additionally, Black people would be naturally associated with others of African origin. Concomitantly, there was a Black Arts Movement to change African American aesthetic values and perspectives. Great emphasis was placed on appearance and the accentuation of natural physical characteristics. Most notable in this regard was the movement toward unprocessed and natural coiffure. It is not incidental that natural hair was uniformly referred to as an "Afro."[111]

Even the names that Black people had come to know themselves by and accept became a part of the critical discourse. The Nation of Islam properly identified European family names as derivative of slavery's legacy. As an expression of Black consciousness, many people, particularly the young, rejected their "slave names." Many children born during this period were given African-inspired names. The Nation of Islam played a significant role in providing some of the fundamental currents for the development of this movement, particularly Malcolm X, who in the last years of his life was the most influential political figure among the activists, artists, and intellectuals of the Black power/Black consciousness movement.

Not since the Garvey Movement of the early part of the twentieth century have we witnessed such widespread concern about color, race designation, and nationality. In fact, it is our observation that these three questions merged to produce a dynamic political culture of the time, unlike any other previous period in African American history. The Black consciousness movement gave legitimacy and broad acceptability to the term Afro-American as representative of an African people, and thus set the stage of the introduction of African American in the late 1980s.[112]

One of the paradoxes in the present debate over race designation is that while, on the one hand, the movement toward African American as a name of choice seems to be advancing, on the other, we also notice that the old dilemma of color distinctions in behavior amongst African Americans seems to have reemerged. The issue of color continues to bedevil our intragroup relations.[113] How much of this is solely internally generated or externally influenced is an important question for social analysis. The answer probably lies closer to a dialectical relationship between the internal and the external. This is not so much an expression of African Americans' independent will as it is the influence of the dominant aesthetic values of white cultural elites over the popular culture. Consequently, whites tend to control the image of Black people in national cultural life. Also, as a people, African Americans continue to suffer from historical discontinuity in their socio-political development from one generation to the next. Unfortunately, one must conclude at this time that as bold as the movement of the 1960s was, African Americans have still not been able to fully liberate themselves from the crucible of race and color.

PART III

BLACK/AFRICANA STUDIES AS DISCIPLINE

Dr. Turner was and continues to be a tremendous influence on my political development. His personal practice and ethics drew from the 3Cs he constantly articulated. He suggested that as Africana scholar-activists, we should be conscious, competent, and committed. As I understood it, consciousness involved being politically and historically aware and attuned to our collective experiences as Black people existing in spaces that attempted to subjugate our lives and ideas. Competence spoke to a work ethic that called for us to render excellent and rigorous intellectual and political engagement on behalf of Black people. Finally, commitment suggested that we be personally invested in this work of education and advocacy, and prepared to do our work continually and consistently over our lifetimes, despite personal or political challenges. Taken together, these principles inform, guide and provide an evaluative tool for my life and work today.

—Agyei Tyehimba

James Turner is one of the most important teachers of my life. He taught and showed me that you can be radically committed to our community while simultaneously being an incredible intellect and human being. He always went the extra mile with me, even though I was not an Africana Studies major. His love and compassion for all of us provided the light that guided us through the university and back into our communities to serve.

—Baye Adolfo Wilson

James Turner at the entrance of the original Africana Studies and Research Center building, ca. 1969.

INTRODUCTION: BLACK INTELLECTUAL INSURGENCY—JAMES TURNER AND THE DISCIPLINE OF AFRICANA STUDIES

JONATHAN FENDERSON

James Turner's writings, institutional commitment, and scholar activism have had a profound influence on the formation, development, and general trajectory of Black Studies in the United States. He has remained at the forefront of Black Studies since its inception as a formal academic enterprise in the late 1960s and labored in the name of the discipline for almost half a century, from 1968 to the present. The collection of writings included in this section represents a remarkably robust approach to the study of Black history, life, and culture.

After rereading and thinking about Turner's writings on Africana Studies, it is difficult to ignore the existence of a scholarly paradox. For those of us invested in Africana Studies, beyond simply staking claim to the production of scholarship on Black people, Turner's writings remain a touchstone and consistent reminder of the intellectual depth, political vision, and radical scholarly critique of the discipline. At the same time, the detractors of Black Studies—and scholars who lay claim to the intellectual project only when it is professionally convenient—tend to ignore Turner's contributions altogether; either as a result of inadvertent scholarly oversight or as a deliberate, self-serving attempt to jettison his work because it fails to fit their preconceived outlook on the discipline. In other words, Turner's ideas are met by two general scholarly habits: on the one hand, there are those who engage with him and attempt to grapple with the imperatives he has placed squarely on the table of Black Studies, and, on the other hand, there are those who elide his contributions.[1] In thinking about a third space and the possibility of a spectrum between these two poles, we notice there are very few scholars who have read Turner's writings on Africana Studies and taken exception in print.[2] Perhaps with the publication of this text, such a group will arise, and we can be certain that Turner would welcome this type of open exchange and constructive criticism.

With hundreds of Black/Africana Studies departments and academic units across the country celebrating their fortieth anniversary and new graduate programs emerging in the discipline every year, the contemporary moment requires that we outline the salient possibilities and come to terms with the shortcomings contained in Turner's work. My introductory remarks here attempt to register Turner's insights, highlight his conceptual contributions, and amplify his thoughts on Black/Africana Studies. This brief introduction positions each piece of writing in its proper context by identifying the historical moment that produced each essay, the publishing site or venue where the piece of writing originally appeared, and each article's location within the general constellation of Black Studies scholarship and critical thought. Turner's six articles that follow are adopted as a way to organize this introduction, appearing as subsection headers. These six sections are followed by brief concluding comments aimed at future generations of Africana Studies practitioners who seek to extend the work of Turner and other activist-scholars like him.

"BLACK STUDENTS: A CHANGING PERSPECTIVE"

"Black Students: A Changing Perspective" appeared in the August 1969 special issue of John Johnson's *Ebony* magazine entitled "The Black Revolution."[3] The article was inserted between the writings of Lerone Bennett Jr., Charles V. Hamilton, Larry Neal, David Llorens, A. B. Spellman, Huey P. Newton, Vincent Harding, Alex Poinsett, Phyl Garland, among others. Though *Ebony* featured small doses of hard-hitting history, cultural analysis, and political stories on a regular basis throughout the 1960s and 1970s—mainly as a result of the contribution of Bennett, Poinsett, Llorens, Garland, and a few others—the magazine never developed a reputation for being a periodical on the radical edge of the Black liberation struggle. That status was granted to publications like the Liberation Committee for Africa's *Liberator*, SNCC's *Student Voice*, the *Black Panther*, a small number of pages of *Muhammad Speaks*, *Negro Digest* (later renamed *Black World*), and a few others. Nevertheless, the appearance of Turner's article in *Ebony*, alongside the work of the rest of the authors featured in the special issue, speaks to Black Power's rising impact upon American society, Black print culture, and African American popular consciousness during the 1960s. Unlike academic journals, *Ebony* was—and continues to be—one of the most popular magazines among African Americans, available in a variety of spaces within Black communities. As a result of being published in the magazine, "Black Students: A Changing Perspective" was accessible to hundreds of thousands of Black people throughout the United States, through their local newsstands, barbershops, beauty salons, corner stores, and in their homes through monthly subscriptions.

Turner penned the editorial while enrolled as a graduate student at Northwestern University. Published a little over a year after the Black student takeover of the bursar's office in May 1968, the essay marks his place as one of the founding architects and engineers of Black Studies in the United States.[4] In addition, the essay is a reminder, on several levels, of the central role played by Black students in both the Black Power movement and the struggle to create Black Studies. The article acts as a reminder first through Turner's role as the student-author, but also through the essay's intended emphasis, topical focus, and compelling thesis, which he painstakingly drives home. The article details the sweeping vision of what historian Stefan Bradley later termed "Black Student Power" and the transformative outlook Black students held for all aspects of American society.[5] Capturing the rapidly evolving outlook of Black students "from Harvard to Tougaloo," Turner connects national figures, local events, and international spectacles of Black Student Power. The essay operates as a historical window into a time period when a large population of Black students were energized by a radical view of the world and motivated by the possibility of ushering this new world into existence.

This essay performs several important functions when it is placed within the larger context of Turner's writings on Black/Africana Studies. First, it effectively jogs our memory about the place of Black Studies in the broader Black liberation movement. While departments of Black/Africana Studies remain liberated zones and lasting reminders of the successes of Black Student Power, Turner makes it clear that American education was understood as one site of struggle out of many. Black Studies departments were beachheads from which radical Black intellectual critique could be launched, complementing other important aspects of Black struggle and activism; they were not fiefdoms to be managed for the pursuit of academic stardom or the amassing of individual and/or institutional wealth. Or, as Johnetta Cole so eloquently puts it, "Black Studies [was] the intellectual arm of the Black Power Movement, [and it] articulates a very different perspective from that of the intellectual establishment."[6] In other words, the fight for Black Studies and the thorough reformation of American higher education were just a small part of a larger fight to improve all aspects of Black life in the United States (and abroad). Black Studies was (and is) not an end, only a means to an end.

In terms of Turner's own thinking, "Black Students: A Changing Perspective" anticipates several questions he would begin to ask about the role of education, the sociology of knowledge and the nature of knowledge production in his later writings. The article also hints at Turner's (and other Black student activists') interest in Africa and the broader Third World, specifically when he cautions the reader about the possibility that the "liberation movement will be maneuvered into a 'bourgeois national movement,' as has happened with independence movements in Africa and Asia." A liberated Africa was on the minds of Black students all across the country, especially students, like Turner, who took courses in African Studies.[7] More specifically, the connections between Northwestern University's renowned African Studies Program, the neocolonial activity of U.S. intelligence agencies, and European colonial interest on the continent made the African anti-colonial struggle a palpable issue for Northwestern's Black students at the time.[8] In fact, during his tenure at Northwestern, Turner worked at the university's African Studies Center and actively lobbied for the participation of Black speakers with radical and anti-colonial sentiments. Not only does Turner's reference to Africa prove that, as James Meriwether has argued, "African Americans reflected on the possibilities for their own situation, with discussion about Africa refracting as well as reshaping debates within black America," but it also offers a glimmer of Turner's commitment to African liberation, which deepened over the years and informed his unique articulation of Black Studies at Cornell University.[9]

"BLACK STUDIES: A CONCEPT AND A PLAN"

Turner produced "Black Studies: A Concept and a Plan" under his new title as Director of the Afro-American Studies Center, after being selected by members of Cornell's Afro-American Society.[10] The students met Turner at the historic "Toward a Black University" Conference at Howard University in November 1968 and felt he was the right person to head the Black Studies program that was in the works at Cornell. In little over a year after participating in the Black student movement at Northwestern, and less than a year after the Howard conference, the twenty-nine-year-old Turner found himself mapping out the details of a Black Studies program and research facility at one of the country's most prestigious universities. Originally submitted as a report to Cornell University's then-president Dale R. Corson, and reprinted publicly in the *Cornell Chronicle* in the fall of 1969, "Black Studies: A Concept and a Plan" is an extremely important document for the history of the Black Studies movement in the United States. Unfortunately, far too many scholars, both inside and outside the discipline, have completely overlooked the manuscript. This is due in large part to the localized nature of the *Cornell Chronicle*, a campus publication

with a circulation too small to cover the entire Cayuga Valley of upstate
New York.

The inclusion of "Black Studies: A Concept and a Plan" in this volume
will, without doubt, draw new scholarly attention to the document and reshape the way we look at both the Africana Studies and Research Center at
Cornell (AS&RC) and the general trajectory of Black Studies in the United States.[11] While much has been written about student protests and the
rebellious climate that created Black Studies, not enough attention has
been paid to the programmatic documents and institutional blueprints for
Black Studies programs and departments. For example, we are all familiar
with the imagery of Cornell's Willard Straight occupation when Black students proudly exited the building wearing bandoleers with clenched guns
in hand.[12] But not many of us know about the document that explicates
the intellectual (and practical) design for the AS&RC—which is the lasting institutional product of the Straight occupation. Revisiting documents
like "Black Studies: A Concept and a Plan" can work to enrich our understanding of the origin of Black Studies by complementing the memories
of radical Black student activism with the historical evidence of a vibrant
intellectual productivity and a rich scholarly tradition.

Perhaps the most remarkable thing about this document is the way that
it is both in and out of step with the (un)conventional vocabulary of Black
Studies advocates at the time, and the way that many of its arguments
are still apropos today.[13] Words like "relevance," "bias," "corrective," "dis-
tortion," "omission," "curriculum," "orientation," "perspective," and terms
like "the Black experience," "Black community," and "urban community
center" saturate the document and ground it in the language of the moment. Variations of these phrases can be found in almost all of the archival
documents and primary literature from the movement to establish Black
Studies. At the same time, key intellectual interventions, like "diaspora,"
and "Africana," were not a part of the popular lexicon, and they represent
Turner's unique vision—an important point I will return to later.

*James Turner with Stan Reeves and other students at burnt out site of
original building housing the Africana Studies and Research Center,
ca. 1970.*

In reading this document, there is a need to draw attention to the way
that Turner maps out the institutional aspects of the Africana Studies
and Research Center and its organizational characteristics as an academic
unit. He envisioned it as an "international center for Black Studies" made
up of teachers, students, artists, and local Black people from the Ithaca
community. And although the scholarly work within the Center would
be both multidisciplinary and interdisciplinary, faculty lines and appointments would be made within the AS&RC. He specifically avoided "a loose
confederation of faculty who hold appointments in other departments and
offer courses under the aegis of their respective departments." He also argued against joint appointments and viewed them as a way to undermine
the integrity of the department. This articulation allowed the academic

unit to consolidate institutional power within the Center and to avoid the conflicting aims of other departments, transitional deans, and anti–Black Studies faculty teaching courses on Black subject matter. The plan for the Center also entailed "a field of study for graduate students," a library, and an urban resident center. Both the ideas for a graduate program and library came to fruition. The AS&RC has bestowed graduate degrees on master's students since 1973 and has recently established a doctoral program, while the John Henrik Clarke Africana Library is currently comprised of close to 25,000 volumes on Black world history, life, and culture. The urban resident center never materialized, and it remains one of the unfulfilled aspirations of the Black Studies project at Cornell.[14] In considering all these aspects—personnel, community engagement, the consolidated power of internal decision making, no joint appointments, an in-house library, and an urban extension center—it becomes obvious that Turner devised a plan that made the AS&RC closely resemble a self-sustained college. The idea of a Black Studies college was not far-fetched during this time period. In fact, many of the student activists explicitly called for "Black Studies Colleges" (or "Colleges of Ethnic Studies") in their lists of demands.[15] Turner, who was one of these students, held on to this idea once he was appointed as a faculty member at Cornell and vigorously worked to bring this concept into being.

*James Turner with Dr. C. Dalton Jones, Africana Studies and Research
Center faculty, and Dr. Meredith Gourdine, a Cornell University
trustee and alum, ca. 1970s.*

"BLACK STUDIES AND A BLACK PHILOSOPHY OF EDUCATION"

The advent of Black Studies also helped foster the creation and proliferation of scholarly journals and publications focused on the parameters of the Black experience. Although publications like the *Crisis*, *Freedomways*, *Phylon*, the *Journal of Negro History*, the *Journal of Negro Education*, and *Negro Digest* already existed, the Black Studies movement ushered in a whole new cadre of journals focused on the Black Studies project and its many facets. Some of these include the *Black Scholar*, established in 1969; the *Journal of Black Studies*, *Africana Journal*, *Black Academy Review*, and the *Review of Black Political Economy*, all established in 1970; *Black Books Bulletin*, in 1971; *Black Images* (published out of Toronto, Canada) and *Journal of Afro American Issues*, both established in 1972; and later journals like *Black Art* (renamed the *International Review of African American Art*) and the *Western Journal of Black Studies*. The point of these journals was to capture, debate, and legitimate the contours of Black life and Black scholarly production. While a handful of these periodicals have managed to survive and flourish, a good number of them ceased publication after a few years. One of these publications with a short life span was *Black Lines*, a journal inaugurated in September 1970 at the University of Pittsburgh by the Black Action Society. This quarterly provided the venue for Turner's essay "Black Studies and a Black Philosophy of Education," published in the journal's second issue in the winter of 1970.[16]

The essay pivots upon a central premise, which Turner uses to both offer a critique and a corrective. The central point is that "education has a definite political function whatever the situation." In the critical portion of the essay, Turner—much like W.E.B. Du Bois in the concluding chapter to *Black Reconstruction*, "The Propaganda of History"—assails the claims of universality and objectivity in American education.[17] He unmasks American education by describing it as "white studies," or "a system of intellectual legitimacy which defines the activities and experiences of white Western people as the universal yardstick of human experience." For both Turner and Du Bois, white studies functions as "more than mere omission and difference of emphasis"; it is "ideological" and "too often a deliberate attempt so to change the facts of history" and other areas of human knowledge.[18] At the same time, Turner uses the political function of education to rethink what Amilcar Shabazz has referred to as "the Black educational tradition" and chart a new course for Black students, Black educators, and Black Studies.[19] Turner argues for the recalibration of Black education to fit the changing social and political context of the period. For Turner, Black education is not only a tool for Black community development and liberation, but Black Studies, as a particular form of Black education, operates as a way to disrupt the process of inculcating white middle-class norms and values in Black students. However, Turner is cautious not to place any lofty revolutionary value on the discipline. In his assessment, Black Studies has the ability to reorient students, but "historical situations make revolutions and revolutionaries, not classroom lecturers." In other words, although Black Studies can be useful in attuning students to the history and unfinished nature of the Black struggle, the fight for a liberated world cannot be won in the academy or in isolated victories at intellectual sites of confrontation.

Much like "Towards a Critique of Social Science" and "Africana Studies and Epistemology," "Black Studies and a Black Philosophy of Education" hints at Turner's sociological training.[20] These three essays are bound by their interrogation of the sociology of knowledge. Collectively, the three articles raise questions about the triumvirate of race, politics, and the social configuration of knowledge.

"BLACK STUDIES AS AN INTEGRAL TRADITION IN AFRICAN-AMERICAN INTELLECTUAL HISTORY"

One of the major arguments launched against the establishment of Black Studies was that, as Michael Thelwell accurately recapitulated, "there is simply not sufficient material in the field to support and justify Black Studies as a major field of academic endeavor."[21] One way that Black Studies advocates responded to this uninformed opinion (or convenient incognizance) was to outline a long tradition of Black scholarship and the presence of ample Black intellectual fodder for disciplined academic inquiry. James Turner's "Black Studies as an Integral Tradition in African-American Intellectual History" is a prime example of this pro–Black Studies rebuttal.[22] Lawrence Crouchett and Ronald Bailey have undertaken similar intellectual ventures. It is these early attempts to excavate the contours of a Black intellectual tradition that paved the way for latter works such as Cedric Robinson's *Black Marxism: The Making of the Black Radical Tradition* (1983), Beverly Guy-Sheftall's *Words of Fire: An Anthology of African-American Feminist Thought* (1995), Winston Napier's *African American Literary Theory: A Reader* (2000), Robin D. G. Kelley's *Freedom Dreams: The Black Radical Imagination* (2002), Kristin Waters and Carol B. Conaway's *Black Women's Intellectual Traditions: Speaking Their Minds*

(2007), and Frances Smith Foster, Beverly Guy-Sheftall, and Stanlie James's *Still Brave: The Evolution of Black Women's Studies* (2009), as well as texts focused explicitly on the Black Studies tradition, like Nathaniel Norment Jr.'s *African American Studies Reader* (2001), Jacqueline Bobo, Cynthia Hudley, and Claudine Michel's *Black Studies Reader* (2004), and Delores P. Aldridge and Carlene Young's *Out of the Revolution: The Development of Africana Studies* (2003), among others.[23]

"Black Studies as an Integral Tradition in African-American Intellectual History" reflects upon a Black intellectual tradition that Turner breaks into four distinct epochs, characterized by the *male* historical actors, prevailing ideologies within the Black intellectual community, and the general sociopolitical climate. He begins with the work of Du Bois and Carter G. Woodson, both of whom he refers to as "the founding mentors," and includes men like E. A. Johnson, Benjamin Brawley, Monroe Work, Arturo Schomburg, Benjamin Brawley, Charles H. Wesley, Charles Victor Roman, and Charles Johnson, all actively researching and writing in the period between 1918 and 1929. A Black feminist or womanist analysis, which is obviously missing, would force him to push this timeline back and broaden it to include Anna Julia Cooper's *A Voice from the South*, the radical activist-scholarship of Ida B. Wells, Josephine St. Pierre Ruffin, Mary Church Terrell, and the Black club movement women, among others.[24] He then follows the initial period with the years stretching between 1930 and 1940, which he refers to as "the emergence of Black Studies as a field." This portion is moved by the work of Joseph Rhoads, Lawrence Reddick, the Association for the Study of Negro Life and History (ASNLH), and the radical "young turks" collaborating at Howard University.[25] Turner referred to this period as a time characterized by the influence of Marxism on African American intellectuals. The period between 1940 and 1960 is described as a low point for Black Studies. He attributes this nadir to the political retrenchment of World War II, the Cold War, and the politics of McCarthyism. In his assessment, the red baiting and political persecution caused the most prominent and productive Black intellectuals to recoil into defensive stances to ward off government-sanctioned attacks.

Then, finally, the last period stretches from 1960 to the year of the article's publication, 1976. Turner refers to this period as "the modern Black Studies movement," which called for the "re-assertion of the intellectual validity of Black Studies." In the article, this period—which would have been the time when Turner was writing the piece—is absent of individual names and instead speaks of a collective critique brought forth by Black student activists located mainly at "Black college campuses." This raises two points: first, it challenges us to remember the important role played by students at historically Black colleges in the push to establish Black Studies; second, it draws attention to the work that scholars need to conduct in order to update this epoch of the Black intellectual tradition and flesh out the historical details of the modern Black Studies movement.[26] The article, coauthored with C. Steven McGann, was initially published in the African Studies Association's *Issue: A Journal of Opinion* in the summer of 1976. It was later republished in the *Journal of Negro Education* in 1980.[27]

"TOWARDS A CRITIQUE OF SOCIAL SCIENCE"

Any reading of Turner's work is incomplete without coming to grips with his firm commitment to a leftist, Black Nationalist project and his conscious suturing of race and radical political economy.[28] Such a position has led some Marxists in Black Studies to argue that he is too "narrow" of a nationalist and some Black Studies nationalists to contend that he is too "Eurocentric" or "dogmatic" in his comfort with Marxism. Needless to say, his work situates him in the interstices of Black radical politics and presents a challenge to doctrinaire impositions and static entrenchments. No essay included in this section captures his left nationalist politics better than "Towards a Critique of Social Science," coauthored with W. Eric Perkins.[29]

The essay, published in the *Black Scholar* in April 1976, builds upon many of the ideas in "Black Studies and a Black Philosophy of Education," while offering a critique of the state of Black political ideology at the time. It connects the American university—"a tool of imperialist and industrial interests"—and American social science, in particular, to "bourgeois philanthropy," "capitalist hegemony," and "America's expanding colonial empire in the South Pacific, the Caribbean, and Latin America." The document is the product of a time period when the Southern African independence struggle was heating up, African American anti-colonialism was cresting, and universities (and other American companies) were being shamed into divesting from apartheid. "Towards a Critique of Social Science" exhibits Turner's transnational awareness and unremitting poise to wed academic critique with social activism; a unique brand of Black intellectual insurgency that typifies his life's work within (and without) the academy.

While the article speaks to the state of the American social sciences more broadly, it also enters into a particular conversation among activists in the global Black radical community. The article appeared shortly after the height of the ideological rift between Marxists and Black Nationalists that occurred in the mid-1970s. This imploded the African Liberation Support Committee (ALSC) and played out on the stage of the Sixth Pan-African Congress in Dar es Salaam.[30] Located in between the two antithetical poles of this rift—which was best represented by the newly converted Marxist Amiri Baraka and the cultural nationalist Haki Madhubuti—Turner attempted to chart a nuanced position while imparting critique wherever it was due.[31] He openly challenges "the new generation of neo-black Marxist intellectuals, in its uncritical adoption of Marxism," especially when "they opt…for a mechanical economism, reducing all social, political, and cultural occurrences as reactions to the economic base." But he also condemns "the degeneration of certain irrational and mystical varieties of Black Nationalism," which he characterizes as "obsolete ideological baggage" that "continues to be defined by under-preparation, mysticism, and bloated black rhetoric." The most stinging critique of particularly narrow forms of Black Nationalism comes across when Turner illuminates the subtextual connection between liberal and conservative "models of cultural pathology" and arguments about the need to (re-)Africanize African American culture—which are most prevalent in strands of Afrocentric thought.[32] This critique is pertinent to contemporary Black/Africana Studies discourse and has been expanded upon by Daryl Michael Scott in *Contempt and Pity: The Social Policy and the Image of the Damaged Black Psyche, 1880–1996*.[33]

"AFRICANA STUDIES AND EPISTEMOLOGY"

In 1980 the Africana Studies and Research Center held a major conference celebrating its tenth anniversary. The event was organized to look back at the ground covered by the discipline during its initial decade and also to chart a new direction by retooling the discipline for the challenges on the horizon. The conference provided the venue for the presentation of one of Turner's most important articles, "Africana Studies and Epistemology."[34] The essay and select papers from the conference were edited by Turner and published independently in 1984 by the Center in a volume entitled *The Next Decade: Theoretical and Research Issues in Africana Studies*. Before moving to discuss the content of the essay, it is important to reflect on the article's initial site of publication. Turner and other members of the AS&RC sought to publish relevant works in-house to avoid the clearinghouse practices and economic interest of conventional publishing companies seeking to capitalize on the new markets opened up by Black Power. As a result, the AS&RC released works like *The Next Decade* and the Africana Monograph

Series, which featured the scholarship of people like Walter Rodney, Hollis R. Lynch, and Houston Baker. This approach to in-house publishing could prove to be valuable in our current "publish or perish" academic climate.

Of all of Turner's writing, "Africana Studies and Epistemology" is the most frequently reproduced and circulated. It has appeared in Delores P. Aldridge and Carlene Young's *Out of the Revolution*, the second edition of Nathaniel Norment Jr.'s *African American Studies: A Reader*, and James Conyer's *Africana Studies: A Disciplinary Quest for Both Theory and Method*. At the same time, the essay is marked by a bit of irony because it is too frequently ignored by scholars enchanted with "the Black Atlantic," "Transnational Black Studies," and other intellectual pursuits that represent Black Studies in the United States as an emaciated, narrow, nationalist enterprise.[35] In fact, Turner's "Africana Studies and Epistemology," along with works by John Henrik Clarke and St. Clair Drake (two people who are part of Turner's intellectual genealogy), could be described as an intellectual prescience to the explosion of African Diaspora Studies.[36] This essay bankrupts the idea that Black Studies is somehow characterized by an "African-American exceptionalism" and narrow emphasis on the Black experience(s) in the United States, as Paul Gilroy has subtly, though consistently, suggested and Rinaldo Walcott and a few others have forcibly argued.[37] To the contrary, the essay is evidence that African American intellectuals (from Du Bois to Woodson to Wells-Barnett to Clarke to Turner) have been among the most fervent in arguing for an international and transnational perspective when thinking about Black people. In fact, Turner borrowed the word "Africana" from Du Bois and Woodson, who both worked heroically, though unsuccessfully, to complete separate Africana encyclopedia ventures.[38]

Turner initiated the use of the term "Africana" as a conceptual intervention in "Black Studies: A Concept and a Plan in 1969, but the article "Africana Studies and Epistemology" provides the most incisive exploration of the notion. It clearly delineates the way he envisioned the term being employed in Black Studies, and how it marks a significant expansion of the discipline's critical lexicon and geographical scope. According to Turner:

> The concept *Africana* is derived from the philosophy of the "African continuum and African consociation," which posits fundamental interconnections in the global black experience.... The *black world* is perceived as patterns within a trilateral relationship between Africa, the African Caribbean, and the African Americas with, understandably, primary concentration on African America.[39]

Although Turner did not perceive that portion of the African Diaspora that fell outside the Western Hemisphere, the concept of "Africana" embraces the entire Diaspora since it rests firmly on the notion of the "black world." Clearly this definition of the term provided Black Studies with a sweeping international vision and outlook that embraced the "global black experience." It is an approach to Black Studies that could be described as the epistemological offspring of Pan-Africanism.[40] The African Diaspora and the African continent are brought into a common purview and organically interconnected by shared histories, cultural expressions, intellectual interplay, and political interactions. Furthermore, the ideas of "fundamental interconnections" and "consociation" offer no hint of an "undifferentiated unity" or an essentialist "African personality." Instead, Turner's conception provides room for a spectrum of possible relations between Africa and the African Diaspora—also within Africa and within the Diaspora—lending room for a broad, critical conversation among different theorists of the African Diaspora. As I have argued before, "this spectrum allows a critical dialogue between Melville Herskovits, Molefi Asante and Afrocentricity, Michael Gomez, Edmund Gordon and Mark Anderson, Paul Gilroy, Brent Hayes Edwards, Robin Kelley and Tiffany Patterson, Sheila Walker, St. Clair Drake and pan-Africanist notions of Diaspora."[41] Many of these scholars, along with several others, have expanded our idea of the Diaspora and opened up the conversation to include places like the Indian Ocean, the "Black Pacific," Europe, and all other corners of the world.[42]

The openness of Africana Studies as a broad, global approach to Black Studies has also led to (mis)uses and abuses of the term, and prompted some more recent scholars to disavow the term (and by extension the discipline) of its political intent and application.[43] It is important to remember, however, that Turner's intellectual intervention mirrored the activist work he was conducting on the ground. Or put another way, his political praxis shaped the intellectual work, and his intellectual work informed his political praxis. He has embodied the same scholar-activist (or activist-scholar) tradition that he hoped the program at Cornell would instill in its students. His central role in the formation of the African Heritage Studies Association in 1969, chairmanship of the African American delegation at the Sixth Pan-African Congress, work with the African Liberation Support Committee, institutional support for Walter Rodney and Hoyt Fuller, participation in the establishment of TransAfrica in 1977, campaign work against apartheid South Africa, and the key role he played in the creation of Cornell University's Council on African Studies were all political projects that connected Africa and the African Diaspora in both practical and intellectual ways.[44] For Turner, this link between scholarship and politics is one of the definitive characteristics that make Africana Studies a unique and independent discipline.

Turner's insistence that Africana Studies is a discipline derives from several important points. First, it is an attempt to forestall the natural attrition that plagues interdepartmental and programmatic claims to institutional space in the American university, which is usually based on disciplines and not fields of study. At the same time, it was (and is) a calculated effort to anticipate and embrace the explosion and utility of "interdisciplinary" work. Or, to put it in his own words, Turner has promoted a vision of Black Studies "that transcends and transforms the boundaries of the traditional disciplines into a new interdiscipline." In addition, he, like most of the initial advocates for Black Studies, believed that traditional disciplinary divisions of knowledge and knowledge production remained outmoded and based on specific Western epistemological assumptions, which have inherent blind spots and lacunae. Such disciplinary partitions and methodological restrictions fail to offer, or strive for, a holistic interpretation of the Black experience. Black Studies scholars like Turner, James Stewart, Maulana Karenga, Delores Aldridge, and Perry Hall did not need to wait on the advent of post-thinkers, Gayatri Spivak's *Death of a Discipline*, or academic acceptance to realize the value of interdisciplinary work. They, like many other Black Studies intellectuals, have consistently argued for a disciplinary structure based on interdisciplinary inquiry.

SYNTHESIS: TRACING A TURNER SCHOOL OF THOUGHT IN BLACK STUDIES

For those of us in the discipline of Africana Studies, ignoring Turner's work comes at a cost. We should ponder what is at stake when we fail to come to terms with Turner's global approach to Black Studies. Perhaps we should ask ourselves, how different would the Black Studies tradition look without his presence and the institutional model of the Africana Studies and Research Center at Cornell? We should also return to his writing—and the works of others like him—to measure the distance Black Studies has traveled in the last forty years (if any). Have we progressed? How much new ground have we covered? And what pivotal ideas have we left behind?

In reading the essays that follow, we should be reminded that they offer only a glimpse into the mind of Turner during a brief fifteen-year period. These articles, falling between 1969 and 1984, do not demonstrate the attention to gender issues he forces his students to wrestle with in the classroom. Nor do they account for his more recent engagement with the literature on Black sexualities and Black Queer Studies. To be just, it was in his course on "Black Intellectual Traditions" where I first read Patricia Hill Collins's *Black Feminist Thought* and engaged the Africana Womanist work of Clenora Hudson-Weems.[45] During that same year, I was first introduced to the budding literature of Black Queer Studies through a graduate student, whose thesis on Black male sexualities was chaired by Turner. These anecdotes should remind us to remain vigilant against any static readings that attempt to freeze Black thinkers into a single past historical moment. Turner—like others before him, including W.E.B. Du Bois, Hubert Harrison, Marcus Garvey, Frances Ellen Watkins Harper, and his own contemporaries, including Patricia Hill Collins, Maulana Karenga, and many other thinkers of the Black intellectual tradition—is not static in his thinking. His ideas grow, change, expand, and sharpen; his thoughts are in motion, and his mind is constantly at work.

James Turner and Africana Studies and Research Center faculty and staff, including staff hired from Ithaca's Black community, ca. 1970s.

Fortunately, the seeds of Turner's thought, praxis, and vision have been, and continue to be, sown among generations of students and activists. I would like to advance the idea that James Turner represents a unique school of thought in the ever-expanding Black Studies project. He has engineered a school of thought that is characterized by a disciplinary design for Black Studies (as opposed to a field of study); a worldwide attentiveness and global frame for the study of Black people; a construction of knowledge that emanates from the sociopolitical and cultural milieu of Black people ("wherever they may be found"); a coupling of race and radical political economy; and a challenge to activate knowledge in the pursuit of social, political, and economic justice. It is a school of thought that looks quite different than the Afrocentric school that Molefi Asante and others have built at Temple or the Dream Team model advanced by Henry Louis Gates Jr. and company at Harvard.[46] Do the tenets of the Turner school remain as applicable to the current state of Black Studies as these other schools of thought in the discipline? Without question, his ideas remain relevant to the contemporary context in which we find ourselves. The series of writings that follow are a testament to a legacy that exhibits great clarity, consistency, resoluteness, and a deep, abiding concern for the well-being of Black people. However, in the final assessment, what is most important—and I think Turner would agree—is the way we utilize these ideas to make history and give birth to a more just world.

Dr. Josef Ben Jochannon and James Turner, March 1979. Cornell University News Service records, #4-3-15. Division of Rare and Manuscript Collections, Cornell University Library.

BLACK STUDENTS: A CHANGING PERSPECTIVE[47]

JAMES TURNER

When he wrote this article, James Turner was a graduate student and organizer of black students at Northwestern University. He is now Director of
the Africana Studies [and Research Center] at Cornell University.

The political socialization of black students is undergoing dramatic transformation. The current trends among black students reflect the changing
perspectives of a cross-section of all blacks in America. The present student
activities, manifested in the demands for Black studies, the formation of
politically active black student organizations, and the search for a viable
and permanent link to their community represent the surfacing of the "internalized revolution," the "revolution" which Lerone Bennett speaks of as
taking place in the "winding corridors of the mind," without which the
revolution in the streets could not succeed. It is the necessary function of
knocking out old psychic structures, and creating new images.

This process of black "re-socialization"—which students have spear-
headed for the past decade—is creating a new consciousness of self and
political awareness of the socio-political and economic institution that perpetuates the dual caste-class oppression of black people in America. New
norms and role models for social performance and cultural attitudes are
being formed, creating for this and the next generation new prototypes for
political action. The present trends are the embodiment and logical development of the perspectives of successive generations of blacks who have
made the most historic liberation struggle in human history. The black liberation movement as a historical demand for justice is perhaps the oldest
resistance movement in existence. Black people have always resisted America; they resisted slavery as they did the involuntary servitude that followed.
Today, the massive struggle being waged by blacks for self-determination is
at the heart of the growing political crisis in America. Not since the abolition movement has there been a parallel period of ferment. Commenting
on the progressive historical development of the movement, Brother Malcolm X once said, "We are creating a generation of black young people
who will know what they want, and they will create a generation who will
know how to get what they want." Black students today are in between

these generations and are a major influence on and product of this transition. Malcolm X is perhaps the single most important influence on black students. From Harvard to Tougaloo, his pictures and political philosophy abound wherever young blacks gather on campuses.

A most salient factor in the contemporary movement is that the dimension and direction of the struggle has been redefined. In a recently distributed manifesto, James Boggs gives the following analysis:

> In the last fifteen years...the Black movement in the United States has moved steadily, and apparently irresistibly, from a struggle for Rights to a struggle for Power, from hope in Reform to realization of the need for Revolution.[48]

The struggle today is to provide blacks with a collective economic base and political control over land. It is essentially student leaders who have been the articulators of these concepts—i.e., Stokely Carmichael, H. Rap Brown, LeRoi Jones, Huey P. Newton. Black students are going through a period unlike any their parents ever experienced—it is a black renaissance and rebirth. Social analyst Harold Baron explains:

> Today, under the slogans of 'Black pride' and 'Black consciousness' we are witnessing a revolution in the role of expectations of high school and college students. Youth in the ghetto are projecting patterns of behavior and action which are totally at variance with the traditional role of 'Negro' as deferential and dependent. At this stage, these new self-concepts are being defined on the basis of black solidarity with Blacks and only secondarily on Blacks' relationships to whites.

Many black college students are not worried about making it in the system, but instead are determined to change it. "Formerly accepted values no longer command assent. Old-established customs no longer govern the daily relations between the races, the sexes, the classes or the generations."[49] Black students were once taken to white universities and molded into the image of their white counterparts, giving rise to what is currently referred to on campus as the Oreo effect: black on the outside but white on the inside. Now black students are rejecting white standards and beginning to realize that they have a better role to play than that of "showcase" or "Model Negro" in white groups. They refuse to be "siphoned off" as the token "accepted" as a means of social status and mobility in white society. Most no longer over-idealize white society and aren't anxious to emulate it. Jeanne L. Noble, Professor of Human Relations at New York University, explains: "On white campuses [black] students want to escape total immersion in white values that they perceive to be...materialistic, racist...[and imperialistic]." At "Negro" colleges, students want to avoid inculcation of black bourgeois culture, which they see as ridiculous, elitist, and self-demeaning as a pursuit of a black imitation of white society.

All over the country black students are openly involved in a struggle over what they can control and attain at universities and colleges that will be of benefit to black people. The issues range over a spectrum including questions of campus social inequities, relevant education for service to the black community, and university expansion that takes the adjacent land and homes of neighboring black families. For example, the University of Chicago has evicted thousands of black people in the Woodlawn Area, the Chicago Circle Campus is threatening blacks in the Lawndale section, and the Illinois Institute of Technology has similar plans for expansion into the surrounding black community on the South Side of Chicago. The pattern is repeated by urban colleges and universities across the country.

Traditional patterns of college admission absorbed those blacks coming from families consciously aspiring for middle-class status, which meant usually that they had successfully accommodated themselves to white cultural standards and had assimilated white criteria for judging themselves and other blacks. However, colleges today are getting an unprecedented number of black youth from urban, working-class communities. These students refuse to adjust themselves to the rules of success defined for them by white men. They have definite ties and commitment to the people from which they come. The contemporary black student passionately resents the idea of obtaining a college degree as a means to escape the black community and refuses to renounce his cultural lifestyles or to remain politely moderate on questions relating to the systematic subordination of black people in America. His concern is for much more than personal identity; for by attempting to know and define himself, he is trying to discover the answers to the future of black people—which are hidden in the present. With each incoming class of freshmen at many colleges and universities, there will be an increasing number of young blacks who do not share the same backgrounds and aspirations of the average middle- to upper-class white undergraduates. For them, the fundamental problem confronting black people is one of survival, and they take it as their responsibility to relate to the problems of their kith and kin. One is reminded of the short poem by Langston Hughes:

Negroes
Sweet and gentle,
Soft and kind
Beware the day
They change their mind.

To be sure, great numbers of black students have begun to change their mind about the material comfort and rewards White America offers those who take their college degree and conform to what the system expects of them. These young people, many of them coming from the most exploited class of the black community, are beginning to question the legitimacy and validity of white normative values and institutions for their lives. The introduction to a student journal produced by blacks at a reputable Ivy League university, which sets the theme and expresses the concerns of thousands of their peers, said in part: "Black America's crisis is our crisis as black students writ large. Simply stated, American universities do not prepare us to cope with our problems in as adequate a manner as it seemingly prepares its white students to cope with theirs. It does not satisfactorily ameliorate for black students a critical problem of our generation; that is, that white society has dictated the terms of our acceptance into the American mainstream. To us, these terms are unacceptable. Therefore, we are now questioning the adequacy of present American standards as a means of attaining self-fulfillment." For these students the prospects of learning what the white boys learn, as some have advised, is to learn how to support and administer the political structure and economic system that subjugates and manipulates black people in every social sphere. There is no argument, as far as they are concerned, about the fact that America is to its core and in the most fundamental sense a separatist, racist culture.

The gallant legal battles and civil rights demonstrations of the past two decades have removed the overt symbols of racism and caused an end to some of its traditional practices but have not significantly reduced their force in shaping American society. For example, take two Northern cities like Chicago and New York, which have some of the best civil rights laws in the country, and have engaged almost two decades of liberal-democratic government; yet their urban black ghettos have expanded and deepened, and social and economic conditions for blacks have steadily worsened, instead of the reverse, even though black people in both cities have had the right to vote and use public accommodations for generations. Racism has become institutionalized in American life, and has taken on a dynamic of its own that is supported by pervasive social practice if not explicitly in legal code. An outstanding urban researcher and social scientist reveals that "the impersonal institutions of the great cities have woven together into a web of urban racism that entraps [blacks] as much as the spider's net holds flies—they can wriggle but they cannot move very far. There is a carefully articulated interrelation of the barriers created by each institution." Thus, the paradox of a "Negro" leader threatening legal suit against black students for fostering separation is ludicrous—to say the least. One can't help but wonder, where was Roy Wilkins's legal action against the white men of the United States Congress who blatantly and illegally threw Adam C. Powell out of the chambers of government? That was the *real* perpetuation of *separation*—of *blacks* from *power*.

Central to the new black student movement is the quest for new values and definitions that are meaningful and appropriate for black people, and which will give substance and significance to their lives. It is in this context that one can understand, as Dr. Gloria Joseph, black assistant dean of students at Cornell explains, "why black students are so insistent on fitting their education more closely to their own world" through demands for Black studies, and calling for development of a Black University (as opposed to traditionally Negro colleges which reflect the curriculum of white institutions). When black campus radicals speak of America as a "white nation," what they refer to, in the main, is that white men have the power to define America thoroughly in their own terms because they *control* the society exclusively and completely. For black men in America the pervasiveness of white images is one of the major components of the control system. The institution of education in any society is fundamentally political, for it is the major socializing agency that induces people to accept and participate in the established social arrangement. In this country the subordination of black people is perpetuated by the educational system, which either refuses to educate or deliberately and systematically mis-educates black children. In order to maintain oppression with stability it is necessary for the system to make those who are educated in its own image. This point is outlined in a position paper by the Black Student Union at embattled San Francisco State College, which reads in part:

> In the black community one of the most blatant forms of oppression is the irrelevant or destructive educational experience of its youth, from elementary school to junior high and high schools, and finally in colleges. There is a denial of the legitimacy of cultural expression among black people, socially, culturally and economically. No atmosphere for self-learning exists in black schools. In San Francisco particularly the dropout rate of Afro-American students has passed the critical stage not because black children are inherently

inferior, but rather because the information that black children receive is alien to them, dealing almost completely with white culture. The heroes are white; the images are white; the teachers, for the most part, are white. There is little in any curriculum which starts with black people as a specifically cultured people. So there is no wonder that black children lose interest at an early age. In high schools and colleges, black students who have already gone through a destructive learning process now have that process increased in intensity. The high school and college curriculums as a whole are irrelevant to the needs of non-white students.

It is against this reality that black students are rebelling. Those who argue that Black studies are a "bunch of soul courses" that will cheat black students in the long run are correct in the first instance—for Black studies are literally the "soul" of education for blacks—but flatly wrong in the latter accusation. In any undergraduate's education not more than one-third of the course of study is devoted to a student's major field of specialization; the remaining two-thirds are spent taking general education electives and degree requisites. The major part of four years of study is not directly related to the specialization of expertise acquired, but is meant to provide the frame of reference and general orientation (in terms of values, motivation and interest) that will determine toward what ends and for whose benefit the knowledge and expertise is to be applied. It is precisely on this point that the argument is made for the need for a black perspective in education for black people. Lerone Bennett goes to the heart of the matter when he says that "black people must have a new frame of reference which transcends the limitation of the white man's concepts." One of those concepts being eschewed is the notion of knowledge for knowledge's sake. Conscious black students want knowledge and skills that are relevant to the experience and conditions of their people. They are determined to provide a purpose for their education; their desire is to develop professional and technical careers tailored to the needs of black people.

The most dramatic product of this movement is the emergence of young, militant leaders who are oriented to the masses and who are replacing the old-guard assimilationist, integrationist leadership. As the ideas of racial solidarity, nation-building and self-determination become the motif of the struggle, the concern shifts to schemes like black capitalism, which seeks to blunt the thrust of the new movement and subverts the people's interest. Recruitment of black college students by industry and business has been accelerated as white power brokers attempt to use naïve, opportunist and middle-class aspiring "Negroes" as middle-level managers to maintain their economic interests and political control in the black community—without relinquishing one iota of power. There is emerging a real danger that the liberation movement will be maneuvered into a "bourgeois national movement," as has happened with independence movements in Africa and Asia, where elite-minded blacks trained in colonial schools take over the colonizer's position or rule but function in the master's best economic interest. There is no fundamental change in the political and economic relationship, which leaves white power still in control of black lives. Witness the recent number of economic enterprises listed as only managed by blacks, but advertised in "Negro-oriented" newspapers and radio stations (most of which are, in fact, owned by whites) as "black businesses" encouraging the people to shop with the "soul brother" and "Buy Black" to help the black community. There can be no self-determination *of any kind* that will improve the conditions of life for the greatest number of black people without a revolution reversing the power and economic arrangements toward the benefit of the masses.

Marcus Garvey once said, "Education is a medium by which a people are prepared for the creation of their own particular civilization, and the advancement and glory of their own race." For educated blacks in America, almost the opposite is true. To be successful to the college level, one would have to ignore the vast omission in course content, and in some instances outright rejection or negation of creative contributions and cultural originality of black folk. A black co-ed explains her experience at a fashionable New England college:

> By the time I reached sophomore year I was emotionally exhausted with the material I had to master in classes. I was taught to worship Western civilization, and I could hardly believe that racial repression was also a fact of history. Balancing inconsistencies and omissions of knowledge is too much for a black student to take alone. When the movement hit Radcliffe—it was a matter of clutching for a straw to save my very soul.

The demand for Black studies is made in response to education in America, which has stifled the development and realization of creative black potential. The need for a relevant educational alternative emerges from those students who recognize that present institutions of higher education are not only European-centered and white-oriented but have little relevance to the total black community, "and who realize the contradiction of allowing themselves to be absorbed into a society that debilitates black people. The black student is more painfully aware that the white university was not made to accommodate him. There is very little which is relevant to him," explains a young man at a large state university. "Further evidence that you are in a white university and one not designed for your kind, is the absence of the kind of food, clothing, cosmetics and music that you are accustomed to. Instead of facilitating the growth of black students, white universities negate their existence and relegate it to trivia."

Black educators and students are just beginning to understand the real truth in the adage that "knowledge is power." Education is a question of power, as Lerone Bennett explains. "It is a question of the ultimate in power. The power to name, to define and to control minds. The truth in the face of this fact is that an educator in a system of oppression is either a revolutionary or an oppressor." For an oppressed people, control over what and how they learn is paramount in determining their destiny and identity, and vitally essential to the larger struggle for self-determination.

The black student movement has moved the road to liberation for black people onto a new plateau of black nationalism. Malcolm X's wife, Sister Betty Shabazz, refers to it as "primary nationalism: a love of the motherland, the family, the language, the folkways and mores of your people. (Call it black awareness, black consciousness or black pride—it's all nationalism)." A Ph.D. student in history at Northwestern University says that "nationalism is a logical and natural development of a people to an oppressive situation." This turn in the movement rejects integration. What dreams there are left among blacks of that utopia is tempered by the recognition that there can be no integration between entities as unequal as black and white in America. This emerging black ideology represents a new awareness of the radical implications of Black Nationalism (the political implication of which, until now, had usually been rather conservative). Of necessity, many of the black radical movements have been involved in a cultural revolution. Northwestern history professor Christopher Lasch has commented that "the radical implications of black nationalism can only emerge once the cultural battle has been carried into the sphere of politics, at which point it becomes clear that Black Nationalism as a political program demands the radical decentralization of power and American institutions and perhaps also the socialization of these institutions....Indeed, one of the potentially revolutionary aspects of Black Nationalism is its capacity to demonstrate that cultural and political questions are always related." For instance, economic (class) exploitation and social (racial) oppression of blacks cannot be separated from the spiritual and psychological (i.e., cultural) chaos in their lives as a result of subjugation to American racism.

The most gallant symbols of this new sense of community and brotherhood among black students are Tommie Smith, John Carlos, and the other black athletes whose heroic demonstration at the 1968 Olympic games forcefully thrust the black liberation movement into the international arena, and captured the admiration and support of black youth all over the country. Defying all normative constraints on them as athletes, as well as the threat to the future of their personal careers, they rose to express their concern for the plight of their people. Only through understanding the depth of this dynamic change in the attitude and political posture of an ever-increasing number of young blacks can we begin to appreciate the revolutionary prospect of their behavior.

The pattern of history has shown that students, intellectuals and disenchanted members of the bourgeoisie (i.e., middle class) have been significant actors in great social movements for radical change, freedom, and national independence for the subjugated masses of their people. Black students are fulfilling their historical role in shaping the destiny of black people toward self-determination and human dignity. The current student movement is confronting the fundamental contradictions in the very foundation of American society; the black student, as he leaves school, will be a pivotal factor in the future political posture of the black community.

BLACK STUDIES:
A CONCEPT AND A PLAN[50]

JAMES TURNER

INTRODUCTION

Here we will examine the meaning and challenge of the Black Presence at White schools and the social origins of the demand for new modes in education (i.e., Black studies). In short, "Black studies is a demand for a new encounter with the Black experience in American education."

In any society, the purpose of its educational system is to provide all members of the society with those skills and tools necessary to maintain and enhance the society. Given the self-defined ethnic, cultural, and social diversity of American people, it would seem as though all subsequent cultural institutions would be equally pluralistic. But higher education in America has traditionally been the exclusive domain of White America. Today, Black students have begun to play a leading role in challenging and changing the status of higher education. Having neither influential input nor functional role in terms of determining content and direction within this almost totally white world, Black students are given little security and assurance.

On college and university campuses, frustration and contempt for the educational system has bred open rebellion against tradition, educational curriculum, and definition of the content of academic study and work. Contemporary Black students feel a keen sense of themselves as an extension of the Black community—a distinct few who seek to gain educational and scientific experience in order to work within the Black community. They hope to channel whatever dynamism they possess into the building of a viable and productive Black community. Increasingly, Black students are seeking to promulgate a conceptual framework within which constructive change may be channeled into the Black community. They seek to build: Thus, a relevant education becomes a necessity.

Among Black college students, particularly those in predominately white schools, there has been a growing identification with the Black community and its problems. At Cornell and everywhere, Black students have begun to question the relevance of their education in relation to their needs and the needs of their community. They have said that the only moral reason for a college's existence is to develop the experience of the society. What does this reason have to do with their presence on the campus, if the only recognition of experience comes from the white community? They have begun to say that perhaps colleges and universities as they now exist are at least irrelevant—and often even destructive—to the Black community. In the Black community one of the most blatant forms of oppression is the irrelevant and destructive educational experiences of its youth, from elementary to junior and senior high schools and finally in colleges and universities. There is a denial of the legitimacy of cultural expression and social facility among Black people. There is little in any curriculum that starts with Black people as a specially and uniquely cultured people. So there is little wonder that Black students lose interest in education, in life, and in society at an early age. But they have now begun to say that perhaps the recognition of one's self is in terms of one's historical presence and social significance. Even further, they are saying that if a college's objective is to make students productive members of society, then that purpose must benefit the entire society, including the Black community. This means that the concept of education, its goals, and its methods have to be re-examined and made relevant to a larger number—and different kinds—of students than those to whom it is now important.

From the very beginning of American history, Black people have formed an economically, socially, and culturally significant part of America. They have contributed to American art, music, and literature; they have been fundamentally important in shaping not only the attitudes and institutions of the Black society, but the whole society as well.

Despite the obvious importance of Black people, however, neither scholars nor the public at large know very much about the precise role of Black people in American life, past and present. Little is known about their position in American society, about the scope, quality, and significance of their contributions to American culture, or about the effects of their actions on the attitudes and institutions of American society.

This ignorance has many sources. At this moment, it is less important to dwell on the sources than to recognize that the ignorance exists and that it must be overcome. Through neglect, a vitally important segment of the nation has been denied a legitimate history and culture. This situation has encouraged among White Americans the growth and spread of ideas and attitudes that are not only incorrect but destructive. At the same time, Black Americans' ignorance of their race's history and culture in America has left them vulnerable to the corrosive effects of American racism, and has reduced their ability to understand and control the forces and attitudes presently shaping their lives.

The long overdue recognition of this omission and of the importance of correcting it has led to the creation at Cornell of a Black Studies Program.

In American education it has been traditional for educators, social scientists, and intellectuals to restrict their consideration of Afro-American life to the topics of "disorganization." There has been a general failure to do the research on the culture and conditions of Black people to allow scientifically validated generalizations. Few social scientists have investigated the "organization" that exists alongside the chaos, and fewer still have attempted to assess the diversity of development within the Black society.

Presently, Black students are being trained to live and work in a White middle-class environment. They are compelled to learn and study the politics, arts, economics, and culture of White people as if Black people, their community, and their problems did not exist. At any rate, the implication is strikingly clear: The achievements of Blacks are inconsequential. The demand upon educational institutions today is for them to make available to the Black student sufficient resources and facilities so that he can develop a high degree of competence and expertise that is relevant to the needs of the Black community. For many, the community from which they came will be the community to which they will return to live and work.

A Black Studies Program seeks to remedy the total indifference of the American system of education to the needs of Black people. The token revision of textbooks to include previously omitted material, and the incorporation of courses in "Black History and Culture" into biased, controlled educational structures will do little to correct the distortions and inadequacies that have led to the present crisis in education. What is needed is a total reorientation of educational and academic practices towards minorities, Afro-Americans in particular. Indeed, such an orientation must recognize the need for a pedagogical as well as a substantive educational revolution. It will mean a radical departure in approach from tradition and orthodoxy in regard to institutional procedure, perception, valuable academic subjects, and organizational relationships.

Black studies is the comprehensive study of the African diaspora and the three primary Black world communities—Africa, North American, and the Caribbean: their people, problems, arts, culture, politics, economics, history, and social development. We respond, as have other educators, "to these legitimate educational imperatives by making the Black experience central to our curriculum design and teaching plan....One significant pedagogical point to which discussion frequently returns is the relationship of a Black perspective to breadth, depth, and excellence in the total curriculum. We believe these are the compatible, that making the Black experience central is in fact a superior means of developing a deep and broadened understanding of the aims, methods, and materials of humanities, the natural sciences, and the social sciences. Far from compromising our commitment to academic excellence, it enhances it."[51]

The development of Black studies programs and the recruitment and enrollment of interested students into such courses of study should, in no way, be construed as a retreat from expanding educational and economic opportunities, particularly as this might be true for Black students. Instead, such programs should be understood as a progressive thrust forward, with exciting, innovative potential that holds out the prospect for improving traditional curriculum. Our basic responsibility as educators is not only to pioneer and develop Black studies as a vital educational field but also to train people who will be intellectually and technically competent. It must be realized that the great historical need in the Black community is to develop serious, creative thinkers, disciplined social analysts, and talented professional workers. Black studies provides the best presently conceived models to achieve these educational needs.

Students will provide important impetus and participate significantly in the direction and development of what will be known formally as the Africana Studies and Research Center, providing a prototype of faculty-student relations. Students will be involved in matters of policy and curriculum and faculty recruitment. Foremost, the Black Studies Program at Cornell will be a community of scholars, teachers, and students.

Its central thrust is towards the creation of an international center for Black studies, with strong emphasis on research, broadly conceived, and effective and innovative teaching in terms of structure, use, method, and content. Most classes will be relatively small (approximately fifteen students per class; larger for such popular lecture courses as Black History and Black Literature, possibly approximately twenty-five). Seminar format and maximum student participation will be encouraged. It is therefore an experiment in scholarship within a specific context and a definite social focus. Among our basic concerns and commitments is the determination to set our skills to a new understanding of the past, present, and future condition of the peoples of African descent, wherever they may be found, with an initial emphasis on America and growing components on Africa and the Caribbean.

Our curriculum plan calls for initial development of comprehensive interdisciplinary courses in the humanities and the social sciences as a basic foundation for the course of study for developing a major. These core courses will be spread across the student's first eighteen to twenty-four months of study. The core of our curriculum begins with the study of political history broken into these three major categories: ancient African history, the history of Africa since European maritime contact, and the subsequent Black diaspora. Additional courses in literature, political science, sociology, and psychology will be built upon an analysis of the various stages of historical experience of Black people in Africa, the United States, the Caribbean, and parts of Latin America.

In Black literature, for example, in the North American context, we will seek to develop in our students a sense of historical perspective for analytical purposes. This course of study will involve looking at Black people during three broad historical categories: the period of slavery, the post–Civil War and segregation era, and contemporary twentieth-century America. The students will be involved in the study of the influence and impact of the social, political, economic, and cultural factors that were prominent in each period and the changes that resulted from transition between historical periods, the purpose being to develop insight and analytical ability for mastery of the subject of Black literature. The same kind of comparative work and analytical framework will be used for study and theoretical development in all other courses in the social sciences and humanities core. Comparative study will involve not only differences across periods of time but also differences and similarities of Black people in the three major geographical areas.

AFRICANA STUDIES AND RESEARCH CENTER: DEFINITION

The Africana Studies and Research Center approaches the controversial and highly significant issue of Black studies in America with five basic assumptions. They affect the character of all that we do and all that we plan to do in the area of Black studies. These are the assumptions.

First, *that Black studies is a field still being born.* This is not to deny the existence of significant and often underappreciated work related to Black studies that has already been done, but it does deny the fact that there is any clear understanding of the specific ways in which a profound mining of the Black experience challenges and transforms the basic educational structures of the nation.

Second, *that the establishing and the defining of the field of Black studies stands logically as a task and a challenge for Black people in America and else-*

where. Others may be called upon for assistance, but the initiative must be ours.

Third, *that the Center and its counterparts on other campuses are in an excellent position to play a central role in defining the field and creating some of the urgently required models.* In this task, of course, we must find ways of combining the thought and activities of those Black persons throughout the nation who are working at the Black studies task, often in scattered and isolated situations.

Fourth, *that a unified, rather than a conventionally understood academic-discipline-bound approach to the creation of Black studies is not only desirable but absolutely necessary.* Indeed, this unified approach is central to the demands of most thoughtful Black student and faculty groups across the country.

Fifth, *that a serious building of this field is the task of years, and not a makeshift program for a few persons to do in several weeks or months.*

BASIC PROGRAM ELEMENTS[52]

Against this background of assumptions, the director and faculty of the Africana Studies and Research Center have been working towards course models, benefiting, of course, from the older hopes and dreams of such predecessors in Black studies as W.E.B. Du Bois, Charles S. Johnson, Ralph Bunche, and Alain Locke, to mention only a few. Already it has become apparent to us that several elements must be a part of any creative, well-structured approach to Black studies. We have understandably sought to include them in our own planning. Among these elements are the following:

1. Serious research in many areas of historical and contemporary Black existence that have been ignored (e.g., social structure in the black community, comparative black urban development in the new world, comparative slavery).

2. The encouragement of those creative artists who are searching for the meaning of a Black aesthetic, who are now trying to define and build the basic ground out of which Black creativity may flow in the arts. Encounters among these artists, on the one hand, and scholars, activists, and students, on the other hand, must be constant in both formal and informal settings.

3. Continuous research on contemporary political, economic, and social policies that now shape the life of the Black community in America and that determine its future.

4. Constant experimentation with the meaning of Black studies for the surrounding Black community, and openness to the possible input from that community into the development of Black studies. The two-sidedness of the experience is essential and must be encouraged.

5. The development of new materials for and new approaches to the teaching of the Black experience, which must grow out of laboratory situations at every grade level.

6. The training of a constantly expanded cadre of persons deeply immersed in the materials, methods, and spirit of Black studies, who can help supply the tremendous demands for personnel in a variety of formal and informal teaching environments. The development of new materials, methods, and curriculum for the teaching of Black children.

7. The creation of consortium models which will make possible the constant interaction of Black students and faculty on northern and southern campuses around certain selected foci of Black studies. This must also expand to the encouragement and development of contacts among Black students, scholars, political leaders, and artists from various parts of the world. It is clear that Black studies cannot really be developed unless we understand more fully both the unique and the common elements of our experiences in the Black diaspora.

8. The gathering and consolidation of those library and archival resources that will facilitate the development of Black studies as it proceeds towards definition.

9. The establishment of good contacts with publishing enterprises, which will not only make available the results of the experimentation and study of the Center, but which will also encourage the increasing number of authors and

researchers who wish to present their work from the heart of
the Black matrix.

10. The gathering, cataloging, and critical analysis of those Black
    studies programs and personnel already developed across the
    nation, so that we may begin with a fuller sense of direction,
    possibilities, and problems. This process began with a
    summer-long seminar in June 1969 and will continue with
    monthly seminars of Black studies directors and several larger
    working conferences at least through the summer of 1971.

The director and faculty of the Africana Studies and Research Center see
all of these elements as crucial to the development to creative models for
the kinds of Black studies programs that will not be palliatives, but significant pathways to the redefinition of American education and of the Black
Experience. They are, therefore, the elements which have guided us so far
in the establishment of the Center.

BASIC OUTLINE OF CENTER DEVELOPMENT

Purpose

We expect to develop an institution that trains teaching and research scholars as well as professional technicians who possess the necessary skills,
technology, and experience to deal effectively with the problems facing
Blacks in this country. We plan to fill the void of competent persons,
efficiently attacking these problems by producing thoroughly prepared
and committed professionals who will deal with such problems as a life-
time career.

The initial conception of Black studies as referring only to Black history
and culture has been superseded by the recognition that technology and
science are related to the modern industrial conditions of Black people in
urban and rural environments. The Black Studies Program must eventually become a center for preparing a new cadre of intellectuals who are
at once precisely trained in scholarship of the Black Experience, and interested in specializing in scholarly work (i.e., teaching, research, creative
arts) in some facet of this developing academic field. Also, it must evolve
into a new kind of professional school concerned with developing and applying the new techniques of planning and economic development in the
ghettoes and rural areas. The intention is to enhance the training of Black
professionals by providing an approach to the problems of Black people in

America, considering their political, economic, cultural, and social needs. Our endeavor is to fashion skills for a purpose and to generate knowledge for the sake of serving: to develop scholarly, technical, and professional careers tailored to conditions and requirements of the Black community.

We will seek the establishment of creative links with our counterparts, i.e., students and educators in other areas of the Black world. We hope to be involved in travel and exchange with parts of the Caribbean, Africa, and elsewhere, with Black scholars, artists, educators, and community workers who are grappling with many issues very similar to those which engage us in North America.

Structure

There will be a primary location: the Campus (Home) Center. This main center of studies will operate on three levels. First, for those majoring in and taking degrees in the program, an intensive two-year introductory sequence has been designed to give students the necessary academic background and perspective to spend the third year doing field work in the urban component of the Center. The fourth year would probably be spent on thesis work. In this sequence, it is expected that the student's first two years will have made him sufficiently sophisticated to initiate an appropriate field project in his third year. The field project would probably then be the subject of his thesis work in the fourth year.

For example: A student interested in the economic aspects of our situation might study, during his year of fieldwork, a particular Black community with a view towards ascertaining both the sources of their resources and the areas, ways, and means by which those resources are drained from the community. After locating the industry, service, or class of commodities which relatively drain the most community resources while returning the least in new resources (jobs, etc.), the students would study and grasp completely all factors which would be involved in establishing a community-owned entity to fill the designated void; factors such as capital accumulation, cooperative organization, and worker-management training programs. If possible, the student would then enlist the community and the Center in a joint effort to do what had to be done. Most probably, however, the students would write a thesis covering what he had already learned and done, while outlining his plans for completing the project. Of course, all aspects of his work will be done in conjunction with the expert assistance available in the community and the Center. It is clear, however, that the student, after graduation, will be continuing work already started, thereby making our educational program relevant, functional, and productive from beginning to end.

Second, the Center will consist of a field of study for graduate students; and third and finally, when the program is sufficiently large, it will be able to provide general survey courses for the student community as a whole, servicing students not in the program who have only an idle interest in our work or who desire only a general knowledge of the situations we will be dealing with. The specializing committed students will then not be hampered in their work, while the program will still provide a general service to the university community.

The program's second locus will be an urban resident center. The urban resident center, based in an urban Black community, will be residential in nature and possess its own faculty. Its functions will be to provide a continued relevance to the community, an arena for field research and experience, and a base for functional community programs. The extension center will accomplish these goals primarily through three mechanisms.

First, the community will be involved in all phases of the Center at all times. All operations and projects will be joint community-Center entities. There will be a constant interaction between the community and the Center as the community people enlist our aid for their particular projects and needs, while we enlist their aid to the same ends. Furthermore, community residents will be welcome to participate fully in the courses given at the Center.

The second mechanism is a free interchange of faculty between the home center and the extension center, thereby ensuring that all faculty are well aware of reality. Perhaps the faculty will conduct research and other projects from the extension center, while analyzing their success, failure, or findings in the home center atmosphere.

The third and final mechanism is that students will always bring fresh insight to both the urban resident center and the home center. At the urban resident center they will energize ongoing community and center projects, while hopefully helping develop new functional operations. When returning to the home center, students will have tested and be freshly prepared to evaluate the curriculum and teaching in the home center in light of its efficiency and effectiveness in preparing them to perform functional jobs. They will be a constant means of evaluating the veracity of data and theory and the validity of method taught at the campus Center.

Recruitment and Admissions

In the recruitment and admission of students, the program will place the highest value on relevant background and experience, along with a commitment to be functional in working on the problems with which the program will deal. While seriously considering such factors as academic training and standing, we must place the greatest reliance on the candidate's relevance to the Black community and his commitment to working towards the solution of its problems. We have neither the time nor resources to operate a race-relations project wherein well-meaning but inexperienced and dysfunctional White students would occupy positions that might be better filled by Blacks. Of course, relevant and equally well-qualified (in background, experience, and commitment) Whites are welcome, but such qualified candidates will undoubtedly be rare.

The Program envisions the existence of two equally legitimate streams of Black students coming to Cornell. Of course, there will continue to be the normally admitted Black students interested in traditional aspects of the university program. We in no way wish to interfere with the recruitment and admission of such students. But we do plan to solicit a second stream of Black students interested specifically and primarily in the problems attacked through our program, students who probably would not consider college at all if such a program did not exist.

In the recruitment of faculty, the program will once again stress relevant background and experience, along with a proven ability to be functional and productive in appropriate spheres. Only through the employment of such persons can we guarantee that all phases of the program will maintain a practical bearing, avoiding the trap of academic over-intellectualization of very real and pressing problems.

Degree-Granting

Degree-granting status is necessary to a strengthening of the program and an accomplishment of its objectives in at least two vital areas: enabling the program to recruit directly and admit those students most likely to both make successful and be successful in the program of the Center; and beginning the vital process of establishing standards of quality and expertise for people and programs operating in the Black community. By establishing real and viable standards of expertise and effectiveness, the programs will make possible a more effective and efficient concentration of the limited resources available to deal with the problems facing us. For example, if the federal government had possessed real and viable standards for who was qualified to do what in the poverty program, the billions of dollars appropriated could have been more effectively used.

Time Table

The home Center will begin full operations in the fall of 1969, hopefully establishing an extension center by 1971, and to degree-granting status by 1972. It is expected that the Center will be able to offer a major with the commencement of full operations in the fall of 1969.

Addendum[53]

While in the interim stages of development, toward a professional school, the Africana Center is organizationally different from other university units called "centers." It is not an interdisciplinary program composed of a loose confederation of faculty who hold appointments in other departments and offer courses under the aegis of their respective departments. As a general principle, joint faculty appointments are avoided because they would compromise the Center's distinctions and the integrity of its purpose. A centralized faculty can better provide a cogent and integrated curriculum. The Africana Center's faculty is multidisciplinary, but they are appointed directly to the Center. Likewise, courses for credit to the extent of comprising a major sequence will be offered directly from the Center. Though the Center provides its own curriculum, course credits for a major and a university degree are presently processed through the Arts and Sciences College, since the Center is not yet a degree-granting unit. The Colleges of Human Ecology, Architecture, Art, and Planning, and Engineering have also approved the Center's courses for their students, and we hope approval from other colleges will be forthcoming. Some courses at the Center have been accepted as appropriate for fulfilling freshman humanities requirements by the university-wide Freshman Humanities Program.

BLACK STUDIES AND A BLACK
PHILOSOPHY OF EDUCATION[54]

JAMES TURNER

With the recent advent of Black studies over the last several years and particularly during the past two years on the campuses of predominately white universities, the very nature of education in relation to the rest of the society has come under scrutiny. Black students in particular have begun to question whether school as normally conceived is fully beneficial for Black people.

Historically the role of education has been two-fold: First, it is to prepare individuals for successful survival in their social environment through the teaching of socially useful skills, and the normative structure of social process (i.e., values and morals) in social relations for both institutional and individual interactions; secondly, to allow the individual to expand his constructive creativity.

Education, therefore, provides both a "tooling" and socializing function. Moreover, at all times, school has the character and direction of the next generation in its classrooms. The point is that education is the process of interpretation, definition, and indoctrination of learning sources. Reading, writing, and arithmetic are not education per se, but are means to an education. Definition determines content and meaning in education. If the primary reason for the existence of college is to develop potential, to refine, and to develop the experience of society, the question is then, "What does this mean for the Black community if the only valid recognition of experience is that of the white nation?" Thus, schools as they now exist are, at least, irrelevant and often even destructive to the Black community. [...]

James Turner teaching one of several seminars at the Africana Studies and Research Center, ca. 1980s.

WHITE STUDIES

For a long time Black people have placed a high premium on and great faith in education as a vehicle for reaching a higher level of survival than they have known most of their lives....Education perpetuates society. However, among an increasing number of Black educators and students there has emerged the conscious realization that education has larger societal purpose. By passing on the collective wisdom, traditional liberal education has functioned to prepare the thinking of Black people to accept white society. American education is functionally tantamount to "white studies."

White studies is a system of intellectual legitimacy which defines the activities and experiences of white Western people as the universal yardstick of human experience. Black studies challenges this assumption and asserts that white is not now nor has it ever been either intrinsically right or complete. However, whites have attributed universal value to their own Anglo-American particularism, and have sought to absorb and distort other cultures in their midst. For instance, white historians will develop concepts which ignore the full dimensions of human history. When it comes to human failings such as greed, barbarity, cruelty, aggression, jealousy, and selfishness they concede that these are attributes common to all men. But when it comes to recording and acknowledging great and outstanding activities and works of men, white scholars will often conclude that peoples are distinguished by achievements, and they are not inclined generally to recognize the glorious incidents in history are the results of shared human events.

It is clear that Black people were never and are not now being educated for the reasons that whites were and are. White students are educated to be rulers and makers of their society. Blacks are taught to synthesize the experiences and memorize [the] conclusions of another people. The consequence of such education is that many Blacks, if not most, are inclined to confuse the interests of our people with that of our oppressor, which creates a situation where we accept white peoples' definition of the problems they cause for us, and solutions they deem acceptable for Black people.

Lerone Bennett makes this point eloquently when he says, "In white-oriented schools, we are educated away from ourselves—away from our people, away from our rhythm, away from our genius, and away from our soul....We must abandon the frame of reference of our oppressor, perceive our own reality....George Washington and George Washington's slaves lived different times and different reality." Black studies must contribute to the development and implementation of a new definition of an end towards which Black children are educated.

Bringing Black students to white universities in large numbers was intended to create greater acceptance of the social system by giving them vested interests in its benefits. Education would assure better occupational status and income and expanding social opportunities. The long-range projection was that education was the medium for producing a larger national Black bourgeois as a stabilizing social class to counteract growing alienation and disruptive currents among the Black masses. However, on white college campuses across the country, Black students turned out not to be as malleable, pliable, or tractable as was perhaps expected by white administrators.

BLACK STUDENTS AND THE COMMUNITY

Black educators should reinforce the development of consciousness and concern for the Black community among students, while making sure that our presence at white schools is not directed against the best interests of our people. Some of the most prominent questions at this point are, "What do we want to educate Black people for? What do we want Black students to do? What do we want them to become?" The Black community needs a balanced range of skilled, communicative, and technical personnel if the concept of Black self-determination is to even have a chance of becoming reality. Black studies programs must move to decolonize young Black minds and to reorient their minds in ways that allow them to make lasting, positive, creative relationships between themselves and their community.

In America, the university, like other [corporate] bodies, is a political microcosm of the society at large. Black educators and students should understand that in a situation of oppression, education is fundamentally political. Through interpretation of the past and evaluation of the present, education has great influence upon the consciousness of a people. For example, history has many meanings for a people. It is especially a record of events, a way of knowing what events of the past have meant to people in terms of their basic political interest and social well-being. It also provides a context for analyzing the forces and mechanisms of social structure that determine the group's position in the process of society. Moreover, education has a definite political function whatever the situation, for it provides individuals with identity, purpose, and direction.

Education is not just the development and teaching of factual information, but is also the primary means for imbuing a people with social values, certain political beliefs, and a specific cultural character. Furthermore, in any social system, teaching is done within definite ideological parameters, which engenders a common frame of reference and orientation among the people. The assumptions a person conceives will in large measure influence the definitions that person will accept, which in turn establishes conclusions held to be truths, thus forming one's perception of reality. Analysis of social process flows from this process.

Amiri Baraka (alias LeRoi Jones) makes an important point when he says, "If you accept the white man's definitions you will share his reality." This is particularly important when you realize that there are two different racial and ethnic populations, whose historical contact and relationship originate in conflict and continue to be hostile, but who both accept the same social definitions; one group is penetrated culturally and dominated politically and economically by the other. Such is exactly the fate that African people in America have suffered ever since the Europeans organized and inspired the slave trade in Africa, and arrested people as political subjects for imperialist empire building.

Therefore, African people must begin to understand and interpret their historical and cultural experiences in new ways and from their own perspective, which will create new dimensions in our thinking and an alternative social philosophy and political direction from our oppressor and political enemies.

Black education must make students consistently conscious of struggle and commitment. Too often the question of cultural values and political ideology is only superficially perceived. It is necessary at this time to define our long-range goals, identify our immediate objectives in order to reach these goals, and put into operation the work needed to fulfill these immediate objectives. Black studies programs must develop Black youth with a revolutionary sense of identity. Therefore, any Black studies program which purports to be educating Black students for fuller participation in the American mainstream is counterproductive to Black people's needs for development and self-control. Moreover, it is essential to our liberation that Black youth are motivated to resist—not accept—the mainstream of the system that apprises and destroys our people.

Brother John Churchville, Black educator and theorist, has written that "with the increased Black Nationalist consciousness which has developed over the past two or three years among a broad cross-section of our people[,] [a] new surge of Black activity has erupted. This activity has serious political-directional implications which necessitate definition and analysis in order that we might see clearly the path we must take toward a correct struggle for freedom."

It is becoming increasingly clear that the Black liberation movement is renewing itself around the basic proposition that black people should control the decisions which affect their lives and shape their destiny. But success in this regard requires more than commitment to idealism and stout passion, more than bold rhetoric and a willingness to be deviant. Intellectually, we must have a social program, and a political plan which translates vision into practical programs. Organizationally, the movement must expand its participation deeper into the problems of the exploited masses of our people. Too much of what has passed for Black consciousness is simply the ritualistic reception of slogans. Those of us who are concerned with Black education realize that we cannot be apolitical because we realize that as an internal colony, our people are engulfed by the oppressor's institutions, and control over content and definition of the learning of our young is a pivotal facet of the liberation struggle.

BLACK STUDENT CADRES

*Students taking a course at the Africana Studies and Research Center,
ca. 1970s.*

Our task is not only to seek immediate political objectives but also to begin a longer term job of creating a recalcitrant cadre of Black students who are committed and equipped to extend the struggle to new levels by establishing institutions which can provide meaningful alternatives in our community for Black youth who do not wish to be absorbed into the "mainstream." Independent Black institutions should be supported as models for self-reliance, while at the same time we accept our responsibility to develop trained expertise that will make such institutions viable with wide-ranging practical significance in the lives of our people.

A chronic problem in the Black community is the dearth of skilled personnel dedicated to developing institutions that will become functionally efficient and socially effective. Such a development necessarily requires an unadulterated ideological commitment to the interest of the Black community. The question of is not an intellectual abstraction; all people are influenced by an ideology of one kind or another. Ideology is a particular group's view of the world; it is their way of seeing their relation to the main processes of society, and understanding the causation of events important to them.

However, even a cursory observation of the beliefs held by many of our people reveals the extent to which they have internalized the ideas and concepts of our oppressors. It has been said that "the art of colonization if it is to succeed means a colonizer sees to it that the victim is not only colonized politically, but also economically and culturally." In other words, the colonized victims develop a "false consciousness," which in our situation means that Black people have absorbed white people's ideology such that it distorts their understanding of our true position in the American social order and severely limits awareness of the ways in which our interests and needs are restricted by the power and social interest of white people as a group.

Exploitation and oppression of Blacks have developed as a way of life in America, and as a basic mode of its social system. Black historian Dr. C.J. Munford makes a poignant comment which most whites and many Blacks would like to avoid: "All white people in America are accomplices in inflicting pain and misery on all Blacks. If there was a correlation between justice and objective social conditions, all whites would stand as condemned murderers in the first degree. The original enslavement of Africans is renewed daily in America."

ROLE OF IDEOLOGY IN EDUCATION

For many professional Black educators, any question of the relationship of ideology to what they teach makes them uneasy. They would most likely be inclined to consider the discussion of Black studies, as we have presented in this paper, as a subjective approach to learning and a sort of sectarian encroachment that would demean the academic quality of their work. But, while it is true that facts must derive from objective discourse, we must not become confused by the façade that education is value-free and above the social system when in fact it is the axis for the developing and refining of ideas [integral to...] the ideology of the society.

Education for Blacks must consider the need to break down "false consciousness." It must seek to reveal to Black people—by facts, by emotionally powerful experiences, and by argument—the machinations of oppression.

A serious problem for Black educators is with the most politically concerned Black students, who are often so socially alienated that they cannot perceive the relevance nor the importance of careful study because of their preoccupation with protest. Such a disposition tends to impede development of political sophistication. In this regard, Albert Memmi has made a salient observation, "The colonized's self-assertion, born out of a protest, continues to define itself in relation to it. In the midst of revolt, the colonized continues to think, feel, and live against and, therefore, in relation to the colonizer and the colonization." Consequently, too many Black activists are merely vociferous political critics who develop a certain emotional rapport with our people.

But liberation is nothing if not a program. A major consequence of the lack of program proposals relevant to protracted (and predicated) struggle is that the Black liberation movement tends to cut off from many important conflicts, and fall into issue-oriented activity where programs are seemingly not as important, and protests seem sufficient. Thus, the discontent of our people lacks direction, and their attention is attached—by default—to liberal reformist programs. We must study in order to be more concise in our social analysis and effective with political action. Therefore, Black studies must be disciplined, rigorous, and demanding with a fundamental commitment to teach competence and intellectual development. The integrity of that learning process must be protected through respect for the distinction between students and teacher and the respective responsibilities implicit to each role.

BLACK STUDIES AND REVOLUTION

However, we should never delude ourselves into thinking or expecting Black studies to be the incubator of revolution. In fact, we should clearly understand that the essential struggle will not be on the campus but in the community, which is the focus for controlling the masses. Furthermore, historical situations make revolutions and revolutionaries, not classroom lecturers. However, guidance can and must be given to those who are serious by preparing them to understand historical circumstances and social conditions that confront Black people.

The best of Black studies programs will—at most—only be able to influence the course of study of some Black students, but will not be in position to control or direct the curriculum they will follow since such programs will not have the power to exact sanctions at white institutions nor at "Negro" colleges as they presently exist. Nevertheless, the effort must be made to complement the thrust of Black liberation movement by ensuring that some of the necessary educational resources are available in order to help sustain the movement and develop our people. This is what serving the Black community should mean—at least in part.

BLACK STUDIES AS AN INTEGRAL
TRADITION IN AFRICAN-AMERICAN
INTELLECTUAL HISTORY[55]

JAMES TURNER AND C. STEVEN MCGANN

The modern Black studies movement, in its present form, appeared in the 1960s as an emergent academic field and a self-conscious component part of the larger social and political movement for Black liberation. In contrast to the 1950s, which had been labeled "the silent generation" by some scholars, the 1960s were times of widespread political unrest and social movements. These currents were enlivened and precipitated by the Black liberation movement in its current stage of struggle for democratic rights, commonly referred to during that period as the "civil rights movement." The Black college campuses were the source of leadership for this movement by young (though not exclusively) activist-intellectuals. The general social climate of self-assertion and political protest released an intellectual ferment that stimulated some Black students and Black scholars in their demand for "Black studies" as a vanguard opposition to an entrenched intellectualism in American society.

The notion of Black studies as a theoretical perspective in academic disciplines and a method of pedagogy challenges that authority and legitimacy of the established intellectualism in American educational institutions which favors the interest of the status quo. Sterling Stuckey, a prominent Black historian, commented that "Black people have met with as great injustices from American scholarship as they have from American life. In fact, colleges and universities have long paved the way for confusion and ignorance, arrogance and presumptuousness, violence and bloodshed in Black-white relations."[56]

The "Black studies" proposition, then, is that though the study of African-American history and culture and the social conditions from economic exploitation and political oppression has been often maligned and distorted in writings from "scholarly" investigations by white academics, the field remains a valid and valuable source of necessary knowledge for teaching and research. This concept has stirred debate and recrimination paralleled by few controversies in the history of American higher education. As a particularistic thrust for independent rediscovery and redefinition of Afro-American history and culture, Black studies involves contending with problems of ideology and power which are long-standing and widespread (if not universal) in American academia. Therefore, scholarly activism and a radical critique of existing theories and analyses of data in the literature (as bodies of knowledge about the relationship of African-American ways of life to the surrounding social order) are of paramount importance to significant groups of Black faculty and students. Concomitant with its academic role is a social role which is concerned with identity problems as related to education and scholarship. The Black studies movement raised questions about *who* would be educated and *how* they should be educated (in terms of the quality and content of learning for Black youth). Black people in America have always been confronted with the problem of sustaining historical connections and ethnic consciousness over each generation of our people through the continuous knowledge of Black history. With the beginning of substantial desegregation of public schools and larger numbers of Black students at predominantly non-Black campuses, the concern for how Black young people were being socialized by their educational environment became a serious "quality-of-mind" issue about the future of the group's collective memory and self-conscious perspective in American society. Harold Cruse, a distinguished social historian and theorist, offered a poignant comment on this issue:

> The further the Negro gets from his historical antecedents in time, the more tenuous becomes his conceptual ties, the emptier his social connections, the more superficial his visions. His one great and present hope is to know and understand his Afro-American history in the United States more profoundly. Failing that, and failing to create a new synthesis and a social theory of action, he will suffer the historical fate described by the philosopher who warned that, "Those who cannot remember the past are condemned to repeat it."[57]

This same issue was the focus of Carter G. Woodson's study, *The Miseducation of the Negro*, thirty-five years earlier. The matter of identity and educational socialization—in all its interrelated group and individual aspects—is central to the concerns of Black educators over serious omissions in established knowledge and distortions in the major national intellectual enterprises and institutions due to Euro-American particularism and ideological bias. The importance of this point was expressed in the writing of an exceptionally insightful and honest white anthropologist: "Social issues and political movements have been intertwined with the search for valid knowledge and expressions of the Black experience in the United States ever since early precursors of modern Afro-American Studies."[58]

The establishment of numerous departments of African-American studies is generally viewed as a recent phenomenon originating in the last ten
years. Though it is true that the field of Black studies is very new in its
present developments, its legacy extends to the earliest beginnings of Black
intellectual history over two centuries ago. Though one can argue that
the notion of Black studies does pre-date the twentieth century, its recent
emergence as an academic field is much more related to the endeavors of
Black intellectuals during the past fifty years. The proper interpretation
and inclusion of the historical role, cultural creation, and social circumstance of Black people in America have been of major concern, especially
to Black scholars in the humanities and social sciences. The development
of the African-American studies in this century can be traced through several stages.

The origins of the modern movement began fermenting in the period
between 1918 and 1929. It was during this period that Black scholars actively participated in the mass awakening of the general Black population,
which was precipitated by the social and cultural flowering of the era. The
second phase of the development of Black studies was ushered by the Great
Depression and marked by the forced parochialization of many Black concerns. By the mid-1930s the question of Afro-American studies was almost
entirely the domain of a Black urban intelligentsia, but it was also during
this period that the idea of Black studies as a separate academic field began
to emerge. In 1940, the advent of World War II began a period of dormancy which lasted until roughly 1960. A lull that was caused by the war
and a gap in the generational shift of Black scholars was accentuated by
the diversion of priorities by many pre-war academicians. The 1960s witnessed the rejuvenation of the civil rights movement, which provided the
atmosphere for the question of Black studies to become a part of the overall
political struggle. Campus protests created the subsequent pressure for the
recognition and proliferation of Afro-American studies programs throughout the nation.

1918–1929: THE FOUNDATIONS OF BLACK
STUDIES

Though W.E.B. Du Bois and Carter G. Woodson are generally considered
the founding mentors with the greatest influence on shaping the roots of
Black studies, it was Du Bois who was preeminent in setting the larger
surrounding movement. "This extraordinary man produced a vast body of
scholarship, literary works, ideological and political writings. His creative

career spanned two-thirds of a century and ended only in 1963, just prior to the flowering of contemporary Black studies."

As early as 1913, Du Bois recognized that the development of what is now known as Black studies could not be possible under the then-present conditions, nor could any correct interpretation of Black people be done by anyone other than trained Black scholars. Writing in the *Annals*, Du Bois notes that "the time has not yet come for the great development of American Negro literature. The economic stress is too great and the racial persecution too bitter to allow the leisure and poise for which literature calls. On the other hand, never in the world has a richer mass of material been accumulated by a people than that which the Negro possesses to-day and are becoming conscious of. Slowly but surely they are developing artists of technique who will be able to use this material. The nation does not notice this for everything touching the Negro is banned by magazines and publishers unless it takes the form of caricature or bitter attack, or is so thoroughly innocuous as to have no literary flavor."[59]

The young Dr. Du Bois, trained in American and German universities, launched African-American studies institutionally when he became the director of the famous Atlanta University Studies Series, which were social and economic analyses of all aspects of Afro-American life. Meticulously researched, this series is still a basic source of the sociology of the Afro-American. During this time, Du Bois also supervised or wrote a series of reports between 1897 and 1903 for the United States Department of Labor, which detailed the social and economic conditions of rural communities throughout the South.[60] This particular set of reports is little known. His massive work, *The Philadelphia Negro* (an important sociological and historical treatment of the Blacks of Philadelphia) is still hailed as a pioneering work of empirical investigation. Du Bois realized that knowledge is a certain measure of power and believed with almost missionary zeal that this power would affect the course of race relations. By careful and sympathetic study, America would learn about Afro-Americans, and how economic exploitation and institutional racism have combined to thwart their development. With Bishop Alexander Crummel, a pioneering nationalist, the young Du Bois was instrumental in the formation at the turn of the century of the American Negro Academy, an organization of intellectuals and activists who desired to create the kind of institutional environment which would nourish Afro-American cultural and educational possibilities. In his important 1897 essay, "On the Conservation of Races," Du Bois talked of perhaps the most important tasks of our movements:

> It is necessary, therefore, in planning our movements, in guiding our future
> developments, that at times we rise above the pressing, but smaller questions
> of separate schools and cars, wage-discrimination and lynch law, to survey
> the whole question of race in human philosophy and to lay, on a basis of
> broad knowledge and careful insight, those large lines of policy and higher
> ideals which may form our guiding lines and boundaries in the practical dif-
> ficulties of every day. For it is certain that human striving must recognize the
> hard limits of natural law, and that any striving, no matter how intense and
> earnest, which is against the constitution of the world, is vain. The ques-
> tion, then, which we must seriously consider is this: *What is the real meaning
> of race; and what has in the past been the law of race development, and what
> lessons has the past history of race development to teach the rising Negro people.*[61]

Du Bois set the contours for the philosophy of racial self-awareness. This
philosophy motivated the flowering of Black scholarship in the early twentieth century. This creative upsurge, which can be dated from the last
decade of the nineteenth and first few decades of the twentieth century,
was associated with the growing urbanization and proletarianization of the
Afro-American masses. Out of this process came greater social differentiation in the Black population and the emergence of a vocal class of Black
intellectuals and political activists who urged Black people to rediscover
their history and redefine their cultural heritage: men like E. A. Johnson,
Benjamin Brawley, Monroe Work, Carter [G.] Woodson, Arthur Schomburg, and others too numerous to mention. [...] Arthur Schomburg would
write in 1913:

> ...I am here with a sincere desire to awaken the sensibilities, to kindle the
> dormant fibers in the soul, and to fire the racial patriotism by the study of
> Negro books. Let us see if we cannot agree to arrange a formula or create a
> basic construction, for the establishment of a substantial method of instruc-
> tion for our young men and women in the material and the useful.[62]

Schomburg became one of the great collectors of Africana materials; the
collection is now housed as a separate branch of the research libraries of
the City of New York and is one of the four most valuable collections of
Africana literature and research sources in the United States.

In 1915, Carter G. Woodson organized the Association for the Study of
African-American Life and History with the following purposes:

1. To promote historical research.

2. To publish books on Negro life and history.

3. To promote the study of the Negro through clubs and schools.

4. To bring about harmony between the races by interpreting the one to the other.[63]

The organization publishes the *Journal of Negro History*, which for sixty years has been devoted to scholarly, analytical, and interpretive research on African, Afro-American, and Caribbean history, culture, and literature. It is one of the oldest continuous academic journals in the country designed to correct the omissions in world history of the people of African descent. The association has gone forward in becoming an outlet for some of the most important and original work on African Americans to date. Woodson himself was a prolific historian, writing many monographs and articles and collecting important documents and letters. An annual meeting was established in which papers were read and discussed, ideas exchanged, and intellectual and academic contacts facilitated. The Association continues to provide a forum for Afro-American scholarship and intellectual activism.

During this period there was a great deal of concentration on the manner in which Black people were portrayed in American history. In 1921, Howard University began publishing the Howard University Studies in History series. The works published during that period included those of Benjamin Brawley, Charles H. Wesley and Charles S. Johnson. Magazines and journals such as *Southern Workman*, *Opportunity*, and *Crisis* became the principle organs in which the concern over Black history was raised.

In 1925, Charles Victor Roman, a physician and contributor to the *Journal of Negro History*, wrote that "what we need is an historical interpretation that will paint us as we are....It is my hope that Negro scholarship will become self-luminous with a brilliancy that will give our race correct historical perspective and lead us to ethnological respectability and racial solidarity which the floods of prejudice have so persistently washed beyond our grasp."[64] Roman's statement not only revealed the usual complaint against the omissions and commission of errors perpetuated by white scholars, but also raised the theme that any Black inquiry must also have a purpose. Investigation and explication are not to exist outside the context of the broader struggle, but must complement and support it (an idea that would be raised loudly in the next generation).

The question of relevancy also prevailed during the Black college rebellions of that era. While many of the issues fought over were academic in nature, the overriding attitude was that Black education should conform to the social conditions and needs of Black people. Because of this, in many instances a number of classes in Black history were added to the curriculum of Black colleges. The support for Black history was not limited to the campus, but was evident in the responsive attitudes and popular support of the masses of Black folk. In 1926, Carter G. Woodson founded Negro History Week, which made the cause of Black academia a mass political issue throughout the Black community.

1930–1940: THE EMERGENCE OF BLACK STUDIES AS A FIELD

The appearance of the Great Depression had a profound effect on the movement for Black studies. The romanticism of the previous decade had been crushed in the economic devastation of this period. The vitality of the 1920s was lost somewhere in the pressing need for survival. Work (or rather, the lack of it) became the pressing issue as the already precarious Black economic condition became unstable. The concentration of Black people on surviving the Depression forced a change in the priority of issues and narrowed the focus of interests. Those who could afford the time to spend on other endeavors did so, but most energies were expended attempting to solve the immediate problem of daily existence.

The issue of Afro-American studies did not fade altogether into obscurity, but the momentum of the previous decade was broken, and the question retreated from widespread debate. However, discussion of Black studies was carried on in major Black scholarly and popular journals and at annual professional meetings. The proceedings of the ASNLH conferences reveal continued concern for a forceful Black studies by some of its members. In 1933, Joseph P. Rhoads, president of Bishop College, called for a scientific evaluation of the Black American's past and the departure from traditional standards which ignore the culture and background of Black people, and noted that the progress of Black social objectives was being retarded by the orientations of many Black educators.[65] Rhoads's statement not only reflected concern for the development of an independent Black inquiry but also the growing rift within Black academic circles.

Rhoads continued his criticisms against the shallowness of much of Black scholarship. In a 1934 article, Rhoads notes that "within recent years 'jazz' has made its advent. Its origin is somewhat questionable, but its relationship to the Negro 'spirit' and 'music' is obvious. It is probable that the Negro is its original producer. Here again we find 'educated Negroes' who are ashamed of the unusual, the new, the novel in the race because it seems to run an uncertain and rather questionable course in its early stages. Instead of studying it with open minds and developing it for noble purposes, we label it is as the works of the devil that are degrading the people; and a no less distinguished scholar, historian, and race leader than Dr. Carter G. Woodson has counseled 'persons who are concerned in social progress' to 'stamp it out.'"[66]

The emphasis of Rhoads's admonitions was that if any Black inquiry was to have relevancy and legitimacy, it must be able to define the conditions and phenomena it observes within the Black population without fear of sanction or lack of recognition from the (white) academic world. His criticisms against Woodson also revealed the latter's precarious leadership role in the movement he helped begin. Unlike Du Bois, Woodson was not able to maintain a progressive stance throughout his career. Woodson was much more concerned with archival accumulation and documentation than with the interpretation of materials.

By 1936, Lawrence Reddick, a young Black historian, began to question the pursuit of Black History solely in terms of quantitative assessments in the context of an alleged neutral objectivity. He complained that the Black intellectual community, which had been shackled by economic conditions that impeded its growth, now found itself imprisoned by the superficialities of the *modus operandi* of white scholarship. In too many instances, Black scholars had become misled by academic objectivity. "Admitting without quibble the correctness in such a view, we must concede that it is a fundamental assumption of the approach presented just now that 'Negro History' is quite different from the study of the Negro. Frankly, the former differs from the latter in that Negro History has a purpose which is built upon a faith. At the sound of such words—purpose, faith—our theoretical objector may again rush forward to protest that the validity of history as history is destroyed if it is urged forward by any other purpose other than the search for truth or sustained by a faith save that invested in the methods and procedures....The very 'father' of the 'scientific' school of historiography, Ranke, has been revealed as a conservative, really a counter-revolutionary, wishing peace so that the ruling class might consolidate their position regained after 1815."[67] In short, Reddick was acknowledging that the dichotomy between intent and purpose is but an arbitrary one.

Reddick's statement delivered at the ASNLH conference was directed against the current method of Black inquiry, but it was also an attack against Woodson and his associates, which widened the split within the Black academic community. It was no longer enough to include Black people in history books, but now history had to be interpreted with the interests of making history congruent with the social objectives of African Americans as an oppressed people. Reddick did not attempt to mandate Marxism as the only method of historical interpretation, but he was clearly against what he considered to be the inadequacy of description that lacked a critique of society which demeaned Black people in the first place. "Summarily, if Negro History is to escape the provincial nature of its first phases, it will surely redefine the area of subject matter in terms of larger focus; recast its catalog of the determinative influences affecting Negro life and reexamine the social philosophy implicit throughout the work."[68]

While historical interpretation was the primary concern, the 1930s also saw the broadening of Black inquiry into the social sciences. A resolution passed during the 1933 ASNLH meeting called for the expansion of the departments of political science, economics, anthropology, English, education, and sociology in Black colleges, and their concentration on Black people in research and teaching. The rising group of young Black scholars who had been educated during the 1920s and early 1930s clustered at Howard University to begin work in the various fields of social science. Scholars such as Ralph Bunche, E. Franklin Frazier, Julius E. Lips, and Edwin E. Lewis resolved to make Black inquiry not just historical documentation but also the exemplification of the motivation, direction, and self-conception of Black people. In 1938, a coalition of Black social scientists inaugurated the Howard University Studies in the Social Sciences to complement the previously published series in history.

By the end of the decade, Afro-American studies began to assume its present form. The preoccupation with history had diminished to include other disciplines as vital components. The idea of Black history changed from its earlier emphasis on a historiography that was descriptive and narrative to a focus upon critical interpretation as well. The significance of this period was in the fact that Black academics were defining the parameters within which Black study should be undertaken. The publication of seminal works forced the recognition of a new radical interpretation of the status of Black Americans and their past. Again in the forefront, Du Bois's *Black Reconstruction in America* (1935), portions of Horace Mann

Bond's *The Education of the Negro* (1934), and A. L. Harris and S. P. Spero's *The Black Worker* (1931) presented the beginnings of the different perspective in Black studies. It was not necessarily a complete Marxist viewpoint (though that position has a compelling argument), but instead is an expansion of resources used to investigate the reality of Black America. Unfortunately, the domination of progressive black scholars was to be short-lived.

It is worth mentioning at this point that during the period just before World War I and through World War II, the migration of hundreds of thousands of Black people from the Southern plantations to the great cities of the Northeast and the Midwest gave rise to a dynamic cultural nationalism. Creative writing and literary criticism flourished, and painting and the plastic arts became significant dimensions of cultural expression. The creation of serious classical Black music (jazz) emerged, and big bands dominated the entertainment of salons of the new urban middle-class. It was a time which gave birth to the concept of the "New Negro," which Alain Locke, Dean of African-American letters and professor of philosophy at Howard University, explains when he wrote this in 1925:

> Recall how suddenly the Negro spirituals revealed themselves; suppressed for generations under the stereotypes of Wesleyan hymn harmony, secretive half-ashamed, until the courage of being natural brought them out—and behold, there was folk music. Similarly, the mind of the Negro seems suddenly to have slipped from under the tyranny of social intimidation, and to be shaking off the psychology of imitation and implied inferiority. By shedding the old chrysalis of the Negro problem we are achieving something like a spiritual emancipation. Until, recently, lacking self-understanding, we have been almost as much of a problem to ourselves as we still are to others. But the decade that found us with a problem has left us only with a task. The multitude perhaps feels as yet only a strange relief and a new vague urge, but the thinking few know that in reaction the vital inner grip of prejudice has been broken.[69]

On the wave of a cultural awakening, Black people exerted their influence upon the cultural forms and enterprises of a modern America. Black intellectuals and artists exerted their influence upon national scholarship and literary affairs, as racial and class inequalities were central to the contradictions of a crisis-ridden America during the late 1920s and early 1930s. The impact of Garveyism (and the Black West Indian influence in general) was critical to the articulation of a widespread militant nationalism among the working class in the Black community. At the same time as writing, paint-

ing, music, and composing flourished and attracted international interest
in African-American culture and its African background, dance and drama
performed by all-Black companies bridged the hegemony of "Hollywood
and Broadway" to revitalize art forms which America has always imported.
During this early twentieth century, the culture of African descendants began to wedge into the very fiber of the larger society and shape and reshape
much of the thinking, behavior, and artistic expression of modern American culture. This is a fascinating period of American history in which the
automobile, the radio, motion picture, and mass consumption were linked
to the cultural rising of Black people and their influence upon values and
art in the larger society. Harold Cruse's major work, *The Crisis of the Negro Intellectual*, marks the beginning of the investigation of this essential
and multifaceted subject, of the importance of this period, and its relationship to the many attempts to create a viable cultural philosophy for the
Black intelligentsia.

In the era of the Depression and New Deal, Black intellectuals struggled
to affect national policy and directions of legislation for social reconstruction. Black scholarship set the tone and provided the institutional
nexus around which the intellectual pursuit of African-American studies
would take place. E. Franklin Frazier and Ralph Bunche were just two
of the scholars whose work influenced national policy and academic enterprise in different ways. Frazier's sociological studies, which assumed
African-American social disorganization, were primary reference sources in
molding the American welfare relationships to Blacks. The current proponents of the theories of "culture of poverty" and "internal Black pathology"
use Frazier's work to support their theses. Ralph Bunche's investigations
of Black political organizations and ideological tendencies were a vital
part of the Carnegie Corporation's massive study of race relations, *An
American Dilemma*, organized by the Swedish economist Gunnar Myrdal.
Positing a position of academic objectivity and value-free research methodology, Myrdal's study became in fact the ideological manifesto for the
integrationist movement. Paradoxically, it was entrenched racism in the
educational establishment which prevented the posturing liberal academicians associated with this major intellectual enterprise from choosing a
director for the study from among the more competent Black scholars.
Available were such people as W.E.B. Du Bois, Charles Johnson, St. Clair
Drake, E. Franklin Frazier, Kenneth Clark, Allison Davis, Kelly Miller,
Ralph Bunche, etc. Those who did participate in the project were relegat-
ed to research assistants. Some of the most valuable monographs by these
social scientists were never published or cited by Myrdal.

1940–1960: INTELLECTUAL HIATUS FOR BLACK STUDIES

By the 1930s the conception of the form African-American studies should take as an academic field (inclusive of all disciplines of scholarship) had been developed, but the theoretical delineation of the salient research tasks had not been solidified. There was not yet the consistent social theory necessary to concretize and unify Black inquiry. The entrance of the United States in World War II provoked a hiatus in the development and expansion of Black studies. The result was the temporary abandonment of independent research and criticism for support of the war effort. Great numbers of the Black men with college training were either in the armed forces or working in the war-related industry. The destruction of the war reduced the number of "artists of technique" and sufficiently slowed the pace of Black studies. However, the distractions of the war were compounded by the repressive red-baiting campaign of Senator Joseph McCarthy.

By the dawn of 1940, the effort of Black scholars who were opposed to the conservative orthodoxy of Black academia had begun to shift the emphasis of Afro-American studies. The views of younger Black scholars in history and the social sciences began to create a radical perspective to Black studies. In that year, W. T. Fontaine noted that "the mind of the Negro scholar today largely because of a defense psychology thrust upon it by social conditions, presents a configuration generally antithetical to democratic-liberal concepts, thought patterns and techniques."[70] But the question of Black studies fell into a period of quiet recess; though there was still interest in the field, the enthusiasm and vitality of just a few years previous had waned. The beginning of academic innovation and a pattern of radical Black scholarship in interpretation of historical events and analysis of contemporary problems were replaced by a more conservative attitude at major Black colleges. The defensive posture of many Black scholars during this period which Fontaine refers to was due in part to the hysteria of the times and a strong anti-intellectual undercurrent in the dominant theme of Cold War politics in America. With the end of World War II, the United States shifted rapidly to a staunch anti-Soviet, anti-communist position. Free thought and critical comment on American society were seriously circumscribed and suspected by influential leaders of government and civic/political organizations. During this period many radical scholars (particularly leftists) and independent-minded liberal intellectuals and artists were persecuted and suppressed. Militant Black scholars, such as W.E.B. Du Bois and Ralph Bunche, and artists like Langston Hughes, Paul

Robeson, and Richard Wright (to name a few) were harassed and restricted by government agents. Associations of progressive Black scholars, such
as the Social Science Division at Howard University (organized during the
previous decade as a monumental beginning for a coordinated and systematic Black studies), were intimidated and soon dissipated.

1960–1976: THE RE-ASSERTION OF THE INTELLECTUAL VALIDITY OF BLACK STUDIES

With expanding economic growth and prosperity and the impetus from
the dynamic force of the civil rights movement, America was nudged toward the direction of a less constrained society. There was a greater sense
of urgency to protect democratic rights of dissent and self-expression. In
this environment, there was a rejuvenation of more independent intellectual discourse in university communities. Student strikes against the general
malaise of the status quo, which has generally afflicted all levels of American education as such; the Black studies movement reflected the most
poignant intellectual crisis in American schools.

Those students who are "the most conscious of the need to have firm
historic roots and contemporary international (Pan-African) ties" represent
an unanticipated maturity in the Black community, necessitating a reex-
amination of the peculiar historical dynamics of the Black experience and
its validity in all aspects of the academic enterprise. As a dimension of
the Black consciousness movement, the utility of Black studies is considered essential to the socialization of socially conscious Black intellectuals,
scholars, and artists—and a Black-conscious intelligentsia committed to
the struggle against the oppression of African peoples. As a variant of the
student protest movement, Black students also are concerned with student
roles in academic decisions, the elite-mass gap, functional relevancy of education to real life experiences, and option for field (community work)
credit and socially oriented values of knowledge.

The issue surrounding Black studies have been analyzed and discussed
with greater intensity and with more space in national media, faculty committee reports, professional journals, and speeches than any other question
in the recent history of American academia. The proponents for Black
studies, by virtue of their position on the crest of a popular struggle for
political and economic emancipation of Black people, are more forceful
and pervasive than their predecessors. Unfortunately, too few of them (and
even fewer white educators) are sufficiently knowledgeable of the intellectual history of the subject they confront. However, Black studies has

risen during this time as a critique of American historiography and as a frame of reference for a critical examination of the foundations of the social sciences (and the humanities as well), and their relationship to many features of the dominant bourgeois ideology. Especial concern is expressed for the necessity of opposition to the manner in which white intellectuals use their knowledge to complement the legitimacy and hegemony of ruling class interests. Also, Black studies denounces the support of conventional knowledge to the persistence of modes of thinking about the basis of the social inequality of Black people deriving from their "deprived culture" and internal pathology. Therefore, the tasks and methods of Black studies are to advocate change in the status quo, oppose the exclusion of Blacks in American education, while contributing to Black cultural consciousness and to a theory of social and political action.

It has long been widely proclaimed among American scholars that their work is independent of political issues. A cardinal axiom in the philosophy of American education is that knowledge and learning—whether science, the humanities, or scholarship in general—are distinct from and should be kept separate from politics and ideology. No issue in the whole affair has agitated more than how the union of politics and knowledge has been essential to the birth and growth of Black studies. Black studies scholars condemn this stance of neutrality as a sham: All groups of people, academicians included, are influenced in their work by their position in society. They reveal that scholarship is political and that the separation between knowledge and politics is artificial and based on a contrived myth about "value-free" knowledge. The influence from the activities and results of science and scholarship are politically significant. This pretense towards neutrality by mainstream scholarship is the source of its large failure and non-credibility; and it is to the enduring credit of Black studies that it is more candid about this question.

Some have been heard to ask, "Can education survive Black studies?" Though Black studies is here to stay in various forms at different institutions, it is more important for us to ask if Black studies can prevail within a context of an entrenched, racist intellectualism of orthodox white academia. For certain, Euro-American domination of university culture and politics has not been overturned.

TOWARDS A CRITIQUE OF SOCIAL SCIENCE[71]

JAMES TURNER AND W. ERIC PERKINS

Nowhere in the Western world has bourgeois intellectual domination been so pervasive as it has been in the United States. Beginning with the rise of the public schools in the nineteenth century, through the development of American higher education, the American bourgeoisie has considered intellectual domination and ideological legitimization as essential to the consolidation of its political and economic rule over a subdued middle class and a divided working class; and for establishment of white supremacy and racial domination in a multi-racial society. The bourgeoisie subverted the original democratic impulse of American education by a pedagogy based upon Anglo-Saxon chauvinism, vocational training, tracking, and of course the denigration and exclusion of particular national and racial groups.

Our interest in this essay is an analysis of how the Afro-American intelligentsia inherited and has been critically influenced by the ideological postures of bourgeois thought, and utilized it in the study of the Afro-American experience. How have such patterns of bourgeois thinking been popularized? How have such patterns of thinking contributed to the total political and intellectual confusion the Afro-American intelligentsia finds itself in? Rather than challenge the methodological and theoretical foundations of orthodox social science, the Afro-American intellectual, with few exceptions, has succeeded in reproducing the worst features of bourgeois thinking: the lack of systematic historical analysis, emphasis on social disorganization, cultural pathology, and consensus over dissent or conflict models. To understand the situation of the Afro-American intelligentsia is to come to grips with the racial and class character of the Afro-American struggle, and the pitfalls of its current domination by an aspiring and upwardly mobile petty bourgeois.[72]

To undertake an analysis of the social character of Afro-American intellectuals, it is necessary to examine some fundamental categories of political economy; the historical genesis of the knowledge industry, its composition, its relationship to the class rule of the bourgeois, and finally the role of the Afro-American intelligentsia within this set of developments. Needless to say, we cannot be exhaustive here, nor do we attempt to put forth the final word on important theoretical and intellectual matters given consideration here. This is part of a larger project, which we see as necessary in this new phase of the Afro-American struggle. We are addressing ourselves to the need for serious and frank discussion, minus the rhetoricalism and character assassination which unfortunately has marked recent discussions. We also feel that it is important to mention that a serious reevaluation of our experiences during the last two decades is occurring, one which should yield important results of ideological self-criticism and non-mechanical and anti-dogmatic conclusions.

We are specifically concerned with the role of ideas in history and the power ideas have in shaping social behavior. Marxism, especially the more orthodox varieties, has been of little use in unraveling the complicated relationship between the economic base and the political, social, cultural, and legal superstructure. Crude economic reductionism predominates in [the] mechanistic brand of Marxism, usually referred to as "Soviet Marxism." It ignores the interdisciplinary approach of Marx: He was simultaneously historian, sociologist, and economist, as well as a partisan political commentator on the great revolutionary developments of his time, like the 1848 Revolutions, the Civil War, and the Paris Commune.

Quoting Marx, the "political economist," these practitioners of "Soviet Marxism" postulate a one-to-one mechanical relationship between development within the economic arena and developments within "civil society"—the legal, social, political, and cultural institutions of a particular social formation. The new generation of neo-black Marxist intellectuals, in its uncritical adoption of Marxism, has become steeped in this orthodox Marxist tradition—a tradition currently under bitter attack.[73] Refusing to dissect the Afro-American experience and the complex cultural and economic foundations of Afro-American nationalism and Afro-American radicalism, they opt instead for a mechanical economism, reducing all social, political, and cultural occurrences as reactions to the economic base. The new black Marxists are merely carrying on the old Marxism. We will return to this theme after an examination of bourgeois social science.

THE NEW LEFT CRITIQUE OF BOURGEOIS SOCIAL SCIENCE

American social science was built on bourgeois philanthropy and the need for the bourgeoisie to legitimize its social-economic dominance and exploitation over the rest of the society. With the rise of the large multiversity, beginning in the late nineteenth century and continuing down to the present day, American bureaucrats began to develop graduate programs of education in the liberal arts, the sciences, and the professions. The results were not without profound consequences: There was the increasing rationalization of education, which led to specialization and professionalization; higher standards and stringent requirements were initiated, and of course, tuition, which excluded great masses from the benefits of college education.[74]

The industrial barons needed this professionally trained intelligentsia to manage business enterprises of the growing corporate economy: business managers in advertising, in state, local, and federal government, and in the emerging service industries. By making education more and more the criterion of success in this bourgeois, democratic society, an essential component of capitalist hegemony was the "education myth." Though they attempted to exert maximum control over American higher education (in contrast to the control of secondary education by elites), to ensure "the Americanization through conformity," they were not entirely successful as pockets of dissent, bohemianism, and finally Marxism creeped into universities.

The social sciences were integral to the maintenance of bourgeois rule not only in the United States, but over America's expanding colonial empire in the South Pacific, the Caribbean, and Latin America. The American colonial empire was also domestic in colonization of the dark-skinned racial groups of the South and West, Indians, Mexicans, and the largest "internal colony," Afro-Americans.[75] Early North American Indian ethnography, for example, produced a wide volume of valuable information and important theoretical insights. Such material, however, merely served the interests of the bureaucrats of the Department of the Interior and Indian Affairs in more effectively controlling the indigenous peoples.

The so-called "primitive societies" of Africa, Asia, and Latin America, with their civilizations of "noble savagery," were repeatedly assaulted by hordes of bush jacket–wearing Englishmen, Frenchmen, and Americans who subjected the interior of their cultures—their sexual and familial arrangements, their gods and their beliefs about man and the cosmos—to microscopic analysis. These people had no influence on the decisions which allowed colonialism to penetrate their world and make them part of abstract European theory. These colonized people were studied so that the Foreign Offices might more effectively exploit and control them through a manipulation of the beliefs which made them act.[76]

Robert E. Park, a father of American sociology and a secret protégé of Booker T. Washington, was instrumental in forming much of the theoretical formulations in the study of race and race relations. His theory of pathology, the marginal man, and assimilation still inform most of the research going on today. His theories of assimilation fit in neatly with the nativist movement operative in early twentieth century which demanded the full scale "Americanization" of Southern and Eastern European immigrants. It naturally related to Afro-Americans, who were the most un-American of Americans, and who would have to assimilate in order to enter the dominant "white" society. His theory of the "marginal man" saw Afro-American culture as a "deviant" variety of "mainstream culture." This theory became the foundation of various theories of cultural pathology and cultural deprivation, prominent in American and Western social science.[77] His conceptual apparatus was adopted by the social engineers who saw the complete reorganization and management of Afro-American culture as the only alternative to further internal moral and cultural decay. Needless to say, such thinking became the foundation of the ideology of "integration," which followed the Second World War, and which produced catastrophic changes in American society.

As a mentor of E. Franklin Frazier, Park's continuous intellectual legacy was established. He wrote on the "Black Bourgeoisie"; of the impact of slavery in completely shattering African culture in the New World; of a lopsided interpretation of "acculturation"; of the disorganized Afro-American family; the dominance of the "matriarchy"; and of urban pathology. His arguments have become part of what one author has called "the folklore of white supremacy and the fakelore of black pathology."[78] They have become part of the ideological armor of white supremacy in combating the Afro-American demand for our full democratic rights.

The curious power of American intellectuals in shaping domestic and foreign policy is too often ignored. Have we forgotten their role, and the role of the university in supporting counter-revolution? "Project Camelot," one of the first of the "counter-insurgency" studies that laid the groundwork for government subversion of political liberty at home and abroad, was a product of Latin American specialists, in political science, psychology, sociology, and anthropology. Intellectuals have dominated the making of foreign policy, and still hold that reign with the likes of Harvard political scientist Henry Kissinger. Domestic policy is dominated by the "think tank" intellectuals of the Brookings Institution, the Rand Corporation, and the Hudson Institute, just to name a few of the better known. James Coleman, a Harvard sociologist, has been one of the leading figures in forming educational policy, policies that have as their result the continued under-education and mis-education of the Afro-American masses. And just recently a group of University of Chicago economists has been advising the Chilean military junta on restoring capitalism, and dismantling the socialist infrastructure created by the socialist-oriented Allende regime. Such collaboration shows us that knowledge is essentially related to political power in capitalist societies.[79]

The student uprisings of the 1960s, conditioned and inspired by the struggle for Afro-Americans' democratic rights, began to offer the first genuine critique of American society in a generation. The era of the Great Depression and the class struggle that it unleashed also produced a wide outpouring of intellectual creativity and criticism of all phases of bourgeois society. This tradition, however, was suppressed by the political terrorism of "McCarthyism" and denied to the post-war generation. The critique of America by this new "intellectual proletariat" centered on an analysis of a number of related phenomena about the university as a tool of imperialist and industrial interests; about the decay of the quality of student education and its increasing irrelevance to social concerns and the wider society; about that false liberalism which produced the likes of "Project Camelot" and Henry Kissinger.

Students during the last decade began to see the university as essential to reproducing capitalist society with its class, race, ethnic, sexual, and intellectual divisions. Education separated manual from intellectual workers: It separated head and hand, and it reproduced and legitimized pecuniary values. Education meant opportunity and success, and the rule of wealth thrived on the pervasiveness of this kind of outlook in society.[80] Afro-American intellectuals have been particularly misdirected by this feature of bourgeois ideology—that college education automatically means economic success. As the last group to enter higher education in significant numbers, black students have been essential to preserving their "myth" and demonstrating its vitality for future generations. This "myth" is a cornerstone of bourgeois democracy and was seriously undermined and "de-legitimized" by the white New Left during the sixties.

A critique of the content and function of the university emerged from this critique. Growing from its analysis of the origins and consequences of the Vietnam War, including the participation of intellectuals in the struggle for Afro-American democratic rights, the critical spirit and radical analysis spread throughout the social science disciplines. Radical caucuses, though minorities, have invaded the disciplines of political science, psychology, anthropology, sociology, geography, economics, and history. This is evidence of a growing politicization of intellectual work and the final exposure of the true nature of "value-free" or "objective" intellectual work.

Knowledge is rooted in and supportive of the dominant socio-economic system. It has ideological functions—that is, to falsify and obscure our understanding of organized exploitation and inequality in wealth, power, and privilege. To radicalize the social sciences is to penetrate the "world of appearances," and reach the essential reality of any given phenomenon.

Marxism has entered the American university, this time through many of these radical caucuses, and their theoretical journals devoted to exposing and dissecting bourgeois social science. Radical economists have introduced Marxian political economy into orthodox economic departments. The theoretical journal, *The Review of Radical Political Economics*, has already produced an important literature on racism and poverty, monopoly capitalism, the structure of the working class, imperialism and military expansion.[81] These young radical economists are by no means immune to criticism, but have initiated serious theoretical challenges to bourgeois economists, who in the economic chaos of the last five years have yet to grapple with their analyses. In addition to their theoretical work, they have exposed the conservative bias of many so-called liberal economists; they have been instrumental in "de-legitimizing" the falsity of state capitalism and the ideological apparatuses that support it.

Alvin Gouldner, William Domhoff, and other logical carriers of the critical tradition of C. Wright Mills have undertaken a similar "ideology critique" of American sociology. In *The Sociological Imagination*, Mills initiated a critique of the dominant varieties of the American sociological tradition, led by the "structuralist-functionalist" interpretation society, with its emphasis on order, stability, and equilibrium. Talcott Parsons's extensive writing was seen as integral to the stabilization of capitalist society following the Depression and World War II. Society is not a system of social variables tending toward harmony and consensus, but a complete whole composed of different groups in competition with each other, and a system that produces uneven social division and unequal share in liberal democracy. Parsons's vision of society was more a rationalization of the differences in power relations among society's various parts, and a disguise for continued management and engineering of conflict.

In Mills's critique of "abstracted empiricism," the tradition of reducing all social phenomenon to a series of mathematical and statistical equations, human motivation, initiative, and will disappear from such theoretical stances. The quantitative method is of some use in allowing us to see certain patterns and regularities in any group of social phenomena but it can never take us the *whole way* in understanding all aspects of society and their inter-relatedness and complexity. He was also poignant in his critique of the "bureaucratic ethos," the vast separation of humanity from the political, social, and economic fabric of society and its ever-growing management by trained specialists. It is this "bureaucratic ethos" which pervades more and more of the life of American society leading to ever accelerating de-personalization, alienation, cultural decay, and social revolt. The bureaucratic social order produces a society of manipulated spectators, who yield to the domination of the political and cultural rule of corporate capitalism. With the advent of the "welfare state," centralization and specialization replaced local autonomy, leading to the "bureaucratization" of every area of life. Nowhere is this more evident than in the chaotic state of our education, welfare, and social service systems.

Alvin Gouldner has built on these arguments of the late C. Wright Mills in his *The Coming Crisis of Western Sociology*, the second volume of his projected multi-volume series on the "Social Origins of Social Theory." No tendency in Western sociological thought escaped his incisive critique: the positivism of early bourgeois sociology, the utilitarianism of the social engineers, the empiricism of the statisticians, structuralism and functionalism, welfare state bureaucratization, and "Soviet Marxism." Linking academic sociology to the reproduction of the dominant capitalist production relation—the total preservation of capitalist legitimacy and culture—Gouldner concludes in the tradition of "Western Marxism" that only a "reflexive sociology" can remedy the "Crisis":

> Starting with the very primitive assumption that theory is made by the praxis of men in all their wholeness and is shaped by the lives they lead, and pursuing this into concrete empirical contexts, one is led to a very different conception of what generates social theory and what it is many theorists are trying to do. Having pursued this conception, one is better able to see just how complex a communication social theory is. It is a complexity that cannot even be glimpsed, let alone grasped, if we fail to see the way in which theorists are entrenched in their theories.[82]

Social theory must criticize itself while uncovering the social relation of capitalist society.

Within history, anthropology, and political science, similar developments have been taking place. A consideration of these will have to await a larger format, but such "ideology critique" in all of the social sciences and the humanities is leading to the radical restructuring of knowledge in American societies, one which is hastening the unmasking of the true character of bourgeois rule.

BLACK INTELLECTUALS AND BLACK LIBERATION

Needless to say the great majority of the Afro-American intelligentsia seems immune to the theoretical and intellectual ferment sweeping the larger society. Clinging to the obsolete ideological baggage of the 1960s, much of the debate, or for that matter serious intellectual work, continues to be defined by under-preparation, mysticism, and bloated black rhetoric. The degeneration of certain irrational and mystical varieties of Black Nationalism heralds the inauguration of a new era within Afro-America. To understand the relationship between the obsolete ideological baggage of the last decade and bourgeois habits of thought necessitates an examination of the Afro-American intelligentsia.

The emergence of the new Afro-American intelligentsia of the late sixties came out of the predominately student-based movement. In many respects, it was the product of corporate paternalism and government intervention. This movement initiated the rebirth of Afro-American nationalism, but not without serious consequences:

> The nationalist tendency among black students is a reflection rather than a source of the present state of consciousness among black people. Because the black student lives most of his life in a paradigm world (the university), this newly discovered black consciousness has no objective referent. It acquires a rather superficial temper because its logic is ingrown. Instead of examining social reality, it blindly latches onto symbols. Instead of critically assaulting social myths and seeking answers to vital political questions, it embarks upon the "politics of identity." In other words, the petty bourgeois black student predictably seeks existential answers to hard-nosed political questions....[83]

This same black student movement has been transformed into the black student intelligentsia: not merely university personnel and teachers, but the entire spectrum of professionals who must procure a college education to practice their alleged skills: state, local, and federal civil servants who man the gigantic welfare state bureaucracy, the public schools' staff, the medical and health personnel in addition to middle level managers in corporate enterprise, lawyers, politicians, and finally that sprinkling of black executives who sit on the boards of directors of the multi-national conglomerates.

The social outlook of this segment of the Afro-American population is social reformism: the philosophy of economic and property acquisition, personal thrift, and moral righteousness. It is an essentially conservative and property-oriented outlook. The past decade's cultural nationalism was not antithetical to this view, since it did not foster an anti-capitalist position. It was even looked at as a way of spurring Afro-American investment and economic opportunity in Africa and the urban black ghettos. The inherent radicalism of this movement was frequently defined by political expediency. The "politics of culture" could not be equated with a "politics of revolution," and since blacks have little power in shaping some cultural components, with the music industry as an example, a politics which pursued "culturalism" was/is self-defeating.

Within Afro-America over the last two decades there has been a "bourgeois democratic revolution"—comparable to the great tide of decolonization and the rise of "neocolonialism" and clientele politics in the "Third World." Within Afro-America, this evolution takes the shape of the control of the petty bourgeoisie over the "Black United Front." The continued success of this segment within Afro-America—moderate civil rights organizations, professional organizations, and the black clergy—is testimony to their support by the white bourgeoisie. This segment represents the internal contradiction for the majority of Afro-America, the working class folks who labor in industry, service, and agriculture. For far too long, this incipient conflict has been cloaked under the rubric of "black unity," which meant license and control by the black petty bourgeois.

Nowhere is this social outlook more apparent than in the philosophies of American intelligentsia, and in the methodologies they utilize in studying the Afro-American experience, which they assert (wrongly, we contend) will advance Afro-American liberation. Let us examine these modes of thought, and show how they extend the presuppositions and content of conventional thought, ultimately preventing the development of any analytical and critical thinking on the Afro-American question. Until such analysis is made, with the assistance of a critical, reflective, and radical social science, the Afro-American experience will be left to be interpreted by bourgeois and liberal intellectuals—black and white—who do not possess the motive of revolutionary self-understanding, but who share the desire for personal and pecuniary gain.

The "Black studies" revolution, a key component of this intellectual reawakening, has done little to eradicate the orthodox thinking on "the grand theory," "abstracted empiricism," social engineering, and cultural pathology of American social science. The Afro-American input into American social science has merely assisted bourgeois ideology in reproducing itself through the Afro-American intelligentsia.

The goals of the Afro-American intelligentsia should be to dissect the social, economic, and political forces which oppress and exploit the black masses—racism, the specific relations of black labor to the American capitalist process as a traditionally "dual exploited" national group; the attempt to control and manipulate black culture through, for example, "Hollywoodization"; the creation of myths which emphasize the so-called "pathology" of Afro-American culture; and the class composition and historical genesis of Afro-America, examining its specificity, as well as its relationship to the dominant society. To date, the Afro-American intelligentsia has been deficient in uncovering "reality" behind the "appearance," leaving our self-understanding and the politics associated with coming to self-consciousness in a vacuum. We must ask why this is so.

The Afro-American intelligentsia, like its counterpart in the dominant society, was trained and is being trained in bourgeois institutions, whose purpose is to support and legitimize capitalist society and Euro-American culture. Consequently, they are taught the social sciences very traditionally and uncritically: One must study the classics and the "chiefs" of the profession or discipline in question, in addition to competing for jobs, status, and grades. When the movement of the last decade emerged, the Afro-American intelligentsia was caught off guard, unprepared and ill-equipped to comprehend the change which surrounded them and the enormous importance of it. The dominant cultural nationalism served a useful purpose in pointing out for us the need to rediscover our heritage, take charge of our lives, define our realities, and make our own decisions. But such practice was not new or foreign to the history of the Afro-American struggle, as we are now well aware.

The intelligentsia did not seek to link our history and culture with the larger movement in the non-Western world for political, cultural, and economic self-determination. Though many militant nationalists exposed the faults of the "ingrown logic" of the integrationist faith in the eventual positive outcome of the American democratic process, it continues to haunt all corridors of the movement. During our intellectual training, we become wedded to bourgeois social, economic, and political theory: Integrationism, black capitalism, the success myth, and possessive individualism are all results of such ideological domination and manipulation.

In "black sociology," for example, models of cultural pathology and cultural deprivation still predominate. Urban communities are seen as locus of social, physical, and cultural disorganization to be remedied by strong dosages of petty-bourgeois culture and welfare state management. Or there is the view that urban Afro-American communities need to undergo "Africanization" to dissolve the degenerate elements of American culture absorbed by the masses. Both views are similar in ignoring the very vital culture, with its belief system and social rules, which flower in our society as mechanisms to facilitate the survival of our people, and which go ignored by our intellectuals precisely because they are not looking for them. These viewpoints were quite common through the last decade,[84] and though black academics and intellectuals claimed their opposition to renegade liberals like Daniel Moynihan or Edward Banfield, their own theoretical perspectives were informed by the ideology and methodology of these neo-racist supporters.

There have been many discussions, and no doubt there will be more before we end, about Afro-American culture needing Africanization, a spiritual and organizational cleansing of the rot from the larger society. This kind of thinking is static and represents the worst kind of theoretical infantilism, seeing the mass of Afro-American people as passive recipients in the social and historical process, not as self-activating men and women creating cultural forms and mechanisms suitable to the oppression that envelopes them. Studies of the Afro-American family are built on the "deviance" and "pathological" models of Gunnar Myrdal and E. Franklin Frazier.[85] Black psychologists engage in the worst kind of mysticism, pitting the abstract values of "blackness" against the real racist and capitalist values of greed, accumulation, and success. The social sciences, particularly as practiced by the Afro-American intelligentsia, rather than challenging the assumption and models of Afro-American intelligentsia, culture, and society, continue to reproduce the same abstract, order-oriented and empiricistic studies criticized by the emerging radical intelligentsia in the larger society. More studies of "breakdown," "disorganization," and "spiritual regeneration" will not assist the *long struggle* for American liberation.

Our history has a long and significant tradition of writing, from George Washington Williams down to Dr. Du Bois. Much of the current history is not based on solid research guided by critically independent questioning and theoretically active inquiry, but on superficial speculation and ideological expediency. History is the "great man theory," as biographies of black leaders, politicians, or businessmen pour out from graduate schools. Or they are empiricistic monographs which study individual communities isolated from the larger social, political, and economic fabric of the dominant white society. This is an artificial and superficial history. This is the ideological history in which black people are forced to see themselves through the prism of white bourgeois categories: as disorganized, deprived, and pathological; necessitating the kind of historical mythology designed to support racism; the worst kind of Eurocentric romanticism. Aside from individual leaders or resistors, like Nat Turner or Marcus Garvey, Afro-

American history is the history of white oppression and of our resistance to that oppression. To struggle against *ahistoricism* is the task of a critical black history. The history being written in the larger society reminds us of an observation which has been frequently forgotten: "that it is men that change circumstances, and that the *educator* himself needs educating."[86]

Within both the popular and academic arenas, the Afro-American experience continues to be locked in the ideological vault of white bourgeois social thought. The first step in recovering the content of our experience is a serious reevaluation of the last two decades' intellectual work and the foundations upon which it was built. Critical work on the early history of the movement has begun, but there is still a long way to go.[87] There is a paramount need to root out the ideology of racist social science by launching a serious and critical intellectual assault. The contours of such a struggle are already taking place within the Afro-American movement,[88] but this is only the *beginning* of a new phase in our development.

Marxism has reappeared, but there is confusion as to why. It has appeared in a serious intellectual vacuum. To our knowledge, no new study of the relationship of Afro-Americans to the developing socialist and Communist movements has been undertaken since Harold Cruse's *The Crisis of the Negro Intellectual* appeared in 1967. Consequently, Marxism to a recent segment of Afro-American intellectuals is conceived as a series of formulae, a rigidly organized and mechanical system of thought unmitigated by the particular reality of Afro-American oppression. Only serious theoretical work, coupled with intense dialogue without personal acrimony between black intellectuals and political activists, can correct this situation.

We must create the kind of social science and theoretical skill that not only foster intellectual debate and analysis, but stimulate thoughts which change our conceptions about the important questions of the Afro-American experience and the nature of our relationship to the larger society. This is no small task, and one with immense political implications. We must first dismantle and "de-legitimize" the legacy of white bourgeois and racist social science, and its methods of research and of organizing and understanding reality.

We must accept our responsibility to understand the reality of our national oppression, and how various forms of political, economic, cultural, and social forces intersect to dominate black people as a systemic process of the social order. What should our guidelines be? A suggestion for this is contained in an important passage from the late French Marxist sociologist, Lucien Goldmann[:]

There are no brute facts. No inquiry, no monograph is ever exhaustive. It only asks certain questions of reality and chooses the facts in the light of these questions. Moreover, in the image that it constructs, the importance given to the different facts, that it accepts for recording, is proportional to what the problems represent for the researcher or investigator.[89]

We must criticize those social theories that promote structural-functionalist consensus models and a static analysis of society's development. We must attack those pseudo-nationalistic tendencies that also promote mysticism, confusion, and theoretical poverty. The adoption of a critical theory will prepare us for the development of a long struggle by giving us the intellectual equipment to analyze and interpret society, to bring our views to larger numbers of Afro-Americans, and to formulate a program for the next phase. A critical Afro-American social theory will also strengthen our intellectual work by making our scholarship the study of our reality, as it is and has been, not as it might have been or as we would have liked it to have been. Finally, it will create the kind of intellectual bases where the dimensions, problems, and tactics of the Afro-American struggle may be discussed, interpreted, and absorbed.

"The philosophers have only interpreted the world in various ways," wrote Karl Marx; the "point, however, is to change it."[90] The message contained in this sentence indicates to us the relation between knowledge and action, theory and practice; and this is still neglected, if not outright ignored. Let us restore this perspective to our future intellectual work. Without it, our struggle will wander in confusion between the anachronistic theory and method of a subservient, moribund, non-regenerative orthodox social science, which facilitates our oppression as a people by rationalizing our condition with racist values and ideological pre-suppositions of the eventual corrective of bourgeois reform.

AFRICANA STUDIES AND EPISTEMOLOGY: A DISCOURSE IN THE SOCIOLOGY OF KNOWLEDGE[91]

JAMES TURNER

> Black Studies begins with the study of Black History...because it is relevant, even indispensable to the introduction and development of all the other subject areas. Black history places them in perspective, establishes their origins and development, and thus aids in critical discussion and understanding of them.
>
> —*Dr. Maulana Karenga*

> We can only understand the present by continually referring to and studying the past; when any one of the intricate phenomena of our daily life puzzles us; when there arise religions problems, political problems, race problems, we must always remember that while their solution lies in the present, their cause and their explanation lie in the past.
>
> —*Dr. W.E.B. Du Bois*

A decade is actually not much time in the span of history. It is only a short period in the life of a new field of study, and it is inadequate for the full development of a discipline and its complements. But, in another sense, it was a long ten years, and as might have been expected, along the way there have been many obstacles, serious challenges, and great demands and expectations. However, the achievements during this time have been nothing short of extraordinary.

It was during the summer of 1969 that the Institute of the Black World organized a two-month project for faculty and students to organize a curriculum prototype that would define the conceptual parameters and explain the scholarly method and purpose for what was generally being referred to as *black studies*.

The summer workshop was followed by a Black Studies Directors' Seminar on November 7–9 of that same year. The approximately thirty participants came from a cross section of private and public institutions of higher education, and all were involved (under different institutional circumstances) with developing program designs and instructional formats as directors for Black studies. The significance of this meeting lies in the fact that it was, in a manner of speaking, the founding convention for the field.

It was the base for professional association between initial Black studies educators, a clearinghouse for exchanging critical information, and the launch of our collective endeavor to articulate and operationalize for academic investigation what we meant by the use of the concept *black experience*. There was a broad consensus that the field of Africana studies is a teaching and research enterprise "that is committed to the interpretation and explication of the total phenomenon called the Black Experience." We delineated four basic tasks for the Black studies scholar: (1) to *defend* (legitimize) against racism and intellectual chauvinism the fundamental right and necessity of Africana studies, at all levels of American education, for all people, but most especially for African American people; (2) to *disseminate* (teach and publish) Black studies social theory and analysis, criticism and historiography, and to reference the work of pioneering black scholars; (3) to *generate* knowledge (research) and codify existing information and predicate contemporary study upon the truths formulated by our mentors; and (4) to *preserve* the acknowledged value of rare and classical texts in the field (archival and library collections), and maintain the scholarly tradition and rich heritage of African peoples and their descendants.

The reader has undoubtedly noticed at this point that I use "Africana studies" and "Black studies" interchangeably. Africana studies is the more formal and proper terminology, while Black studies is the more common usage. On this matter I agree with Professor John Henrik Clarke:

> I prefer to use the phrase "Africana Studies" to "Black Studies." Black is an honorable word, and I am glad to see so many people lose their fear of using it, but it has its limitations. Black, or Blackness, tells you how you look without telling you who you are, whereas Africa, or Africana, relates you to land, history, and culture. No people is spiritually and culturally secure until it answers only to a name of its own choosing—a name that instantaneously relates that people to the past, present, and future. As the Caribbean writer Richard B. Moore has said in his book *The Name 'Negro': Its Origin and Evil Use*, "Slaves and dogs are named by their masters. Free men name themselves."[92]

Africana studies is essentially about renaming self in the world of knowledge and human relations.

The conference organized by the Africana studies and Research Center at Cornell University was the nexus and logical sequence to the IBW meeting. Some of the key figures from the first meeting were participants at this conference, such as Lerone Bennett, Vincent Harding, William Strickland, Stephen Henderson, and Howard Dodson.

An introductory essay to a topic as large as the subject of Black studies will inevitably be selective and representative of the perspective of the writer. However, this book of selected articles is reflective of our continuing intellectual and pedagogical interest in the vitally important task of assessing the progress of the field. The tenth anniversary was certainly a milestone in the life of the African Studies and Research Center. It rather naturally occurred to us that this would be a very appropriate occasion to assemble an interdisciplinary group of prominent scholars in Africana studies, colleagues from other departments and programs from universities across the country, and a selection of some of our best students over the past decade to exchange ideas about research and teaching experiences. The gathering surpassed our most optimistic expectations and has been widely hailed as the most significant coming together of Africana studies scholars since the Institute of the Black World meeting.

The development of the Africana Studies and Research Center is quite indicative of the typical pattern generally associated with the concept of the modern Black studies movement. We trace our origins to the second black renaissance of this century during the 1965–75 period, a time of extraordinary intellectual and social ferment and artistic creativity in the African American community. This period has been generally referred to as the high point of the black (arts) consciousness/black power movement. Black students at predominantly white campuses were most often (though not exclusively, as Howard, Jackson State, Fisk, North Carolina A&T, Atlanta Universities, and others were significant) catalysts for promoting the Black studies proposition at the university and college levels. Black students joined concerned educators and intellectuals in point out "the urgent necessity for including the study of African American experience." Though we refer to a modern stage in Black studies, we must hasten to point out the fact that, contrary to a broadly held belief, Africana studies is not a recent development. As the author has explained in a previous monograph, the field has a rich intellectual legacy extending from at least the early nineteenth century, based on the worlds of such people as Edward Wilmot Blyden, Martin Delany, Frances Harper, Benjamin Brawley, and Casely Hayford, and from the beginning of this century, with W.E.B. Du Bois, Carter G. Woodson, Leo Hansberry, Arthur Schomburg, Charles S. Johnson, J. A. Rogers, and Ida B. Wells, to name a few. We shall discuss this point further later in this chapter.

There is a unique character to this contemporary stage in the intellectual history of the study of people of African descent. Our social roots (fertilized as they were by the challenges for change of the 1960s) gave rise to an intellectual perspective that proposed that Black studies would supersede the traditional disciplines by pursuing a holistic structural interpretation in its research and teaching methodology of the black experience. Essentially this means a commitment to an interdisciplinary approach in the construction of both social theories and research paradigms of the various dimensions (i.e., social, cultural, political-economic) of African American societies.

The concept *Africana* is derived from the philosophy of the "African continuum and African consociation," which posits fundamental interconnections in the global black experience. Consequently, curriculum is predicated upon a model of Black studies that begins with the African background and next the transformation—slavery—into the African diaspora, from which the African American experience derives textual meaning. The *black world* is perceived as patterns within a trilateral relationship between Africa, the African Caribbean, and the African Americas with, understandably, primary concentration on African America. Moreover, all segments of the black world population live under social conditions directly related to the international political economy of advanced industrial capitalism. Africana as a construct is congruent with James Stewart's theory of an "Expansive Model of Black Studies." His paradigm is based on a methodology of Black studies that transcends and transforms the boundaries of the traditional disciplines into a new *interdiscipline*. An expansive model in Black studies constitutes an investigative emphasis with an ethnographic orientation. Philosophically, its argument is that a more accurate understanding of African American sociocultural and politico-economic realities is achieved "if the research concerns emanate from their [African American] experience and phenomenological frame of reference."[93] If it is true, and I certainly contend it is, that Anglocentric (or so-called mainstream) scholarship on the black experience is biased towards person-centered variables and *internal* causal contingencies, and attributional schemes with person (group) change implications, then Africana studies is an "alternative presuppositional perspective"[94] that gives at least as much investigative emphasis to systemic institutional-centered variables and external causal contingencies that affect the life chances and social conditions of black people. Africana research "which attempts to emanate from the perception and experience of those under study is more apt to illuminate the fact that psychological and behavioral and cultural processes are inextricably linked to their economic-political, social, and situational contexts. Such considerations move the research away from ethnocentric analysis and more toward (systemic) and ethnographic ones," which is a far more socially useful research on black people in American society.[95] Stewart's concept *expansive* also assumes a "historical tradition of the linkage between scholarship and activism while simultaneously reflecting the constraints imposed by the contemporary social knowledge and the application of knowledge to promote Black liberation and human dignity."[96]

This is a specifically Black studies conceptualization of the role for black intellectuals in terms of their active relationship to the ongoing institutional and organizational process of the African-American community and the oppression and racist inequality that it confronts. An expansive approach to Black studies presumes that education is based on a philosophy of history. [Abdul] Alkalimat, [Ronald] Bailey, et al., refer to the criticality of a historical focus that elucidates qualitative developments in dynamic human processes; that is, the interpretation of history as social analysis in order to provide an analytical paradigm for the assessment of significant events and quantitative changes in the configuration of society. They posit, particularly in *Introduction to Afro-American Studies*, a philosophy of history that associates events with specific time frames, which reflects continuities and discontinuities in the complex forces that shape society's configuration. This process is commonly referred to as periodization of the black experience. However, to achieve an expansive model in Black studies, the purpose of history must be for higher intellectual exposition than recording and describing the facts of events. Evidentiary statements in historical documentation must give more than a chronicle and should present instead an interpretation that penetrates the social meaning, in human terms, of the important *stages* in the movements of history.

As a methodology, history in Black studies constitutes the foundation for theoretical construction of an analysis of the fundamental relationship between the political economy of social developments and the racial divisions of labor and privilege, and the common patterns of life chances peculiar to the social conditions of black people. Basic to the teleology of Africana studies is the application of knowledge to promote social change. This primary tenet has been the focus of some controversy. The basis of controversy concerning Africana studies is related directly to an extant perception that Black studies is at variance with the societal zeitgeist. Though the expansive model subsumes the traditional academic approach, it nonetheless conflicts with the reigning ideological premise that knowledge should be pursued for the sake of knowledge, per se. The assumption is that scientific investigation is a value-free process. This argument ignores what some scholars have identified as the "unscientific nature of the scientific enterprise." Research is a social product, and the values and assumptions of the investigator are, more usually than not, congruent with the dominant ideas and prevailing forces that govern the status quo. In the real world virtually all scientific research is geared to one sort of problem or another that changes society progressively. Funded research in the sciences is concentrated, for the most part, on such concerns as military weaponry, food and animal production, reclamation of marine life and water resources, transportation and communication technology, industrial and farm productivity, and medical cures. Knowledge is pursued for enlightenment of social experiences. Art is contemplated more for abstract, existential properties. Even the deliberations on aesthetics are not without social purpose. The humanities are all too frequently the bastion of white racism and national/cultural chauvinism, as they serve to perpetuate a basic Eurocentric philosophy of history, language, literature, music, creative production, and sociology of society by essentially omitting and derogating non-European peoples and their projects.

In his discussion of the relationship of Africana studies to traditional disciplines, James Stewart states that

> it is important to keep in mind that it [i.e. Black studies] seeks to (a) fill a wide gap in the existing intellectual arena and (b) to resurrect a formal linkage between the academic and social formations. The intellectual task is not then simply to pick or choose among the conceptual and methodological toys of traditional disciplines, but to re-conceptualize the social fabric and rename the world in a way that obliterates the voids that have inevitably occurred as a result of artificial disciplinary demarcations. It is by renaming the world—that is, by employing linguistic conventions that specifically meet the needs of Black studies, per se, as opposed to imitating the conventions of traditional disciplines—that the power of forgotten voices to speak to the living can be restored. This latter claim implies that *history* has a preeminent hierarchical position in the context of the academic project of Black studies, with insights from other foci of inquiry serving to clarify patterns of historical continuity and change.[97]

Pedagogically and intellectually, Africana philosophy seeks to "rename the world" and broaden the knowledge base for all of us through the concept of Afrocentricity in Black studies.

The Black studies proposition at the empirical and conceptual levels relates to fundamental methods of acquiring knowledge and organizing curricula from which we all receive education. In recent years black educators have criticized with growing intensity the limitations in Anglocentric assumptions and, particularly, the notion that there are ultimate or absolute truths derived from universal research. The process of accepting new theories in the academic community is not simply a matter of adopting explanations of experimentally verified empirical observations, but of accepting competing conceptions of reality and dissimilarities of reference language. Moreover, a scientific theory is more likely to be a conceptually relative entity in the sense that the language of one theory may not be translatable into the language of its predecessor in the same field of research. The major propositions characterizing the mainstream of academic research conclude that empirical laws of social regularity should be the basis of predictions; that social scientists should be disinterested, objective observers of social phenomena and their works (value) free of normative content; that all expressions or normative judgments are reducible to emotive expressions and thus of limited theoretical worth or, at least, open to suspect. However, the major disciplines have a primal tendency to reduce all problems of understanding to technical problems of information gathering and gauging variables.

The dominant fields of knowledge thus surreptitiously support the status quo, because the *normative judgments* germane to its technical procedures, and applications of their findings, are generally ignored and do not face the test of critical examination or empirical verification. Indeed, the normative principles are so ensconced in the conceptual orientation that they are not even recognized as such. For all the contention and support lent by American intellectuals and educators to the possibility of, and need for, value-neutral social theory, the product of the mainstream too often "turns out to be disguised ideology." This is not necessarily a condemnation; the essential point being made here is summed up in the following proposition: If there are grounds for holding that facts of nature are seen through a paradigmatic scheme, in effect there are grounds for believing social facts are not independent of conceptual paradigms used to investigate them. Dr. Lorenzo Morris is particularly poignant on this point: "When social statistics are perceived as meaningful in America, it is because they relate to values in American society. Conversely, when the conditions of Black and White Americans...are compared, no social statistic can be completely neutral unless it is also completely meaningless."[98]

The theoreticians of Black studies use the basic social science concept of the sociology of knowledge to explain the legitimacy of the idea that the position of black people in the social structure not only offers peculiar insights, but also represents a specific meaning about social truth. Further-more, all knowledge is a perspective on shared experience.

A. Olomenji argues, in a manuscript soon to be published, that one's point of origin, the place from which one looks out at the world, will large-ly determine what and how one perceives. A collective perception acts as a filter through which all reality is screened and transformed into a practical belief system. The collective perception and belief system defines a people's reality, as well as what that reality means. The collective worldview pro-vides a basic framework for viewing what exists in the world, as well as a basic supposition of how the world operates. A belief system reinforces the common assumptions of a collective perception. It is the practical and cen-tral reference for all action.

Professor Wade Boykin has pointed out that "there is inherent subjec-tivity and bias in the research enterprise....One's assumptions are actually so critical in determining the nature of one's research enterprise."[99] We have come to realize with increasing clarity that presupposition effective-ly modifies perspectives and is the source of a priori bias. Boykin explains that "truth" in science is based considerably on a social-cultural-consensual reality.[100] This "consensual reality," vis-à-vis the black experience, actually translates into ideational hegemony of Anglocentric presuppositions and perspective. To be sure, ethnocentrism, prejudice, and ignorance are factors that influence the intellectual tone of many white educators, particularly in terms of their attitudes towards Africana studies. However, Boykin has made an even more salient observation of common Anglocentric bias. He postulates what he calls the Law of Personal Presuppositions:

> You will rarely find a researcher-scholar concluding anything in his or her
> research that is inconsistent, contradictory, or threatening to his or her own
> self-definition, self-statement, and value system.[101]

In as much as the raison d'être of Africana studies, at least partially, is to critically redefine significant aspects of conventional knowledge both in social theory and social values, proponents of Black studies have had to contend, and continue to do so, with long-standing bias in education, especially in curriculum, that is widespread at virtually all levels and in-stitutions in American academia. Professor Sterling Stuckey, a prominent black historian at Northwestern University, has commented: "Black people have met with as great injustices from American scholarship as they have from American life. In fact, colleges and universities have long paved the way for confusion and ignorance, arrogance and presumptuousness...in Black-White relations."[102]

With the beginning of substantial desegregation of public schools and larger numbers of black young people at predominantly non-black campuses, the concern for how young black people were being socialized by their (new) educational environment became a serious "sociology of knowledge" issue throughout Afro-America. Harold Cruse, a Black studies professor at the University of Michigan and a distinguished social historian and political theorist, offered a poignant comment on this issue: "The further the Negro gets from his historical antecedents in time, the more tenuous become his conceptual ties, the emptier his social connections, the more superficial his visions. His one great and present hope is to know and understand his African-American realities in the United States more profoundly. Failing that, and failing to create a new synthesis in history and the humanities and a new social theory, he will suffer the historical fate of intellectual subterfuge."[103] This very same issue was the focus of Harvard-trained African American historian Dr. Carter G. Woodson's seminal study, *The Mis-education of the Negro*, thirty-five years earlier. Woodson observed:

> The "educated Negroes" have the attitude of contempt towards their own people because in their own schools as well as in their mixed schools Negroes are taught to admire the Hebrew, the Greek, the Latin and the Teuton and to despise the African. These "educated" people, however, decry any such thing as race consciousness....They do not like to hear such expressions as "Negro Literature," "Negro Poetry," "African Art," or thinking (B)lack.[104]

This matter of identity and educational socialization—in all its interrelated social and individual aspects—is central to the concerns of black educators over serious omissions in established knowledge and commission of distortions in the major intellectual enterprises because of exaggerations of Euro-American particularism and its ontological bias. The importance of this point was expressed to writing of an exceptionally insightful and honest anthropologist, Charles Valentine: "Social issues and political movements have been intertwined with the search for valid knowledge and expressions of the Black experience in the United States ever since early precursors of modern Afro-American Studies."[105] The dean of African American social science, Dr. St. Clair Drake, social anthropologist and professor emeritus at Stanford University, reports in a significant study recently published in the respected journal, the *New York University Education Quarterly*, that since 1974, "Black Studies grew steadily and became entrenched [during] the next five years, though there were some erroneous reports in newspapers and magazines during 1974 that such programs were in decline."[106] In fact, he contends that "the Black Studies field has become institutionalized in the sense that some of its values are being accepted by the educational system."[107] One of these was the concept that "an ideal university community would be multiethnic with ethnicity permitted some institutional expression and with Black Studies being one of the sanctioned forms" as the caste structure in American higher education slowly transforms into an emerging form of pluralism.[108] But there is continuing resistance, based largely upon ideological and theoretical bias, academic nationalism, and competitive interests, and some behavior whose motivation can only be explained as racist. In this respect it is important to realize that "at least 250 programs devoted to the study of the Black Experience in the United States exist today. Half of these have been operating since 1970, and of the sixty-four that were granting degrees in 1971, all except four have continued to develop. All give some attention to the implications of an African origin for Black people in the New World, and increasingly a 'diaspora' frame of reference focuses some attention upon the Caribbean and Latin America for comparison with the United States."[109]

Sociologist Wilson Record, of Portland State University, conducted a study in 1972 and 1973 of Black studies on fifty campuses across the country for the purpose of assessing their impact on university procedures for curricular innovation and faculty recruitment. He suggests that the effect of the dynamic development of Black studies in postsecondary education has effected changes such that "colleges and universities would never be quite the same again."[110]

The establishment of numerous departments of African American studies is generally viewed as a recent phenomenon originating in the last ten years. Though it is true that the field of Black studies is very new in its present developments, its legacy extends to the earliest beginnings of black intellectual history over two centuries ago. Though one can argue that the concept of Black studies does predate the twentieth century, its recent emergence as an academic field is much more related to the endeavors of black intellectuals during the past fifty years. The proper interpretation and inclusion of the historical role, cultural creation, and social circumstance of black people in America has been of major concern, especially to black scholars in the humanities and social sciences. The development of African American studies in this century can be traced through several stages.

The origins of the modern movement can be traced to the ferment that began between 1918 and 1929. It was during this period that black scholars actively participated in the mass awakening of the general black population that was precipitated by the social and cultural renaissance of the era.

The second phase of the development of Black studies was ushered in by the Great Depression and marked by the forced parochialization of many black concerns. By the mid-1930s the question of Afro-American studies was almost entirely the domain of black urban intelligentsia, but it was also during this period that the idea of Black studies as a separate academic field began to emerge. In 1940 the advent of World War II began a period of dormancy that lasted until roughly 1960. There was a lull that was caused by the war and a gap in the generational shift of black scholars that was accentuated by the changing of priorities by many postwar academicians. The 1960s witnessed the rejuvenation of the civil rights movement, which provided the atmosphere for the question of Black studies to become a major innovation in higher education. Campus protests created the subsequent pressure for the recognition and proliferation of Afro-American studies programs throughout the nation. However, once these programs were established, they were confronted with the essential task of academic construction—of organizing curriculum and developing pedagogical methodology. Essential to this task was the selection of source materials as reference and texts for classroom instruction. The teaching function was to be the foundation for most of the programs. As a "new" field there was the immediate challenge of developing prototypical courses that could serve as beginning models for standardization and cross-reference of courses between the various departments and programs. Each instructor was responsible for developing his or her own individual syllabi. But if the program were to grow and become effectively institutionalized and regularized, there were going to have to be coordination between instructors in a given program in order to achieve a reasonable degree of systematic organization of courses for effective interface and a logical symmetry in intellectual focus. There had to be a meaningful division of academic endeavors that would provide a basis for integrated learning from one course to another in a program.

There are specific functions common to all disciplines, and they are in two dimensions. First, the intellectual parameters of the field must be relatively clearly established with rather apparent theoretical configuration. Second, the ideational and analytical "meanings" of the discipline—that is, what characterizes what we do as different, and significantly, from what is done in other disciplines—must be delineated. In sum, a fairly commonly adhered-to definition of the raison d'être of the field must emerge: for example, what is the consequence of "Afrocentric" perspective for the pursuit of truth? This difference must not be different for difference's sake; moreover, it must comprise a *significant* difference in the social construction of knowledge. It should challenge and enrich the learning process and provide a *particular* symbolic ethos of the discipline. This means that Black studies would (and should) not serve as a secondary appendage or an intellectual afterthought to another established discipline (what would be essentially a modicum of black content in an erstwhile "Europerspective" subject). This raises the question of whether African American studies composes a discipline in its own right and could contribute academically to the development of new knowledge. Other related questions are: Can the field generate new theory? Does Black studies have a viable intellectual tradition of research investigation and scholarly literature?

There is a great deal of discussion among scholars and educators about what constitutes a discipline. For instance, is a course on Biology and Society, biology or sociology; is Art History, art or history; is History a science or an orientation to factual information within the humanities? What about Social Psychology; is it an academic bastard without sufficient specific identity and legitimate claim to a parent discipline, or is it on the frontier of theory as a consequence of cross-fertilization between and within traditional structures of knowledge? If Political Science is a discipline, what is its cogent theoretical definition and a characteristic explanation/ description of its methodology?

The point is, we think, that knowledge is being packaged with new labels and in different arrangements, representing the realities of modern society. Though the initial questions may seem important, they may not be relevant or germane. Nonetheless, these questions about Black studies as knowledge reveal a complex argument couched in, and implied by, theoretical development stemming from dominant mainstream criteria concerning adequate theory (empirical interpretive, critical) and converging trends and opinions among the most institutionalized and professionally prestigious academic disciplines concerning self-referential evidence supportive of the Black studies criteria.

The fact that most of the major arguments in history, social science, anthropology, arts, literature, and the humanities derive from Euro-American particularism in experiences that have been held to be generalizable to the universe reflects a dialectic historicism operative in modern Western theoretical development. Black studies represents a disillusionment and critique of "certified knowledge," and the historical currents of disillusionment with the mainstream are also a current of progressive contribution towards a more adequate social analysis and public policy. Therefore, Black studies is a "reconstruction discipline," as a synthesis of what its criticisms imply, convergence with theories reviewed, and the philosophic methods of its pedagogical emphasis. If the reconstruction method is, itself, a workable procedure, we have in Black studies a way of arriving at new theory. Black studies is a conceptual paradigm that principally tells us, like other academic discourse, what counts as a fact and what problems of explanation exist. It is commonly accepted among social scientists that "what we take to be an action, and even its proper description, is internally related to the interpretations that are intrinsically constitutive of it." But an action, to some extent, can be judged according to the linguistic and conceptual structure through which that action is filtered. A social science bereft of an analysis of the interchange between the subjective and the objective is thus a social science orientation that condones a tendency of "uncritical acceptance of ideological bias" of both a cultural and moral sort. Thus, conclusions about what constitutes a significant contribution to knowledge reveal that a similar filtering process is operative in such evaluation.

This debate, I am sure, will continue to go on and, in my judgment, should go on, because of its intellectual importance and significance in redefining and reformulating issues of theory and methodology. Undoubtedly we can expect continued contentious relations with many non-black educators and even with neoconservative black intellectuals who have gained a sort of prominence as clients of the new right (and, for that matter, the old right wing) thrust directed at all institutions of American society—education notwithstanding, I suspect that we will have to come to grips with the reality that ours is not just a protracted contention, but that, as is true in most other arenas of race relations, the difficulties Black studies scholars will confront, because of the prevailing institutional forces in American education, are endemic. Nonetheless, there has been an impressive degree of "settling in" that provides a firmer foundation for the next decade. Many of our colleagues who began a decade ago in Africana studies have been able to achieve relatively permanent, tenured positions at a cross section of colleges and universities in the country.

A recent catalog by Greenwood Press indicates that there are approximately twenty serious academic journals and magazines devoted to Africana studies. There are better than a half dozen professional associations whose central purpose is the support and advancement of Africana studies as an academic discipline and the cultivation of scholars. There has been a sound basis in the development of conceptual and theoretical clarity. Though there has been some wane in funding resources for research and a falloff in interest by major publishing houses in recent years, the productivity of scholarship in the field has been steady, evidenced by a discernible increase in the quality and in the quantity of published manuscripts. In spite of the obstacles there have been some major publications in the past few years worthy of note: *The Shaping of Black America*, Lerone Bennett; *The Harder We Run*, William Harris; *Survival and Progress: Afro-American Experience*, L. Alex Swan; *Black Americans and the Political System*, Lucius J. Barker and Jesse McCorry; *Langston Hughes: Before and Beyond Harlem*, Faith Berry; *There Is a River*, Vincent Harding; *Black Women Novelists*, Barbara Christian; *The Slave Community*, John W. Blassingame; *How Europe Underdeveloped Africa*, Walter Rodney; *When and Where I Enter*, Paula Giddings; and the recently published *Principles of Black Political Economy*, Lloyd Hogan.

This list could be much longer; it is not meant to be exhaustive. My intention is to give a representative sample of the scope and caliber of scholarship characteristic of the field. Perhaps most significant of all has been the publication of two widely used introductory texts in Africana studies. The two-volume set, *Introduction to Afro-American Studies*, an edited collection by Peoples College, and the more recent, first single-authored text, *Introduction to Black Studies*, by Maulana Karenga, have made critical contributions to the standardization of the Black studies curriculum. These introductory texts are vitally important to conveying a coherent definition and common identity to the discipline. Ultimately, the consolidation of Africana studies will be predicated upon a foundation of an integrated, standardized curriculum.

While we have good reasons to enjoy a reasonable sense of satisfaction at this stage, the path ahead will not necessarily be unobstructed. The conservative mood in the country is impacting educational policy. Dr. Faustine Jones, of Howard University, has identified definite patterns of erosion in commitment to inclusion of formally neglected and oppressed national *minority groups in the* educational system. With the election of the Reagan administration there emerged neoconservative political action groups that began targeting public sources of information and public education for political assault as part of their version of a "holy" war to safeguard the "soul" of the republic from what they perceived to be unwelcome ideas. Prominent among these self-initiated guardians of society are organizations like the Committee for a Free World, which began in 1981 and issued the following statement: "We are persuaded that the struggle for freedom may in the end be won not on the battlefields but in books, newspapers, broadcasts, classrooms, and in all public institutions."[III]

Their rallying cry is for an ideological war to control America's mind. We can expect that such political chicanery will induce encounters, at the institutional level, which will challenge us to stand firm on the ground we have achieved thus far. It is precisely because of this kind of raging conservatism, which is being mobilized as a retrogressive social movement, that Africana studies is all the more essential to the preservation of the modest gains made by African Americans over the last decade. There will very likely be those who will ask, with the transformations of society toward greater technological concentration in the scientific and computer age of the 1980s and 1990s, if Black studies is feasible or necessary. Stewart has pointed out in this regard that "the current socialization of students" prior to entry into higher education is undeniably generating a careerist mentality. This trend has its counterpart among Black studies faculty, many of whom face continuing subtle and overt harassment by non–Black studies colleagues. Many of the first faculty in the field are gradually deemphasizing involvement in community activities as they have succumbed to (or have been seduced by) the orthodox norms of academic traditionalism in their pursuit of careerist aspirations for legitimacy and acceptability for purposes of job stability and security. Younger faculty have not been quite as engaged by commitment to community outreach and the wedding of intellectual and social activism on behalf of the liberation of the black community.

This phenomenon is denying Black studies both a critical bridge to the potential beneficiaries of applied scholarship, that is, the external community, and a source of power to facilitate the continuation of innovative projects in the face of renewed opposition. Dr. Robert C. Johnson, writing on "Why Colleges and Students Need Black Studies" in the *Chronicle of Higher Education*, states that academically and vocationally Black studies are important for a variety of reasons. Some of his reasons are as follows: one-third of all children born in the country are Black, Hispanic, Asian, American Indian, and so forth; 25 percent of the population consists of racial ethnic groups; many regions (particularly urban centers) and institutions (that is, urban public schools) are rapidly approaching a black and Hispanic majority; and the vast majority of the people in this world are racial ethnic groups of non-Anglo linkage. He concludes that "for the most part, the majority of the students in American institutions of higher education are being grossly underprepared to function in a multiethnic, multiracial, multicultural world."[112] Dr. Eleanor Traylor indicates a similar point when she states: "Moreover, in a country as culturally plural as the United States, we enjoy the large opportunity to educate our children multi-culturally and multi-linguistically. And because of the nature of our world today, nothing is more desirable than multi-literate citizens whose respect for one another transforms old enmities or superstitions threatening the very existence of the planet itself."[113]

The research department of the New York Urban League recently collected a tri-state study of New York, Pennsylvania, and New Jersey to ascertain the kind of mentor relationships black students have in graduate schools. Their findings revealed that for most of these students there was no significant mentor relationship to encourage and guide them in their study. This is clue, in part, to too few black faculty in American higher education. In the *Chronicle of Higher Education*, Charles Farrell reports that "virtually no gains are being made in increasing minority representation in the faculties and administrations of predominantly white colleges, according to many educators familiar with academic recruiting."[114]

This observation is supported by a special investigative study of the shortage of black professors by the *Wall Street Journal*. The *Journal* found: "In few industries today are Blacks as scarce as in higher education. In predominantly white schools, Blacks usually make up only about 1 percent of the tenured and non-tenured faculty. Princeton University has only 9 Black faculty out of a total staff of 581. The University of Michigan has 20 out of a total of 684—and that's the highest percentage of Blacks in the Big 10."[115] The University of Pennsylvania had 31 black faculty in 1972 and it has 31 black faculty in 1984. The situation is getting worse because the potential pool is getting smaller. For the past five years the number of blacks applying to arts and sciences graduate schools has steadily declined. Between 1975 and 1980 Harvard, Yale, and Princeton each produced a total of ten or fewer black undergraduates who went on to earn their doctorates; Howard University produced 275. Institutions such as Morehouse College in Atlanta have been far more successful than most white institutions in encouraging black students to go on to graduate school. Black colleges educate only about a quarter of the black undergraduates, but over half the blacks with new Ph.D.s got their undergraduate education there.

The vice-provost and dean of graduate studies at Stanford University, Gerald Lieberman, says, "Part of the problem is a national climate of indifference and even suspicion toward affirmative action. Many colleges seem to have developed a 'plateau mentality' that does nothing more than maintain present ratios of minorities and whites."[116] An associate director of the American Council on Education's office of minority affairs, Sarah Melendez, says, "It is very clear that there is an underrepresentation of minorities on faculties and administrations."[117]

The future prospects are not good, as there is little, if any, expectation of improvement. The prognosis is that the situation will get worse as minority faculty are terminated by denial of tenure and through the syndrome of "last hired, first fired" during programs of retrenchment and fiscal austerity. Currently the proportion of black faculty in American higher education is 4.0 percent. Lorenzo Morris points out, "The data on the status of Blacks from 1975 through 1977, however, show that progress in all areas of higher education has slowed down and in areas like professional education, it has come to a standstill."[118] In a special report, "Participation of Black Students in Higher Education: A Statistical Profile from 1970–71 to 1980–81," prepared by the National Center for Educational Statistics and released November 1983 by the U.S. Department of Education, the following summaries were offered. During the first half of the 1970s:

> The large increase in Black enrollment coincided with the expansion in both federal legislation and federal policies aimed at reducing barriers to higher education for minorities and low-income students. By 1975 the percentage of Black high school graduates who enrolled in college was the same as that for whites (although high school graduation rates were still lower for Blacks than whites). Black enrollment at the post baccalaureate level did not experience an equivalent upsurge. In fact, by 1976 there was a smaller proportion of Blacks in graduate and first professional schools than there had been in the early 1970s.

During the last half of the 1970s:

> Black participation in higher education stabilized in most areas. The number of Blacks who enrolled in college remained about the same, in spite of the fact that the number of Black youth eligible for college increased by almost 20 percent. The number and proportion of degrees awarded to Blacks remained about the same at the bachelor's, doctor's, and first professional levels, while there were substantial declines at the master's level. The number of Blacks receiving master's degrees declined 16 percent, four times greater than the decline for non-Blacks.

Doctoral degrees awarded to black students for the years 1976, 1979, and 1981 were 3.6, 3.9, and 3.9 percent, respectively. Though the data are not firm for the past three years, there is evidence that indicates trends of decline in black student enrollment in both undergraduate and graduate schools. Professors Laurie Hatch and Kent Mommsen, from their study of racial gaps in education, report that "from this analysis two major points emerge. The substantial and widening racial gap in American higher education is accounted for primarily by remaining inequities among males."[119]

The pattern seems to be significantly related to the Reagan administration's cutbacks and changes in federal aid to higher education, particularly the government's support for need-based financial assistance to students and guaranteed low-interest loans. The shift has been especially severe among indigenous black males.

The trends of the 1970s and 1980s appear to have some rather direct implications for the progress of Black studies, in the long term, if not immediately. Fewer African American faculty would mean that there is a lessened likelihood that students will have mentors who will introduce them to Africana studies and encourage them to seriously consider academic careers in the field. There will also be a diminishing potential source of new colleagues necessary to further the field. Relatively fewer black students in American higher education will reduce the natural constituency and bridge of support for the field. How these problems are resolved or transcended will impact as much, critically, upon the future of Africana studies as will the ongoing discourse on questions related to ontology and epistemology.

PART IV

PAN-AFRICANISM AND INTERNATIONALISM

Africana Studies as a theoretical approach or a method of inquiry is by definition an outlook which presupposes the binding and oppressive limitations of identities imposed by particular forms of colonization within state formations, all of whom emerged as part of a Western European imperial project. As a proponent of, and seminal figure within, the field of Africana Studies, the work of James Turner has always reflected this understanding.

—*Jared Ball*

Amiri Baraka and James Turner, head of the North American delegation to the Sixth Pan-African Congress, Tanzania, 1974 (source: Black World/Negro Digest, 1975).

INTRODUCTION: JAMES TURNER AND THE PRACTICE OF PAN-AFRICANISM

LATASHA B. LEVY

James Turner's intellectual and political contributions transcend political categories. Often regarded as a Black Nationalist with a sophisticated analysis of class struggle and political economy, his teaching, writings, and commitment to institution-building have advanced a distinct, progressive vision—one that fuses black consciousness with a radical tradition of activism. While Turner has been able to navigate a wide range of Black political circles, his sophisticated engagement with the histories, cultures, and social conditions of the Black world makes him an important figure in Pan-African politics.

An examination of Turner's Pan-African writings and politics offers a unique opportunity to engage critically the full range of intellectual and political expressions within a Black Studies paradigm. Without question, Pan-Africanism influenced the Black Studies movement as well as a range of Black liberation struggles and cultural formations that sought transnational "linkages" against imperialism, colonialism, and capitalist exploitation. Since the late 1960s, Turner has figured prominently in the modern Pan-Africanist tradition by modeling a progressive Pan-African praxis. Under his direction, the Africana Studies and Research Center's scholarly interrogation of the "global Black experience," in addition to its direct engagement with local and transnational politics, was indicative of Turner's Pan-African orientation. That orientation provided an important blueprint for building a tradition of scholar-activism that was central to the Black Studies project from its inception. To be a Pan-Africanist intellectual meant that theory, praxis, ideology and activism were constantly entangled—each fueling the other.

Since the early stages of his own political education, Turner was exposed to intellectual and activist circles that were astute in examining global systems of racial oppression and class exploitation. Indeed, Turner's political education rested on a Pan-African worldview that valued African culture and philosophy, but it also propagated the necessity of coordinated resistance to colonialism and its racial imperialist dimensions across the African Diaspora. In a 2011 interview with former students Jonathan B. Fenderson and Candace Katungi, Turner describes the ideologies and institutions that helped to shape his political consciousness as a young Harlemite. He recalls the National Memorial African Bookstore at the corner of 125th Street and Adam Clayton Powell Boulevard, where he attended lectures given by Black Nationalist leaders such as Malcolm X and Queen Mother Moore. His informal education was also shaped by Pan-African activists Elombe and Kwame Brath as well as Richard B. Moore, the Caribbean activist and member of the African Blood Brotherhood who fused Black Nationalist and Marxist ideologies. Moore's bookstore, the Frederick Douglass Book Center, also located in Harlem, served as an educational center that exposed Turner to the writings of W.E.B. Du Bois and contemporary African politics.

These formative experiences guided Turner's vision of Black Studies as an inherently global intellectual enterprise that was vital in the struggle for Black liberation. Due to these early experiences, Turner recognized education as a critical site of resistance to white domination. He reasoned, "Domination impacts all spheres, not just in terms of command over the body of a people, over their labor, but also over their cognition, over their cognitive abilities, over their consciousness, over the way that they looked at themselves and looked at others."[1] In this sense, Black Studies was not just about diversifying the curriculum to include the contributions of African people; it was a battle over epistemology, interpretation, and the production of knowledge—a battle over consciousness and social change.

Turner deployed the "Africana" concept as a transnational framework for the study of the "global Black experience," conceptualizing the Black world according to "patterns within a trilateral relationship between Africa, the African Caribbean and the African Americas." Though Europe and Asia were very much a part of the Africana Center's engagement with the Black world, Turner emphasized the experiences of African Americans as a focal point of Black Studies. This focus on national specificity, however, did not preclude global interactions and comparisons, nor did it advance an African American version of "U.S. exceptionalism." Instead, the scholarly examination of the history and culture of Black communities in the United States was integral to understanding the context that gave rise to Black Studies. For Turner, anchoring Black Studies in the United States provided an opportunity to engage in comparative and transnational studies, identify points of cultural continuity and distinction, and contemplate opportunities for political cooperation.

Similarly, Turner asserted that any comprehensive study of the Black experience must include a critical examination of African history and culture that did not rest on static or undifferentiated conceptions of Africa or romanticized notions of an African past. Africana faculty members were often required to develop expertise in more than one geographical area, and students were trained to consider the relationships across the Diaspora. If we consider the paradigms and curriculum designs that defined the early years of Black Studies, the transnational character of Black Studies makes it clear that the recent articulation of Diaspora Studies is not new. Even more, Africana Studies in particular (and Black Studies more broadly) invested in Diaspora politics in practical ways.

The four essays in this section provide a window into Turner's theory and praxis. He outlines important interventions that revamp Pan-African historiography and model a progressive Pan-African politics. Turner was not concerned with cultural idealism and romantic abstractions. Rather, he was actively involved in cultivating transnational relationships for the purpose of Black liberation. As activist Sylvia Hill, founding member of the Southern Africa Support Project, explains, "Pan-Africanism is not a thing. It's not a static entity of ideas. It's a dynamic process."[2] Turner's writings in this section perceptively capture this process as a Black Studies practitioner and scholar-activist.

PAN-AFRICAN PRAXIS

The first two articles in this section were published amidst Turner's direct involvement in two significant Pan-African formations: the African Heritage Studies Association and the Sixth Pan-African Congress. The first article, "Africa: Conflict in Black and White," coauthored with South African scholar Rukudzo Murapa, speaks to a critical development in the Black Studies movement: the founding of the African Heritage Studies Association (AHSA) in 1969. The AHSA was born out of the protest movements of the 1960s, and its aim was to recover African Studies as a Black Studies project. Tensions between Black scholars of African Studies and the white male intellectuals who dominated the field erupted at a meeting of the African Studies Association (ASA) in Los Angeles in 1968. A caucus of Black scholars, led by Afrocentric historian John Henrik Clarke, challenged the racial chauvinism of the white Africanists and their refusal to consider Black scholars for leadership positions within the organization. When the ASA failed to address the marginalization of African people to the satisfaction of the Black caucus, members staged a takeover of the 1969 annual meeting in Montreal, which solidified an official break away from the ASA and the establishment of the African Heritage Studies Association as a separate organization. Through the convening of the AHSA, Black scholars of

African Studies committed themselves to a dual mission: (1) to further the "exploration, preservation, and academic presentation of the historical and cultural heritage of African peoples" in Africa and in the Diaspora, and (2) to intervene in U.S. foreign relations in support of African liberation movements.[3]

James Turner, wearing a Northwestern University sweater, as student leader and incoming director of the Africana Studies and Research Center, ca. 1969–70.

Turner played a central role in mounting a challenge to the ASA. At the time, he was a graduate student in sociology at Northwestern University and had connected with sociologist and activist St. Clair Drake, who played a pivotal role in developing Pan-African scholarship as part of the Black Studies intellectual mission. While at Northwestern, Turner also studied African history and worked as a graduate assistant at the university's renowned African Studies Center. There, he raised concerns about the Center's record of inviting only white speakers to give lectures and presentations.[4] Additionally, in the spring of 1968, Turner helped to coordinate the student sit-in at Northwestern that demanded a Black Studies program. His direct involvement in the occupation of the ASA annual meeting was an extension of his activism in the Black student movement and a broader struggle against mis-education and educational apartheid. The ASA's refusal to integrate its leadership or to make a public statement in support of the anti-apartheid struggle only confirmed suspicions that the field of African Studies, founded in the 1950s during the height of anti-communist hysteria and African independence movements, provided an intellectual home for white male scholars to serve government agencies and neocolonial politics.

Turner and Murapa published a short but cogent indictment of the African Studies Association soon after the Montreal meeting. Not only do they confront the "arrogance of white scholarship" and the marginalization of Black scholars of African Studies; they vehemently rejected the ways in which white Africanists attempted to frame Black Studies and African Studies as separate and unrelated. Indeed, the collaboration between Turner and Murapa represented a symbolic and practical unity between African American and African experiences. It was also emblematic of the relationship between African and African-descendant scholars that was nurtured and sustained through the AHSA. Grounded in an African-centered scholarly approach and a Pan-African politics, the AHSA cultivated a strong network of scholars and activists across the Diaspora. Turner served as the president of the AHSA 1972–76 and 1982–84. Notably, his contributions to the development and leadership of the AHSA were concurrent with the planning and development of the Africana Studies and Research Center at Cornell. Both created institutional bases for Pan-African scholarship and activism.

Turner's commitment to supporting Pan-African networks led to his involvement in the planning of the 1974 Sixth Pan-African Congress (Six PAC), which sought to mobilize international support for liberation movements in Southern Africa against Portuguese colonialism and apartheid.

He published the second article in this section, "Sixth Pan-African Congress 1974: Historical Perspective," during the Six PAC's preparatory stage. The 1974 Congress was the first of the Pan-African Congresses to take place on the African continent, and it was by far the largest, attracting more than five hundred participants.[5] In 1973 Turner was chosen to serve as chairman of the North American Steering Committee, which included Julian Ellison of the Black Economic Research Center and Sylvia Hill, who also served as secretary general.

*Participants at the Sixth Pan-African Congress (source: Black World/
Negro Digest, 1975).*

Turner's article serves as an overview of Pan-African history, beginning in the nineteenth century and maturing into a series of Pan-African Congresses during the first half of the twentieth century. It had been nearly three decades since the Fifth Pan-African Congress in Manchester, England, and Turner sought to highlight the historical significance of Six PAC by placing it in the tradition of the Manchester meeting. Led by radical Pan-Africanist George Padmore, the 1945 Fifth Pan-African Congress attracted an array of Pan-African visionaries, including C.L.R. James, Amy Ashwood, Ras Makonnen, Julius Nyerere, Jomo Kenyatta, Kwame Nkrumah, and W.E.B.

Du Bois. The Congress also coincided with an international meeting of African trade unionists, which added another dimension to its radical vision and broad participation. By all accounts, this Congress represented a transformative break in the history of the Pan-African Congress movement that called for revolutionary, anti-colonial struggle (rather than reform) and leadership and participation of the African masses (rather than elites). Its legacy continued to inspire Black liberation movements across the Diaspora in subsequent decades.[6]

Turner opens the article with a quote that underscores the Six PAC's intention to follow in the tradition and spirit of the 1945 Pan-African Congress. He writes, "The discussions were initiated by Africans. An attempt was made for us to act, not react." Indeed, Kwame Nkrumah issued a call in 1969 to convene a Pan-African Congress on the continent, a feat that was especially challenging in previous decades due to Cold War repression, surveillance, and constraints on travel. Julius Nyerere, president of Tanzania, agreed to host the Congress, which took place in June 1974 in Dar es Salaam—widely considered the seat of Pan-Africanism.[7] During its initial stages, veterans of the Fifth Pan-African Congress (including Nkrumah, Nyerere, and C.L.R. James) endorsed the Sixth Pan-African Congress.[8] While the initial call came from Africans, Pan-Africanists in the Diaspora, especially from the United States, played a central role in its organization.[9]

As an overview of Pan-African history, Turner's article anchors Six PAC within a long tradition of Black liberation struggles, but it also theorizes Pan-Africanism in innovative ways. Guided by the central role Africans played in the initiation of the Fifth and Sixth Pan-African Congresses, Turner places African agency squarely within Pan-African historiography. Instead of rehashing a U.S.-based Pan-African historical narrative, Turner draws our attention to what he calls "parallel developments" on the African continent in order to reframe Pan-Africanism as a "cross-fertilization of ideas and experiences" that emanated from "both sides of the Atlantic." This point was significant given Six PAC's mission to mobilize transnational support for African liberation movements.

Along with highlighting a history of Pan-African activity on the African continent, Turner reframes Pan-African history by focusing on "fundamental relationships" rather than cultural continuity. For Turner, three fundamental relationships ("between Africans and Europeans"; "between Africans and other oppressed peoples"; and "between different classes, groups, and communities within African societies") provide a more useful frame for the examination and praxis of Pan-Africanism. Given that much attention had been focused on changing the first fundamental relationship, Turner urges a critical examination of the other two relationships in order to confront the tensions and contradictions that impede social transformation. "Between 1919 and 1945," Turner explains, "the internal contradictions of tribal and linguistic differences, class distinctions, traditional versus modern social practices, definitions of the positions occupied by women, and youth, *etc.*, were all subordinated to the overriding desire to change the relationship between the colonizer and the colonized." Although these internal contradictions proved to be a formidable challenge at the Sixth Pan-African Congress—resulting in the deepening of ideological cleavages—Turner, acutely aware of the issues at stake, used history to foreground his reflections prior to the convention.

Interestingly enough, Turner's emphasis on fundamental relationships is instructive in considering the ideological tensions that engulfed the Sixth Pan-African Congress. The relationships between (conservative) nation-states, for instance, changed the course of Six PAC's mission when certain progressive, oppositional groups in Africa and the Caribbean were barred due to the presence and influence of state leaders—a fundamental issue that ultimately led C.L.R. James's protest of the Congress. In addition, the "race vs. class" debate strained the relationship between African liberation movements and Black activists from the United States, which was especially tenuous given the relatively privileged status of African Americans who were also a "stateless" entity with little tangible power. Cleavages within the North American delegation, often framed as a "two-line struggle" between Black Nationalists and Marxists, also were intensified by masculinist ideologies and sexist practices.[10] Turner found himself at the very center of these debates, and his call to confront fundamental relationships within groups and between communities proved to be a prescient observation.

Given the ideological splits that emerged during the convening of the Sixth Pan-African Congress, historian Lerone Bennett resolved that Pan-Africanism "died" at Six PAC.[11] But for many of the Congress participants and organizers—including Turner, Sylvia Hill, Oliver Cox, James Garrett, Ka Flewellen, Loretta Hobbs, Geri Augusto, and Amiri Baraka—the debates at Six PAC were an important and necessary development in political education, especially for Black activists from the United States.

Despite Six PAC's many challenges, its legacy can be gleaned from the renewed commitments among Black activists from all over the world to wage local struggles in support of the anti-colonial and anti-apartheid movements in Southern Africa. For Turner, this meant utilizing the resources of the Africana Studies and Research Center to popularize the struggle and provide a platform for African revolutionaries to gain support from communities of intellectuals and activists located in the U.S. and throughout the Diaspora. It also meant coordinating efforts to intervene more forcefully in U.S. foreign policy. Undoubtedly, Six PAC contributed to a series of anti-apartheid formations in the United States. Of great significance are Turner's contributions as a founding member of the TransAfrica Forum, established in 1977, which in many ways fulfilled the call of the Six PAC and attracted the leadership and support of a number of the Congress organizers.[12]

SCHOLAR-ACTIVISM AND CONTEMPORARY AFRICAN POLITICS

James Turner and Africana students and faculty donating farming tools to the Kerenge Ujamaa village in Tanzania.

Turner's commitment to Pan-African praxis remained a defining component of his scholar-activism. The articles "Universal Education and Nation-Building in Africa" and "The Political Economy of American Investments in South Africa" dispute any claims that Pan-Africanists are largely preoccupied with origins and romanticized notions of history and culture rather than with modern Africa and post-colonial politics. As was the case with many activists and intellectuals of the period, Turner was well versed in contemporary international politics, especially developments in Africa, which is arguably no longer a dominant current within academic circles.

In 1971 Turner published "Universal Education and Nation-Building in Africa" in the *Journal of Black Studies*, which aptly describes the critical dilemma of mass education in new African states. Though education was a cornerstone of nation-building and modernization, Turner illuminates the undue strain that uncoordinated education systems had on developing nations. By using conceptual frameworks from sociology, political science, and economics, Turner argues that serious and expensive errors were made in the planning of mass educational systems, creating a dysfunctional relationship between universal primary education and political and economic development. Inevitably, rapid educational expansion also raised the economic expectations of urban youth, who became disenchanted by the nation's incapacity to employ the growing rate of graduates. Here, Turner provides a thoughtful critique of the post-colonial condition. In his estimation, educational development in most of West Africa had the unanticipated result of perpetuating the elite-mass gap as well as ethnic divisions. The article examines the interrelationships between education, politics, and economics, and cogently argues that education must be carefully coordinated for the purposes of nation building. This position mirrored early Black Studies imperatives to train students for service and leadership in the development of their communities.

Similarly, Turner intervened in national debates about the role of U.S.-based corporations and government agencies in the maintenance of the oppressive apartheid regime in South Africa. Published in 1979, his "The Political Economy of American Investment in South Africa" article contains an incisive analysis of racial capitalism and its central role in shaping of "geopolitics." This study also makes use of sociological methodologies, painstakingly detailing the myriad of ways that the apartheid regime enacted violence on the African populace. Compellingly, Turner asserts that descriptions of the apartheid system as "just a method of racial segregation" or as "pure race prejudice" grossly misconstrues its "fundamental nature and purpose" of integrating Africans into a system of *white domination* and *absolute power*. Furthermore, Turner implicates both indirect investment and inaction as equally culpable in reinforcing oppressive white-minority rule. Without question, Turner's anti-apartheid activism was yet another manifestation of his Pan-African praxis. This is critical to note given the ways in which much of the scholarship on the anti-apartheid movement tends to divorce this worldwide struggle from a history and tradition of Pan-Africanism.[13]

THE STATUS OF PAN-AFRICANISM IN CONTEMPORARY BLACK STUDIES

Turner's writings in this section set out to articulate the meaning of Pan-Africanism in relation to the Black Studies project. These essays make it clear that Pan-Africanism is not an abstraction. It is real poli-tics—committed to both the vindication of Black histories and cultures, and practical engagement with contemporary political struggles. Turner's work also demonstrates that Pan-Africanism is not static or immutable and speaks to many of the criticisms and mischaracterizations of Pan-African ideologies. Viewed from this perspective, the call for Pan-African unity does not trivialize differences nor encourage a uniform "sameness." Uni-fication, whether on the continent or throughout the Diaspora, must be understood as *strategic* and always in negotiation with the material effects of white supremacy, capitalist exploitation and Western imperialism.

An engagement with Turner's work raises pertinent questions regarding the status of Pan-Africanism within Black Studies. Undeniably, the turn to-ward Diaspora Studies and Black Transnationalism in recent years emerged alongside a rejection of Pan-Africanism among some Black Studies schol-ars. In light of Turner's writings, we should continue to ask what exactly fuels the dismissal of Pan-Africanism. Far too many mischaracterizations rest on a stigma that fails to engage progressive and radical expressions of Pan-African ideology and activism. Black Studies can only be strengthened by a more accurate interrogation of the "cross fertilization of ideas and experiences" and the fundamental relationships that lie at the heart of Pan-African activity. Certainly, criticism of Pan-Africanism as masculinist and elitist has raised legitimate concerns about the potential reproduction of oppressive ideas and systems of domination and inequality. Yet the whole-sale abandonment of Pan-Africanism to the point of non-engagement may have anti-intellectual and counterproductive consequences.[14] Rather than retreat from blind spots and contradictions, Turner's work invites intellectual exploration as foundational to social transformation.

Reading Turner's work into these tensions is instructive as we seek to fortify Black Studies and re-imagine an intellectual and activist agenda that speaks to contemporary realities facing Black world communities. What would a progressive Pan-African praxis look like today? How do scholars engage in the politics of Diaspora or the politics of difference? What are the alternative models? As we contemplate opportunities for transnational cooperation in the face of post-colonial and neoliberal challenges, Turner's Pan-African praxis offers a model that is fluid, transformative, and profoundly invested in the cause of liberation—a cause no less important today than it was during the early stages of the Black Studies movement.[15]

AFRICA:
CONFLICT IN BLACK AND WHITE[16]

JAMES TURNER AND RUKUDZO MURAPA

The encounter at the International meeting of the African Studies Association in Montreal, October 15–18, 1969, must be viewed in the context of the endemic conflict between black and white scholars in America. The disruption of the plenary session and the subsequent panel discussion at the Queen Elizabeth Hotel was a contemporary manifestation of historical schisms between Blacks who attempt to work in the field of Black Studies (i.e., Africa and the African diaspora) and the Whites who dominate and control this field.

The opposition, as it unfolded in Montreal, was not simply directed at the "lily white" composition of the African Studies Association. Of equal concern was the fact that black scholars have been continually consigned to a marginal position, and have been forced to languish in the underground of the academic world. This is largely due to a process of white racism that relegates the legitimacy and validity of black scholarship by not providing adequate professional recognition and financial and institutional support. But of primary concern is the conviction among Blacks that the intellectual activities, i.e., research and publication of white scholars, functioning, historically, under the auspices of such organizations as the A.S.A. and its Canadian and European counterparts, have been responsible for a legacy of misinformation and distorted concepts about Africa.

*Faculty member Rukudzo Murapa and James Turner in conversation at
the Africana Studies and Research Center, ca. 1970s.*

Moreover, the arrogance of white scholarship is evidenced through continuous exclusion of black scholars in the process of debate and review
over data and theories concerned with black people as presented by white
men. We recall the writings of W.E.B. Du Bois several decades ago, which
took opposition to the "Hamite hypothesis," so popular then among white
scholars, as did Leo Hansberry and Carter [G.] Woodson, with the attempts of white anthropologists and historians to sever Egypt and the
Northeastern "Horn" in the [Mediterranean] area from the historical flow

of African development. However, to protect their positions of prominence in the field, white men resorted to a game of denying the intellectual capacity and scholarly competence of Blacks. It was common for white men to refer to black scholars who concentrated their academic work on the study of black people as "race men." The implicit accusation was that they (Blacks) could not be objective scholars in the study of black people, since they, themselves, were Black. Yet, the same judgment was never conceived as applicable to white men who study their own culture and the experience of European people. In order to defend their assumed ability and prerogative to study black people, white intellectuals continue the argument by concluding that being Black did not give one special insights in African Studies. In fact, white scholars concluded that Blacks in the new world had become so separated and alienated from their African roots that there was no link between them and Africa which would inform them in ways not open to white researchers. Indeed, all of this suggested that white men were, in fact, better able, from all respects, to study black people. White men have taken it exclusively upon themselves to define the content and parameters of the subject, and the method for the field of study. Thus, by talking and listening to each other, only, and [by] sharing basic assumptions, they construct their own definitions and criteria for scholarship, with no mind given to the ideas and works of black men in this field long before them.

Their frame of reference is a product of their own formation and determinant of what they accept as fact. Rarely do they pay credit to or refer to such Black Africanists as Carter [G.] Woodson, Edward W. Blyden, J. A. Rogers, Leo Hansberry, W. Alphaeus Hunton, Lorenzo Turner and W.E.B. Du Bois, to name a few among the many. Among the so-called prominent Africanists, there are very few who have had any exposure to the Schomburg collection and similar Africana collections at Howard, Fisk, and Atlanta Universities. For white scholars, black people are the object of their research designs unilaterally conceived and projected. They visit and study Africa for personal interests and academic promotion and commercial publication—all of which is to further perpetuate, not only their prestige, but also their claim to the legitimacy of their scholarship. Seldom do they go to Africa to study for the benefit of Africa and its people. White scholars have consciously and systematically not permitted a situation of parity and reciprocity to evolve between them and black scholars. They have always asserted the right to judge and to critique the work of black intellectuals on the basis of criteria constructed without the participation of black people. In the final analysis, the burden of proof is always upon the black scholar. He had to carry his work to the throne of white academe to be evaluated and adjudged as to its validity and, indeed, his own legitimacy as a scholar. The wiles of such white imposition and presumptuousness have led white academics to conclude, with their usual air of finality, that Black studies refers to Afro-American studies and not at all to Africa. They argue that the two are discontinuous and disparate experiences and fields of study—there is still no modesty in the face of evident ignorance.

The work of such figures as William W. Brown, Timothy Fortune, Martin Delany, Alexander Crummell, Langston Hughes, Countee Cullen, Alain Locke and Sterling Brown, again to name just a few among the many, are rarely even footnoted in white scholarship. The question, historically echoed by black intellectuals, is, how can Whites claim competence to judge when virtually all of their work, by its gross omissions, reflects them as dismally ignorant of the nature of the black experience and the vast body of literature written by Blacks from as early as the colonial period to the present[?] On what basis do they make such an evaluative judgment and comparative conclusion?

In the final analysis, the incident in Montreal was more than a performance of black self-assertion; it was and is a challenge to the criteria of competence, definition, and direction of white research in Africa. Black scholars in Montreal and elsewhere demonstrated a clear determination to arrest and change this situation by assuming full control of the nature of study and definition of scholarly work in Africa. We are fully convinced that the weight of historical evidence proves that exogenous definition, no matter how sympathetic, is far from being comprehensive and satisfactory.

Another area of concern expressed in Montreal was that white scholarship has often been a hand-maiden of white Western, industrial and political international interests. The structure of financial support given to such organizations as the ASA and AAI gives considerable credence to this suspicion. Petitions for support of research [from] these organizations are directed to foundations related to corporate institutions [that] maintain colonial investments in Africa [and] who are often influential inspirators of neocolonial designs on the continent. Thus, the claim of "value free" and academic neutrality falls on its face. To paraphrase Fred Burke, considered by some a prominent Africanist[,] seldom have studies of politics in Africa been achieved in the context of political neutrality.

SIXTH PAN-AFRICAN CONGRESS 1974: HISTORICAL PERSPECTIVE[17]

JAMES TURNER

An entire generation of African, Caribbean and U.S. political activists were influenced by the ideas and strategies projected in the Fifth Pan African Congress....The discussions were initiated by Africans. An attempt was made for us to act, not just react.

In the 20th century, there has been a restless movement, inevitably destined to change the shape of the world, among those whom Fanon calls "the wretched of the earth." It was W.E.B. Du Bois who, in 1903, foresaw that the color line—the relationship between the oppressor and the oppressed—would be *the* question of the 20th century. Those who participated in, or were affected by, the Pan African Congresses have been part of this tremendous world movement. If we are to consider the five Pan African Congresses which convened between 1919 and 1945, we should understand them within the context of the international socio-political situation at the times of their occurrence. We should understand that Pan Africanism itself developed from early roots on both sides of the Atlantic, growing out of exchanges of ideas and concrete experiences among Africans. And we should understand that these earlier Congresses posed for the first time in an international context the basic questions facing African people. These were questions of relationships, as well as of specific conditions.

The Congresses represent marking points in the Pan African movement. One would be mistaken to consider only these five meetings in order to understand the overall drive of African people for liberation and development. In particular, we should be conscious of other forces in the total struggle, such as the impacts of Marcus Garvey and the mass-based [Universal Negro Improvement Association (UNIA)], the emergence of socialism as a "rational choice" for oppressed people, and the African and Asian independence struggle, with their internal core of trade union and mass party movements.

But because of the people these Congresses motivated, and the questions [raised at these] Congresses, they are important for our view of the total struggle. They form a necessary background for those who will take an interest in the Sixth Pan-African Congress.

The five Pan African Congresses took place between the two World Wars. In that period, the Third World was milked of men and material; the lands of the colonial peoples changed hands as dictated by the fortunes in war of European states; the Great Depression hit African communities in the U.S., and in the African and Caribbean states, much harder than it did the people of Europe. Lynching and Jim Crowism were at a peak in the U.S. The first concrete fruits of the Russian revolution began to make impact on world politics. It was a time of flux and change.

The Trinidadian Sylvester Williams had organized a Pan African Conference in 1900 which W.E.B. Du Bois, the prime mover behind the subsequent meetings, attended. But Pan Africanism had begun as a political force years before either the Williams conference or the Pan African Congresses.

Distinguished visiting scholar Shirley Graham Du Bois (widow of Dr. W.E.B. Du Bois) lecturing to students and faculty at the Africana Studies and Research Center, ca. 1970s.

THE FUNDAMENTAL RELATIONSHIPS

Since the European colonization of Africa, and the slave trade which created overseas communities of Africans, three sets of relationships have evolved which have determined the extent of our peoples' freedom, material well-being, and potential for self-reliant, dynamic development. Pan Africanism has been used as an ideology by Africans struggling to change one, two, or all three of these relationships. These relationships are:

1. *Between Africans and Europeans.* This has been primarily a relationship of African dependency, [and] of subordination of the interests of the masses of African people to the development and maintenance of Europe's economic-political system: capitalism. It is this relationship which has been given the most attention by all five previous Pan African Congresses.

2. *Between Africans and other oppressed peoples.* This has been at best a stunted relationship in modern times. The scope and direction of the relationship have been defined almost entirely by the oppression under which non-European peoples exist, due to the control of the world by capitalism and imperialism. The resulting mal-development and international contradictions within Asia, Africa, and South America (Latin America) make difficult the forging of new directions for social, economic, and political intercourse among the different peoples. But, as we shall see, by the time of the Fifth Pan African Congress, this relationship also merited serious political consideration by Pan Africanists.

3. *Between different classes, groups, and communities within African societies and communities.* Between 1919 and 1945, the internal contradictions of tribal and linguistic differences, class distinctions, traditional versus modern social practices, definition of the positions occupied by women and, youth, *etc.*, were all subordinated to the overriding desire to change the relationship between the colonizer and the colonized. By the time of the Fifth Congress, however, even this third relationship had grown in importance on the Pan African political agenda.

ROOTS AND CROSS-FERTILIZATION

This short article cannot give an in-depth history of the development of Pan Africanism. [B]efore turning to examination of the five Congresses themselves, we should sketch briefly the earlier cross-fertilization of ideas and experiences which helped give rise to Pan Africanism. Towards the end of the 19th century, the relationships referred to above precipitated a parallel development of many institutions, organizations, and ideas among Africans in the United States, parts of Africa, and the West Indies.

At the time, almost all of Africa and the Caribbean were colonies of European powers. In Africa, the Europeans had finally managed, in most places, to quell overt African military resistance, and were consolidating their political and economic administrations in order to effectively alienate the land and exploit the labor of the Africans. Racist laws, taxes, and other actions proscribing the freedom and development of Africans abounded. The Caribbean area was undergoing a similar period of the consolidation of colonial power and a capitalistic, plantation-style economic system. Africans in America were reeling from the abrupt end of Reconstruction.

Some of us are familiar with the movements and individuals which emerged from these conditions in the U.S., but less familiar with parallel developments in Africa. For many of the same reasons that separate Black churches became vehicles for political protest in the U.S. and in the English-speaking Caribbean, the African churches and various "independent" religious movements became mediums of political, as well as religious, expression. Some of the political aspirations of Africa were couched in the more acceptable terminology of Christianity.

For example, there was a movement in Africa akin to the [African Methodist Episcopal Church (A.M.E.)] movement in the U.S. It was called "Ethiopianism," and it began in South Africa at the turn of the century, then spread to Nyasaland (now Malawi) and the Congo (now Zaire) via the Chilembwe and Kimbango Movements, and to Uganda via the Malaki Rebellion.

Among individuals, John Chilembwe, a militant Nyasaland minister, figures prominently, corresponding in some respects to Henry Highland Garnet and Bishop Henry M. Turner in the U.S. Chilembwe came to the unfavorable attention of colonial governments in his region when he wrote an eloquent protest against Africans being called to fight on behalf of Europe in World War I.

Several of the early Black ministers in the U.S., including Bishop Turner, visited their counterparts in South Africa; some of the activist ministers from Southern Africa attended schools in U.S. There was naturally exchange of ideas and some insight into the similarities of oppression and basic problems facing our people.

West Africa also gave birth to independent African churches "whose adherents were thinking in African terms and so testifying to the Pan African vision." There had been for some years Africans such as Martin Delany and Africanus Horton, whose heritage went full circle, from Africa to enslavement in the West and back to West Africa. They wrote political tracts and edited newspapers which took the wider view of African problems beyond their own states (Sierra Leone, Liberia, or Ghana) to a West African, and even continent-wide perspective.

It was also in East and Southern Africa that the movement was transformed from religio-political to more overtly political. (In particular, several figures associated with the growth of African nationalism in South Africa, including Isaka Seme, one of the founders of the [African National Congress (ANC)], went to school in the U.S.—again the opportunity for cross-fertilization.) The period of time concurrent with the holding of the Pan African Congresses saw the rise of many African nationalist organizations, including the All-African Convention of 1935, the Rhodesian African organizations, the Nyasaland National Congress, the East African Association, the Somali Youth League, and the Kenya African Union. All of these, while focusing heavily on problems of a particular nation-state, contributed to the growth of Pan African thought.

Among the early organizations which played dynamic political roles in West Africa were the Fanti Confederation (1868), the Aborigines' Rights Protection Society (Gold Coast), and the West African National Congress. This last organization was created in 1820, when a conference was convened by Casely Hayford at Accra "to coordinate the economic, political, and social aspirations of the progressive Africans of the four West African Territories (Nigeria, Gold Coast, Gambia, Sierra Leone)." These African organizations emerged around specific conditions within states, but they also form part of the base in the development of Pan Africanism.

THE FIRST FOUR CONGRESSES

The first Congress organized by Du Bois was held in Paris in 1919, concurrent with the Paris Peace Conference at which the European powers hammered out the end of World War I. One of the main reasons of the Congress was world-wide Black concern for the fate of the African colonies in the negotiations. Fifty-seven delegates came to the first Congress from fifteen countries, nine African and the rest American, European, and Caribbean. The largest number of delegates was from the West Indies. The delegation was not, for the most part, composed of people who traveled to France for the meeting. (Very few Black people had that level of mobility.) Instead, they were individuals who were in France at the time for reasons connected with the War. In fact, Du Bois later related that all European governments refused to issue travel visas to would-be delegates.

Since Germany's colonies in Africa (including parts of present-day Kenya, Tanzania, Togo, the Cameroons, and Namibia) were up for grabs, the African delegates found it a critical time to bring to the world's attention, while all eyes were focused on Paris, the total question of the treatment of Africans in the colonies. The First Congress appealed to the new League of Nations, in an act of faith which later proved futile, to oversee the "political, social, and economic welfare" of the Africans. But the Congress also listed five key areas of concern, which were identified as involving Africans and people of African descent, and which formed the essence of the relationship between Africans and Europeans at that time. Their points [were]:

1. The alienation of African land and ruthless exploitation of Africa's natural resources;

2. The role of European capital and of individual and corporate concessionaires in Africa, with the resultant drain of excessive profits from Africa to Europe;

3. Exploitation of Black labor and inhumane labor conditions;

4. The deliberate policy of inadequate education of Africans, especially in technical fields;

5. The repressive colonialist-run state and prevention of African participation in political activity.

Thus, the first Pan African Congress was one of the first international arenas in which Africans initiated their own discussion on the question of land, capital, labor, education, and the nation-state as it affected African people.

The Second Congress, in 1921, was held simultaneously in London, Brussels, and Paris. One hundred and thirteen delegates attended. This time, the largest contingent (41 delegates) came from Africa. Once again they came primarily as individuals, with some few representing organizations. Again, appeals were made to the League of Nations concerning African land and labor, and even on the question of self-government—an idea certainly inimical to the designs of the European colonial powers. Special concern was voiced for the barbaric crimes committed by the Belgians against Africans in the then Congo.

The Third Congress was held in two sections, one each in Lisbon and London, in 1923. Of the two, the Lisbon meeting was far the more important. A dominant role was played by the *Liga Africana*, an association of Africans in Portugal and its colonies.

The *Liga* was a federation of African associations which represented several million Black people. Again, the basic question of land, labor, education, and political rights were broached. Three of the most important demands were:

1. "The development of Africa for the benefit of Africans, and not merely for the profit of Europeans..."

2. "The right of Blacks to bear arms in their own defense..."

3. "The organization of commerce and industry so as to make the main objects of capital and labor the welfare of the many, rather than the enriching of the few."

In 1923—at the height of entrenched colonialism in Africa and the Caribbean, naked repression of America's Black community, and years before the Third World began in earnest to look at a socialist alternative—these were bold ideas.

By the time of the Fourth Congress, Du Bois planned for a site "nearer other African centers of population." He sought to have the Fourth Congress as a series of meetings in Jamaica, Haiti, Cuba, and Martinique or Guadeloupe. The colonial powers quickly thwarted this plan by making sea transportation unavailable. So, in 1927, the Fourth Pan African Congress was held in New York. For obvious reasons, African participation was low, although West Africa was well-represented. The items on the agenda did not deviate from the basic ones previous Congresses found important.

In 1929, would-be organizers of a Fifth Pan African Congress were insistent on an African site. They tentatively selected, for accessibility, the North African city of Tunis. The French government then informed the

Congress planners that such a meeting could be held anywhere in France, but nowhere in Africa. Obviously, there was fear of the potential of a Pan African Congress on African soil. It was not until after World War II that circumstances allowed for the convening of the Fifth Pan African Congress at Manchester, England, in 1945.

More political commentary has been made on the Fifth Congress than on all of the others, and justifiably so. The names of many of the participants alone were enough to stamp the Fifth Congress indelibly into African political history. These were people of dynamic political energy, intent finally on a plan of action to change the relationships and conditions affecting African people. To mention a few, there were: Du Bois, Kwame Nkrumah, George Padmore, C.L.R. James, Jomo Kenyatta, Mrs. Amy J. Garvey, Ras Makonnen, I. T. Wallace-Johnson, Ken Hill, J. C. deGraft-Johnson, Mark Hlubi, Obafemi Awolowo and Nnamdi Aizkiwe.

But what is really more important to our political understanding of the impact of the Fifth Congress than a list of the prominent participants was the *tone* of the meeting, and the *political issues* considered. The Congress organizers, the Pan African Federation (headquarters London) made use of the fact that representatives of many Caribbean and African labor and farm workers' organizations had just attended an international labor meeting in Paris. For the first time, it was possible for delegates to be drawn from a wide cross-section of African and Caribbean society, imbuing the Congress with a special tone of concern for the aspirations of the masses. From the U.S., there was also representation of a wide cross-section of organizations then acting as political focal points in the Black community, including the NAACP, the UNIA, fraternal organizations, newspapers and church groups.

There were major sessions concerned with changing the relationship between Africans and Europeans, entitled variously: "Imperialism in North and West Africa"; "Oppression in South Africa"; "The East African Picture"; "Ethiopia and the Black Republics (Liberia and Haiti)"; "The Color Problem in Britain"; [and] "The Problem in the Caribbean."

Resolutions of [a] political, economic, and social nature were passed for each of several geographic areas, including a special set of resolutions on South West Africa (Namibia), the Congo and North Africa, and the so-called protectorates of Bechuanaland, Basutoland, and Swaziland. Special consideration also was given to the struggle of Afro-Americans, and it was recognized that "the successful realization of the political, economic, and social aspirations of the 13 million (Black people) in the U.S. is bound up with the emancipation of all African peoples...."

The overwhelming political conclusion of the Fifth Pan African Congress was that political independence—an end to colonialism—was a necessity in order to change the first fundamental relationship, that [is,] between Europeans and Africans.

For the first time in the history of the Congresses, the delegates also specifically expressed solidarity with the struggles of other oppressed people against imperialism, mentioning by name the people[s...] of India, Indonesia and Vietnam. While it was understood that oppressed peoples shared a common enemy, the sentiment of the Fifth Congress was that the changing of their status vis-à-vis Europe had priority in the political strategy.

Many of the delegates, by the time they left Manchester, had already begun to translate analysis and definition of the problem into organization. Several were destined to play primary roles in the shaping of the subsequent struggle for African political independence. Kwame Nkrumah, of course, stands out in this respect.

One final facet which is vital to an assessment of the Fifth Congress was the Declaration to the Colonial Workers, Farmers, and Intellectuals. The declaration was a call to action which just began to touch on the third of the fundamental set of relationships. It was the beginning of a recognition that the purpose of all the political, economic, and social change being advocated, *and the principal actors in the struggle*, must be the masses of the African people, including all segments of society. In part, the declaration states:

> We affirm the right of all colonial peoples to control their own destiny...(to be free) from foreign imperialist control. We say to the people of the colonies that they must fight for these ends by all the means at their disposal....The Fifth Congress therefore calls on workers and farmers of the colonies to organize effectively...and the intellectuals and professional classes to awaken to their responsibility. Today there is only one road to effective action—the organization of the masses.

An entire generation of African, Caribbean, and U.S. political activists were influenced by the ideas and strategies projected in the Fifth Pan African Congress. The Fifth Congress, as did the first four Congresses, raised in an international (Pan African) context the fundamental relationships affecting African people, as well as the specific adverse conditions arising from those relationships. The discussions were *initiated* by Africans. An attempt was made for us to act, not just react. The Congresses helped give impetus and sustenance to the political work of many people in the

African fight for independence. A balanced assessment of the five Pan African Congresses must conclude that they occupy an important place in the continuum of ideas and movements in the struggle for African liberation and development.

THE POLITICAL ECONOMY OF AMERICAN INVESTMENT IN SOUTH AFRICA[18]

JAMES TURNER

A prominent specialist in African-American relations, with many years of experience in African affairs, remarked recently that the world is full of little known places, which most Americans only become conscious of when catastrophe brings them to notice, or when they become the focus for a clash of big power "interests" threatening world peace. Vietnam was such a place until the middle 1960s, when American soldiers were sent there in the thousands. Until then, few Americans would have known where to look for Vietnam on the map. Africa is another area of the world which has been obscure for most people in America.[19] Even though the American connection pre-dates the founding of the republic, only a few times has Africa been brought dramatically to world attention.

During the late 1950s and early 1960s the upsurge of independence for African countries brought the continent into focus as symbolic of a new era of emergence from colonial domination by the greater mass of the world's people. The Congo crisis of the 1960s and the subsequent murder of that tragic country's first Prime Minister was another incidence of international attention. Relatively few Americans would have known Angola was an African country before Henry Kissinger made a speech in Detroit on November 24, 1975, in which he accused the Soviet Union and Cuba of changing the balance of international relations by intervening in an internal struggle for power in Angola, and warned that continued involvement would affect "other relationships." Then, in 1977, there was fighting in the southern Shaba provinces of Zaire, which was initiated by attacks from disaffected Katangese insurgents coming across the border of neighboring Angola; and American military support, indirectly, to protect the dubious regime of President Mobutu Sese Seko. The news from Zaire was followed almost immediately by last year's grave international crisis sparked by the three-way fighting among Eritrea, Ethiopia, and Somalia in the "horn" of Africa. The point is that swiftly moving events in Africa are producing strong political undercurrents which influence American foreign policy planners, and the pace of the country's deepening entanglement in African affairs moves considerably ahead of the public's consciousness of this reality. The critical question now is whether the near confrontation between the big powers in Angola and then Zaire was incidental and has significantly abated, or whether it will emerge again over the issues at stake in southern Africa. It appears that conditions are present which make southern Africa one of the areas of the world where internal conflicts can produce major big power confrontations that could threaten international peace.

Geopolitically, southern Africa has become, and promises to remain for some time, a tinderbox of acute political conflict. The stakes in southern Africa are great[;] the area is rich and produces some of the most important industrial resources in the world. The area stretches from Zaire and Tanzania in the north to the Republic of South Africa in the south[,] encompassing twelve nations in a region larger than the United States. It is militarily strategic because of its critical location, which is bounded on the east by the Indian Ocean and in the west in by the South Atlantic. The shipping lanes around the Cape of Good Hope are vital for the transport of petroleum from the Arabian peninsula to the oil-dependent industry and life style of the United States and its allies of Western Europe and Japan, and are the only effective alternative to the Suez Canal, which is vulnerable to the endemic conflicts of the Middle East. The geopolitics are colored by an important racial factor; of a total regional population of one hundred million, the European descendants are less than five percent and live mainly in South Africa (approximately 4.2 million), with another two hundred and eighty thousand in Rhodesia (Zimbabwe to the Africans).

South Africa alone is a very rich country. It is responsible for eighty percent of the world's gold and diamonds and is the third largest producer of uranium.[20] But not all the countries are so well endowed naturally. The richest hub of the region (Rhodesia-Namibia–South Africa) is under the domination of minority racist, White, settler regimes. South(ern) Africa is the only component of industrialist capitalist society in the modern world in which racial domination is the most basic principle of social organization. The White minority governments have successfully repressed challenges to its hegemony and dissension of all kinds, while consistently defying international pressures for internal reform. Oppressive conditions and resistance to change in the areas of southern African forced under minority White control make social conditions ripe for bitter conflict, with escalating violence. Southern Africa is a system of racial, political, and economic exploitation, whose means of production rest essentially upon the labor of African workers.

Over the past decade there has been a growing debate about the United States' relation with minority racist governments in southern Africa. The discussion and mounting protests have concentrated primarily on the role of America-based transnational corporations in the region. Impetus was given to these concerns by the spread of mass African rebellion throughout South Africa from the urban reserve of Soweto in the summer of 1976, when tens of thousands of Black students, workers and unemployed carried on a running confrontation with South African authorities. Though the Africans were unarmed, the "Soweto uprising" was the most serious threat to the government since the Sharpeville protest and consequent massacre on March 21, 1960, when a quarter of a million Black people gathered outside police stations all over South Africa to protest the offensive "pass laws." In Sharpeville, police fired into an unarmed crowd of five thousand, killing sixty-nine and wounding two hundred people, many of them women. The death of Steve Biko—founder of the Black Consciousness Movement—while in detention in September 1977 and a subsequent wave of government suppression, bannings, and arrests of Black community leaders and civil rights activists have added new urgency to the issue. Steve Biko's stature in South African society has been compared to Dr. Martin Luther King's role in the United States. The debate over cutting off bank loans from the U.S. and withdrawing corporate investment from South Africa is intensifying. A large number of church groups, coordinated by the New York–based Interfaith Center for Corporate Responsibility (an agency of the National Council of Churches), have launched a campaign against U.S. bank loans to South Africa. Church-sponsored groups have also challenged U.S. investments in South Africa at the annual stockholder meetings of Ford, General Electric, IBM, Goodyear Tire & Rubber, Motor Oil, Union Carbide and many other corporations. University investments in corporations with major South African holdings have also increasingly become the focus of those in this country who are opposed to apartheid. A growing number of American unions have passed resolutions declaring that they would withdraw deposits of their pension funds from banks extending loans to South Africa. In an indication in growing public support for some form of government action, a Harris public opinion poll released in December 1977 showed that forty-two percent of those Americans polled favored preventing any new investment in South Africa, compared with thirty-three percent against. Particularly important, in this regard, is the growing opposition movement in the Black community, whose population is of African descent, to apartheid and racist, minority rule in South Africa.

The word *apartheid* literally means "separate" in Afrikaans, [a] language derived originally from Dutch which is spoken by about sixty percent of South Africa's White population. The remaining forty percent of the White population are descendants of British settlers. The Afrikaans, through control of the Nationalist Party, have governed the country un-interruptedly since coming to power in 1948. From the Nationalist government the theory of apartheid or separate development [between] the African and European components of the population was firmly established as the primal policy of the state. Consequently, South Africa now has all the institutions of a police state, which were being built at the same time the factories, roads, bridges, mines, and telecommunication system were being constructed as the infra-structure for the country's economic expansion.

South African is a rich and beautiful country, but it is a land of stark contrasts. Fewer than four million "Europeans" in the population enjoy a standard of living as high as that of the world's richest countries, while the African majority of eighteen million lives in poverty as severe as in the poorest undeveloped nations. The social differentials between the privilege of South Africa's White population and the misery of its African and Colored people reflect the racial exploitation of labor which is fundamental to the country's social organization. The African labor force is subjected to [a] higher degree of extra-economic coercion than workers in most undeveloped countries; and racial inequality, too, is more highly regulated and acute there than in any other industrial country. Whites in South Africa comprise eighteen percent of the population but take home over seventy-six percent of the wealth created every year; they receive sixty-eight percent of the income, while Blacks, eighty-two percent of the population, are left with only twenty-three percent of all the wealth. While Africans contribute over two-thirds of South Africa's labor force, White workers earn on the average eight times as much as their Black fellow workers. In 1970, the ratio of African to European per capita income was 1:17; in 1971, the gap [was] 1:20 and was reported to be growing still wider.[21] A 1972 survey revealed that over eighty percent of all Africans live below the poverty line—that is[,] the whole family earns less than twenty-five dollars a week. The breakdown of wage differentials by occupational categories are instructive: in manufacturing (per month) 518 rands (1 rand = $1.40) for Whites and 109 rands for Africans; in retail trade, 230 rands for Whites and 70 rands for Africans; [and in] mining, 663 rands for Whites and 71 rands for Africans. The average annual per capita income in South Africa for Whites is $2,373.60 in contrast to $117.60 for Blacks (reported in the *Financial Mail*, December 13, 1974). The average unskilled wage for an African man as of August 1974 was $93.00 per month.

The White minority has expropriated, for its use, permanent legal rights to eighty-seven percent of the country's best land (including every major village, town or city in the country) under the government's policy of apartheid or separate development of the races. This policy restricts legal African residence to the remaining thirteen percent, "which consists of 276 separate, non-contiguous native reserves, grouped into eight Bantustans of African homeland." These lands are the poorest and least developed areas of the country, without any modern industrial infrastructure, e.g., there are no major cities or ports, few roads or railroads, insufficient electrification and living space, inadequate health facilities, and restricted educational opportunities. The state spends approximately $340 a year on educating each White child, and education is free and compulsory only for Whites. Ninety-three percent of Whites of high school age are going to school; for Blacks the figure is 8.9 percent. Whites can live and work wherever they choose; African men and women have to carry passes, [and] may live and work only where the stamp in the passbook—put there by a White official—decrees. Whites vote and make laws in parliament; Blacks have no vote. Whites organize trade unions and strike for higher pay, Blacks go to jail for striking, and their trade unions are given no legal recognition. There are more than one million migrating laborers in South Africa, men who are forced to leave their families behind in the Bantustans while they work on a yearly contract, living in compounds or hostels. Taken together, these social conditions reproduce the poverty and the oppression of the Black population.

All of this by the conscious design and the carefully constructed system called apartheid. Taken literally, this term does mean physical separation (of the races), but to think of this system as just a method of racial segregation would be to misunderstand its fundamental nature and purpose. Over three hundred years of South African history, with the increasing dependence of the White economy on African labor, White policy in fact has always involved the domination and use of the Africans, first as land and house serfs, then as mine workers, now as factory workers. Seven out of ten workers in South Africa are Africans. They constitute ninety percent of the work force in agriculture, forestry, fishing, and mining; sixty-five percent in electricity, gas, and water; sixty-seven percent in services; sixty percent in construction.[22] South Africa is a unique society in which the intensity of racial cleavages is in direct proportion to the degree to which skin color and racial origin have become the basis of one's relationship to the means of production. A White skin is the best insurance against falling below a certain level, and a Black skin marks all, with few exceptions, as members of the class with nothing but labor power to see—and at a low price. The wealth generated by industrialization is systematically channeled away from the African population whose labor has produced it, and into the enforcement of apartheid and White prosperity more generally.

Social differentiation of the components of the population on the basis of racial characteristics initiates a social division of labor, which forms the material foundation of all social relations. Social differentiations engenders the development of a racist division of labor; that is, racism at the point of production in workshops, plants, mines, factories, in agriculture and the service industries, in all aspects of production. This racist division of labor, which [characterizes the] apartheid system [...] , is manifested in racist occupational classifications, racist wage differentials, racist training and promotion practices and so on. The perpetuation of the racial economy and Bantustan spatial organization plays a crucial role in the denial of equality in all spheres of South Africa's life—economic, political, and social.

Therefore, apartheid is a system designed to use Africans for the creation of wealth which then guarantees the exclusive benefits of that wealth to Whites. In essence, apartheid is a national state policy utilized as a basis for government by European settlers in southern Africa to solve a dual problem for themselves: the desire to integrate Africans into the mechanisms of production while at the same time ensuring the continuance of White domination. Thus they both seek to draw the African majority into their industrial society and to shut them out as well. They were able to do this by depriving the Africans of their political rights, their power to organize, their ability to build their bargaining strength. This is the real meaning of apartheid. It is a whole system employed by a White minority to perpetuate its position of absolute power. It aims not at ending the interaction between Blacks and Whites but at controlling the terms of that interaction for White benefit.

Apartheid has done much more than provide a privileged standard of living for White workers. Its most important effect has been to provide an extremely profitable climate for investment. International corporations have always recognized this fact, and much of South Africa's fairly spectacular growth was financed by foreign investment. United States involvement has been particularly important because it provided not only much of the capital necessary for developing key industries, but also the licenses, technology, and personnel which, in many cases, were even more important than the capital itself. Profits from the apartheid system and its excessively low paid African labor are enormous; U.S. companies admit to a seventeen percent (and better) rate of profit. Besides investments, the five leading capitalist powers (U.S., Britain, Japan, West Germany, and France) had a total trade of $7,827 million with South Africa in 1976.

The development of the South African economy since World War II is one of capitalism's great success stories. Virtually a frontier society in 1945, South Africa today boasts the most highly industrialized, technologically sophisticated economy on the African continent. With the fastest rate of economic growth (after Japan), the country has been and continues to be very attractive to foreign investors. South Africa enjoys a comparatively high degree of freedom from the symptoms of underdevelopment typical of African economies; however, it is critically dependent on foreign investment and trade for sustaining the solvency of its highly diversified economy. The country's total foreign liabilities were 16.5 billion rand in 1975. It is precisely this inflow of foreign capital and technology which has helped absorb the costs of industrialization, thereby easing the burden on the state, which can allot correspondingly more of its resources to the enforcement of apartheid policies and the repression of opposition. Dynamic economic growth and the unswerving support of overseas investors have encouraged White South Africans to ignore external criticism of their country's apartheid system. Foreign investment (and the steadfast political and military support that follows) has done more to shore up the system than any other consideration or set of factors. A fourth of the total capital investment in South African enterprise is foreign; transnational banks hold some sixty percent of the total assets of the country's twenty largest banks. Overseas finance (including the United States government's Export-Import Bank) provides credits to enable South Africa to buy abroad what it cannot produce at home. Much of the capital equipment essential to South African industry, which has become extremely import-intensive over the past few decades, is supplied by the United States. Western European and American business has been making the vital contributions all along the way, financing and equipping the economy, nurturing the growth of a strong police and military, and guaranteeing the tacit political support of Western governments. It has been estimate[d] that eighty percent of South Africa's private industrial production is under foreign control or influence. Professor Ruth Milkman makes an important observation[:]

> The historic role of Western corporations investing in and exporting to South Africa in the post war years has been to help make possible its rapid economic growth and diversification. Because the vast bulk of the wealth generated by this economic growth is channeled into Whites in South Africa, in gross disproportion to their contribution to the economy, the very

process of industrial development has strengthened the hegemony of the White minority over the African population.[23]

The enormous police and military capabilities of South Africa's White minority government have grown in direct proportion to the inflow of foreign capital. Beyond their strategic role in the economy American corporations in South African provide a crucial political contribution to apartheid. United States investment in trade in South Africa creates a material bond between American corporation and the status quo regime. This 'bond,' created by profits, provides the minority regime protection from meaningful sanctions. On this very point, South African industrial editor for the *Sunday Times*, Tony Roenderman, ask[ed] the question: What is the significance to South Africa's security of the combination of sanctions and the guerilla war which as forced the White Rhodesian Government to concede to demands for Black rule? He says that there is no significance for South Africa necessarily and offers the following candid comment:

> Though this country does not have a big brother to shield it against an economic boycott, it has a number of advantages of its own which Rhodesia does not enjoy; a large, well-developed economy, virtual self-sufficiency in everything but oil. Strategic importance to the West, a long coastline, and its own not inconsiderable counterthreats.[24]

Former Senator Dick Clark's subcommittee on African Affairs said in its report, *U.S. Corporate Interests in South Africa*, that private U.S. banks played a crucial role in "directly assisting the South African government in its efforts to attain economic and strategic self-sufficiency." Transnational investors are contributing to South Africa's urgent campaign for economic self-sufficiency, in anticipation of the day when international sanctions will be imposed upon the country (as in neighboring Rhodesia in 1965). Direct American investments in and trade with South Africa helped generate the reserve which foster the economic growth of the country, and loans by U.S. banks give the government flexibility necessary to maintain apartheid. It is precisely because of the vital linkage between foreign capital and White minority rule in South Africa that anti-apartheid forces have become concerned with the divestment issue in relation to the role of American corporations and banks in that country.

Many of America's largest companies are active in South Africa; more than three hundred and fifty companies have subsidiaries there—including twelve of the top fifteen and fifty-five of the first one hundred companies ranked in [the Fortune] 500. To most U.S. companies, South African offers an attractive business opportunity; return on investment has been higher than in most developing and many developed countries, and the size of American investment there has grown steadily over the last two decades. At the end of 1966 American direct investment in South African was 490 million dollars. Ten years later the dollar value of U.S. direct investment had more than trebled, reaching a figure of at least $1.7 billion by 1977.[25] However, between ten and fifteen corporations account for some seventy-five percent of the direct American investment in South Africa.[26] Furthermore, U.S. investment in South African is heavily concentrated in a few major areas of the industrial economy, so that, for instance, American companies dominate the auto and oil industries—controlling over forty percent of the oil market.

Recent estimates indicate that the major investors are:

- Mobil—$1.3 billion

- Caltex—more than $225 million

- General Motors—$150 million

- Ford—more than $100 million

- Chrysler—$45 million (South African unit merged with South African–owned company in 1976)

- Union Carbide—over $100 million

- Kennecott—$130 million

- Phelps Dodge—over $100 million

- General Electric—more than $125 million

- ITT—$50–$70 million (though minor position in South African–owned company since 1977)

- IBM—8.4 million

American companies have at least $1.665 billion of direct investments in South Africa, comprising seventeen percent of all direct foreign investment there.[27]

To this point, we have been discussing direct investment in the South African economy—but an even greater amount of American capital goes to South African in the form of indirect investment. This consists primarily of loans to governmental agencies, businesses, or commercial banks. In addition, American banks have over $2 billion in outstanding loans to South Africa, accounting for thirty-three percent of all loan claims against the country. The major part of American loans to South Africa has been made by Chase Manhattan, Citibank, Manufacturers Hanover Trust, Morgan Guaranty and Bank of America. There are two aspects of bank loans to South Africa that make them especially vital to maintaining White minority rule. First, they have come primarily during periods in which South Africa has faced serious economic and political instability. Second, the recipients of these loans have generally been prominent institutions of the apartheid government. It is a truism that the White minority in South Africa fervently desires to maintain political and economic control of the state. Apartheid is the system they have devised to assume this position of supremacy.

The South African government is unique among Western industrialized nations in its degree of intervention in the economy. The government has set up a number of parastatal corporations such as: Electricity Supply Commission; Armaments Development and Production Corporation of South Africa; Industrial Development Corporation; Uranium Enrichment Corporation of South Africa; South African Coal, Oil and Gas Corporation; and the Iron and Steel Corporation—to ensure their command over the most strategic sectors of the economy under their control. They are among the largest enterprises in the country. In any analysis of the South African economy, it is important to understand that it is an economy directed and dominated by political as well as economic factors. In fact, the public (parastatal) corporations have been growing far more rapidly than private business enterprises, thereby setting the stage for escalating state intervention in the economy in the future. This growth of the public sector is a crucial part of the overall design to maintain the racial supremacist structure of South African society. It accounted for only six percent of new gross domestic fixed investment between 1950 and 1969, eight percent in 1965, eleven percent in 1970 and seventeen percent in 1975. Conversely, the private enterprise share of gross domestic fixed investment fell from sixty-five percent in 1950 to forty-nine percent in 1975. Describing the public corporations, which are state financed and controlled, the *Quarterly Bulletin* of the South Africa Reserve Bank reported that "social responsibility" rather than the profit motive *per se* has been the rationale of their establishment and direction. The ruling Nationalist Party has gone to absurd lengths on occasion to insure that apartheid regulations are followed even when regulations are a detriment to the overall economy. It is logical to assume that they are designing their whole economy to foster their political position and not to weaken it. To be sure, any foreign investment must fit into the integrated economic and political plan designed by the government.

The significance of foreign control or influence goes beyond their direct contribution to the total amount of capital invested in the South African economy. Equally important are the transfer of technology and managerial skills in sectors of the economy which are absolutely critical to its diversification and future growth. As important to South Africa's economy as the actual amount and direction of capital flow is the ability to import capital goods from abroad. Thus the stability in foreign trade is at least as crucial as investment, though the latter directly facilitates the former by providing foreign exchange.[28] United Nation's economist Sean Gervasi, writing in a recent United Nation's publication on foreign investment in South Africa, reported:

> The importance of capital is of more than purely quantitative importance. In many instances capital inflows are in fact the finance for purchasing sophisticated goods, especially machinery, which cannot be made in South Africa....What this means is that foreign 'capital' cannot be replaced simply by finding new sources of finance in South Africa. The capital imports are in fact irreplaceable commodities for sustaining economic growth.[29]

British economist John Suckling, a lecturer at York University, has attempted to clarify the importance of these "irreplaceable commodities." He suggests that the input of technological knowledge, managerial expertise, and capital goods has been the most important role of foreign investment. He estimates that about sixty percent of the growth in South Africa's domestic product between 1957 and 1972 could be ascribed to "technological change," two-thirds of which was the result of new technology entering the country through foreign investment. American investment has increasingly been directed into the most rapidly growing sectors of the country's economy. Much of the equipment essential to South African industry supplied by the American investments has figured particularly prominently in such "critical sectors" as capital goods, computers, transportation and energy.

The U.S. is actually the second ranking foreign investor in South African industry, behind Britain, which accounts for about sixty percent (or approximately eight billion dollars) or total foreign investment. However, U.S. capital holdings are more important to the economy than their comparative size would seem to suggest. American capital has gone increasingly into the high technology section of enterprise, e.g., cars, computers, electronics, petroleum and petrochemicals, and ore processing. In addition, U.S. banks are now the biggest lenders to South Africa, with outstanding credits of nearly three billion dollars, as we have seen. Virtually all American firms in South Africa not located in auto manufacturing, oil refining, computers, or mining operate in high technology and/or heavy engineering industries. They manufacture intermediate capital goods which are then used by other manufacturers in the country. They provide the implements or expertise necessary for the construction of major public and private work projects. They produce goods for finished consumption which are of recent invention and make use of complicated production processes. For instance, South Africa has no major domestic computer firms; the market is dominated by several American companies (which include the most prominent names in the field—International Business Machine, National Cash Register, Burroughs, Control Data Corp. UNIVAC-Sperry Rand, Honeywell, to name a few). IBM is the largest supplier and servicer of data processing equipment in the country and controls approximately fifty percent of the computer market, conducting twenty-five percent of its business there with the South Africa government.[30] The strong demand for electronic data processing equipment in South Africa is in part the direct result of apartheid. Limitations on the employment of Africans, Indians, and Coloreds, and influx control of these peoples to the urban industrial areas, legally reserved for the Whites, put a premium on automating such tasks. Certainly, it is the industrialized character of the South African economy that requires sophisticated data processing devices, as well. The managing director of Burroughs South Africa said as much in March 1971:

> We're entirely dependent on the U.S. The economy would grind to a halt without access to the computer technology of the West. No bank could function; the government couldn't collect its money and couldn't account for it; business couldn't operate; payrolls could not be paid. Retail and wholesale marketing and related services would be disrupted.[31]

Of course, what is not said is that many of the uses of American computers go far beyond such benign or normal administrative business/economic functions. There are at least twelve governmental departments (analogous to cabinet level departments in the U.S.) which are largely devoted to controlling the life of everyone outside the White population. Such institutions can keep track of twenty-two million non-White South Africans, and can direct or certify the decisions of these individuals make as to residence and employment. American computer technology is used directly in administering the "Book of Life" information about millions of Coloreds and Asians. Likewise, the Group Areas Act, which controls the residency and movements of these people, could not be enforced without the storage of individual records on sophisticated computer terminals like those provided by IBM. Without the service of computers from the United States, the infamous "passbook" system for Black people, which provides detailed information at the fingertips of South African authorities for the most minute regulation of the African population, would be inoperable, South Africa has one of the largest daily prison populations in the world—over one thousand Africans are prosecuted every day for just pass law violations. The assistance which American computer companies give to the South African government is at least as crucial to maintaining apartheid as the administrative services they provide in the private sector.

The three American automobile manufacturers produce more than sixty percent of South Africa's vehicles. The auto industry is one of the most dynamic forces in the expanding South African economy. Because this industry incorporates high technology and has substantial linkages with major other sectors of the economy, and produces a valuable product, the government views it as a strategic resource, as an instrument for achieving industrialization. Therefore, the auto industry stands as a cornerstone of the economy; by 1970 this industry was contributing seven percent of South Africa's GNP and accounting for fourteen percent of total investments.[32] More to the point of our concerns, foreign automobile manufacturers have become deeply involved in business relationships with the South African government's strategy for internal security and military defense. In South Africa the majority population is considered not only as a political opponent but a potential military enemy. Therefore, the direct contribution by Ford and General Motors to the South African security apparatus—in terms of increased sales of armored trucks, tanks, troop transport, and all variety of vehicles to the military and police—has invidious implications for the domestic affairs of that troubled country.

South Africa realizes the importance of research for economic growth, but also recognizes that it is too small to support the costs for its own effort to advance science and technology. Connection with foreign science and technological research is vital. One sector of the South African economy which has been as a substantial beneficiary of United States and Western Europe activities there is the arms industry. The country is virtually self-sufficient in production of all but the most sophisticated arms. A Stockholm research organization has estimated that South Africa's Western partners supplied it with at least $1.1 billion worth of war materials between 1965 and 1975. In flagrant violation of the 1964 UN embargo on arms to South Africa, the USA, France, Britain, Israel and West Germany continued openly and surreptitiously to arm the apartheid regime. Army Chief of Staff, General H. J. Martin, was quoted in South Africa's *Sunday Express* of December 22, 1968, as saying that South Africa was working on its own nuclear weapons. After India set off its first nuclear explosion in 1974, Dr. Louw Alberts, vice-chairman of South Africa's Atomic Energy Board, emphasized that South Africa is able to produce atomic bombs. "Our nuclear program is more advanced than that of India," he said, as the London *Times* of July 12, 1974, reported. It was estimated in August 1977 that South Africa is indeed on the verge of having an experimental nuclear device, and could test a hydrogen bomb trigger within eighteen months. Reportedly, by 1980 South Africa could jump into the H-bomb club. South Africa's budget for 1977–78 of $1.9 billion allocates eighteen percent of total for the military, up twenty-one percent over the previous year. Meanwhile, the government of Pretoria claims it could not find the fifty million dollars required to build the urgently needed 20,000 houses for African residents of Soweto.

Perhaps the bottom line in any analysis of American investment in South Africa as an accomplice to apartheid must come to rest on a very basic question: the contribution of economic enterprise and technology to coercion—coercion ultimately based on the ability of the government to subject the vast majority of its population to direct violence and terror, as a means of universally disenfranchising a distinct section of the populace as a public policy based on criteria of race and concepts of racism.

Last year the National Council of Churches made public documents which had come into its possession, but were previously considered confidential, that indicate that General Motors had entered into a covert contingency agreement with the South African military. The arrangement was made for American owned automobile plans to be converted to military use in the event of a national emergency. In 1967 the *Financial Gazette* reported in reference to Ford and GM that "[i]n times of emergency or war, each plant could be turned over rapidly to the production of weapons and other strategic requirements for the defense of South Africa." During World War II, Ford and GM plants were used for military production, assembling tens of thousands of vehicles and other equipment.[33] It appears that these corporate giants, with their monopoly of the auto industry, continue close ties with the ruling Nationalist Party. In May 1977, following the nationwide protest and resistance to apartheid initiated by the rebellion in Soweto, two important memos from the General Motors Corporation, previously secret, outline the company's contingency plans to be put into effect "in the event of civil unrest." The first of these memoranda was dated May 6, 1977, and the other July 20, 1977, from managing director of GMSA, W. C. Nott, to D. Martin, regional director for Africa in the U.S. They reveal clearly the close identity of interests between the South African government and a major U.S. investor.

General Motors has over $150 million invested in two plants in Port Elizabeth. It is instructive to note that, of more than 3,600 workers in both plants in 1977, only 432 were Africans. In a cover letter, Mr. Martin pointed out: "To avoid focusing attention on it, we are approaching this entire matter on a low-key, but maintain close liaison with the Civil Defense Authorities. Many management personnel have been briefed on the overall pattern of control and there is close cooperation between companies in the industrial areas."[34] The documents begin with an assessment that South African industry "is poorly prepared to handle industrial disruption and civil unrest," and reveal that the company has accepted the designation of GM facilities as "National Key Points" by the National Key Point Committee of South Africa. This means that plants will be placed at the disposal of the national authorities of the government when it declares the country in a state of emergency. Within the concept of these plans, plant personnel who have military training and who still have training commitments are encouraged by the authorities to join a local commando unit. Each of the plants will have one or more all-White male GM Commando units, even though the total number of White and Colored workers for General Motors are 1,744 and 1,464, respectively. To further emphasize the unequivocal racial focus of the plans, the document explains its primary assumption as follows:

> It is assumed that almost 100 percent of the White employment at GMSA would not be party to creating or stimulation civil unrest and that the populations groups would be African and Colored. The White employee group would not be party to such action and could be relied on to take action to contain it...pending the arrival of law enforcement authorities.[35]

These memos indicate that GM intends, on the occasion of domestic strife, to turn its White workers against Colored and African workers, and perceives the potential for social unrest in racial terms only. The managers of the auto company seem to relate the interests of the firm solidly with the minority regime, to the extent actually assuming that it would cooperate with South African troops in suppressing protest and political action by the African and Colored majority. There is no reflection of sympathy or understanding of the plight of these people and their demands for social justice. It is a sad commentary in American business leadership that the premier corporation of the United States would have such an unfortunate interpretation of social problems in South Africa and the responsibilities towards the people of that society. In 1971 eighty-six percent of American investors in South Africa told *Newsweek* that they favored apartheid. A director of Union Carbide told the same survey, "Majority rule would be bad for South Africa and bad for business." An executive of International Harvester said, "I have a lot of sympathy for what the government is trying to do—I wouldn't want hundreds of Africans running around in front of my house." We can continue this scenario through other major sectors of industrial investment in the economy, e.g., petroleum, mining, agriculture, construction, telecommunications, etc.—illustrating their institutional support directly, if not inadvertently, to minority rule in South Africa. But suffice it to say that it is widely acknowledged that the United States is deeply implicated in the structure of the South African state, by virtue of the significant foreign holdings in that country owned by American firms such as Ford and GM, while business publications like *Fortune*, *Business Week* and *Forbes* argue that their presence in South Africa is a positive factor in encouraging economic progress and the American philosophy of equal opportunity. They contend that as they contribute to economic growth, there is produced evolutionary change in social patterns which improves the welfare of all South Africans, and most especially the Blacks. *The counterargument is that there is not fundamental conflict between industrialization and apartheid.* Furthermore, the social, legal, and institutional rigidities in South Africa have led many people to question the ethics of investment there. Indeed, this is the heart of the debate over the divestment issue.

Much of the contemporary literature on South African political economy centers on the thesis that industrialization will undermine apartheid. The contention focuses on the debate over whether apartheid and industrialization can coexist in tandem, or whether the rationalizing force of capitalist development will ultimately modify the traditional principle of social organization that is embodied in apartheid. The most widely held view justifying continued investment in South Africa insists that fundamentally industrialization and apartheid are incompatible. The kernel of this position—often referred to as the "progressive force" argument—is that as investment and the GNP rise, so must the demand for African workers because of insufficient labor supply from the White minority. Consequently, the Africans will become more secure in the labor market. As their job status, income, and standard of living are upgraded, this will inevitably lead to full and equal integration into society on all levels. This being the case, apartheid will become increasingly irrelevant, as economic, political, and social distinctions fade into history. The belief that apartheid can be modernized out of existence rests upon assumptions about the historical roots and function of racial oppression in South Africa.

There are two primary factors presented to explain the development and persistence of discrimination against Africans and Asians in this country. The notion is that apartheid is pure race prejudice, and as such is regarded as essentially irrational behavior preserved by the abnormal degree of Afrikaner primordial attachments, stemming from cultural and social exclusiveness. The second factor purports to explain the motive for apartheid as a function of the desire of the White working class in South Africa to gain and protect a privileged position in the labor market. This is considered to be more rational than race prejudice in that with the economic expansion and increased productivity, White workers could be taught that there would be more in general; therefore, their living standard would not be adversely affected by greater inclusion of Africans. The essential flaw in this set of assumptions about racial domination in South Africa is its (incorrect) contention about the relationship between economic growth and racial oppression. It ignores what is in many ways a more basic force in the history of the country: the development of an economy based on cheap and powerless African labor. From this dimension of South African history, apartheid has been a sophisticated mechanism for regimentation and regulation of forced Black labor upon which the dynamism of South African capitalism has risen. There had been a great deal do consistency between economic development and the disenfranchisement of the Africans. "There is substantial evidence for the view that race relations in South Africa have in large part consisted of the imposition of new and more refines methods for forcing Africans to be at the disposal of White employers at low wages."[36]

Rather than acting as a liberalizing influence, economic growth has been accompanied by intensified repression of the African populace. For instance, between 1950 and 1975, direct investments in South Africa by U.S. corporations increased by more than one thousand percent. African wage rates, however, remained clustered around subsistence levels in all sectors, including manufacturing where U.S. investments are concentrated. The last ten years have seen intensification of political repression and land dispossession, the creation of the Bantustans and the exclusion of the Africans—all at the same time as there was rapid economic growth. There has been greater control rather than relaxation. It is so clear, from even the briefest examination of history, that the years of maximum economic growth have been also years of mounting political domination and economic exploitation for the great majority in South Africa. In 1969, the gap between the average monthly pay for South Africa's White and Black industrial workers was $259. By September 1975 the gap had risen to $453, despite wage increases. In 1975, the average Black industrial worker was earning $125 a month[;] his White counterpart earned $589. The poverty datum line, that is[,] the absolute minimum income on which a family can survive, was calculated at $149 a month for a Black family in Soweto in 1975.[37] In other words, by 1975 the average Black worker was still being paid less than survival wages, despite Polaroid's "reforms" and the wide-scale activities of U.S. corporations. It is also interesting to note that South African government propaganda has claimed that Black workers in South Africa are much better treated than in all other independent African states. Professor Julian Friedman refutes this assertion as erroneous in a comparative study done for the United Nations. His findings are that African workers in South African are actually in worse condition than in some other African countries.[38] The evidence supports an incontrovertible conclusion that apartheid and industrial capitalism have flourished in tandem, and the "industrialization undermines apartheid" thesis is not sustained. Perhaps the preoccupation in the literature with this thesis has not advanced our understanding of the peculiar character of racial capitalism in South Africa.

Over the past few years, in response to growing criticism of the role of U.S. investments in South Africa, there have been voices from within the business community that advocates the position that corporations could be persuaded to work determinedly for social justice. The hope would be that major companies would make a good faith effort to develop internal policies that would oppose apartheid. To date it is more wish than fact. The so-called "Sullivan principles," named after Rev. Leon Sullivan, a member of the Board of Directors of General Motors, pledge American firms doing business in South Africa to abolish discrimination among their workers. Professor Ferguson, a scholar with diplomatic experience in Africa, said in a recent issue of *Foreign Affairs*: "To expect business in South Africa to exert its influence to redistribute political power in a fashion which threatens its very raison d'être is to ascribe to that community an unwanted altruism."[39] A 1978 report of the Senate Subcommittee on African Affairs noted that "[c]ollectively, U.S. corporations operating in South Africa have made no significant impact on either relaxing apartheid or in establishing company policies which offer a limited but nevertheless important model of multi-nation responsibility."

The special challenge that the Southern African region poses to U.S. foreign policy derives from two aspects of the situation that have yet to be discussed with clarity in the policy debates.[40]

The first and most important of these factors in the fact that the fundamental dynamic in the situation is a contest for control of the South African state. This is a revolutionary struggle for sovereign power, and not one to implement "civil rights." The latter struggle cannot begin, realistically, until the elements that control the state commit themselves to the recognition of equal social, political and economic rights for all members of the South African society. Such recognition is absent from the present regime and counter its basic philosophy or to the version it has of its own security. The only social force in South Africa that is deeply committed to apply the precepts of the Universal Declaration of Human Rights to all South Africans is the exploited Black masses. Only when the state is responsible to them will there be a chance to see human rights implemented in South Africa. I believe that it is in the interest of the United States to encourage and speed up this process whereby the masses make the state accountable to themselves, and to promote such a process with a minimum of suffering and violence, but with a recognition, as well, that lack of such fundamental change also means enormous suffering and violence.

The second factor is the perception among the Western industrial powers that the mineral resources, economic continuity and location of South Africa are critical elements not only to each of them, specifically, but to their collective well-being. There is the assumption, reinforced by the perspectives engendered and propagated by the Trilateral Commission, that the Western industrial nations will rise or fall together. The relevance of South Africa to this perception is rooted only in the belief that were Communist states, White or Black, to gain a foothold in the area, important strategic resources would be denied to Western powers, and that were there to be any substantial disruption of the economic position of the privileged White communities in the Southern African states, the economic and social and thus political well-being of the Western world would be seriously harmed. There is the sense that, already quite apart from threats of Soviet gain, South Africa has become a structural source of tension in the political economies of Western states. The local White communities are seen as a surrogate for Western interests. There is too little faith in the possibility of mutually beneficial relations between Western states and future Black regimes.

Thus the growing priority of Southern Africa rests on the twin factors of the need for a genuine revolution in the political structure of South Africa, and the perception of a threat to collectively significant Western interest[s] by such a revolution.

This dangerous duality places the Western powers, [which] wish somehow to achieve a settlement in the region that is humane not only in its outcome but also in its methods, in the middle of the confrontation. Consequently, we meet with opposition and suspicion on both sides [: the] Blacks [...] charge, not without reason, that the Western states seem to place their priorities on preserving their capital and privileges enjoyed by their White kinfolk; [...] the Whites [...] charge that we interfere and hasten a social cataclysm "too ghastly to contemplate." The southern African situation seems to be one where the middle way is not the right way, the compromise solution is no solution, [and] where the internal settlement (which is limited by what the oppressive regimes feel is necessary to preserve their privileges and standard of living) is no settlement at all. Moreover, for the Western governments to take no action is not necessarily for the Western countries to be uninvolved, because private and business involvement in the South African system has become substantial. Government inaction may mean simply the continued reinforcement of Western supports to the oppressive regimes.

The ruling minority in South Africa is a racially exclusive group, drawing on the deepest felt traditions of religion and history to justify their self-definition. They are also extraordinarily rich, drawing on exclusive control of the state, and use of that control to regulate and exploit cheap labor in order to perpetuate their position. The Afrikaner believes in the so-called curse of Ham. He believes that his historic trials and victories are blessings of God and indications of his destiny to rule himself and dominate his laborers. They are not assimilable. He is an anachronism in the Western world, which, once, too, shared many of his basic beliefs, unfortunately, but which also learned that a deeper commitment to freedom and peace coupled with the dispersion of power among the formerly enslaved and colonized peoples made change necessary and possible.

The Afrikaners would not pose a serious threat to these deeper commitments in the Western world if they did not control the South African state, if they controlled a state with a territory more commensurate with the needs for a decent, but not super-privileged life of its four million members. The Afrikaner program for survival, "Separate Development," is neither separate, since the terms are dictated by the ruling minority, nor development, since the resource base available to the masses is so limited. The Western states can set the limits of their support for democracy in southern Africa at disengagement. To be genuine, this would require the withdrawal of corporate and non-governmental involvement. In that case the victory of the African masses would seem to be inevitable, though perhaps very costly in human lives and well-being, not only because of the violence required to overthrow minority rule, but because of the violence done to the population day-in-and-day-out so long as the present system lasts.

UNIVERSAL EDUCATION AND
NATION-BUILDING IN AFRICA[41]

JAMES TURNER

This paper is concerned with an analysis of facts socially relevant to the formative significance of compulsory education for nation-building—i.e., its relationship to political advancement and economic planning. Specifically, the focus is on primary education and political economy. Decisions about educational planning are of economic as well as political concern and consequences.

The basic proposition of the paper is that structural education—i.e., the educational system of a polity—has direct social relevance for political development in new African nations. It has been usually thought that schools are apart from politics, an agency to equip young people with the basic skills of literacy. Prima facie evidence shows that the critical role of education is societal adaptation to increase the role specialization and structural differentiation in the achievement of political capacity. It has generally been accepted as a truism that a primary need of African states during their post-independence period was for immediate and widespread programs of elementary education. Our hypothesis is that, contrary to the role of education in the technologically and industrially advanced states, compulsory primary education is politically dysfunctional for new African states and political unification.

A conceptual framework for studying social change is most important in the African context. The first priority of all African governments is to make societal communities of their new states. The combined disciplines of sociology and political science, and to a lesser extent that of economics, provide the analytical rubric. The theoretical approach is essentially structural-functional, as developed by Robert Merton.[42]

Our operational definitions are as follows: "Functions refer to those observable consequences or characteristics that relate to the adaptation of a system or relate to its maintenance and continuity. For characteristics that make for or aid in adaptation, the term 'functional' will be used, while the term 'dysfunctional' will refer to those which weaken or lessen the adaptation of a system."

Functional and dysfunctional aspects of the educational system will be examined only as they are relevant to political process and the social structure. Primary emphasis will be placed upon those educational functions directly concerned with the process of building a unified and viable national state.

AFRICAN SCHOOLS AS CHANGE AGENTS

The school in Africa is inevitably an agent of change. Most of the leaders of national independence movements were African intellectuals, as well as many of the rulers of the new states.[43] In recent years, increasing attention has been given to education as a process for change in social relations and a primary mechanism for nation-building. African states, for the most part, expanded the overall provision of education with considerable enthusiasm and expectation. There seems to have developed in Africa a "mystique" of education: "With the popular faith in the efficacy of education as the motor of social improvement, it is not difficult to understand why the control and planning of education became, often even before independence, a political issue of crucial magnitude."[44]

It is true that education is an essential factor in the modernization process, and for affording the people the advantage of participation in the technological activities of the modern world. Nationalist movements produced at least two crucial political and sociological changes: (1) an end to overt colonialism and a shift of state power; (2) rising social expectations on the part of the people. Millions of Africans perceived education to be the primal achievement as a passport to a better life and the higher standard of living promised as the objective of the struggle for national independence. Of course, this notion of the central importance of education for social improvement and economic opportunity has been cultivated during the colonial experience, but has been intensified with a new sense of legitimacy following political independence. The growing quest for education demanded a rapid expansion of educational systems in most new African states, particularly on the primary level. Political leaders who wished to stay in power had to comply with this major public pressure for increased educational opportunities, even though the educational system absorbed a disproportionate amount of the budget, and such a program might put an undue strain on the financial capabilities of the country; the demand could be met only at the expense of other areas of national economic development, and other forms of investment. But most, if not all, political leaders accepted the axiom that education is the basic component in nation-building and thus the foundation from which the economic progress of Africa would spring. The reasoning was patent: in a modernizing society where personal achievement tends to supersede and replace ascribed status and primordial relations, only education could open the door to political participation, social opportunities, and economic advancement. Education, then, was to be the panacea, though the precise relationship had not been fully worked out.

> The existing statistics studies apply to the well-developed countries where data is [sic] available. Although little is known at present about the role of education in lifting an economy at an early stage of development, there is a presumption and a certain amount of historical evidence that education is one of the main prerequisites to the movement forward into sustained growth.[45]

It would be expected, in view of the scarcity of available financial resources, [that] the African governments would allocate funds with greater certainty concerning the best possible economic return. But, as in all governments, political considerations interfere with planning. Political leaders in Africa feel a sense of urgency about eliminating the stigma of illiteracy which makes their countries appear inferior and offends their senses of national and human dignity. Education is not only viewed as the key to technological modernization, but also as an effective means by which to diffuse a sense of African dignity, produce feelings of national spirit and identity, and create an atmosphere for political integration.

> [T]he school emerges as the heart of the civic education of the political community....In all cases the school system is the basic factor in the development of civic interest and loyalty, and the chief instrument for that purpose.[46]

From a general sociological perspective, the emergence of the modern state depends essentially on the universalization of citizenship. African education has to be especially concerned with children and young people as future citizens of modern states. There are some tasks of socialization performed by the school which relate directly to political loyalties. Mobilization of African communities to take part in the social transformation that followed political independence could be greatly facilitated by expanding educational facilities to increase the level of popular political consciousness. Literacy is the key to wider communication with the people. Such development, however, poses a growing political dilemma for African governments and ruling parties. "As political awareness grows with education so too do economic anticipations."[47]

It is the relationship of this growing politicization, particularly of the urban-dwelling population with at least primary education, and their increased economic expectations to political development, which is the concern of this paper.

UNIVERSAL PRIMARY EDUCATION IN AFRICA AND POLITICAL DEVELOPMENT

During the terminal stages of colonialism, education was highly valued as an indispensable base for all progress; and this value was carried over and elaborated during the immediate post-independence period. "This faith in education is a fundamental datum which any calculation about Africa's future must reckon with."[48] The spectacular achievement of independence by relatively few educated Africans gave greater credence to the benefits to be derived from mass education, and made it difficult for Africans to accurately and objectively assess the appropriate place of education in the broader spectrum of economic planning and political and social construction. Most African leaders had been educated in Western Europe or America and had become firmly convinced that compulsory education was the sure road to political democracy, social equality, and governmental efficiency. Furthermore, they were aware of the literacy gap between the so-called modern world and Africa. The familiar orthodoxy was that education would reduce cultural fragmentation and local parochialism within a larger cultural matrix, and is required for development of Africa's manpower needs necessary for economic and political development. Generally speaking, African nationalism has been a populist movement, proclaiming the "rights of man" and advocating a sense of national solidarity predicated upon a common education available to all. Education became virtually an individual right, an opportunity intimately linked with building a sense of nation. But there is evidence of a difficult and expensive lesson about the role of educational expansion and politics in the growth of young African nations.

> Earlier optimism concerning the inevitable returns to investment in schooling is now being replaced by a more guarded attitude concerning the possible role of education in development. The rapid expansion in primary school provision has created a new and formidable problem, that of unemployment among individuals with a few years of basic schooling. Paradoxically, at the same time that the new states argue for a major effort in the provision of schooling, they are unable to utilize its products effectively in the context of development.[49]

In sum, it is evident that education is as critically important a factor in economic change in Africa as it has been in political change. But serious errors in planning have been made by assuming that rapid and spectacular consequences in economic development and political advancement can come from education. Nigeria is a classic illustration of such erroneous planning, which precipitated a dysfunctional relationship between universal primary education and political advancement and economic development.

COMPULSORY UNIVERSAL EDUCATION IN NIGERIA, AN ILLUSTRATIVE CASE

Beginning about mid-1952 politicians in Southern Nigeria began to call for free, universal, and compulsory education. S. O. Awokoya, then Minister of the western region, warned that "education development is imperative and urgent. It must be treated as a national emergency, second only to war. It must move with the momentum of a revolution."[50]

The next year, the eastern region Minister of Education R. I. Uzoma, presented his government's education policy, emphasizing universal primary education [U.P.E.]. By January 1955, U.P.E. was begun in the western region. From 1954–1955, primary school enrollment rose enormously: "from 457,000 to 811,000 (or from 35 percent to 61 percent of the 5–14 age group), the number of primary school teachers increase from 17,000 to 27,000 and primary schools rose from 3,550 to 6,270."[51] The regional government's spending on education increased from £2,223,000 in 1953–1954 (35 percent of total expenditure) to £5,359,000 (47 percent of the total expenditure) in 1954–1955.[52] Two-thirds of this increase in local government spending was for primary school grants-in-aid. During the 1955 school year, the western region spent £2.4 million on construction of primary school buildings and a total of £5 million for the four-year period between 1954 and 1958. Two years later, the eastern region abolished all primary school fees, and primary school enrollment between 1956 and 1957 rose from 775,000 to 1,209,000 (or from 48 percent to 73 percent of the age group). The number of primary school teachers increased from 29,000 to 40,000 and primary schools from 5,060 to 6,986. Spending for education rose from £3,573,000 in 1956 to £5,000,000 by 1957, the greater part of total expenditures going to primary school education. Primary school expenditures alone increase from £2,102,000 to £4,449,000, representing about one-third of the region's total budget.[53] The Nigerian political leaders were convinced that widespread literacy was essential for a functioning democracy and an effectively modern polity. Universal primary education as a political creation served to relate the political leaders with the masses; it was a classic example of welfare politics. However, with each passing year, the financial cost of education on central and regional governments was becoming an increasing burden. The governments in both regions were soon compelled to ask their people to pay for "fee-free education." The government levied a raise in education rates. The levy was not received well by the people, either too poor or unwilling to sacrifice for education. After all, the politicians had created considerable fanfare over their promises of free primary education.

Anti-tax riots broke out in some parts of the western region. The discontent caused serious political defeat for the ruling political party—the Action Group—in the western region, and played a part in the decentralization of power. In the eastern region, though the government temporarily avoided the embarrassing issue of payment (fees were eventually reintroduced in the eastern region), it became fiscally irresponsible, which led to significant political ramifications. In the East, Nigerian leaders began, for the first time, to refer to primary education as an "unproductive social service" and to express concern over "political problems of unemployment in the future." The region's dilemma was pointed out by Alvan Ikoku, a member of the Eastern House of Assembly.

> Before the new Constitution came in, North and West were getting more farms, roads, and attention to their cash crops than the East. The East was paying more attention to opening schools and hospitals. So they outpaced us in their economic development and we outpaced them in our social development and services. The result [of] the division is that we have to foot a heavy bill for social service.[54]

Also, the problem of education finance had the effect of intensifying Catholic-Protestant rivalry and projecting it to the center of the political spectrum with consequent effects on the unity of village life, the effectiveness of local government councils, the nature of electoral campaigns (the composition of the NCNC leadership was altered), the views of political leaders, and the general effectiveness of many of the major decisions made by the regional government.

As Nigerian politicians came to power, they became directly responsible for the consequences of their actions and could not dismiss as easily the British warning over dangerous effects of rapid educational expansion. Education competes for limited resources with other forms of investment, and educational expenditures must be justified by some form of economic return. Moreover, the very magnitude of U.P.E. confronted Nigeria's political leaders quickly with politically explosive questions of how to pay for a scheme which cost far more than they had envisaged and which was producing primary school graduates faster than the economy could absorb them.[55]

> Now a little more than ten years after Awokoya's stirring statement of intention, some disquietude has begun to appear. No longer do people tend to give unqualified approval to all kinds of educational expansion. Reservations about what has happened and about some existing plans derive from several sources and take on different forms. The most evidently dismaying fact is that primary school leavers are piling up in towns where not enough employment opportunities exist for them and where they are straining housing and water supply facilities, burdening ill-paid relatives and turning to delinquency. Politicians have begun to sense this situation as a potential source of social trouble. Just behind this issue lies the vast percentage of the Nigerian budgets (well over 40 percent of the Eastern and Western budgets) that is being spent on education, particularly primary education. The money so spent is being withheld from industrial and agricultural investment that might provide an increased national income and more jobs. Also, the quality of the primary system has been called into question.[56]

The growing concern of Nigerian politicians over mounting unemployment among young people was indicated in the 1960–1965 development plan which displayed an increased interest in agriculture, commerce, and industry as opposed to the 1955–1960 plan which stressed the social services. But in spite of substantial school fees in 1961, education in the eastern region took 45 percent of the budget, and its recurrent costs are rising despite efforts to curb educational expenditures. The 1964 revenue and expenditure projections point to 60 percent of the budget going into education. Furthermore, the pattern of educational development in Southern Nigeria has ruptured the nexus between primary schooling and salaried employment.

> Given the sluggish rate of growth in lower job opportunities in the modern sector of most African territories, it is probable that any nation which succeeds in expanding its primary school enrollments beyond 50 percent will be faced with growing unemployment among school leavers.[57]

It is not too great an overstatement to refer to Nigeria as the India of Africa in reference to the educated underemployed and educated unemployed. Also, the pattern of educational development in Nigeria contributed to the growth of ethnic consciousness; ethnicity grew parallel to the development of the nationalist movement. Voluntary associations and tribal unions grew up, whose origins derived largely from the realization by a few literate members that their groups were behind some other group (or groups) in respect to schooling, which facilitates propensity to explain events in ethnic terms. "Nigerians and their leaders do not as yet look up to the schools as instruments for the conscious fostering of a Nigerian consciousness or solidarity."[58] Ethnicity and urban unemployment, and their resultant societal problems, play no small role in the current tragic political conditions in Nigeria. It is evident that at the stage of her economic development, Nigeria cannot afford free universal primary education. Attempts to institute it arise from erroneous educational thinking, political planning, and lack of economic foresight. Scarce resources have to be apportioned according to certain investment priorities that will have the effect of directly stimulating economic growth and increasing political capacity. The goal of universal primary education may eventually be more securely reached when it is not hastily pursued, but perceived as a progressive development to be coordinated with other aspects of economic planning and political development. In attempting to use educational expansion as an impetus to broad political development and economic productivity, greater cognizance must be given to the basic fact that the proportion of population inputs into the educational system that will be economically productive is a function of both the level and rate of development.

THE IMPACT OF EDUCATION UPON SOCIETY-POLITY RELATIONS

To be sure, our underlying interest in the role of education in political development does result in our giving somewhat more attention to the consequences of educational process for the polity than we give to the influence of political factors upon education. It would seem that attempting to analyze the relationship of different educational patterns of development to political consequence amounts to treating educational systems as independent variables and political systems as dependent variables. In fact, the educational system is a creation of the polity.

> The tendency to exaggerate the determinative role of one particular variable among a number of interrelated variables is common in the social sciences and is most marked in special efforts to give high visibility to a previously underemphasized variable.[59]

However, the relationship between education and polity is one of recipro-cal dependence, "of mutual stimulus and response." Since this paper takes as its focus the impact of education upon the polity, our primary concern is with the political burden and tension created by educational imbalance in developing countries. Certain patterns of educational inputs have demon-strably had political destabilizing consequences for recent African states. But greater attention to education as an instrument to be manipulated and interrelated to all aspects of economic development in political planning can lead to greater control and direction of social change with a minimum of political vulnerability.

> Deeper insight into the circumstances under which particular educational patterns lead to undesirable political consequences may also provide guide-lines for development planning, for determining what educational 'mix,' what educational pyramid, what curricular content, what timing and spac-ing of educational inputs will be supportive of the interrelated development of society, the economy and polity.[60]

In Durkheim's terms, an educational system is both the product of a given society and the institution that determines the society will endure. Howev-er, the specific task of education in developing states differs from the role of education in the developed and technologically advanced countries. In the latter, progress in economy and society proceeded development in ed-ucation, but in new African states the situation is almost in reverse order; educational systems must be geared to a future objective, to a society and an economy as yet undetermined. The burden of socialization of schools in young African states is also heavy because of the absence or undevelop-ment of other cultural agencies. In modern industrial countries, the school had only a modest socialization task to perform; it mainly supplemented or embodied influences readily and abundantly available outside the school.[61]

The political development process is an interminable interaction among the processes of differentiation, equality, and the integration and adaptive capacity of a political system. Change and increase in any one of the processes has a concomitant affect for change and increase on the other processes—i.e., increased capacity may lead to or require greater differen-tiation and less inequality. This conception of the political development process involves a notion of a development syndrome comprised of three primary principles:

> 1. Differentiation, as the dominant empirical trend in the historic evolution of human society; 2. equality as a core ethos and ethical imperative pervad-

ing the operative ideals of all aspects of modern life; and 3. capacity, as not only the logical imperative of system maintenance, but also the enhanced adaptive and innovative potentialities possessed by man for the management of his environment [human and nonhuman] through increasing rationality, applied science and organization technology....In these terms, political development can be regarded as the acquisition by a political system of a consciously sought, and qualitatively new and enhanced political capacity as manifested in the successful institutionalization of (1) new patterns of integration regulating and containing the tension and conflicts produced by increased differentiation, and (2) new patterns of participation and resource distribution adequately responsive to the demands generated by the imperative of equality.[62]

The potential integrative role of education in nation-building and political development is widely acknowledged. Literacy, as well as attitudes congruent with modernization, is crucial for effective political penetration by government as well as for meaningful citizenship. Education has a cardinal role in producing the skilled manpower and organization necessary for modernization; i.e., modern communications systems are made possible by mass literacy. However, rapid educational expansion may also have disunifying consequences which, in the short run, may outweigh the integrative expectation on which such integration has been predicated. Premature and extravagant effort to impose or realize equality may so disperse meager resources that the capacity of the system is severely limited, if not terminally damaged. The essentially significant factor is whether equality or capacity receives primacy in ultimate political decisions. Most African governments are caught in cross-pressures, which, ironically, demand simultaneously the burdening of the educational system, especially at its base, and the achievement of rapid economic development.

The ability of a government to establish and sustain a program of social and economic development is greatly improved, in the short run, if it can focus its resources on both human and physical "centers of strength." The consequence of educational expansion—with the limited absorptive capacity of most West African economies today—is to aggravate the problem of unemployed students and second-generation aspirants. There is little benefit to be gained from turning out graduates for whom the labor market is not ready, who will then become frustrated and disaffected. There is much to be gained by conserving academic resources for spheres more immediately vital to the economy. African economies are still very largely imposed upon subsistence agriculture and pastoralism, and only a small fraction of the total population is engaged in wage and salary employment.

> Part of the difficulty of absorption is due to the education system producing the wrong kinds of education. The balance between primary, secondary and higher education; between general and vocational studies; between humanities and science; or between institutional and in-service training—all these need to be blended in the right proportions if education is to be a help rather than a hindrance to economic development.[63]

The widespread assumption that there is a direct relation between education and upward mobility derives from the fact that in most developing African states there is a very close association between education and occupational mobility. This is the consequence of the weakness of the private sector, from the fact that most opportunities for salaried employment are in the government service, and from the fact that recruitment in service emphasizes educational qualifications.

> In most contemporary African states, employment opportunities within the modern economic sector are dominated by the demands of government and other public agencies. This bureaucratization of the employment structure confers a high premium upon educational qualifications.[64]

Philip Foster (1963) further concludes that "that the association of limited employment opportunities in the modern sector of the economy, the domination of these opportunities by government agencies, with the lack of ancillary mobility mechanism, places a far greater premium upon possession of formal education than characterized Western economies at earlier stages of their economic development."[65] The symbolic significance of education in political development for African countries is explained by one writer: "To newly independent nations, education, particularly in its higher levels, is a symbol of national prestige in much the same manner as a steel mill."[66]

The built-up bureaucratization of the occupational structures in African states as a result of predominating rationalization of educational criteria during early stages of development can lead to the polity being shaped by bureaucratic dominance. The consequence of bureaucratic expansion, especially during early phases of the political system, is political weakness. "Premature or too rapid expansion of the bureaucracy when the political system lags behind tends to inhibit the development of effective politics."[67]

The extent of bureaucratic involvement in politics of developing African countries is exceptionally high. Such structural imbalance in the polity can, and usually does, lead to administrative bottleneck (the condition is accentuated when there is inadequate modern organization technology, which is much the case in Africa), economic inefficiency and ineffective political planning and operations, which lead to general social stagnation. There is also the potential for severe rigidity in social mobility and class cleavage. "Bureaucracy constitutes a special sub-cultural segment—the high prestige strata of the society."[68]

However, the problem of dysfunction is not wholly or even mainly one of structural imbalance in the polity. The main limitation on the absorption of the educated in Africa is their high price relative to average national output per member of the population. In African countries where most people are illiterate, the primary school graduate whose only skills are reading and writing commands a wage disproportionately higher than a farmer's income in terms of the value of their respective contributions to national development. Farming is the essential sector of virtually all African economies. The output of the educational system is comparatively more costly in new nations.

> A university graduate who in a rich country, commences at a salary about equal to a miner's wage, may in a poor country receive five times a miner's wage. In consequence, all production or provision of services which depends on using people is much more expensive, in relation to national income, in poor than in rich countries. The poor countries may need the educated more than the rich, but they can even less afford to pay for or absorb large numbers.[69]

In the United States, for example, the cost of eight years of primary education for every child is about 0.8 percent of the national income; in Ghana it is 2.8 percent and in Nigeria, 4.0 percent. One of the primary reasons for the greater cost of education in the African countries is that, while the average salary of primary school teachers in the United States is less than 1½ times per capital national income, in Ghana and Nigeria a primary school teacher gets five and seven times, respectively, the per capita national income. If the cost of education is to be kept within taxable capacity, to allow for sufficient investment in social overhead capital for economic advancement, widespread provision of education belongs to a stage of development where the premium for education has already diminished to reasonable proportions.[70] Considering the high cost due to the high ratio of teachers' salary to average national income, the time it takes to train large numbers of teachers properly (so that quality is not sacrificed, as was true of the Nigerian case), and the subsequent high cost of employing and utilizing the educated product, the goal of universal primary education might be better set for twenty years ahead or more, rather than for the immediate future as proclaimed in the zenith of the independence movement. Distribution in the occupational structure in developing African countries should be a function of the level of economic development.

Africana Studies and Research Center faculty, students, and members of the Black community in Ithaca on a study abroad trip to Ghana, West Africa, ca. 1970.

Current educational development at the present state of development in most of West Africa, with Guinea in some respects an exception, has been malintegrative in the modernization process in at least two principal ways: (1) education tends to perpetuate the elite-mass gap; (2) education tends to facilitate and even exacerbate, division among different ethnic, regional, and parochial groups, which is dysfunctional for political unification. The characteristic result of dispersion of educational facilities in a decentralized educational system, in culturally fragmented societies where primordial ties tend to remain transcendent, is proliferation into an increasing number of separate units tending to strengthen ethnicity and regional parochialism.

However, quite to the contrary, it is education's role in nation-building to forge a larger sense of national identity.

EDUCATION, SOCIAL MOBILITY, AND STRATIFICATION IN AFRICA

An important aspect of the colonial legacy for societal advancement in Africa is the uneven impact of development on different ethnic or static groups, or in different regions. It is an empirical fact that some groups, areas, and individuals are at independence more developed and have an inherent advantage over those that are less developed.

> It is a sad fact that once the process of development starts in one sector of a society the inequalities within that society tend to increase.... Trade, labour and enterprise are apt to move toward progressive areas, leaving the poor zones still poorer.[71]

The unevenness was caused by a number of factors—i.e., the differential capacity or receptivity to education on the part of indigenous cultural groups, the favoring of one group or area against another by the colonists and in many instances the result of the fortuity of the impingement of modernizing influences. Whatever the reasons, expansion of occupational roles in the modern sector of African countries after independence has been characterized by a gross imbalance in status and social positions. The skewing of social development of unequal advantage in favor of already better-developed demographic groups or geographical regions is the essential dilemma facing African governments. The struggle to counter, correct, or to maintain the social imbalances is often at the center of the domestic political spectrum in the new African states. The basic question facing the new states in Africa is whether to emphasize equality or capacity. The process of uneven development tends to continue according to its own logic and dynamic unless deliberate measures are taken to apply opposing influences. The most widely accepted premise for political development has been egalitarian political policies and provision for equal access to education. But it is the suggestion of this paper that by emphasizing capacity in social and political development it is more functional for political unification, economic growth, and general nation-building. The proposition is that capacity will produce greater equality if resources are also deliberately allocated to ensure regional equality and also to spur advancement in the less-developed areas.

Social mobility in Africa is often marked by generational discontinuity. After the wave of Africanization following independence, first-generation elites were brought into available upper-level occupational positions. But because economic development had not kept pace with the production of potential elites, and because of the preemption of political and bureaucratic structures by the incumbent group, who became entrenched, the channels for upward social and political mobility have been drastically restricted for second-generation aspirants. There develops a bureaucratic-authoritarian tendency which is detrimental to social democracy; competitive politics as a vehicle for political mobility is progressively diminished. Ironically, the frustrations and disaffection of second- and third-generation aspiring elites are accentuated and aggravated by the extraordinarily high rate of upward mobility of the preceding generation. On the other hand, the incumbent, older generation of political and bureaucratic elites in control of state power fear displacement by or loss of power to a new class of better-educated technicians and managerial and administrative specialists.

> When an essentially static society marked by widespread illiteracy and a predominance of ascriptive criteria moves toward a dynamic and modernizing society where education is the principal criterion of upward mobility and stratificational position, each successive wave of better educated persons presents a challenge to his predecessor. This phenomenon largely explains the prevalence of generational discontinuity.[72]

The relationship between the two elite groups is critically determinative of future political development in many, if not most, African countries.

UNEMPLOYED SCHOOL LEAVERS AND THE ANOMIC POTENTIAL

Aside from the costs of universal primary education, if attained with the speed projected by its political advocates, it raises the problems of absorption of the enormous output. Unemployed school leavers are essentially an extension of the generational discontinuity phenomenon among elites downward into the mass stratum of the population, "Throughout West, East, and Central Africa today—at a time when all of these countries want to quicken the pace of development—masses of young people"[73] are crowding the cities in search of work that for the most part is nonexistent. Many of these job seekers and aspirants to modern, urban life began their education when the main determinant of high occupational status and social mobility was a primary school certificate, but by the time they finished, economic, political, and social conditions had changed drastically.

> The problem in an important sense is often created by the introduction of mass primary education mainly for political considerations. Subsequently, a gross imbalance has tended to develop between the great expansion in the educational system and the comparatively limited growth in the economy and in the occupational structure. The result is a vast and nearly uncontrollable school leavers [sic] whose political orientation toward the polity is marked by disaffection and alienation, and whose behavioral disposition is basically anomic.[74]

African politicians are becoming very aware of the jobless semi-literates who represent a potential for political eruption and social instability. The question is whether individual countries have the capacity to achieve the higher rate of economic progress necessary to match the expectations people have of improvements in their living standards, as well as keep abreast of the rising rate of population increase—which is estimated at two to three percent a year for most of the countries in Africa. At least one observer thinks that "this type of unemployment…is not self-correcting, nor will any simple expedient solve it."[75] The value of literacy has been reduced and no longer commands or carries the high premium it once did because of expanded educational systems, and it becomes increasingly difficult to secure wage or salary jobs in the modern-market exchange sector of the economy. Primary school leavers are imbued with extravagant expectations and considerably estranged from indigenous traditional culture and rural farm life in societies where the agricultural sector of essentially export economies engages 75 percent or more of the working population. The economy depends on one or two primary cash commodities that earn well over half the total national earnings from world trade. The widening gap between African background and primary school milieu and socialization, and alienation of African school children from traditional rural life is socially, economically, and politically dysfunctional for political development and economic advancement. For in a predominantly agrarian society most primary school leavers are needed to improve local agricultural skills, technology, and production. But seeking livelihood and living space outside the rural farm area will cause serious overcrowding of the urban areas and burden the government further with heavy expenditures it can ill afford for amenities.

The Ashanti survey, conducted shortly after World War II, produced evidence that 95 percent of the boys who completed primary and secondary schools went to the towns and would not follow traditional rural occupations, even in an area as rich as Ashanti.[76] Similarly, a Nigerian leader complains of the problems caused by this migration syndrome:

> Our people are lethargic about agriculture. To our school children, in our primary and secondary schools, when we talk of going back to the land it seems to them like a fairytale because we have been so saturated with the colonial type of education, which is the education on pen-pushing. There is no technical touch in our education system, it is all pen-pushing and recitation—so that when we talk about going back to the land, even our sons laugh at us.[77]

The most serious long-run sociopolitical problem facing African countries is unemployment among school leavers.

CONCLUSION AND OBSERVATION

New African states are currently engaged in the task of nation-building, which requires the evolution of political procedures adequate for successful interaction of all sections of the polity. Parochial particularisms must be replaced in the political sphere by national ideology, which can raise the level of political culture by developing among the populace a level of political action and political commitment to a societal entity that transcends primordial ties.

Proper socialization of the members of society is essential to the social unity upon which effective political institutions must rest. The rapid expansion of the educational program tends to produce short-run misallocation of resources, excess capacity, and certain forms of human capital that cannot be employed fully with political consequences of great concern. Because of the predominance of government in economic development in new African states, the governing politicians are provided with the opportunity to manipulate the disposition of students.

Also, the government can regulate the output of the educational system to correlate with opportunities in the occupational structure and in accordance with manpower needs for overall societal development. The needs of the new states are for progress in industrialization and rationalization of agriculture, and to reduce the politically destabilizing aspects of educational development. Cognizance must be taken of education's function as both a consumer good and a production good in the polity.

The development of modern industries is a slow process, and it is futile and erroneous to propose that heavy investment in education by itself is an adequate means of promoting effective developmental objectives of a new country. Investments must be increased in areas other than education in order to create nonhuman capital that will provide employment opportunities for school leavers and social overhead capital for investment in the improvement of the social, cultural, and material environment—i.e., roads, buildings, market centers, communications, and transportation equipment. This will facilitate technological development, increase agricultural production, and, very conceivably, attract a more highly skilled labor force to agriculture as the population comes to think of primary education as compatible with a higher level of farming organization. Historically, societies have developed politically when predicated upon a solidly productive and advanced agricultural sector. Without these concomitant changes in the society, through political direction and social engineering, education will not live up to the expectations for it. Rather than serving as a vehicle for economic advancement, excessive diffusion of primary education may be a hindrance because of its diverse impact upon political stability. Further, investment in educational development will realize the best returns, in terms of beneficial social effects, when industrialization and urbanization have complementary development. Deliberate development of the major resources available in a developing African country, in a uniform and coordinated system, is likely to have more favorable political consequences than insisting on a large-scale primary education, or on a crash program producing a large reservoir of high-level manpower.

PART V

THE POLITICS OF RACE

Dr. Turner is all about seeing all of us strive to make our own paths: showing us how to never to be silent when it counts. From the moment I walked through his office doors in 1996, Dr. Turner let me be the Black Puerto Rican woman that I am. I could write about the Young Lords Party and engage in passionate debate with intellectual integrity. He taught me to trust my voice, my truth, and my politics. Dr. Turner's guidance and mentorship has kept me going in the rough times in this world of scholarship and activism.

—*Rosa Clemente*

As a scholar of Africa and the African Diaspora, Dr. Turner's conception of race has had a tremendous impact. Not only does my study of Rastafarian repatriation to Tanzania in the age of decolonization assume that the histories of Africa and its Diaspora are mutually constitutive, but it argues that race, long assumed to be solely a diasporic issue, is indeed relevant to African history. Turner's very definition of Africana demands a more expansive treatment of race in all its complexity: a globalizing construct and reality with local resonance.

—*Monique Bedasse*

James Turner and internationally renowned writer James Baldwin, artist-in-residence at the Africana Studies and Research Center, ca. 1970s.

INTRODUCTION: JAMES TURNER AND THE SOCIOLOGY OF RACE

ANTHONY P. BROWNE

RACE, RACISM, AND WHITE SUPREMACY

Throughout the African Diaspora, white supremacy and racism have had an enduring impact on virtually all aspects of political, economic, social, and cultural life. Since the seventeenth century, the socially and historically constructed European conception of race "created" an inferior group consisting of those phenotypically designated as African-descended and a superior group comprising those of European extraction. Subsequently, within this framework, Blackness became associated with bondage, inferiority, and social death, and whiteness with freedom, superiority, and life.

The United States was founded and structured on the ideology of white superiority and the divine right of domination and, thus, white racism. White supremacy as reflected in the "natural" basis of racial hierarchy was legitimated by academia through racial discourses in philosophy, literature, and the sciences that professed to be value-free. The philosopher Charles Mills discusses this ideology as a racial contract that has negatively affected non-European nations across the globe. The racial contract is the system of rules, laws, values, and understandings upon which the political system of white supremacy rests—that is, the exploitation of nonwhite peoples for the material, social, psychological, and cultural benefit of those who are white. Such a contract, by necessity, does not recognize people of color as having full rights as citizens or, indeed, as human beings. This is because the larger purpose of the contract is the differential privileging of the whites with respect to the "other" who experienced the exploitation of their bodies, land, and resources, and the denial of equal socioeconomic opportunities. In short, white supremacy can be thought of as the normalization of white racial domination. This normalization produces and reproduces myriad cultural, political, economic, and social advantages and privileges for the dominant group and limits such advantages and privileges for Blacks and those deemed "other."

A voluminous social science literature has irrefutably documented that racism and white supremacy are an endemic structural phenomenon, not simply at an individual level or an isolated occurrence in the past. That is

to say, racism consists of beliefs and institutional arrangements that reinforce the superiority and inferiority of racialized groups. As many scholars
have argued, racial outcomes are not primarily the product of individual
"racists" but of the institutionalization of racial domination into a racial
structure that shapes the life chances and opportunities of the various races
at all levels. Social patterns of inequality based on race are routine and standard in the functioning of our social system and are perpetuated through
media, texts, schools, language, laws, cultural traditions, and patterns of
interaction. For example, the racialized power exercised by Europeans encompasses the symbolic power to classify Blacks as an inferior "other," the
political power to preclude basic rights, the capacity to mobilize the resources of the state to enforce segregation and inequality, the social power
to deny inclusion in civil life, and the economic power to privilege whites
in jobs and wealth creation.

*Faculty member C. Dalton Jones in the classroom, teaching students
about the structures, pedagogy and education, ca. 1970s.*

However, despite inequities in power between dominant European groups
and people of African descent, racialized social systems are not fixed, and
neither are the ideologies that accompany them. Due to mass-based social
movements of the 1950s and 1960s, for instance, the racial structure of

the United States underwent a fundamental transformation that, after 350 years of struggle, led to the eradication of state-sponsored white supremacy. But racialized social systems like that in the United States possess the remarkable capacity to be resilient and the post–Civil Rights era spawned the development of more insidious forms of racism such as "color-blindness" that denied the existence of racism and would prove more challenging to combat.

TURNER AND AFRICANA SOCIOLOGY

The work of the noted Africana sociologist James Turner builds upon the tradition of an impressive group of Black sociologists, including W.E.B. Du Bois, Anna Julia Cooper, and Oliver Cox, who argued persuasively that comprehending the role played by race in social structure—in organizing myriad inequalities, in informing government policies, and in shaping identity—needs to be properly understood in order to substantively address its pernicious impact. His stature derives from authoring some of the seminal works in the field as well as the development of the Africana Studies and Research Center at Cornell, one of the earliest academic departments of its kind in the United States. The nascent Africana Studies movement of the late 1960s and early 1970s was often dominated by scholars in the humanities—namely, history and literature. But Turner's work along with a coterie of newly minted sociologists raised important questions that interrogated the nexus of America's capitalist political economy, white supremacy, Black working-class marginalization, and Black self-determination. This group developed a variety of theoretical and conceptual frameworks that included nationalist, Black Marxist, Afrocentrist, and Black feminist approaches to understanding the conditions that shape Black life. In doing so, they utilized social science tools to provide explanations that illuminated the process of social change, subordination, and resistance within and across the African Diaspora. Turner, like many of his colleagues, had long been dissatisfied with the major explanations of inequality offered by mainstream American sociology. Explanations based on flawed Eurocentric theoretical models that often focused on supposed deficits in the culture and social structure of African American communities. For example, many leading theorist of the time argued that Blacks did not value education and that matriarchal families were the primary causes of inequality. Instead, Africana sociologists, like their earlier intellectual forebears, undertook research that would counteract racism and improve the life circumstances of people of African descent by locating the underlying causes of persistent Black inequality in the racially based allocation of power, privilege, and resources. These interventions in the structures of knowledge provided a counter-narrative to the Eurocentric perspective that buttressed white hegemony while presenting itself as supposedly objective, scientific, and value-free.

Throughout his career, Turner's output represents a holistic approach that influenced at least four subfields in the discipline: the sociology of race; social stratification and inequality; political economy; and the sociology of power and resistance. Turner's corpus sought to facilitate a vigorous debate within the Africana and Black Studies movements regarding the crucial role played by structural forces—namely, the power of political, economic, and cultural structures in both constraining and enabling opportunities for those in the African Diaspora.

SITUATING THE ESSAYS UNDER REVIEW

Throughout the history of Blacks in the United States, scholars, activists, and writers concerned about the Black condition have offered a variety of approaches to ameliorating Black marginalization. The four articles reviewed in this essay appeared while critical questions were raised about the significance of race in the post–Civil Rights era. On the one hand, members of the dominant group asserted that Civil Rights legislation of the 1960s effectively ended racial discrimination and that any remaining inequality was due to shortcomings in the Black community. On the other hand, African Americans maintained that the Civil Rights laws addressed issues of liberty, not equality. As such, the long freedom struggle and the granting of civil rights did not address deep, racialized inequities rooted in more than three centuries of white supremacy. They maintained the inequities did not magically disappear with the Civil Rights legislation of the 1960s; but rather the impact of historic and contemporary political and economic inequality continued to be injurious to the life chances of African Americans.

James Turner at the State of Black America Conference, hosted by the African Studies and Research Center, ca. 1980s.

Turner and others argued persuasively that the freedom movement was defeated in its next phase as it shifted the focus from "liberty" to "equality," and sought the redistribution of wealth and power. This laid bare the racial commitments of the dominant group to preserving white supremacy and the attendant political, economic, social, and cultural structures that support its dominance. Turner's approach contributed to frameworks that facilitated the intersection of Pan-Africanist and African-centered Marxist traditions by providing a robust theory of social oppression undergirded by key concepts such as political economy, white nationalism, class struggle, displacement, and resistance. Turner elucidates how structures of white domination can shape the everyday existence of Black people, but he also provides a way forward by delineating how these structures and their inherent contradictions can assist in vigorously and forcefully resisting race and class oppression.

Accordingly, in the rest of this introductory essay, I will analyze the core arguments in the articles under review. I will examine empirical, methodological, and theoretical contributions, as well as limitations and directions forward. The conceptual tools deployed allowed Turner to focus on urgent questions impacting the Black condition, including the social effects of power differentials, the mechanisms by which social inequality is racialized and reinforced, and the macro- and micro-dimensions of modern racial inequality. These research questions continue to animate the work of scholars who probe the intersection of race, social structure, and power. In sum, Turner's work sought to initiate social change through intellectual leadership, which helped to foster the creation of new and richer interpretations of power dynamics, oppression, and social possibilities, all of which would inform a more practical and emancipatory political and social agenda.

Several interrelated themes emerge prominently in the four essays that shape Black life chances: the role of internal colonialism; the role of the Black middle class and Black capitalism; the impact of technology and displacement; and the impact of racism and white supremacy. Each will be addressed in turn.

INTERNAL COLONIALISM

Turner utilizes internal colonialism theory in the essay "Blacks in the Cities: Land and Self-Determination" to analyze the urban crisis, "the inherent political and economic contradictions caused by race and class oppression and exploitation" of people of African descent. He traces the trajectory of Black marginalization through time and space, from chattel slavery through sharecropping and the industrial economy of the northern cities. Each period is marked by virulent forms of white supremacy that consigned Blacks to the economic, political, and social periphery.

Turner's work delineates the centrality of internal colonialism theory in facilitating a comprehensive understanding of the oppression faced by large cross sections of the Black community. As applied to Black America in the 1960s and 1970s, internal colonialism theory also evolved in part from Marxism's engagement with the so-called "Black Condition." Despite later critiques by some social scientists about its applicability to the experiences of Blacks in America, Turner's conceptualization eschews the pitfall of other theorists by circumscribing internal colonialism as a *system* of inequality grounded in the lived experiences of the Black poor and working class, thereby acknowledging class cleavages in the Black community and the integration of the Black upper class into America's political economy. He defined internal colonialism as a *geographically based* pattern of racialized subordination by the dominant power for their material benefit. Turner's conceptualization of internal colonialism emphasizes the intersection among various elements of racial oppression—inequality, political marginalization, institutional segregation, and cultural domination. This subordination produces the outcome of *systemic and durable* inequality evidenced in policies and practices of myriad societal institutions, including systems of employment, education, health, cultural production, and finance. Then as now, the context of Black lower-class social oppression reflects this definition, including persistent patterns of inequalities in the areas of residential segregation, incarceration, wealth, education, health, and employment. These indicators of social well-being are also reflective of conditions faced by former colonies throughout the Black world.

As the essays demonstrate, Turner is at his most effective when he theoretically and empirically grounds his insights in the lived experiences of the most marginalized segments of the Black community. For activists, political leaders, and pragmatic scholars, however, the essays could have been made more indispensable if they outlined steps in the development of a bottom-up political movement that was capable, over time, of mobilizing support for public policy initiatives and Black-led approaches to alter the seemingly intractable patterns of racial inequality. Perhaps prescriptive recommendations were beyond the scope of the essays, and certainly no scholar can provide definitive strategies to bring about racial justice. Nonetheless, in the post–Civil Rights era, given the repression by the state during the Civil Rights and Black Power eras and the demobilization of social movements by many African Americans in favor of electoral politics, Turner's reimagining of new Black social movements would have been invaluable in providing a broad outline for a potent moral vision, broad-based mobilization, and feasible programs to tackle the plight of the Black poor and working classes.

THE BLACK MIDDLE CLASS AND BLACK CAPITALISM

The unprecedented class bifurcation in the African American community that occurred in the post–Civil Rights era continues to shape debates about race, social responsibility, and culture. As the Black middle class and upper class became ascendant politically, socially, and culturally, scholars like Turner critically assessed the broader implications of their rise in light of the pervasive discourse of post-racialism promulgated by the dominant group. In the essay "Implications of Class Conflict and Racial Cleavage for the U.S. Black Community," Turner sought to discern the consequences of this development particularly as it related to the Black poor and working classes. Turner was prescient in his observation that "if one projects this trend for two or three decades and takes even a cautious view of prospects for further improvement in educational and jobs opportunities available to the children of these years, the likelihood is that there will be a far more visible and influential black middle class by the end of the century than there is now." He proceeds to ask a salient question: What kind of power and influence will this new class exercise? He notes that "their status would rise, their degree of subordination would diminish, and their potential political influence will become substantial." But given the context of durable white nationalism, he cautioned that this new middle class would gain little control over the nation's productive wealth, and its economic power will therefore remain limited. Surely, neither Turner nor his contemporaries could have imagined the exponential increase among the ranks of the Black middle and upper classes, or the election of a Black president at the beginning of the twenty-first century.

The rise of the Black political and economic elite was concomitant with the erosion of life chances of the Black poor and working class. Turner provides a succinct historical account outlining the many commonalities between Black Americans and those on the African continent subjected to "external" colonization. His work advanced internal colonialism theory by documenting the movement from direct to indirect rule and the mechanisms used by dominant groups in this process. Turner's analysis also anticipated a phenomenon that would take root several decades later—which is the rise of the race-neutral bourgeois Black politician whose political orientation and governance often advanced the interest of the larger society over and against the interest of the Black masses—thus pointing to the fact that internal colonialism can also mean that members of the subordinate community may support the policy agenda of the larger society. Turner was quite perceptive is his comment that members of the Black upper class would increasingly gain political influence at the local and national levels but this power would largely support their class interest.

During the post–Civil Rights era, we have witnessed the ascent of race-neutral Black politicians who pursue racially diffuse electoral and governing strategies by avoiding issues specific to African Americans. While largely deemphasizing race, these candidates advocate universal policies they contend would benefit everyone, rather than any particular group.

Perhaps ironically, as many observers have concluded, these were often pyrrhic victories whereby as Black communities understandably basked in the symbolism of these candidates attaining office, their communities, however, received very little in the way of substantive public policy that would fundamentally address pressing social and economic concerns. A cursory review of Black social welfare indicators strongly suggests that this group has lost ground economically and socially as their communities during the post–Civil Rights have been marked by mass incarceration, underemployment, and joblessness.

An underdeveloped area in the essays centers on the role of the Black upper classes. In the context of the time they were written, a dominant strain of internal colonialism theory was rather dismissive of a progressive role that this class could play. Indeed, as members of this class actively participated in denigration of the freedom movement, the commodification and depoliticization of race consciousness, it was surely understandable that some would look askance at their possible contributions to racial justice. Yet, viewing the Black upper class through such a narrow lens, Turner's analysis obscures possible sources of resistance within the Black middle class that leaves no space for an African-centered Black middle class that would use its wherewithal in service of a more racially egalitarian society.

THE ROLE OF TECHNOLOGY AND DISPLACEMENT

Turner's work also highlights an issue that is often overlooked in discussions of race—that of the role of capitalist technology in constraining Black opportunities. In the essay "Blacks in the Cities: Land and Self-Determination," he posits that technology is rarely a neutral actor, in that it often represents the class and racial interest of those who control it. From the cotton gin to automation to telecommunications, Black labor has been disproportionately and adversely impacted because these developments gave capital greater flexibility from political and social constraints as it sought to maximize profit. By the 1970s, technological advances increasingly made cheap Black labor less crucial to the operation of American capitalism, with the result that for the first time in American history, segments of the Black population became "surplus labor." To be more specific, technology played a crucial role in hastening the collapse of the industrial economy, the relocation of jobs from urban centers, and the eventual globalization of production. In each of these interrelated developments, Black labor was most negatively impacted as the jobs lost were primarily unionized and were replaced—if at all—by poorly paid service work with minimal benefits and opportunities for advancement.

Turner's warning about the dangers of the redundancy of Black labor would later prove to be prophetic as mass incarceration increasingly became a tool to control Blacks locked out of the labor market. Policing and corrections would become prominent tools in the social control of Black populations designed to contain further uprisings, ensure a measure of social stability, and protect the economic and political interests of the dominant group. As a result, the state, during the post–Civil Rights era, moved from a rather nominal concern with the social welfare of Blacks to oppressive social control where criminality and deviance were racialized, creating a vicious cycle of punishment that further impoverished and marginalized large cross sections of Black poor and working-class communities.

RACISM AND WHITE SUPREMACY

The essay "Inequity in the System: Racism in American Society and on College Campuses" reflects a major theme in Turner's work that centers on understanding the roots of white supremacy, its pernicious impact, and strategies to mitigate its power. He writes that American history is replete with examples that show "a profound commitment to dividing society along racial lines with the intent of constructing a system that exploits African labor in order to maintain the power, privilege and prosperity of European Americans." Echoing W.E.B. Du Bois, Marcus Garvey, and Malcolm X, Turner observes that America's social system produces racialized consciousness, where most Americans view the world as natural—and influences beauty, status, prestige, and worldviews. Here Turner highlights how white supremacy not only silences the perspectives of Blacks, but also devalues them—culturally, aesthetically, intellectually. Therefore, given this systemic devaluation, people of African descent must resist the disempowering lens of white supremacy by developing an affirmative cultural identification with the African continent.

The educational system, Turner writes, is one of the major mechanisms in society that perpetuates and legitimizes white supremacy, race, and class inequality. This is largely unrecognized by many Americans and is perhaps most visible in narratives of success where the ubiquitous dominant ideology dictates that upward mobility is simply the result of individual effort and ability. This assumption reinforces the widely held belief that the relative material success enjoyed by whites is a function of cultural and behavioral differences—especially with regard to work habits, delayed gratification, persistence, and the value placed on education. This ideology not only reaffirms the status quo by erasing whiteness of its privileges, but also reinscribes widely held notions about supposed deficits of people of African descent as the primary causes in their continued inequality. In addition, given America's long history of white domination, Turner reminds us that education also plays a major socializing role in furthering Eurocentric hegemony by legitimating forms of knowledge, values, and traditions that are often detrimental to the social and psychological well-being of people of African descent. As a corrective, Turner—echoing the work of Carter G. Woodson, John Henrik Clarke, and Ron Walters—makes the forceful case that education must be utilized as an instrument of liberation. That is to say, given its enormous socializing power, educational institutions must remain contested spaces where African Americans continue to wage a struggle for the development of culturally relevant curriculum, to increase their social mobility and life chances, to develop their communities, and to affirm their humanity—often over and against a racist educational system designed to protect unearned white privilege.

The hostile climate that pervades many college campuses is representative of a contested space. Beginning in the 1980s, colleges and universities reported dramatic increases in racially motivated acts of hostility toward the Black presence at historically white institutions. Their presence was negatively framed as a result of lower admission standards, which in turn undermined the status and prestige of the institution. As a corrective, Turner suggests that white supremacy must be directly confronted to alleviate the racist climate and transform college campuses into spaces where Black students would thrive both academically and socially. In doing so, institutions must commit to substantially increasing the presence of Black students, faculty, and administrators, as well the institutionalization of robust Africana Studies departments. If fully implemented, these actions would undoubtedly revamp the structure of higher education while providing students with the cultural, intellectual, and practical tools to positively impact their communities. Nevertheless, the question remains, absent the use or threat of force, what consistent leverage can be deployed by Black students, faculty, administrators, and alumni to force colleges and universities to incorporate these socially necessary proposals.

Similarly the political system remains a site of struggle for African Americans in the quest for self-determination. Due to the vast inequities in power, the racial interest of the dominant group are protected by institutions and policies designed to safeguard their advantages. Within this vein, Turner indicates that the designation "post–Civil Rights era" is a tacit recognition of a milestone in the twentieth-century experience of African Americans as well as the recognition of the passing of a significant political era. In other words, the Civil Rights movement was aborted before it could effectively transform America's social, political, economic, and cultural institutions because Black advancement was framed as a threat to white interest. Toward this end, intellectuals and policymakers aligned with the dominant group and shifted the spectrum of American politics to a renewed radical conservatism that was insidiously and sometimes overtly aligned with reactionary white nationalism. Turner makes the case that white nationalists used race to shape the backlash campaign against the Black freedom movement as it began to address economic inequality. The dominant group feared that full equality would require a massive redistribution of wealth and power, which stoked considerable white anger, resentment, and fear that further Black progress would come at the expense of their privileged status. Consequently, white politicians in both major political parties used coded language—law and order, welfare, and big government—to appeal to their white constituents by framing Blacks as undeserving and dependent.

Turner was quite prophetic in noting that these were ominous reminders that America's racial dilemma remained unaddressed. In fact, as he concludes, the color line had been revitalized for the post–Civil Rights era. During this period, the ideology of color-blindness has been effectively mobilized to delegitimize discourses that regard racism as a persistent structural problem. Proponents assert the fundamental equality of all racial groups that not only includes rights, but also life chances. Therefore, subscribing to a post-racial, color-blind perspective allows members of the dominant white majority to contend that race no longer affects an individual's or group's social or economic well-being. Since it focuses on perceived individual and group shortcomings, the color-blind perspective is widely embraced by many whites who not only view themselves as politically progressive but also profess their adherence to an ideology that does not see or judge individuals by the "color of their skin." Those who support this premise, which essentially denies the existence of white privilege, also contend that race-based programs and policies foster racialized thinking and thus racial division, which is injurious to the social fabric. This articulation of color-blindness is a further reminder that the power relations that undergird white dominance persists despite the formal dismantling of state-sponsored white supremacy and is a sobering reminder that America will remain a racially unequal society as long as the political economy and culture reflect white hegemony.

JAMES TURNER AS SCHOLAR AND PUBLIC
INTELLECTUAL

The publication of these essays helped establish James Turner as a major public intellectual of the Black social condition whose work remains extraordinarily broad and influential. This impact extended far beyond the confines of the academic community and elevated Turner to the status of a widely read public scholar. Turner's corpus of scholarly material is distinguished as publicly accessible and intellectual, decades prior to the emergence of a more recent cohort of Black public intellectuals. As a public intellectual, he has spoken to countless community groups, civic organizations, and leaders throughout the African Diaspora, bridging the spheres of academia, community, and nation. Despite the increasing number of preeminent Black public intellectuals over the past two decades, Turner continues to stand without equal as one of few sociologists whose work informed the Black liberation struggle.

As the essays reviewed here demonstrate, within the Africana Studies movement, Turner has been a pivotal sociologist in making the case for the discipline's relevance for not only understanding the roles played by racism, capitalism, and white supremacy, but also in offering strategies to alleviate Black marginalization. The essays highlight Turner's theoretical and empirical research in various subfields that consistently address policy implications. He is a social scientist of provocative ideas and insights, with long-standing interests both in asking the right questions and in providing insightful explanations about the interplay of white domination and Black resistance across time and space. For more than forty years, his innovative sociological concepts and macro-sociological, historical, comparative, and trans-disciplinary theories have been cited, broadened, applied, translated, and used to explicate conditions in the African Diaspora. To be sure, Turner's work contributed greatly to the cross-fertilization of sociology, history, politics, and economics as he forcefully argued that understanding how social systems functioned was integral in the struggle for Black self-determination. If an overarching theme can be drawn from the preceding discussion, it is this: Those committed to social justice must remain vigilant in combating the legacy of inequality and injustice wrought by white supremacy that continues to undermine efforts to bring forth a more racially just and egalitarian society.

BLACKS IN THE CITIES: LAND AND SELF-DETERMINATION[1]

JAMES TURNER

> In the modern world, the era of neocolonialism, the class struggle has be-
> come a race struggle. In other words it is not only a class struggle, but racial
> too. Race forms the class struggle in the modern world.

> *—Kwame Nkrumah*

In any analysis of "the urban crisis in America," our point of reference must be the inherent political and economic contradictions caused by race and class oppression and exploitation of African people in the United States.[2] For the dialectics of these contradictions have moved the Black Liberation Movement to a struggle to confront the specific social and economic relationships on which the American political structure and economic system is based. The history of racism in American life reveals that there has been an elaborate conspiracy to deprive African people in this country of political rights and economic security through control of the land.

Today this process has manifested itself in the metropolitan cities in a new form of colonialism, organized as the urban ghetto. James Boggs describes this process: After centuries of the most ruthless exploitation of the land, first as chattel slaves and then as sharecroppers, Blacks have now been driven by the mechanization of agriculture into the major cities of the North. There they are herded and confined to segregated reservations (i.e., ghettoized slums), forced to make homes out of dilapidated dwellings that have been worn out by whites who have abandoned them for the suburbs to escape the expanding Black population.

Against these exploiters and overseers, the Black community is now struggling for its self-determination as a colony against an imperialist power; conscious that any serious improvement of the condition Black people depends upon their ridding themselves of the whole parasitical white structure comprised of a huge network of absentee entrepreneurs and administrators. This network includes landlords, merchants, realtors, racketeers, and politicians, union leaders, licensing and inspector bureaucrats, university and school administrators, doctors, lawyers, and policemen.[3]

In reconstructing and defining the nature of the Black man's condition in America, the United States must be seen as a colonial oppressor and Blacks "as a people within the territorial confines of the most powerful capitalist country in the world." However, in order to understand the situation of the African colony in this country today, it is necessary to understand the nature of colonialism. The major argument against the use of the colonial analogy as a model for analyzing the oppression of Black people is that the African community does not have separate territory. But separate does not seem to be the most essential factor in distinguishing a colonial situation.

The author uses the term *colonial people* rather than *colonial territory* since territory may be developed while the people become less developed. There is a kind of development of underdevelopment. Throughout American history, Blacks were never given access to large amounts of land, rural or urban. This is the essential social relations between a colonial people until the relationship is ruptured, wherein the colonial people do not receive enough goods, services, education, health resources, etc., to produce and reproduce themselves in a fashion conducive to an accumulation of wealth with their colony. In fact, the separation of a whole people from the means of production makes Black people in this country the archetype of a colonial society.

Roy Innis describes the peculiar character of domestic colonial oppression of blacks as follows: "Oppression can occur in one's homeland or in the homeland of the oppressor and the latter has been suffered by two great people—the Jews and the American Blacks."[4] The most conspicuous and significant historical factor relating to the system of exclusion and exploitation of Black people has been the calculated design to maintain them exclusively in a property-less status. In such a position, Black people have always had to turn to and depend on white people for every single one of their needs. This situation confirms the colonial captive position of the Black population. Without control over any significant portion of the area they occupy, and not having ownership of any capital instruments or means of production, Black people are not simply oppressed, but are victims of super-exploitation. The lack of command over land left them without any basic resources essential for self-sufficient development of the ability to exercise political influence to protect their social interests or even their lives. This situation continues into the present. It is instructive to ask, for example, if Black people comprise 47 percent of the population of Newark—then why don't they occupy anywhere near 47 percent of the land? It is important to point out that this condition is related to another peculiarity of our caste domination. That is, the police force of the urban Black reserves (ghettos) are virtually all white and completely controlled and responsible to the interests of the white community. The election of prominent "Negro politicians" to political office in Cleveland and Washington, DC, has not altered this pattern of relationship of Black people to land and resources and control over area occupied, such control being basic for political power and economic development.

The cities and the rapid pace of urbanization of the African American population raises vital questions for the direction of the struggle in the 1970s. For the past several decades the African population of the great metropolitan regions has been increasing at a more rapid rate than the white population. In fact, over half of all Black people now reside in the central areas. Many urban affairs experts are projecting within the next few decades, Blacks will constitute 25 to 50 percent of the total population in at least ten of the fourteen largest cities. Much has been said about the migration that has transformed the African population from rural to largely city-dwelling people. But it is seldom understood that the movement of Black families into the inner cities beginning with World War I and accelerating through World War II was caused not simply by the pull of industrial jobs in the war industry but, essentially, the mechanization of agriculture which forced them off the land into Black political colonies in the big cities of the North and West.

As technology has transformed American social organization, so, too, has it altered the form of Black colonization. Millions of Black people have been uprooted from the land without the security of corresponding increase in urban employment and have been confined to small pockets of land in the city consciously reserved for their limited use, and which are inadequate to their needs. There are not sufficient goods and services and resources for Black people to provide for themselves. Medical facilities are appalling, ghetto schools are institutionalized agencies for the perpetuation of ignorance, public transportation and sanitation are worse than inadequate, and there is a real absence of any means by which people can become self-reliant. These conditions in big-city Black colonies is a classical reflection that Blacks have become the great surplus of labor. There has been a vital shift in the dynamics of our situation from the economics of uselessness which poses crucial questions of survival.

The destiny of Black people has always been tied to our value of America as a profit-making investment. The modern urban dwelling population is rapidly outliving its usefulness as a source of cheap labor, and, furthermore, corporate capitalism is not willing to train Blacks for productive use.

This is a dangerous situation. With increasing urban rebellion threatening damage to white property, our danger to national stability begins to clearly outweigh any value we may maintain for white interest. As the value of Blacks becomes less than their potential danger as a threat of serious social rupture and upheaval, the nature of their condition becomes colonial, primarily for containment and captivity.

There was the belief among some Black theoreticians of the possibility of the Black people gaining political control of the cities through default as white people flee to the suburbs to escape the flow of African immigration. However, this pattern is accompanied by a suburbanization of industry which removed the tax base and which would leave Black people no viable economic infrastructure or source of support for necessary municipal and social services. At the same time, plans are being designed to create local urban mergers, thus creating larger metro regions as the primary level of government and political organization. This would effectively deprive the inner-city population from obtaining any meaningful political power and, most important, any control over significant land use with productive value. The purpose of metro regions is to maintain Blacks' colonial status.

But this plan was not sufficient, as Black people could still pose a threat as a rebellious and tumultuous force, threatening those financial and industrial institutions that could not be easily uprooted and transported to the suburbs. Thus, neocolonial plans such as urban renewal and model cites were designed to effectively move Black people away from the inner city and the commercial hub of the city by scattering them around the periphery of a city and Balkanizing the community so that they are left in a strategically defenseless position. In addition, highway development schemes and urban housing construction are used by white people to repossess the land as they make way for housing and commercial schemes that are intended to attract larger numbers of white people into returning to the city. This is the context in which the proposed plan to build the great New York State office building on the Harlem site must be understood. Those "Negroes" who have supported the plan have argued that it would bring great economic development to the Harlem area[,] but the question they tragically overlook is economic development for whom—which is the essential question.

It is not difficult to imagine what the dynamics of economic spinoffs from the construction of that building will be and the effects it will have on transforming the community and the African people there. Even before the building is completed there will be an anticipation of need for a myriad of social services for the white people who are to come there to work, which will attract a deluge of white business development. It will not be long before there will be talk of the need to provide good quality cultural centers in the vicinity; and the white office workers will operate to effectively move Black people out in less than a decade and reconstruct this area to fulfill their own needs and interests. Such a development will break up the possibility of this historically rich African population developing into a strong political and economic unit to advance the interests of Black liberation. It has been said very often in recent times that America is the Black man's battleground. By logical extension, the city is the front line of the Black man's struggle, for it is within the city that our oppression is most politically rationalized and economically sophisticated, and the military occupation of our communities most intense and extensive. But the city also contains the greatest contradictions and antagonism.

James Boggs writes in a recently distributed manifesto that "Blacks in the United States are an underclass in the most highly advanced capitalist society in the world. In [their] total number far exceeding the organized working class in the United States and the population of most nations[,] they are concentrated at the hearts of major cities, experiencing every day the contradiction between the spectacular material development of this country and its extreme backwardness in human relations, between the actual misery and degradation of their daily lives and a constantly beckoning world of abundance and ease. This contradiction drives the Black Movement towards social revolution."[5]

Any serious attempt at liberation must involve a plan to create a political cadre that will work to organize Black people in the great metropolitan areas, and develop strong, independent Black political organizations which will move our people toward capturing control over all institutions that are within the area they occupy. Involvement in domestic politics will not be directed by a belief in the liberal fallacy of social progress through political participation in electoral politics—which only lubricates the mechanism of neocolonial design—but instead to create friction in that system by pushing it to expose to the people the fact that the white controllers cannot and will not provide for their needs, secure their interests, or protect their lives.

Political elections should be used to place Black nationalist–oriented party members in office who will claim the African areas autonomous city states and develop and create planned economies based on African socialist models directed toward self-reliance. This intermediate political activity will begin with the people where they are and confront the monopolistic, capitalist ruling structure with greater contradictions, thus heightening the level of conflict between the Black colony and white controllers, and providing a vehicle to increase the level of nationalist consciousness among Black people and calling their attention to the need for power to control their lives, land, and resources to secure their welfare.

Simultaneously, there must be political plans laid to encourage and support budding cooperative developments and the building of Black cities which are taking place in budding cooperative developments; and also the building of Black cities which are taking place in some parts of the South now. In a sense, this would mean using the urban Black colony in the city areas as a hinterland for support of Black nation-building in areas in the South where Black are in great numbers. In addition, it would translate geographical dispersion—which has been a liability in the sense of territoriality and thus common nationalist-orientation among Black people—into a means by which we help them understand that such dispersion is a source of weakness. Therefore by these means we can stress the need for concentration over common territory that will provide Black people with a strategic advantage in the struggle over control over land and resources.

In conclusion, [I make] two fundamental political assumptions, which are as follows:

1. The success or failure to mobilize African people in the great metropolitan centers can make or break the current thrust of the liberation movement.

2. Without control over land, resources, and production, there can be no self-determination for a people.

Their survival will always be a question of concern, the social conditions of their lives will always be tenuous at best, and their future will hinge on the whims and wishes of others.

IMPLICATIONS OF CLASS CONFLICT AND RACIAL CLEAVAGE FOR THE U.S. BLACK COMMUNITY[6]

JAMES TURNER

For the proponents of social change, nothing is more important than to understand and make use of the dynamics of the situation within which they must function. In the case of the U.S. black community, the dynamic forces and resulting necessities and possibilities for effective progressive action are unusually complex. The black community is culturally and racially isolated within American society, kept apart by white-generated definitions of racial and other cultural attributes required for admission to the mainstream. By these definitions a line of racial cleavage is maintained. In addition, American Blacks are divided horizontally into a middle class and a working class, like the rest of U.S. society. This is the result of socioeconomic forces operating through all American institutions, except that the racial cleavage line means that the black middle and working classes are subclasses, enjoying only secondary status within each national class.

Though Blacks own little property, existence of a black middle class is possible because class membership in the modern world is not simply a matter of property ownership. The working class is inherently propertyless, and all owners of means of production are automatic members of the bourgeoisie, but a substantial and influential though subordinate part of the modern middle class now consists of professionals and technicians who by virtue of their credentials, skill, or competence are able to serve the manipulators of productive wealth and are well paid for doing so. While inheritance of a substantial block of property or wealth provides assured passage into the upper power-wielding strata of the bourgeoisie, having parents with the requisite racial and other cultural attributes and the economic means to provide a higher education is sufficient for entry into the lower bourgeoisie. The same criteria, with appropriate qualifications, apply to membership in the black middle class. Since there are some opportunities, though circumscribed, for the acquisition of limited property, surplus income, and higher education there is upward flow of recruits from the working class, thus providing both white and black middle classes the options for dynamic growth. Since these new recruits originate at social levels which do not equip them with the cultural attributes required for upward mobility, it is a function of education, training, and other socializing processes to make good the deficiency. A few recruits escape or do not succumb to those co-optive influences, but usually find their upward progress halted at an early stage. The middle classes maintain both their cultural and socioeconomic homogeneity despite dilution from below.[7]

Class is a nationwide socioeconomic phenomenon, resulting from operational characteristics of society's basic institutions; but classes are not homogeneous. They are subdivided by many lines of major and minor social cleavage. The criteria of cleavage are primarily, though not exclusively, racial and economic. They are maintained by applying such readily stereotyped discriminators as pigmentation, facial contours, language, tastes (in dress, food, and music), behavior patterns, and the like. These cleavages create intra-class hierarchies, ordered according to the scale of values by which each of the cultural attributes is measured, e.g., race and national origin. Manipulation of cultural values and employment of visible characteristics as discriminators are important tools for the management of power on behalf of the higher-status subclasses. Racial cleavages help to reinforce class distinctions by providing additional barriers to mobility. Racial and cultural diversity, a purely historical and an inherently enriching phenomenon, is transformed into a tool of social management and human degradation.

There are times when historical forces and social movements blunt the edge of the tool and bring about evolutionary changes in the balance of de facto power among subclasses. New accretions of power can sometimes be used to initiate and carry through changes in de jure power and class structure which goes well beyond what was inherent in the system. That is, a dynamic discontinuity may be brought about. The situation facing American Blacks today has this potential, but the actual outcome will depend on the perceptions, aspirations, strategic acuity, solidarity, and discipline of black middle-class leaders and their essential relationship with the black working class. This calls for the propagation and spread of a common understanding of current processes and their potentialities.

Since 1954 there has been a gradual but accelerating change in the processes of black middle-class formation. With few exceptions, entry into this class was via one of the southern black colleges[,] where education and certification provided under the aegis of white-dominated boards of trustees were seldom adequate to permit entry into white-dominated occupational structures. The fifties, and especially the sixties, brought about a number of changes. Blacks began to gain access in larger numbers than before to educational institutions hitherto reserved mainly or exclusively for whites. Curricular and other changes in some black colleges and universities improved their status and that of their graduates. Middle-class job opportunities in white-dominated organizations became available in greater numbers. If one projects this trend for two or three decades and takes even a cautious view of prospects for further improvement in educational and job opportunities available to the children of these years, the likelihood is that there will be a far more visible and influential black middle class by the end of the century than there is now.

The burning question is what kind of power and influence this new class will exercise. Merely by its existence and growth it will weaken the force and effect of cultural and racial cleavage within the national middle class. Its status will rise, its degree of subordination will diminish, and its potential political influence will become substantial. But it will gain little control over the nation's productive wealth, and its economic power will therefore remain miniscule. A similar process in the former colonial countries gave rise to a national bourgeoisie which led the struggle for independence. Seldom was political sovereignty employed to achieve increased economic sovereignty, which would have required an escape from domination by foreign capital and enterprise. Seldom, too, was political sovereignty viewed as providing an opportunity and responsibility to work for the benefit of the nation as a whole. More often, independence conferred a license to initiate a process of middle-class economic aggrandizement. Those able to do so began acquiring title to land and other natural resources at the expense of the peasantry. Incentives were offered for foreign industrial investment, subject perhaps to local participation and provision for the employment of local personnel in positions hitherto closed to them. Employment or participation in foreign commercial and financial enterprises which continue to dominate the international trading economies of most former colonies became an important objective. Advanced degrees from Western or Western-style domestic universities, available only to the well-to-do, became a condition for obtaining the well-paid jobs offered by government, universities, and the professions. As a result, most ex-colonies have strong neocolonial ties to metropolitan capitalist countries, and a well-entrenched Westernized elite or comprador class which depends on and profits greatly from its country's willingness to cooperate with the world capitalist system.

The interests of this class are the interests of multinational firms. Inevitably, neocolonial economies are guided and energized by investment and other economic decisions made abroad by decision makers whose main concerns, as regards their satellites, are to maintain high profits and good public relations. The governments of these peripheral capitalist countries necessarily become both politically and economically subservient to overseas influences.[8] Though independence has succeeded in eliminating or greatly attenuating the lines of cultural cleavage that formerly divided the colonizer from the colonized, it has in most cases been accompanied by a sharpening of class divisions within former colonies because the newly powerful national middle class has now an interest in acquiring an economic power base and protecting its privileged position vis-à-vis world capitalism. Internal cultural differences, reflecting the extraordinarily varied ethnic evolution of African peoples, have often been transformed into lines of cleavage to help define and maintain emergent class divisions. Nigeria and Uganda are examples.

Exceptions to this neocolonialist line of evolution are rare among newly independent states. They have occurred only where leaders have provided an ideology, both idealistic and pragmatic, in opposition to capitalist domination, and have succeeded in blocking the efforts of middle-class influentials to follow a self-serving path. Perhaps the outstanding example of consistent movement in a non-capitalist direction is that of Tanzania under Nyerere's leadership. An idealistic ideology which became increasingly pragmatic under pressure of such events as the barracks mutiny and the Zanzibari revolution of January 1964, the subsequent merger with the island state, and the successful repulsion of several attempts at seizure of power by bourgeois politicians has been the focal point of action. Conversely, Ghana provides the major example of revolt against an initial non-capitalist line. Nkrumah's ideological and analytical guidance were not matched by adequate pragmatism, with the result that his political organization collapsed under continual pressure from a disaffected middle class and its professional military allies. Though the quality of leadership is crucial, as these examples suggest, it can no more fully explain what happened in these two countries than it can anywhere else. Tanzania had the advantage of having been a neglected trusteeship territory with a very small middle class, little foreign investment, and few strong ties to the world capitalist network. Ghana had a strong foreign-dominated trading economy and perhaps the most extensive, sophisticated, and solidary middle class in sub-Saharan Africa. Frustrated with Nkrumah's failure to permit them to fulfill their potentialities as a national bourgeoisie, they turned against him, assured of support from the capitalist powers. Leadership thus interacted with history to produce results that are partly predetermined. Nyerere might have failed, Nkrumah might have succeeded, given different perceptions and strategies in each case.[9]

This capsule history is relevant because the situation of American Blacks, as often remarked, resembles that of a colonized people. As the black middle class gains power and influence, it will begin to see the fulfillment of its aspirations in terms of closer ties to the national capitalist establishment. Lacking an effective counter-ideology and an independent power base, the American black community will inevitably evolve into a kind of internal neo-colony. Though racial discrimination will persist, it will be attenuated for members of the black middle class as they acquire and adopt the credentials, skills, tastes, and behavior patterns required for entry into the national middle class. By the same token, class divisions and cultural differences within the black community will be widened and deepened. The black middle class will begin to believe that assimilation into the white middle class is in prospect, and with the characteristic myopia of class it will presume that the same is possible for the entire black community. Both beliefs will be illusory. Whites will continue to maintain as much of a racial cleavage line as possible in order to hold their position of dominance within both the middle and working classes, while the increased upward mobility of upper-income Blacks will enhance their class consciousness and drive a thickening wedge between them and the black working class. Possessing no territorial unit over which to exercise full political sovereignty, middle-class Blacks will nevertheless gain increasing influence within urban and county governments, both locally and nationally. These powers, though limited by lack of durable support from black working-class voters, will be used, like those in bourgeois-dominated ex-colonies, to promote middle-class interests. Outside investments will be encouraged in urban ghettos as a means of providing more technical and bureaucratic jobs and satellite small business opportunities. Political empowerment will occur but will remain that of a subclass, subject to good behavior; economic gains will be real enough for the fortunate few but will be neocolonial, generating little economic power.

What has just been described is only the most probable, not an inevitable, course of events. A less probable but possible alternative exists. The situation in the United States conceivably permits, though it does not favor, the development of a black-oriented non-capitalist ideology and strategy based on the use of political power to achieve independent economic power within the framework of American society. One major tenet of such an ideology would have to be opposition to racism in all its manifestations, implying among other things, respect for black culture and history, and an effective equalization of socioeconomic opportunities. While this implies integration into American society, it neither implies nor requires assimilation into any non-black cultural stream. A second major tenet would be espousal of a non-capitalist form of economic organization for the black community, implying reduction and eventual elimination of class differences. Not only is this necessary to the preservation of cultural diversity without cleavage, it is also essential if ownership ties to the national capitalist establishment are to be minimized. While no economy, not even those of the USSR and China, can function independently of the world capitalist network, many can and do maintain control over their own decision processes. Unlike neocolonial regimes, their economic and social progress is internally energized and guided, subject only to constraints that no society or community can escape. The American black community, even though engulfed by American society, can achieve analogous control over its own destiny, but only by pursuing a non-capitalist path. Such a path is essential to the development and execution of a sound political strategy, for only a non-class-conscious approach can lead to the full mobilization of mass voting power on behalf of the black community as a whole.

Why this must be so can best be understood by remembering that black progress thus far has resulted mainly from court decisions and legislation affecting civil rights, and has been very much of a middle-class phenomenon, with little benefit sloshing over or trickling down to the working class. While mass voting power has been successfully mobilized in a few instances—though too often through alliance with and subservience to old line urban political machines—it has had a strong middle-class bias, frequently including reliance on white liberal support, and has failed to demonstrate durability. Durable political power requires mass support which has not been forthcoming because the narrow scope of black progress has done little to arouse the enthusiasm of black workers, welfare recipients, and the unemployed. Only a genuine and increasingly effective effort to produce real and direct benefits—not trickle-down benefits—for those at the bottom of the income scale can alter this state of affairs. Only so can the black vote be durably mobilized and its potential as a revolutionary force for black liberation realized.

Forces at work in the black community constitute a classic example of a dialectical process at work. The ideological predispositions of the American black middle class and its perceptions of self-interest reinforce a process of class expansion and political empowerment which seems to promise black liberation but is in fact divisive and destined to produce internecine strife. The ruling class of an ex-colony has the satisfaction of exercising sovereign political power no matter how limited its economic sovereignty may be, and of standing at the top of both the socioeconomic and the cultural hierarchies. The top class in an internal colony has neither of these satisfactions, but is subject to the perpetual frustration of its legitimate aspirations. Just as the well-to-do and highly cultivated German and Spanish Jews, suffering an exacerbation of anti-Semitism following the influx of low-income and poorly educated East European Jews, created lines of cultural cleavage between themselves and Jewish ghetto dwellers, so will upper-crust American Blacks increasingly differentiate themselves from their working-class brothers. The newly elected chairwoman of the board of the NAACP, Attorney Margaret Bush Wilson, is reported (*Newsweek,* January 27, 1975) to have proclaimed, "I consider myself an aristocrat...character, competence, accomplishment. That's my definition of aristocracy."

The best that can be hoped from this state of affairs is something that must be called pseudo-development. Centered around a core of black businessmen, small property owners, professionals, and public and private bureaucrats, there will be an emphasis on the creation of monumental structures as opposed to the development of people. This will strengthen the forces of exploitation and underdevelopment which already weigh heavily on the black working classes. Driven into ever greater dependence on the street economy and various forms of rip-off and crime, the working class will become an increasing threat to middle-class security and aspirations. Emphasis on law and order will undermine concerns for progress and create an environment in which the police, courts, and politicians will become ever more adept at inflicting the visible crackdown on petty criminals and social marginals and receiving invisible payoffs from powerful outside criminal and real estate interests.

The recent erection or a huge New York State office building on 125th Street in Harlem, purportedly for developmental purposes, is a case in point. Because it will provide some additional lower-middle-class employment opportunities in the borough, it is currently leading to the preemptive purchase of nearby property by outside capitalists bent on catering to the white collar workers and transients which the building and its satellite activities will bring to the neighborhood. This displeases black storekeepers and professionals in the vicinity, drives illicit business onto side streets, now mainly residential, and displaces or inconveniences those now living there. Those who benefit will be outsiders and the more mobile members of the black middle class; the sufferers will be all the poorer and weaker members of the community. Examples of pseudo-development, including the well-known cases of "urban removal," could easily be multiplied, and all would demonstrate that the typical processes of capitalist middle-class expansion, including those dubbed "black capitalism," benefit a few, injure many, and diminish the humanity of all.

The alternative to this outcome does not lie in a continued or increased emphasis on civil rights legislation and enforcement. Consider, for example, what might happen if some miracle suddenly eliminated racial discrimination as a fact of American life. Middle- and working-class Blacks, subject at last only to the disabilities of economic deprivation and low social status, would compete on culturally equal terms with white Americans of their own class. The competition would be unequal, because of the heritage of socioeconomic disadvantage from which both black classes suffer. Progress toward proportional representation of Blacks throughout the occupational structure of each class would be exceedingly slow, and would probably never be attained. Disillusionment would set in, particularly among lower-class Blacks[,] who would experience the greater hardships, class divisions would be sharpened, and the possibility of a middle- and working-class alliance to work for racial equality—the analytical equivalent of national independence for external colonies—would no longer exist. The neocolonial syndrome would still be operative. Equality of civil rights, desirable as it is for its own sake—as is national independence—is no more sufficient as a goal of social action than independence has proved to be.

While there is no chance that a civil rights miracle will occur, black intellectuals and political leaders must recognize the need for, and the possibility of a more fundamental, a more revolutionary, approach. In so doing they will possess an important advantage, as members of an internal colony, over their counterparts in external colonies. For an external colony, independence is a logical first step. Once achieved, there is a loss of political leverage on the metropolitan power. An internal colony, by contrast, is compelled to seek gains by operating within the system of representative government and bureaucratic decision making, being thereby granted an opportunity to exercise leverage on the system. Where the numbers of the colonized minority are sufficiently large and concentrated, as in the case of American Blacks and their potential allies, the leverage inherent in a durable mobilization of mass voting power is exceedingly great. To do this, a firm sense of the politics of the situation is required. But politics without ideology is opportunism, ideology without strategy is rhetoric, and strategy without tactics is futility.

The ideology must be both idealistic and pragmatic: idealistic in the sense of offering a morally and materially better world, for otherwise it can never engage the emotions of leaders and followers to the extent needed for a long and successful struggle (witness the difference between North and

South Vietnam); and pragmatic in the sense of being non-Utopian, that is, of promising a future which could be a logical and attainable outcome of the present situation, though not the most probable outcome. Such an ideology would be idealistic because what it seeks is not inevitable, and pragmatic because what it seeks is possible.

The strategy must be patient and cautious, suited for the long pull, deferring the achievement of revolutionary changes until a series of fundamental reforms has prepared the ground. That is, it must be a strategy of struggle. This means that its adherents must be disciplined rather than flamboyant, and willing to work invisibly for the small gains of the moment rather than to become imposing public figures. Above all, they must be liberated in Fanon's sense of having accepted the need to sacrifice personal status, material comfort, and perhaps even life for the sake of helping to bring about a permanent lifting of oppressive constraints. Struggle requires large numbers of such psychically liberated people, not only among the leaders but in the rank and file.

The tactics must be those of working inside the system, though on its fringes[,] where system powers can be manipulated for initially small but increasingly large gains, rather than outside the system, which is a power vacuum. The first large objective should be to bring about major reforms, involving true structural changes (and not mere cosmetic tinkering) in the welfare system, education, administration and enforcement of so-called justice, drug traffic, and the exploitative practices of landlords, merchants, and financial institutions. Such changes would embody the substance of racial equality, which "rights" do not. The second large objective would be to create a black-controlled non-capitalist economic system, for if "black capitalism" could become a reality, it would merely change the existing internal colony into an internal neo-colony, characterized by class and cultural conflict among Blacks.

The structural core of such an alternative system would consist of community-owned, worker-managed enterprises, or producer cooperatives, based on fully democratic participation at all levels. Since such enterprises would be small, and would be created in ethnic communities isolated from the mainstream, they would not be a threat to the American system. This is what would make their creation politically feasible. Smallness is a virtue in other respects, too. The overwhelming majority of American privately owned enterprises are small, completely overshadowed by the corporate giants, yet providing the basis for a relatively independent life of work for millions of people. Small worker-managed enterprises also provide better opportunities for egalitarian participation in decision making.

Models of analogous non-capitalist systems are available, and would re-pay close study. One is the Tanzanian program of transforming traditional farm villages into fully participatory, cooperative communities, governing their own affairs but receiving assistance from governmental sources. An-other is Algeria's more widespread establishment of producer cooperatives operated under a regime of worker self-management in both the agricultur-al and non-agricultural sectors. Unlike Yugoslavia, which adopted a system of worker self-management in the early fifties as a reaction against the cen-tralized Soviet system, Tanzania and Algeria have moved in a non-capitalist direction without following a communist path. One of the prime virtues of an economic system based on fully participatory worker self-management is that it carries the principles of democracy over from the political into the economic sphere, as Jaroslav Vanek (economist at Cornell) has pointed out in several of his many writings on the subject.

Before either of the two major tactical objectives specified above can be openly and seriously pursued[,] there will have to be a long period of preparation. Ideological, strategic, and tactical ideas must be examined with great care, clarified, and then elaborated into a cohesive statement. This is a first step. Next there must be a systematic effort to develop a force of dedicated proselytizers who would organize study groups in which potential followers would be led systematically through reading and dis-cussion to an understanding of the alternatives and, it would be hoped, to an acceptance of the core program. The final preparatory step would be or-ganization of a political movement aimed at mobilizing mass voting power and exercising political leverage behind the sequential achievement of the tactical objectives.

During the action phase it would be extremely important for cadres and candidates to recognize the need for sequencing steps in such a way as to match one's own evolving capabilities and also those of the opposition. In particular it is necessary to mobilize support as one goes, and not to go too fast. Every new adherent, for example, can help with the cultural rehabili-tation of the psychically crippled victims of existing oppressive mechanisms as each is subject to reform, and thus create further adherents. As in China during the decade or two of land reform and cultural rehabilitation which preceded the final communist assumption of power, each step would rein-force the next; reform measures liberate some oppressed individuals[,] who then help to liberate those still oppressed. An example of a good tactical move for this initial phase is the request by the Brownsville Community Federal Credit Union to be assigned responsibility for delivering welfare checks, a task now handled by commercial banks. Not only would this bring direct benefit to welfare recipients, but it would increase their awareness of the potentialities of black political action and create links to the black political vanguard. Many potential tactical moves of this kind must exist. Because achievements would be slow in coming[,] it will be necessary to maintain tactical flexibility without loss of strategic clarity or a weakening of discipline. The ability to do this is what identifies a serious struggle.

As political leverage increased through the first tactical phase[,] there should be a shift to moves aimed at facilitating the creation of worker-managed enterprises. One such move might be legislation explicitly designed to authorize the creation of worker-managed, community-sponsored enterprises. Another need would be credit facilities tailored, like those in agriculture and home building, to the specific requirements of a worker-managed system. Parallel to this could be a system of urban land grants, in which deteriorated or substandard housing and land would be acquired by eminent domain and turned over to community organizations to be rehabilitated and rented by worker-managed enterprises under community auspices. In still another parallel to government aid to agriculture, urban land grant colleges could be established to train workers in technical and administrative skills, and to help operate a producers cooperative extension service for the explicit benefit of black workers and their self-managed firms. To give such measures an explicit black focus without becoming subject to charges of black racism would be a problem but not an insoluble one. Perhaps a serious and careful handling of the idea of reparations would prove useful, but there may be other ways as well. One of these might be to form an alliance with socialistically inclined white radicals, if they could organize sufficiently to undertake serious political action. In that case, there would be no need to confine the idea of worker management to the black community, although formulas should be devised which would assure priority to black development. Blacks and other non-white ethnic minorities, because they stand to gain most from such a movement and can argue most effectively from the bitterness of their own experiences, should be its initiators and prime energizers. It can be expected that middle-class Blacks are likely to become disaffected in larger numbers, and thus liberated, as realities fail to fulfill hopes, and may therefore be a major source of leadership. Leaders and followers must be recruited from among black people, especially those at low income levels. Without such solidarity there is small likelihood that our history can be diverted from its usual ambiguous path toward a movement of greater human promise.

INEQUITY IN THE SYSTEM: RACISM IN AMERICAN SOCIETY AND ON COLLEGE CAMPUSES[10]

JAMES TURNER

Racial conflict in higher education mirrors the racism in American society. In order to combat the problem, African American students must understand its roots.

Racism in America is older than the United States. Its institutionalization began one hundred and ten years before the meeting of the first Continental Congress in the mid-18th century, when it adopted the Constitution and the Bill of Rights. Some of the first racist laws were enacted in Virginia in the 1660s, clearly demonstrating that racism constitutes a fundamental contradiction in the American body politic.

From its very inception America has espoused a belief in the principles of "...One Nation, Indivisible, Under God, With Liberty and Justice for All." However, it should be clear that these beliefs, which our children are taught to recite in school as self-evident truths, are in fact distortions of the truth.

A very different reality is evident: a profound commitment to dividing society along racial lines with the intent of constructing and perpetuating a system that exploits African labor in order to maintain the power, privilege, and prosperity of European Americans. Racism has a long and sordid history rooted in the culture, institutions, and religion of this country. One of the oldest justifications for the inhuman practices associated with racial subjugation was that it was ordained by God.

The legacy of this radically conservative political agenda is manifested in a tradition of gaping racial inequity, which is evident in contemporary American society. It is critically important for African Americans, particularly students, who potentially are on the cutting edge of change, to understand that racism is a system that was devised specifically to maintain a hierarchy in which the preferential treatment of Whites would be secured for posterity. Conversely, this same hierarchy perpetuates the exclusion, exploitation, underdevelopment, poverty, and brutality of African Americans. The United States is a highly racialized society in which all significant goods and services, wealth and power, are distributed through this intricate racialized criterion.

The socialization process in this country produces a racialized consciousness, a lens through which Americans view the world as naturally as they breathe, eat, or make love. Likewise, beauty, status, and prestige are defined and perceived by this same racialized criterion. However, racism is not a natural phenomenon; but it is a human invention, socially constructed to manipulate resources to benefit a specific group. Thus, racism critically shapes two fundamental aspects of American culture: (1) attitudinal or ideological, which encompasses belief systems, and (2) institutional or behavioral, which is manifest in the social structure. Plans to execute change in race relations tend to focus on problems associated with the former, while ignoring those more fundamental issues inherent to the latter. However, it is precisely this latter dimension that is most salient to the continuity of institutional practice, its abiding effect on society, and resistance to change.

RACISM AND EDUCATION

From this historical and conceptual institutional framework, we can more effectively analyze interracial relations, as well as better understand the interaction between racism and education. Education plays a reciprocal role in that it is influenced by, and is a primary conveyor of, the history, traditions, and values of society. Education is critical to the socialization process, because it transmits the established knowledge of the collective experience as perceived by the dominant group. It is less an agency of change, and more a conservator of the status quo.

Because of its centrality to social mobility and life chances, education is pivotal to maintaining the racial hierarchy and perpetuating competition for status and opportunity. Despite this fact, Africans in America have invested much energy, resources, and hope in this institution, recognizing that it is an essential component to self-determination and the redefinition of self; that it provides a basis for competition and a means of acquiring skills to develop their communities. In order to do more than merely survive, African Americans realize that they must confront this challenge in their quest for education, circumventing where necessary and breaking down when possible, the racist barriers that permeate the educational system.

Slavery was the defining experience for Africans who were compelled to the so-called "New World" by European interlopers. A standard feature of enslavement was compulsory, imposed ignorance. Until and unless this confinement to the abyss of illiteracy was transcended, no other options would be possible. During slavery, the denial of education was used as a front-line strategy to preserve existing patterns of segregation. Precisely because of the critical role of education, it was inevitable that the main focus of the freedom movement was educational opportunity. In this vein, the strategic victory against segregation in education, *Brown vs. The Board of Education* (Topeka, [Kansas]), in 1954, established a legal precedent that opened the way for the Civil Rights Bills of 1963 and the Voting Rights Act of 1965. This was the golden age of Civil Rights.

DIVIDED AMERICA/DIVIDED CAMPUSES

In the wake of these achievements, a formidable opposition developed to block any further advances and even this swelling tide of progress. The Civil Rights Movement has reached an impasse and is practically stalemated.

Present-day conditions are referred to by historians and sociologists as the "post–Civil Rights" era. This reference is a tacit recognition of a milestone in the 20th-century experience of African-American people in the United States. At the same time, it indicates the passing of a significant political era. The Civil Rights Movement was aborted before it could effectively transform Americans' social, political, economic, and cultural institutions into egalitarian and democratic principles. The high ideals that motivated the struggle for racial equality and an integrated society a generation ago have been severely curtailed. Intellectuals and policy makers have shifted the spectrum of American politics to a renewed radical conservatism that is not so subtly aligned with reactionary White nationalism. This resurgence has gained new inroads in both political parties, which are determined to undermine and reverse the programs enacted during the Civil Rights Movement. These are bleak reminders that America's racial dilemma has not been resolved. The color line is still in place and has indeed been revitalized. Public opinion polls reveal that society is sharply divided by race on all major social issues. This is no less true for race relations in institutions of higher education.

To the chagrin of educators and college administrators alike, reported incidents of racism in the cathedrals of higher learning are on the rise. Racial antagonism and angry conflicts increasingly characterize relations between Black and White students on the campus of America's historically White colleges and universities.

The presence of Black students on these campuses has always been problematic. From 1826, when the first African student graduated from college, Black students have encountered obstacles in their quest for meaningful lives through education. In 1954 scarcely one percent of the students enrolled at traditionally White colleges were African American. By 1978 more than half of all Black students were attending such institutions. This was a dramatic change due directly to the success of the Black liberation struggle against apartheid in America. However, there is never an easy walk to freedom. Beginning in the 1980s, reports of racial confrontation from around the country began to surface with increasing frequency.

Even in the hallowed halls of the ivory tower, hostility toward Black students has risen dramatically. This rise seemed to correlate with the election of Ronald Reagan; it intensified throughout the Reagan-Bush years. According to the National Institute Against Prejudice and Violence, since 1986 more than 250 colleges and universities have reported racist incidents. These include some of the most reputable schools in the country. Incidents have ranged from racist graffiti scrawled on buildings and in restrooms, to racist slurs and caricatures transmitted in student publications and on campus radio. More serious acts such as death threats and physical assaults have also been documented. Racism can be both overt and covert. Covert racism is the most pervasive form of racism in higher education.

African-American students attending historically White institutions must expect to confront a situation in which they will be a very small minority in an essentially White environment. The trend since the mid-1970s has been toward erosion of the numerical gains for Black student enrollment, especially in the case of African-American males. Black students are marginalized, in part, because of limited options for meaningful mentor relationships, due to the very low numbers of African-American faculty. Black faculty constitute less than two percent of the national total. Future prospects are not encouraging, as the pipeline from graduate schools producing new Black PhDs has narrowed significantly during the last decade. Black students are further alienated by academic advisers who seek to dissuade them from enrolling in African-American studies classes.

Recently, a most insidious development has taken place: a series of bogus accusations by White students, mostly women, claiming to have been assaulted by Black students. A co-ed at SUNY Old Westbury told the campus police last November that she was attacked and stabbed by an African-American male while walking on campus. She later confessed to fabricating the incident.

Debates over Afrocentricity and a curriculum of inclusion are flashpoints for heated exchange, but also provide opportunity for positive change that could ameliorate racial discord on campus. However, it is affirmative action that generates the most controversy. Black students and faculty, whatever their backgrounds, find themselves viewed as beneficiaries of lower standards. Politically conservative students aggressively protest policies for recruitment, admission, and financial aid for "minority" students. They will often accuse administrators of encouraging race-specific programs, but their real motive is to reduce, if not deny, access for African-American students.

CONFRONTING THE PROBLEM

Most college administrators shy away from controversy and want to avoid tension at all costs. Their response to racial problems is most likely defensive, a short-term public relations campaign aimed at controlling damage to the image of the institution. Individual incidents are isolated from the broader racist milieu and characterized as aberrant. Occasional suspension of an offending student is considered a resolution to systemic racist problems. Superficial measures such as inviting prominent African-American intellectuals to lecture for a day, or campus dialogues on racism sponsored by the Dean of Students office are proposed as therapy against racism. A few colleges have proposed that students take one or two courses in non-Western cultures. Such a step is necessary but not sufficient to deconstruct the patterns of White supremacy in the curriculum and institution as a whole. College and universities most likely to be successful in combating racism are those that (1) have well-established African-American studies departments, (2) actively hire Black faculty, (3) appoint Black administrators to decision-making positions with real power, and (4) empower Black students by asserting the value of diversity to quality education and the principle of equal participation of all students in every aspect of campus affairs.

However, it was socially conscious student activism that provoked positive change a generation ago. In the final analysis, it is Black students who must set the parameters of their campus experience. They must not allow others to define the terms of the discourse. Analytical skills must be cultivated by studying the impact of institutional racism on the conditions of the African-American community from an African-centered standpoint. African-American students must develop and sustain effective organizations that can present and defend their interests in campus affairs, and elect their representatives to funding and decision-making boards open to students.

Effective organization will also provide a base for social networking and leadership development. It is absolutely imperative for Black students to support each other. Black student organizations should cooperate in order to sponsor serious political symposia and cultural events on campus that inspire consciousness raising and that spiritually uplift their community. Racism often goes unchallenged because of apathy. African-American students should study the heritage of Black people in order to solidify a self-actualizing identity. Apolitical behavior must be replaced by commitment to the principles of academic excellence, and social responsibility to the legacy of their forebears who fought and the fight for freedom that made it possible for them to be on campus today.

AFRICANA STUDIES AND CRITICAL RACE THEORY: FIFTY YEARS AFTER BROWN[11]

KIMBERLÉ CRENSHAW

It takes my breath away to contemplate that more than twenty-something years ago, I walked in these doors, and it has been my good fortune to be able to mark my arrival here as the beginning of an intellectual journey. And I'm delighted that it brings me back here to a continuing, existing Africana Studies and Research Center now marked by this important moment. It is really momentous, given the constant threats that the Center has always been faced with since its inception. So the fact that it is not only still surviving, but thriving, gives me untold pleasure.

I am happy to return home to the Africana Center bearing tales of the world that I encountered just outside these protective halls and to speak about the many gifts that I received here: principally the gifts of insight, the gifts of perseverance, and a sense of self that made my survival possible. It has been a memorable and eventful journey, and like all seasoned travelers, I have stories that I am anxious to tell, all of which commemorate the value of good home training. The topic consequently reflects my interest in sharing an immensely personal story on the interface between Africana Studies and critical race theory, a school of thought that I have been closely associated with since the earliest days of my engagement in the legal profession. Now, against the sometimes seamless way we tend to think that we've always been what we have eventually become, I want to examine the particular ways that Africana Studies—and, by extension, other projects grounded in the study of a racialized people—contributed to, paralleled, and presaged one of the most significant and contested intellectual movements in the law. As an early critical race theorist, I am interested in telling the story not only to honor my roots, but also to underscore the need for strengthening the intellectual and institutional ties between Africana Studies and critical race theory. I also want to highlight the importance of student activism and the important role that students play in creating an intellectual movement; and to let them know that the work you do today is likely to transform the institutions you occupy tomorrow.

The current backlash against critical race theory (an expansive vision of racial justice), in particular, is powerful and profound. It comes as we celebrate the fiftieth anniversary of *Brown v. Board of Education. Brown*, which, it seems, is feted far more than it is honored in practice. The symbolic value of *Brown* has been outweighed by the yawning contradiction between how it is celebrated and its doctrinal marginality. All three of us—Derrick Bell, Charles Ogletree, and myself—have been going all around the country, taking up various positions in the debate about *Brown*. We tame the conversation when it becomes blunt and celebratory; we lift *Brown* up sometimes when it is dismissed as a meaningless act of judicial paternalism. The range of conversations that we've taken up has been dizzying.

Dr. James Turner, Harvard law professor Charles Olgetree, former Africana graduate and social justice lawyer Soffiyah Elijah, and actor and activist Danny Glover, who was part of the struggle to establish Black/Africana Studies at San Francisco State University in the late 1960s.

Fortunately, today my departure from *Brown* is a little bit different. I want to identify and trace the contests that were opened up over the meaning of educational equity in the pursuit and construction of social knowledge. More specifically, I'm interested in thinking about *Brown* not simply as a repudiation of segregation in public education; instead, I'm interested in fleshing out the trajectory of a particular institutional and ideological vision of educational equity, one that eventually came to confront the narrow parameters of what *Brown* was interpreted to mean within the very institutions that produced it—namely, the institutions of American law schools.

Let me start this narrative in a personal way, first, by locating myself in a particular generation. I would call myself a part of the post-*Brown* generation—the generation that came to universities and professional schools a scant decade or so after the first critical mass of black students matriculated in significant numbers in white institutions. I would say we were the beneficiaries of our predecessors having barreled through the initial walls of exclusion. That first generation, roughly from the mid- to late 1960s to the mid- to late 1970s, suffered through the initial shock of the black presence in white elite institutions. They are the ones who bore the brunt of what happened when, for example, rooming in the dorms with white students—such as being watched curiously when pressing their hair and facing questions about it; or asked questions about what they were eating; or confronting questions based on all kinds of stereotypical presumptions. They were the ones who had to encounter white professors who did not think they had the right to be there and no curriculum or courses that even anticipated that blacks would ever be part of these institutions. They were the ones who set the stage for Black Studies programs here at Cornell. Our predecessors struggled to create the Africana Studies and Research Center, Ujamaa Residential College, a culture, and set of expectations that were handed down to those of us who then came to fill their places.

I believe that it was both the institutional space that they created as well as a culture of entitlement at such schools that emboldened the post-*Brown* generation to take on one of the most resilient and well-defended white institutions in the nation—namely, American law schools. As it would turn out, the Africana experience not only prepared us to wage ideological and institutional battle within America's elite law schools; it also provided the wherewithal to struggle against our erstwhile allies—the liberal Civil Rights community, on the one hand, and the radical white intellectual community, on the other hand. In fact, as argued in our edited collection *Critical Race Theory*, the movement emerged as a simultaneous engagement with both. It was a radical critique of traditional Civil Rights liberalism and a racial critique of radical legal thought. Both, I contend, were enabled, in large part, by the ideological and institutional environments that were created and nurtured by the first wave of scholars and student activists who created the space that we literally stand in today.

One experience stands out vividly in symbolizing the unexpected contests in which I engaged at law school. I had occasion to meet a certain Civil Rights leader and, to stay true to my promise, I am not going to mention his name. He was the leader of a major Civil Rights organization. It just so happened that he was a close family friend with a colleague of mine here at the Africana Studies Center, Randy Brock—whose name I want to lift up here. His mother had the occasion to introduce me to this Civil Rights leader. I will never forget: he was eating some soul food in their kitchen. She introduced me to him, saying that I was matriculating to Harvard Law School in the fall. He barely skipped a beat, kept eating, looked up briefly from his plate, and asked me whether I had, in fact, been accepted. I was taken aback by the tone of this question because it seemed as though he regarded the statement as a wishful hope on my part rather than a factual reality. Just beneath the surface of his barely interested demeanor lurked an expression of doubt about my legitimacy, my bona fides, a doubt that I usually associated with white racism. I quickly suppressed that thought; this was a Civil Rights leader of some stature, after all. Once I assured him that, indeed, I had been accepted and was in fact going to Harvard Law School in the fall, he took an even more confrontational stance; "So what did you study at Cornell?" Here I thought I had him. I remember thinking, "Surely he'll understand the seriousness of my commitment, my intentions to my people, when I tell him that I was a graduate of the Africana Studies Center at Cornell. What better indicator could there be of my preparation to fill the ranks of black lawyers trained, ready to join the struggle, than he?" I couldn't have been more wrong. He commenced a blistering attack on the Center, accusing it of intellectual charlatanism, on me for being unprepared and foolish, and on my parents for wasting valuable resources on such learning—which, at best, was most appropriate for perhaps high school instruction, but unsuitable in the curriculum of higher education. Not only did he fail to offer me any words of encouragement—he predicted in no uncertain terms that, given my mis-education, I would need remedial help and was likely to flunk out of Harvard Law School. He said he would have counseled me to take more respected and established coursework, such as sociology and psychology.

Needless to say, I was shocked. Yet in the tirade lay a trove of meaning that revealed the full extent to which the integrationist vision had animated the thinking of this leader and others like him. It was perhaps the source of the malaise that characterized the slow pace of change in higher education, particularly in American elite law schools. His vision, his orientation to black people, not only reflected a breathtaking manifestation of intra-racism, but profound ignorance about the contours of white supremacy in higher education. I was shaken by the encounter but not remotely bowed by it. Little could he know how wrong he was about the Africana Studies Center and how it had prepared me for law school. He would be hearing from me again.

Africana Studies provided and exposed us to the essential building blocks of a critical consciousness, a consciousness that provided the conceptual framework to identify, analyze, critique, and resist the operation of white supremacy in the institutional and ideological practices of mainstream legal education. Not only did Black Studies provide a critical consciousness; it also fueled a generation of students to confront and transform the conditions and the practices of legal education. It immunized us, if you will, against exposure to the ambivalence, even from our closest allies. At the risk of using an inappropriate metaphor—given the militaristic engagement that our country is engaged in right now—to a certain extent Africana Studies created guerilla intellectuals who would go deep inside mainstream institutions and live to tell the story of our engagement. Live to find our way back home.

If Black Studies as a discipline produced, say, the Marines, I would say the Africana Studies Center produced the Delta Squads. We were the forces that were unleashed in the comfortable and hallowed halls of American law schools. Dr. Turner, in particular, was our drill sergeant— our instructor. He was the one who showed us how to do the things we needed to do; how to map where we were. He reminded us what the institutional battles were all about. He was the one who let us know that there was an objective to be fought in these engagements, to decipher the map, to know where it was that we were going and where we were coming from. In Africana Studies, we were taught the essential tools of survival in hostile terrain, to go deep into that terrain, and to do work there. We learned the importance of teamwork and community in intellectual production and in the development of our epistemologies. We learned the importance of reaching out to allies when they are necessary, the importance of mobilizing masses and coordinating smaller formations when those are necessary. In Gramscian terms, we learned to engage in the war of position.

*James Turner teaching a graduate seminar at the Africana Studies and
Research Center, with graduate student Kossouth Snyder, 1974.*

Contrary to the instinct of my nemesis, a true leadership for the next phase of the struggle was being forged right here in the Africana Center. Traditional Civil Rights leaders—the so-called "race men"—thought that they had arrived, but again, as Gramsci noted, it's only after the outer walls of the fortress have crumbled that the sturdy structure of the racial state revealed itself. So it was with higher education. They mistook milling about in the fortress courtyard for access to the inner sanctum of power. Confused about where they were and how to push further inside, they were rendered ineffective at this stage of institutional struggle. It took the "unqualified" insurgents, those of us who "wasted our time" in Africana Studies centers, to go deeper—and that is the story that I want to tell.

I mentioned two conceits in this narrative. I am nostalgic about and I am partial to Africana Studies and to Dr. Turner in particular. I came to Cornell, walked into Ujamaa and into the Center, and I knew this was the place for me. Africana was the gathering place where rhetorical conversation and posturing took a backseat to real learning and discursive engagement. It was formed in the throes of institutional struggle. Our courses reflected an encounter with a nationalist orientation, epistemology, and pedagogy. We did not actually understand, in those terms, the full measure of what we were being exposed to by that point. The concepts were clear and illuminating—central were the situated and socially constructed nature of all knowledge, or the politics of knowledge production, as it were. Not only was this the prism to engage key issues (such as the relationship of the academic enterprise to the liberation of African people), it also brought into view the legitimizing function of mainstream disciplines as they shored up the status quo. Uncovering the structural terms and the stabilizing function of the academy would eventually find expression as we future law students uncovered the role of law in insulating the status quo. Claims of neutrality, objectivity, and the dominant edict against all bias were regularly deconstructed through specific examples. Vivid examples were drawn from a range of sociologies that pronounced the black community as "pathological." Attributional discourses were unpacked and debated. We were exposed to the tensions between constructs that framed racial inequality in terms of our personal agency—our fault—versus frameworks that understood the structures of white supremacy and their continuity in contemporary society. We looked through specific lenses to explore such policies or orientations such as the Moynihan Report, the Philadelphia Plan toward black capitalism, the rise in incarceration rates, and urban renewal. All of these were examples of a political and legal embodiment of knowledge that was naturalized within relationships of white racial power.

These policy reviews similarly provided the substance of the claims that contemporary conditions of black America were far from the product of individual initiative in an open opportunity structure, but instead were the exercise of particular policies against our communities. In Africana Studies, we addressed and visited the differential histories of African versus European immigration, in particular how structures of white supremacy bent and made an express ramp to the fast track called "whiteness" in American society. We discussed various frameworks seeking to capture race as a variant of class arrangement, variously positioned either as wholly contained as a class matter or relatively autonomous from class. Finally, we learned to read the racial climate, the unmistakable trends in the economy, in politics, and in culture that spelled retrenchment long before mainstream leaders noticed the discernible nip in the wind of racial reform. These are just some of the intellectual tools, the critical frameworks provided by Africana Studies. Equally significant was the expectation, reinforced through a rigorous reward system—known as Dr. Turner's grading—that intellectual engagement and production would proceed in the teeth of institutional struggle.

Almost every year there was some sort of threat to the survival of the Center, some way in which the conditions of learning might be upended. The relationship between politics and education was thus normalized. In fact, we expected anything we were struggling for to be contested. If it was not raising eyebrows, then its potential to disrupt a disempowering status quo was put into question. I mean here to give a snapshot of Africana Studies, as I remember it, in establishing a baseline of intellectual and institutional preparation.

I thought, though, that going to Harvard was going to be in some ways a replication of what I had going on at Cornell. There was not an Africana Studies Center, but there was one institution there, Derrick Bell and under his wing I had hoped to nestle. I was rudely disappointed though, in 1981, when Derrick Bell took a deanship at another law school. It was the first time he left Harvard, an action that set about a series of events that, in my view, led to an emergence of critical race theory.

It might be useful to paint the picture of the players on the stage, as it existed in 1980, specifically at Harvard, but also at other elite law schools. By this time, there was a critical mass of African American students and other students of color beginning in the early to mid-'70s. We were again one generation behind those who had really broken down the walls. While the institution adjusted its recruitment policies to admit greater numbers of students of color, it did not understand these policies in terms of correcting forms of illegitimate exclusion or providing access or resources to communities that had been underserved by an elite focus on corporate or mainstream interests. Instead, the admissions of students of color proceeded along the idea that it was good to put a thumb on the scale for the underprivileged. Affirmative action for African Americans and other people of color was not good, but it was temporary. It modernized the law school, which was seen as a separate value from a merit-based logic of admissions.

While the admission of students might forgo the merit-based decision-making, faculty and curricular issues were a different matter altogether. Harvard's faculty remained stubbornly exclusive—two black faculty of more than seventy implied nothing more than a basic "pool problem." The pool problem itself was not deemed grounded in or reflective of racial power, nor was it the responsibility of the school to fix it. Merit was somehow lifted out of the economy of racial power to reflect some intrinsic value: variously called intellectual "candle power" or sheer intellectual brilliance. Something that could be quantified and roughly measured through markers such as attendance at an elite law school, high grades, officer status on a law review, a Supreme Court clerkship, perhaps a Wall Street practice, followed by a friendly call from a law school dean facilitated by a shepherd or mentor. The happenstance that these biographies perfectly match those who have populated these institutions during segregation was utterly uncontroversial. Indeed, it confirmed rather than challenged the logic of merit. In the ultimate self-referential act of deserving, most law professors seemed to be saying, "I deserve to be here, so everybody who mirrors me deserves to be here as well."

The dependent proposition that any of them naturally deserve to be there, when the terms of deserving were fashioned in the vortex of white supremacy, was never challenged by Civil Rights advocates, who, in fact, maintained friendly relationships with their liberal allies. An easy alliance seemed to have settled. After all, Harvard was not a redneck, backwoods, racist institution in the South. In its cool, airy halls reigned a sensibility of modern, technocratic efficiency that manifested little tolerance for outright racism. Integration at the faculty and curricular level would come when people of color would prove their worth in terms that the institution could honor. I believe this was a tacit agreement that liberals in these institutions felt they had a right to rely on. They were wrong.

In the fall of 1981, a class arrived coming from many different parts of the academy and Civil Rights community. This was the second generation, those students weaned on everyday conditions of struggle in their undergraduate institutions. One might rightly say that this was an entitled generation, those of us who felt we had a right to an education that facilitated our own understanding about how to address the needs of our community. The notion that we were to wait until the institution deemed our interests worthy of resources was not an alien concept, but it was not a concept that gave us any pause whatsoever. We were very disappointed that Derrick Bell had left and we understood why. We understood, too, that his courses had to continue and that teaching them provided a unique opportunity for advancing the integration of the faculty through minority hiring. So a small group of us approached the dean to ascertain what plans he had in place to teach Derrick Bell's course and to bring other people of color onto the faculty. His stunning retort set the stage for a protracted battle over affirmative action and identity, which revealed the apologetic stance of many Civil Rights leaders and the conservative underbelly of liberal legal consciousness.

James Vorenberg (the dean of Harvard Law School at the time) was no Bull Connor. He was a liberal rights attorney who was good friends with Derrick Bell, a mentor of sorts to Charles Ogletree. In our constellation, he was a man who uttered the words that set the stage for the battle: "Wouldn't you prefer an excellent white professor over a mediocre black one?" This stunning rhetoric revealed what some of us had come to understand as the liberal face of institutional exclusion. Merit was objective, impartial, and *aracial*. Indeed, racial perspectives and experiences were in an entirely separate universe, a universe of bias and prejudice, quite apart from neutrality. Of course, those of us who had come out of the Black Studies tradition identified it for what it really was—the deployment of a specific pattern of racial distribution that suppressed the racial contours, even of those who invoked it in good faith. Vorenberg really believed that his articulation was right and righteous and in believing that we would be pacified by this, he was probably affirmed by his Civil Rights colleagues as well as past generations of some students. Moreover, Vorenberg challenged us in our demand for the Constitutional Law and Minority Issues course. In his mind, there was nothing unique or compelling about such a course. It had been merely a concession to Derrick Bell that was revoked the moment he resigned. "What was so unique," he asked us, "about such a course that couldn't be gathered through a more piecemeal fashion; taking con law here, legal aid there, perhaps housing, and (when offered) an employment discrimination course?" In effect, Vorenberg was asking us—as he no doubt had asked any number of other students—to recite and justify what kind of learning we were asking for.

Past generations of students had not yet been fortunate enough to constitute a critical mass to unpack this institutional and ideological response. They knew something was missing in the treatment of race in the curriculum, but were not equipped to launch an effective collective response. Moreover, the claims that there were no qualified professors anywhere in the country to come to Harvard Law School may have struck a chord for those who may never have been instructed by a person of color. They had a hunch that this institution was wrong, but not a strong enough experience from which to wage institutional warfare at that point.

Our generation took the challenge up because we had the tools to do so. Our first response was to unpack the institutional conditions under which the reigning notions of merit were forged. We drew directly from Black Studies critiques of objectivity and neutrality in the fields of sociology, political science, history, and so forth. We highlighted the fact that while Vorenberg's cohort was assembling their credentials, lawyers of color were developing new knowledge and new approaches. They were completely reordering law to achieve ends for which the law was never intended. We noted too that the disaggregated knowledge that Vorenberg would have willed on us was precisely the argument used to attack Black Studies. We knew the difference between an education based on the occasional, random, and altogether unsatisfying moments when mainstream courses dealt with the "race problem" and education based on foregrounding the black community, and examining the conditions under which it was constructed, policed, and resisted. We knew as well from our policy studies that the law played far more than a liberationist role. Indeed, the law's tenure as a discourse of reform was minimal. It was minuscule compared to its far longer history as a discourse of racial disempowerment. This part of the story of law was not being told in our classrooms. In fact, when race came into view, it was only for a moment to celebrate the inevitable corrective that *Brown v. Board of Education* was meant to represent. It was not to challenge the pervasive way that law constituted white supremacy.

On the rare occasion that race did enter the classroom, it was either through a transgressive act on our part, playing against the active expectation of a detached and disembodied legal reasoning—or it was through an objectifying request on the part of the law professors to testify about what it meant, how it feels to be a racial object. How it feels to be confined to a ghetto, to be a victim of racial profiling, or to be affronted with a racial epithet. The minority testimony would then serve as a text to be examined and prodded to reveal the difficult and complex task of law to remain neutral in the face of such emotional appeals. The classroom's accompanying demand for racial testimony stood in stark contrast to our experience of discussing race in our Black Studies classes. Knowing that productive racial discourse was possible without apology and without transgression enabled us to imagine a classroom dynamic in an area of study that the law school was refusing to provide. The rejection of our demand itself constituted precisely the ideology of neutrality that we were set to uncover and contest. Thus, when the dean finally offered his compromise—a three-week course featuring Jack Greenberg and Julius Chambers—we immediately boycotted it. Our histories of institutional struggle helped set the stage for what we would do after the boycott. We took our education in our own hands and established an alternative course.

The story would not be complete without revealing the role some of the Civil Rights colleagues played in denouncing us as "racist" for having repudiated the dean's course. Drawing from their own struggles with Black Power movements a decade earlier, Civil Rights spokespersons such as Bayard Rustin and Carl Rowan, scholars such as Martin Kilson, leaders of the Legal Defense Fund, and the Urban League denounced our efforts as reverse racism. The same terms used to denounce SNCC in the '60s—the emerging Black Power discourse and consciousness—was deployed by Civil Rights leaders across the board. Our Black Power move was seen as the infusion of the irrelevant characteristic of race into the academy. To the Civil Rights integrationist perspective, it was the same as a Bull Connor sensibility being infused into Harvard Law School.

Interestingly, in the context of institutional struggle over integration, critics seemed initially unaware of the contradiction into which they themselves had walked. On the one hand, the very core of our argument was that the traditional criteria were inherently racially exclusionary, and that experience and perspective provided another vector of qualification. This vector of qualification was not only defensible but—given the history of legal education—was an absolute imperative if white supremacy was going to be dismantled. If Civil Rights leaders' rejection of our basic argument was to stand, then their own support of affirmative action was partial and apologetic. Without a foundation to critique exclusionary credentials, race affirmative action was, in fact, a preference. It was an excuse for departing from objective standards because there was no other vector of qualification. In this moment, their conceptual failure to advance the cause of affirmative action was embarrassingly revealed.

Our alternative course takes us to Derrick Bell. What we decided to do was to pool all of our resources from each of our student organizations and bring professors of color from all over the country to Harvard Law School, to both educate us and reveal that there was a deep trove of qualification across the country. We chose Derrick Bell's book, and in his book, there is in the very first page a lithograph of Tommie Smith and John Carlos as they stood in the 1968 Olympics in their black-fisted, Black Power salute. That picture, in the first page of a law book, told us a valid story about the project that Derrick Bell was up to. It was clear that in the same way that Carlos and Smith were engaging in the race, but engaging in the race not as people who happened to be black, but as black American athletes on the world stage who were not framing their grievance as something private back home and domestic, but something of global significance. The fact that they were doing it in the face of the American media's repudiation was the interventionist, aggressive, in-your-face kind of stance that Derrick Bell was bringing into the law school.

So what was it that he was repudiating in that book? He was repudiating the traditional way that legal scholarship was going to be articulated. He was repudiating the idea, number one, that the measure of legal scholarship was its ability to reconcile with traditional values, its ability to uphold values of federalism, its ability to uphold values of institutional separation of powers. The interests of the black community were not supposed to be part of the articulation. So what Derrick Bell was doing right then was saying what's important about legal ideology is not whether it can be reconciled with these preexisting values, but whether it advances the interests of the African American community. That was a direct echo of what was happening in Black Studies programs. That is what we heard. That is what we picked up.

To make a long story short, here is what happened: We brought people in from around the country. They each taught a chapter of Derrick Bell's book. These people who came in from across the country formed the first group of critical race theorists. The students who took the course—myself, Mari Matsuda, a range of others—ran the course and then became part of critical race theory. What we had was a common text and a context. We had an experience where we recognized that we were the second and third generation of racial integration and would take up the process of challenging the ideology that made our exclusion in those institutions seem reasonable. We had a text that directed us and helped us think about and put together the relevant histories, the relevant ideas to make those projects work. At the end of the day, having this common text and context helped us realize what we had in common. It helped us answer the question that the dean asked us: "What is so important and compelling about a course in constitutional law and minority issues?" We were able to figure that out through Derrick Bell's text and the assistance of other scholars of color.

Let me fast-forward to what I consider the challenge that critical race theory faces today. There is a longer conversation about how our stance in the law school then had to take up a struggle with white leftists—who understood the critical dimension of law but did not understand the racial dimension of law. While they were engaging in a process of encouraging people to challenge structures and institutions, they did not mean for us to challenge the organizations. So when we went into those organizations saying, "OK, well, let's talk about how ideology shapes these arrangements, let's talk about the relationship of legal ideology and white supremacy, let's talk about what's missing in critical theory and how it's not capturing racial disempowerment," we were accused of "Mau-Mauing" the organization and tearing it apart. The full circle goes back to the '60s. They told us, "Oh, we've been through this one before. This is what happened when we got kicked out of SNCC. We're not letting you kick us out of our own organization." So there was this sense that "we have been there, done that—we are not going down that road anymore." Now whether or not it was apocryphal, whether they were there or just borrowing other people's experiences, we were never able to determine fully.

Where we stand now with critical race theory is at a very important juncture. I tend to describe it as one of racial laissez-faire-ism—a return to old *Plessy* type of ideas that had never been fully repudiated in law, and that go on to justify ongoing racial inequalities across the entire social plane. We've been celebrating *Brown v. Board of Education* with an implicit belief that it repudiated *Plessy v. Ferguson*, and on a doctrinal level, it may be true. But on an ideological level, I'm not so sure how much *Brown* actually repudiated *Plessy*. Remember this one point about *Plessy*: It made an argument that segregation was not unconstitutional because it was symmetrical. Whites could not sit in black cars; blacks could not sit in white cars. Now there is inequality to that symmetry to be sure, but as we all know, segregation was about more than the symmetry of who could sit in what cars. It was about the lived social experience, the meaning of symbolic subordination, the consequence of that deeply structured separation, and a social structure that actually told African Americans, "If you want to be made equal, you've got to prove it to us through this system of separation and segregation that we've established."

Now, the very same argument—that symmetry is the way you measure equality, not the social context, not the historical meanings, not the difference in the life experience between blacks and whites—is a similar kind of argument that is being played out in affirmative action and other race-conscious remedies today. Take, for example, *Richmond v. Croson*, one of the most important Civil Rights cases that repudiated affirmative action. What was the argument? The argument is that there is reverse discrimination going on when people are not treated symmetrically, when black people are treated differently from white people and white people are treated differently from black people. Equality, on the other hand, is found when they are treated the same. So, if a white person can't get a special dispensation, then a black person shouldn't get the special dispensation. Now, we know that just like in *Plessy v. Ferguson*, symmetry did not tell us everything about inequality, and neither does color-blindness today tell us everything about racial inequality.

So just to put a point on it, we know that there is a general recognition that a whole world of difference exists between living a life as a black person and living a life as a white person. There is an asymmetry in the lived experience of race in this country. White students will tell you this, and [Andrew] Hacker did that study some time ago and said, "How much money and damages do you think you should get if you accidentally turn black?" And white students said, "Fifty million dollars wouldn't be too much." Therefore, there is an implicit recognition that there is an asymmetry in race. Racial laissez-faire-ism tells legal institutions, tells legislators that this asymmetry cannot be taken into account. It cannot be taken into account to redistribute racial value and access—not even by legislatures who want to take into account these differences in order to create a more egalitarian world.

What is the meaning of this? I would contend that the future for Africana Studies and critical race theory is one that engages in deep ideological contestation over color-blindness. Color-blindness is the virtual lunch counter for the twenty-first century. Color-blindness is where we have to pull up a seat and engage in discursive disobedience, refusing to allow race to be taken off the table, refusing to allow our condition to be seen as the natural consequence of our choices or simply the consequence of people deciding that they don't want to pursue lucrative professions. We have to take seriously the lessons that Black Studies taught us and continue to contest the ways in which legal structures use some of those ideas of neutrality to justify our exclusion.

As a concluding point—and here I am going to come full circle back to some of the insights from Black Studies—what we have to be prepared to engage in is the fact that, at this point, racial struggle is not necessarily waged by everybody who looks like us. This is one of the basic lessons I learned the moment I sat down with the Civil Rights leader who told me that I was going to flunk out of Harvard Law School. Our task must address the need to remove from conservatives, the right wing, one of the most effective attacks that they have been able to make on the Civil Rights constituency—the creation of African American spokespersons who carry a deeply anti–Civil Rights position into contemporary society. Color-coded as black, there is confusion among the masses about what these people really represent—and you all know exactly whom I am talking about. I will just offer a final quote from a good friend of mine, Luke Harris, who said that it is time for us to distinguish between our Mandelas and our Buthelezis. I think Africana Studies and critical race theory give us the critical tools for this important work in the twenty-first century.

AFTERWORD

SCOT BROWN

James Turner's writings helped define a discipline born of struggle. These works are the product of the multiple roles he played in the making of Black Studies: as student leader, administrative architect, and theoretician. Turner's studies of Black Nationalism/Pan-Africanism, Africana Studies epistemology, race, and social stratification are influential beyond their areas of topical concern. Even recent trends toward the examination of intragroup restraints on freedom and the intersection of identities and forms of oppression—racism, patriarchy, classism, ethnic conflict, and homophobia—borrow heavily from the language and logic of self-determination, autonomy, and solidarity so clearly exemplified in the works of this collection.

When students like Turner rallied in the 1960s, it was difficult to find texts on any aspect of the Black experience in American university libraries or bookstores outside of historically Black colleges and universities and other noteworthy exceptions. Book titles in African American, African, and African Diaspora subjects are currently among the most sought after by university and commercial publishing companies. Correspondingly, the Black Studies discipline has grown exponentially since the first department was won by the student-led struggle at San Francisco State University in 1968. Currently there are hundreds of departments and programs at colleges and universities. Numerous public school districts offer classes in African American Studies. The Black Studies intervention has also been a catalyst for diversity among the ranks of faculty in traditional academic departments, most noticeably in the humanities and social sciences. Other new disciplines such as Women's Studies, Chicano and Latino Studies, Asian American Studies, Native American Studies, Sexuality Studies, and Atlantic Studies have moved forward along a pathway forged by the Black Studies movement.

New studies are only beginning to explore the historic evolution of Black Studies, from social movement to established discipline. This process of "institutionalization" has dramatically reformed academia while also making concessions to its norms and modes of operation. More than four decades removed from its mass-movement origins, Black Studies (also known as African American Studies, Africana Studies, African Diaspora

Studies, etc.) has grown to become an essential component of elite higher education. Recent years have seen a steady growth of PhD programs. Unlike prior generations of faculty who were trained in traditional fields of study, a significant portion of new PhDs have majored in Black Studies at the BA level and continued to do so throughout their graduate years. These developments are clear milestones in the cultivation of scholars with extensive training in interdisciplinary approaches to instruction and knowledge production.

The trend toward further professionalization has regrettably coincided with increasing psychic distance from the ideals articulated by those who agitated for Black Studies in the latter 1960s. Black Studies as a social movement functions, for the most part, as a conduit for historical memory or references to legacies of prior struggle. It is a past evoked typically in recognition of sacrifices made by those who came before us. The movement, though, leaves us with so much more. The powerful student-activist imagination that informed early conceptions of Black Studies—as a community-centered force—has enduring value for epistemological strides forward. As questions about the future of the discipline persist, we, as students of Dr. Turner, are convinced that encounters with the works of contributors to the early Black Studies vision are necessary for the advancement of an Africana Studies paradigm capable of responding to current challenges facing African and African-descended world communities.

NOTES

1. Joy Ann Williamson, *Black Power on Campus: The University of Illinois, 1965–75* (Urbana: University of Illinois Press, 2003); Noliwe M. Rooks, *White Money/Black Power: The Surprising History of African American Studies and the Crisis of Race in Higher Education* (Boston: Beacon Press, 2006); Fabio Rojas, *From Black Power to Black Studies: How a Radical Social Movement Became an Academic Discipline* (Baltimore: Johns Hopkins University Press, 2007); Stefan M. Bradley, *Harlem vs. Columbia University: Black Student Power in the Late 1960s* (Urbana: University of Illinois Press, 2009); Ibram X. Kendi, *The Black Campus Movement: Black Students and the Racial Reconstitution of Higher Education, 1965–1972* (New York: Palgrave Macmillan, 2012); Martha Biondi, *The Black Revolution on Campus* (Berkeley: University of California Press, 2012); Delores Aldridge and Carlene Young, eds., *Out of the Revolution: the Development of Africana Studies* (New York: Lexington Books, 2000).

2. John Henrik Clarke, "The Influence of Arthur A. Schomburg on My Concept of Africana Studies," *Phylon* 49, nos. 1/2 (1992): 4–9; Jacob Carruthers, "John Henrik Clarke: The Harlem Connection to the Founding of Africana Studies," *Afro-Americans in New York Life and History* 30, no. 2 (2006); Sony Ramsey, "Caring Is Activism: Black Southern Womanist Teachers Theorizing and the Careers of Kathleen Crosby and Bertha Maxwell-Roddey, 1946–1986," *Educational Studies* 48 (2012): 244–65.

3. James Turner, interview by Scot Brown, Ithaca, New York, November 2010.

4. David Emblidge, "Rallying Point: Lewis Michaux's National Memorial African Bookstore," Publishing Research Quarterly 24, no. 4 (2008): 267–76.

5. Ralph Crowder, "The Historical Context and Political Significance of Harlem's Street Scholar Community," Afro-Americans in New York Life and History 34, no. 1 (2010): 34–71.

6. Richard Cloward and Lloyd E. Ohlin, Delinquency and Opportunity: A Theory of Delinquent Gangs (Glencoe, IL: Free Press, 1960).

7. Harrison E. Salisbury, The Shook-Up Generation (New York: Harper & Row, 1958).

8. Kalonji Olusegun, email message to editor, September 2011.

9. Harold Williamson, Northwestern University: A History, 1850–1975 (Evanston, IL: Northwestern University, 1976), 328.

10. Ibid., 329.

11. Lawrence de Graaf, "Howard: The Evolution of a Black Student Revolt," in *Protest!: Student Activism in America*, eds. Julian Foster and Durward Long (New York: Morrow, 1970), 319-344.

12. Ibid.

13. Roland J. Hinz, Kathryn Ogletree and James Turner, "Black Student Statement and Petition to Northwestern University Administrators, Received Monday, April 22, 1968," *Northwestern University Library*, accessed May 19, 2012, http://exhibits.library.northwestern.edu/archives/exhibits/1968/Documents.html.

14. Williamson, Northwestern University, 338.

15. "Northwestern Cool after Sit-In," Chicago Defender, May 7, 1968, 3.

16. "James Turner to Speak at Core Forum," Chicago Defender, August 17, 1968, 11.

17. "500 Coming to Meeting of Educators," Chicago Defender, June 5, 1968, 3.

18. "Cornell Continues to Have Problems," New York Amsterdam News, April 18, 1970, 10.

19. George Davis, "The Howard University Conference," Negro Digest 18, no. 5 (1969): 44.

20. "The Black Studies Thing," New York Times, April 1969, 65.

21. Candace Katungi and Jonathan Fenderson, "'Committed to Institution-Building': James Turner and the History of Africana Studies at Cornell University, an Interview," Journal of African American Studies 16, no. 1 (2012): 128.

22. Michael Scailes, "The Meaning of the ASA Black Caucus at the Eleventh Annual Meeting in Los Angeles," Africa Today 16, no. 2 (1969): 13.

23. Ibid.

24. Ibid.

25. John Henrik Clarke, "The African Heritage Association: Some Notes on the Conflict with the African Studies Association and the Fight to Reclaim African History," Issue: A Journal of Opinion 6, nos. 2–3 (1976): 5–9; Ronald W. Walters, Pan Africanism in the African Diaspora: An Analysis of Modern Afrocentric Political Movements (Detroit: Wayne State University, 1993), 366–70.

26. Brown, "Interview with James Turner," 38.

27. Clarke, "The African Heritage Association," 5–11; Walters, Pan Africanism in the African Diaspora; Michael and Martin William West, eds., Out of

One, Many Africas: Reconstructing the Study and Meaning of Africa (Urbana: University of Illinois Press, 1999), 97–106.

28. Brown, "Interview with James Turner," 44.

29. George Shepherd, "The Black Revolution and African Studies," Africa Today 16, no. 2 (1969): 1–2.

30. John Henrik Clarke, "African Studies in the United States: An Afro-American View," Africa Today 16, no. 2 (1969): 10–12; Sterling Stuckey, "Relationships between Africans and Afro-Americans," Africa Today 16, no. 2 (1969): 4–9; Rukudzo Murapa and James Turner, "Africa: Conflict in Black and White," Africa Today 16, nos. 5–6 (1969): 13–14.

31. "Straight Crisis: Five Years Later," Cornell Daily Sun, April 19, 1974, 13, 18.

32. "Up in Arms—April, 1969: Willard Straight Hall," Cornell Daily Sun, September 16 1980, 44; "Timeline of the Events as They Unfolded," Cornell Daily Sun, April 16, 1990, 1; "Straight Crisis: Five Years Later," 13.

33. Agyei Tyehimba, "Challenging White Cultural Hegemony, Advancing Black Liberatory Education: The Black Student Struggle for Black Studies at Cornell University, 1968–69" (Master's thesis, Cornell University, 1997); "Blacks Repulse Intruders," Cornell Daily Sun, April 20, 1969; "White Break-In Attempt Stirs Dispute over Cops," Cornell Daily Sun, April 20, 1969.

34. "Black Students Leave as CU Accedes to Demands," Cornell Daily Sun, April 21, 1969.

35. "AAS Statement," Cornell Daily Sun, December 13, 1968, 4.

36. "Perkins Replies to Afro Demands," Cornell Daily Sun, December 13, 1968.

37. "James Turner Views Africana," Cornell Daily Sun, February 2, 1972, 1.

38. "Turner Discusses Black Problems," Cornell Daily Sun, November 20, 1969, 3.

39. "Turner Views Black Studies," Cornell Daily Sun, February 20, 1970, 12.

40. Kwame Anthony Appiah, "W.E.B. Du Bois and the Making of the Encyclopedia Africana, 1909–1963," http://www.blackpast.org/?q=perspectives/w-e-b-Du Bois-and-making-encyclopedia-africana-1909-1963.

41. "Turner Views Black Studies," 1.

42. "James Turner Views Africana," 1; Boniface Obichere, "The Significance and Challenge of Afro-American Studies," Journal of Black Studies 1, no. 2 (1970): 161–77; Nathan Hare, "A Torch to Burn Down a Decadent World," Black Scholar 2, no. 1 (1970): 2–5.

43. James Turner, "The Political Sociology of Racism and Systemic Oppression: Internal colonialism as a Paradigm for Socioeconomic Analysis; Theoretical Nexus in Afro-American Political Thought: Nationalist Responses to Racist

Oppression from Emigration to Pan-Africanism," (PhD diss., Union Institute and University, 1975).

44. S. Eversley Bradwell, "Always Room at the Top: Black Students and Educational Policy in Ithaca, NY" (PhD diss., Cornell University, 2009).

45. "Experimental College at Cornell Based upon Ujamaa," New York Amsterdam News, September 23, 1972.

PART II

1. Robin D. G. Kelley, *Freedom Dreams: The Black Radical Imagination* (Boston: Beacon Press, 2002), 62.

2. Ibid., 193.

3. Manning Marable writes in 1983: "The genocidal logic of the situation could demand, in the not too distant future, the rejection of the ghetto's right to survival in the new capitalist order. Without gas chambers or pogroms, the dark ghetto's economic and social institutions might be destroyed, and many of its residents would simply cease to exist." Manning Marable, *How Capitalism Underdeveloped Black America* (Cambridge, MA: South End Press, 1983), 253.

4. C.L.R. James, *The Black Jacobins: Toussaint L'Ouverture and the San Domingo Revolution* (New York: Vintage Books, 1989), 244 (emphasis added).

5. Angela Y. Davis, *Women, Race & Class* (New York: Vintage Books, 1983), 18.

6. Some durable examples of such texts include Hazel V. Carby, *Race Men* (Cambridge, MA: Harvard University Press, 1998); Joy Ann James, *Shadowboxing: Representations of Black Feminist Politics* (New York: Palgrave, 1999); Patricia Hill Collins, *Black Feminist Thought: Knowledge, Consciousness, and the Politics of Empowerment* (Boston: Unwin Hyman, 1990); Audre Lorde, *Sister Outsider: Essays and Speeches* (Trumansburg, NY: Crossing Press, 1984); June Jordan, *Some of Us Did Not Die: New and Selected Essays of June Jordan* (New York: Civitas Books, 2002); bell hooks, *Ain't I a Woman: Black Women and Feminism* (Boston: South End Press, 1981); Cathy Cohen, *The Boundaries of Blackness: AIDS and the Breakdown of Black Politics* (Chicago: University of Chicago Press, 1999); Barbara Smith, *Home Girls: A Black Feminist Anthology* (New Brunswick, NJ: Rutgers University Press, 2000).

7. See Combahee River Collective, "A Black Feminist Statement," in *This Bridge Called My Back: Writings by Radical Women of Color*, ed. Cherríe Moraga and Gloria Anzaldúa (New York: Kitchen Table Press, 1981), 210–18.

8. Safiya Bukhari, "Coming of Age: A Black Revolutionary," in *The War Before: The True Life Story of Becoming a Black Panther, Keeping the Faith in Prison & Fighting for Those Left Behind*, ed. Safiya Bukhari and Laura Whitehorn (New York: Feminist Press, 2010), 10–11.

9. See, for example, Scot Brown, *Fighting for US: Maulana Karenga, the US Organization, and Black Cultural Nationalism* (New York: New York University Press, 2003); E. Frances White, "Africa on My Mind: Gender, Counter Discourse, and African American Nationalism," and Wahneema Lubiano, "Standing in for the State: Black Nationalism and 'Writing' the Black Subject," in *Is It Nation Time?: Contemporary Essays on Black Power and Black Nationalism*, ed. Eddie S. Glaude Jr. (Chicago: University of Chicago Press, 2002).

10. Combahee River Collective, "A Black Feminist Statement," 212.

11. Ibid., 211.

12. Ibid., 212.

13. Ibid., 214.

14. Bukhari, "Coming of Age," 56–57.

15. Frantz Fanon, *The Wretched of the Earth*, trans. Richard Philcox (New York: Grove Press, 2004), 149.

16. See Jared Sexton and Steve Martinot, "The Avant-Garde of White Supremacy," *Social Identities* 9, no. 2 (2003): 169–81; and Frank B. Wilderson III, "The Prison Slave as Hegemony's (Silent) Scandal," *Social Justice* 3, no. 2 (2004): 18–27.

17. See, by way of direct and indirect discussion, Daniel Widener, *Black Arts West: Culture and Struggle in Postwar Los Angeles* (Durham, NC: Duke University Press, 2010); William Van Deburg, *Modern Black Nationalism: From Marcus Garvey to Louis Farrakhan* (New York: New York University Press, 1997); and Rod Bush, *We Are Not What We Seem: Black Nationalism and Class Struggle in the American Century* (New York: New York University Press, 1999).

18. William L. Patterson, *We Charge Genocide: The Historic Petition to the United Nations for Relief from a Crime of the United States Government Against the Negro People* (New York: Civil Rights Congress, 1951).

19. Fanon, *Wretched of the Earth*, 1.

20. Originally published in *Black World* 20, no. 2 (January 1971): 6–13.

21. We have taken these extensive quotations from Rev. C.T. Vivian's recent book, *Black Power and the American Myth* (Philadelphia: Fortress Press, 1970), because we believe it is a valuable treatise and deserves attention.

22. Parentheses and brackets are the author's.

23. These varieties of Black Nationalism are not rigidly delineated nor are they mutually exclusive categories. Any individual or Black Nationalist organization usually assumes any number of combinations of these varieties.

24. In fact, after Nigeria and the Africans in Brazil, the Black people of America constitute the single largest African group in the world.

25. C.J. Munford, "Black National Revolution in America," in symposium, Utah State University, May 1970, 5–6.

26. Julius Lester, "From the Other Side of the Tracks," *The Guardian*, April 19, 1969, 13.

27. Christopher Lasch, professor of history at Northwestern University, unpublished manuscript, 1968.

28. For a discussion of this point, see John Horton, "Order and Conflict Theories of Social Problems as Competing Ideologies," *American Journal of Sociology* 71, no. 6 (May 1966): 712.

29. Horton, "Order and Conflict," 702.

30. Quoted in Bill McAdoo, "Pre–Civil War Black Nationalism," *Progressive Labor* (June–July, 1966): 40. Cf. W.E.B. Du Bois: "We are Americans, not only by birth and by citizenship, but by our political ideals, our language, our religion. Further than that, our Americanism does not go. At that point, we are Negroes, members of that vast historic race....We are the first fruits of this new nation, the harbinger of that black tomorrow which is yet to soften the whiteness of the Teutonic today....As such, it is our duty to conserve our physical powers, our intellectual endowments, our spiritual ideals; as a race, we must strive by race organization, by race solidarity, by race unity to the realization of that broader humanity which freely recognizes differences in men, but sternly deprecates inequality in their opportunities of development," as quoted in E. U. Essien Undom, *Black Nationalism* (Chicago: University of Chicago Press, 1962), 28–29.

31. Sethard Fisher, "Essay Review—Negro Life and Social Process," *Social Problems* 13, no. 3 (Winter 1966): 344.

32. Frank Kofsky, "Malcolm X," *Monthly Review* (September 1966): 44.

33. Louis A. Coser, *The Functions of Social Conflict* (New York: The Free Press, 1964), 87–88.

34. E. Franklin Frazier, *Race and Culture Contacts in the Modern World*, 1st ed. (New York: Knopf, 1957), 311.

35. Lerone Bennett, *Confrontation: Black and White* (Chicago: Johnson Publishing Company, 1965), 10.

36. Cf. Erik Erikson, "The Concept of Identity in Race Relations," in *The Negro American*, ed. Talcott Parsons and Kenneth B. Clark (Boston: Houghton Mifflin, 1966), 247.

37. Originally published in *The Black Scholar* 1, no. 2 (1969): 18–27.

38. Eric Williams, *Capitalism and Slavery*, 2nd ed. (London: Deutsch, 1964).

39. Aimé Césaire, *Discourse on Colonialism* (Paris: Présence Africaine, 1955), 22.

40. Bloke Modisane, "Why I Ran Away," in *An African Treasury*, ed. Langston Hughes (New York: Crown Publishers, 1960), 26.

41. The psychological implication of racial discrimination for the black man in white society have produced numerous studies. This question seems to have been summarized by John Dollard. "The upshot of the matter seems to be that recognizing one's own Negro traits is bound to be a process wounding to the basic sense of integrity of the individual who comes into life with no such negative views of his own characteristics," in *Caste and Class in a Southern Town*, 2nd ed. (New York: Harper, 1949), 184.

42. RobeR.E. Park, *Race and Culture* (New York: The Free Press, 1950), 356.

43. James Baldwin quoted by Thomas F. Pettigrew in *Profile of the Negro American* (Princeton, NJ: Princeton University Press, 1964), 10.

44. Stokely Carmichael, "Toward Black Liberation," *Massachusetts Review* 7, no.4 (Autumn 1966): 639–40.

45. Evelyn Rogers, "Is Ebony Killing Black Women?," *Liberator* 6, no. 3 (March 1965): 12–13.

46. Robert Penn Warren, *Who Speaks for the Negro?* (New York: Harcourt Brace and Co., 1965), 20–21.

47. Erik H. Erikson, "The Concept of Identity and Race Relations," in *The Negro American*, ed. Talcott Parsons and Kenneth Clark (Boston: Houghton Mifflin, 1966), 232.

48. Lerone Bennett, *Negro Mood* (Chicago: Johnson Publishing Co., 1964), 49.

49. Rupert Emerson and Martin Kilson, "The American Dilemma in a Changing World, the Rise of Africa and the Negro American," in *The Negro American*, ed. Talcott Parsons and Kenneth Clark (Boston: Houghton Mifflin, 1966), 640–41.

50. St. Clair Drake, "The Social and Economic Status of the Negro in the United States, in *The Negro American*, ed. Talcott Parsons and Kenneth Clark (Boston: Houghton Mifflin, 1966), 35.

51. Erikson, "Concepts of Identity," 230.

52. John O. Killens, "The Meaning and Measure of Black Power," *Negro Digest* 26, no. 1 (November 1966): 36.

53. William K. Kgositsile, "Has God Failed James Baldwin?" *Liberator* 7, no. 1 (January 1967): 11.

54. Killens, "Measure of Black Power," 33.

55. Bennett, *Negro Mood*, 55.

56. Gerald McWorter, "Negro Rights and the American Future," *Negro Digest* (October 1966): 36.

57. Emerson and Kilson, "The American Dilemma," 638.

58. Frank Kofsky, "Malcolm X," *Monthly Review* 18, no. 4 (September 1966): 44.

59. Alex Haley, *The Autobiography of Malcolm X* (New York: Grove Press, 1965), 242–43.

60. George Breitman, ed., *Malcolm X Speaks* (New York: Merit Publishers, 1965), 269.

61. Lewis Coser, *The Functions of Social Conflict* (New York: The Free Press, 1964), 87–88.

62. James Farmer, "Mood Ebony," *Playboy* 13, no. 2 (February 1966): 126.

63. Aimé Césaire, *Toussaint L'Ouverture* (Paris: Présence Africaine, 1961), 31.

64. Farmer, "Mood Ebony," 126, 177.

65. Farmer, "Mood Ebony," 178.

66. Originally published in the Center for African American History and Culture, Occasional Papers series 1, Temple University, Philadelphia, PA, 1992, under the authorship of Bettye Collier-Thomas and James Turner.

67. F. Z. S. Peregrino, "Be Known as Negroes," *The Star of Zion*, January 19, 1899.

68. *Afro-American Ledger*, September 25, 1915.

69. "'African-American' Favored by Many of America's Blacks," *New York Times*, January 13, 1989; *Freedom's Journal*, August 29, 1828, 178.

70. Mary Frances Berry and John W. Blassingame, *Long Memory: The Black Experience in America* (New York: Oxford University Press, 1982), 389–96; for a discussion of the relationship between race designation terms and skin color, see F. James Davis, *Who Is Black?: One Nation's Definition* (University Park, PA: Pennsylvania State University Press, 1991), 5–6.

71. The distinction is made in terms of the African presence in America as captive laborers, as a consequence of European expansionism and colonialism. The original presence of Africans in the Americas was as free seafaring explorers and traders, who were familiar with the North American hemisphere long before the arrival of Christopher Columbus and others.

72. Ira Berlin, *Slaves without Masters: The Free Negro in the Antebellum South* (New York: Pantheon Books, 1974), 6–8, 108–11, 151–52, 195–98, 247–49, 265–69; E. Franklin Frazier, *Black Bourgeoisie: The Rise of a New Middle Class* (New York: The Free Press, 1965), 13–15.

73. Frazier, *Black Bourgeoisie*, 136–37; E. Franklin Frazier, *The Negro Family in the United States* (Chicago: University of Chicago Press, 1966), 165, 197–200.

74. "The 'Colored People' of the West Indies," *Christian Recorder*, June 23, 1866; "White Is Right in Haiti," *Chicago Defender*, January 1, 1946; "Color Prejudice," *Indianapolis Freeman*, February 6, 1904; Thomas H. Jackson, D.D., "Who Are We?" *Christian Recorder*, March 10, 1881; "Color-Blind Negroes," *The Star of Zion*, January 19, 1899; "The White Negro," *Washington Bee*, August 5, 1911; "The Mulatto—Crux of the Negro Problem," *Philadelphia Tribune*, April 12, 1924; "Condemns Employers and Housewives Who Ask for 'Light Colored' Help Only," *Baltimore Afro-American*, September 12, 1931; "Sees 'Light-Skinned Aristocracy' in Race," *Chicago Defender*, November 18, 1944; "Negroes Are Color Crazy," *Negro Digest*, March 1965, 86.

75. "Should the Word African in Our Denominational Title Be Changed?" *Christian Recorder*, September 3, 1870; "Not Negroes but Africans," *Indianapolis Freeman*, January 7, 1893; Sterling Stuckey, *Slave Culture: Nationalist Theory and the Foundations of Black America* (New York: Oxford University Press, 1987), 199–215; Berry and Blassingame, *Long Memory*, 389–91; "'African-American' for 'Blacks' Signals a Return," *New York Times*, January 6, 1989.

76. Monroe Work, *The Negro Year Book, 1931–1932* (Tuskegee: The Negro Year Book Publishing Co., 1933), 20; Berry and Blassingame, *Long Memory*, 391.

77. Editorial, *Provincial Freeman*, March 17, 1855.

78. "The 'Colored People' of the West Indies," *Christian Recorder*, June 23, 1866.

79. As early as 1837 some free black leaders in the Moral Reform Association, emphasizing that they were Americans, questioned the need for retaining "Colored," or any other race designation. For discussion of this issue, see Howard Holman Bell, *A Survey of the Negro Convention Movement, 1830–1861* (New York: Arno Press and the New York Times, 1969), 50–53; and *The Colored American*, September 2, 1837, 2–3; February 10, 1838, 19; March 29, 1838, 38–39.

80. For over a decade the A.M.E. Church intensely debated the issue of removing African from the denominational title. For a sample of the articles discussing this issue and the general question of race designation, see in the *Christian Recorder*: "The Word African in Our Denominational Title Should be Retained," August 27, 1870; Rev. Benjamin Tucker Tanner, "Americans: Not Negroes," March 14, 1878; and Rev. Benjamin Tucker Tanner, "Americans and Negroes: Both," March 28, 1878 (Tanner's response to J. W. Cromwell, editor of the *People's Advocate* who argued for Negro); Rev. B. J. Brooks, "Our Church Title," April 22, 1880; Rev. E. Ferguson, "The Word 'African,' and Consolidation," April 22, 1880; Rev. John B. Bagwell, "Who

We Are," December 23, 1880; J. H. Scott, "Who Are We?" December 30, 1880; Rev. Benjamin Tucker Tanner, "Who Are We?" January 13, 1881; Wm. E. Walker, "Who We Are," January 20, 1881; Rev. A. J. Kershaw, "Who Are We?" January 27, 1881; J. H. Scott, "Who Are We?" February 3, 1881; Thomas H. Jackson, "Who Are We?" March 10, 1881.

81. While color consciousness was evident early in the nineteenth century, it wasn't until after emancipation that practice based upon color values becomes institutionalized in social relations that are internalized in the newly emerging black communities.

82. Editorial, *The Star of Zion*, December 9, 1897.

83. In 1878 Everett J. Waring proposed Afro-American as an alternative to Negro and Colored. A member of a very prominent family, Waring was born free in Columbus, Ohio, in 1859. A graduate of Howard University's law school, Waring was the first black attorney to be admitted to the bar in Maryland. "Everett J. Waring Dead," *Baltimore Afro-American*, September 5, 1914; "The Term Afro-American," *New York Age*, January 2, 1892.

84. Bruce, a former slave, was very dark-skinned. Born in 1856 in Piscataway, Maryland, he knew about the most devastating aspects of slavery. Possessing little formal education, through sheer determination he was able to develop journalistic skills. Bruce wrote extensively for the black and white press. In 1884, his famous column head "Bruce Grit" appeared in the *Cleveland Gazette* and in the *New York Age*. It is around this time that Bruce and Fortune developed a relationship. During the early 1890s Bruce worked with Fortune in the Afro-American League and in the Afro-American Council. Their relationship appears to have deteriorated by 1895. Almost two decades later, Bruce and Fortune worked together in the UNIA, an organization funded by Marcus Garvey. Rayford W. Logan and Michael R. Winston, eds., *Dictionary of American Negro Biography* (New York: W. W. Norton & Company, 1982), s.v. "Bruce, John Edward [Bruce Grit]," by Ernest Kaiser, 76–77.

85. "Its Origin Dates to Ante-bellum Days," *The Ledger*, June 18, 1898.

86. T. Thomas Fortune, a journalist and civil rights advocate, was born in 1856 to slave parents in Marianna, Florida. His ancestors were a mixture of Africans, Indians and whites, among them Thomas Fortune, an Irishman who was his paternal grandfather. His father, Emanuel Fortune, served in the Florida constitutional convention of 1868. Prior to launching his journalistic career, T. Thomas Fortune attended Howard University for a short period of time during the late 1870s. Fortune was a key figure in the founding of the National Afro-American League, which was a major forerunner

of the **NAACP**. Logan and Winston, *Dictionary*, s.v. "Fortune T[imothy] Thomas," by Emma Lou Thornbrough.

87. "The Color Line," *The Star of Zion*, December 2, 1897.

88. Beginning in 1877, with his critique of "Colored Society in Washington," Bruce was outspoken against blacks who prided themselves on their white antecedents, and who promoted the idea of class distinctions based on color. Willard B. Gatewood, *Aristocrats of Color: The Black Elite, 1880–1920* (Bloomington: Indiana University Press, 1990), 160–61; "Color Line in Churches," *Christian Recorder*, October 22, 1885; "Our Correspondent Resigns," *New York Age*, February 28, 1885; Charles W. Chestnutt, "What Is a White Man?" *The Independent*, May 30, 1889, 693–94; "Color Blind Negroes," *The Star of Zion*, January 19, 1899; "Color Prejudice," *Indianapolis Freeman*, February 6, 1904; Nannie H. Burroughs, "Not Color but Character," *The Voice of the Negro* 1, no. 7 (July 1904): 277–79; "The White Negro," *Washington Bee*, August 5, 1911.

89. Bettye Collier-Thomas and Sharon Harley, "Race, Class and Gender in the Upper South: A Comparative Analysis of Black Women in Baltimore, Maryland and Washington, D.C., 1890–1920," paper presented at the annual convention of the American Historical Association, 1984; Gatewood, "The Color Factor," in *Aristocrats of Color*, 149–50; E. Franklin Frazier, "Old Families and New Classes," in *The Negro Family in the United States* (Chicago: University of Chicago Press, 1939), 405–6; Burroughs, "Not Color but Character," 277–79; "Women Hardest Hit by Invasion of Yellow Spectre," *Baltimore Afro-American*, May 23, 1931; Melville J. Herskovits, "The Color Line," *American Mercury*, September 1925.

90. "Dear Bishop Harris, Negroid Does Not Mean Any More than Afro-American," *The Star of Zion*, December 15, 1898. This is a letter signed "Bruce Grit" from John Bruce in response to an article written by A.M.E. Zion Bishop C. R. Harris who supported Afro-American as the race designation.

91. Ibid.

92. "Our Women Not 'Negresses,' Insult to Our Women," *Indianapolis Freeman*, November 17, 1906; in 1932 and in 1937, the *Baltimore Afro-American* conducted a reader's survey to determine the preferred race designation among black Americans. In discussing Negro, a number of respondents indicated a dislike for "nigger" and "negress" as terms independent and derivative of Negro. For surveys of African American preferences in selected cities, see in the *Baltimore Afro-American*: "Voters Choosing Word 'Negro' in Lead in First Week's Balloting," February 27, 1932; "Word 'Negro' Leads Others," March 12, 1932; "Word Negro Leads Other Designations for Racial

Group," March 19, 1932; "How to Begin an Argument," July 24, 1937; "How to Extend an Argument," July 31, 1937; and "How to Extend an Argument," August 7, 1932.

93. Monroe Work, *The Negro Year Book, 1916–1917* (Tuskegee: The Negro Year Book Publishing Co., 1918), 43.

94. "The High Cost of Propaganda," *Negro World*, August 14, 1926.

95. "Negro Is an Honorable Name," *Negro World*, June 1, 1930.

96. Monroe Work, *Negro Year Book, 1912* (Tuskegee: The Negro Year Book Publishing Co., 1913).

97. Monroe Work, *Negro Year Book, 1931–1932* (Tuskegee: The Negro Year Book Publishing Co., 1933), 18–26.

98. For a survey of attitudes and opinions regarding Negro as an appropriate race designation during the years 1930 to 1960, see *The Schomburg Center Clipping File, 1925–1974* (microfilm). For public surveys of African American preferences in selected cities, see citations to *Baltimore Afro-American* in footnote 26.

99. Amy Jacques Garvey, ed., *Philosophy and Opinions of Marcus Garvey*, Studies in American Negro Life (New York: Athenaeum, 1969), 2:18.

100. Ibid.

101. Ibid., 2:22.

102. For a survey of attitudes and opinions regarding the capitalization of the term Negro, see "Negro—Capital 'N' & Name Controversy," *Schomburg Center Clipping File* (microfilm). Journalist Lester A. Walton argued persuasively for the capitalization of Negro and its use as a generic race term. For Walton's views, see "Wants Letter 'N' Capitalized: Lester Walton Writes Letter to the Associated Press," *New York Age*, May 1, 1913. For a discussion of the capitalization campaign and a listing of white periodicals and newspapers who capitalize Negro, see Work, *Negro Year Book, 1931–32*, 22–26.

103. For publications which reflect the Black consciousness/Black power movement, see *The Black Scholar, Black World, Liberator, Muhammad Speaks, Journal of Black Poetry*, and the SNCC newsletters and position papers. The *Liberator* is an excellent example of the metamorphosis which occurs in the political thought of African Americans. For examples of juxtaposing "Negro" and "Black" as paradigms of political attitudes, see the *Liberator* for the period 1967–1968. Launched around 1960, this publication styled itself as the "voice of the Afro-American protest movement in the U.S. and the liberation movement of Africa." Widely read by radical intellectuals, it accurately reflected the political attitudes of the period. During the latter part of 1967, the magazine suspended usage of the term Negro in the titling of articles and began exclusive use of the terms Afro-American and Black. The only excep-

tion to this policy was the publication of "Negro Revolution," an article by Harold Cruse. Negro continues to be used, however, in lowercase and as a term of derision.

104. For information regarding the Nation of Islam's usage of the phrase "the so-called Negro," see *Muhammad Speaks*.

105. Lerone Bennett, "Liberation[,] integration or separation dilemma is called false choice by advocates of transformation," *Ebony*, August 1970; Lerone Bennett, "The Terms Defined," *Ebony*, August 1970.

106. Amiri Baraka, "The Congress of Afrikan People: A Position Paper," *The Black Scholar*, January–February 1975, 6–7; Peter Bailey, "What African-American Nationalism Means to Me," *Negro Digest*, December 1967, 31–33; James Turner, "Black Nationalism: The Inevitable Response," *Black World*, January 1971, 4.

107. Benjamin Goodman, *The End of White World Supremacy: Four Speeches by Malcolm X* (New York: Merlin House, 1971). See also George Breitman, *Malcolm X Speaks* (New York: Pathfinder Press, 1989).

108. Lerone Bennett, "What's in a Name?" *Ebony*, November 1967.

109. W. Burghardt Turner and Joyce Moore Turner, eds., *Richard B. Moore, Caribbean Militant Harlem: Collected Writings, 1920–1972* (Bloomington: Indiana University Press, 1988), 237. For history and analysis of the uses of the term Negro, see Richard B. Moore, *The Name "Negro": Its Origin and Evil Use* (New York: Afro American Publishers, Inc., 1960).

110. Malcolm X, *Malcolm X on Afro-American History* (New York: Pathfinder Press, 1989).

111. C. Eric Lincoln, "How Negroes Rediscovered Their Racial Pride," *Negro Digest* (July 1961): 71–76; William E. Cross, Jr., "Toward a Psychology of Black Liberation: The Negro-to-Black Conversion Experience," *Negro World* (July 1971): 13–27; Simon Podair, "The Black and White of It," *Negro Digest* (March 1967): 38–43.

112. "'African-American' for 'Black' Signals a Return," *New York Times*, January 6, 1989; "'African-American' Suits Me Fine," *Washington Post*, February 19, 1989; "'African-American' Favored by Many of America's Blacks," *New York Times*, January 31, 1989; "For Blacks, a Debate on New Terminology," *Philadelphia Inquirer*, April 21, 1989; "Identity Crisis," *Upscale*, June–July 1991; "Colored Again," *Emerge*, April 1991; "Most African-Americans: Don't Call Us That," *Philadelphia Daily News*, January 28, 1991; "Honoring Heritage with a New Name," *Post-Standard*, February 15, 1991.

113. Alice Walker, "Embracing the Dark and the Light: For Black Black Women and Whiter Black Women Who Wish to Struggle Together Over the 'Dirty Little Secret' of Color in African-American Life," *Essence*, July 1982; "Is Skin

Color Still a Problem in Black America?" *Ebony*, December 1984; "Light vs. Dark: Why Skin Color No Longer Makes a Difference," *Ebony*, May 1988; "Effi Barry Reveals: Mayor Wanted Her Skin Darkened to Protect His Image as a Black Man," *Jet*, July 23, 1990.

PART III

1. A brief list of scholars who have seriously engaged Turner's ideas about Black Studies in print, and particularly his notion of Africana are Delores Aldridge, Talmadge Anderson, Mario Azevedo, Karanja Keita Carroll, Anani Dzidzienyo, Jonathan Fenderson, Milfred C. Fierce, Munashe Furusa, James Garrett, Darlene Clark Hine, Clenora Hudson-Weems, Maulana Karenga, Marquita Pellerin, Patricia Reid-Merritt, and James B. Stewart.

2. Winston Van Horne, "Black Studies, Names Controversy," in *Encyclopedia of Black Studies*, ed. Molefi K. Asante and Ama Mazama (Thousand Oaks, CA: Sage, 2005); Molefi Asante, "Sustaining Africology: On the Creation and Development of a Discipline," in *A Companion to African-American Studies*, ed. Lewis Gordon and Jane Anna Gordon (Malden, MA: Blackwell, 2006); Molefi Asante, "The Pursuit of Africology: On the Creation and Sustaining of Black Studies," in *Handbook of Black Studies*, ed. Molefi K. Asante and Maulana Karenga (Thousand Oaks, CA: Sage, 2006).

3. James Turner, "Black Students and Their Changing Perspective," *Ebony*, August 1969, 135–40.

4. The Black student group at Northwestern was named "For Members Only." The name was a way of not only signifying the all-Black nature of the group, but also a rhetorical play on the (all-)White country clubs located throughout Evanston, which frequently had signs posted out front that read "For Members Only." Turner was a graduate student, but the group consisted of mostly undergraduates. See Lerone Bennett Jr., "Confrontation on the Campus," *Ebony*, May 1968, 27–31, 32–34; and Northwestern University Black Students, "If Our Demands Are Impossible, Then Peace Between Us Is Impossible Too," in *Black Nationalism in America*, ed. John Bracey, August Meier, and Elliott Rudwick (Indianapolis: Bobbs-Merrill, 1970), 476–85.

5. Stefan Bradley, *Harlem vs. Columbia: Black Student Power in the Late 1960s* (Urbana: University of Illinois Press, 2009).

6. Johnetta Cole, "Black Studies in Liberal Arts Education," in *The Black Studies Reader*, ed. Jacqueline Bobo, Cynthia Hudley, and Claudine Michel (New York: Routledge, 2002), 21–34.

7. In addition to taking courses in African Studies at Northwestern, Turner was also one of many students who came under the influential orbit of St. Clair

Drake, who taught at Roosevelt University in Chicago, maintained Pan-African connections to progressive leaders and radical activists throughout Africa, and vociferously argued for a liberated African continent.

8. There is a documentary on Melville Herskovits and the central role he played in the development of African Studies, called *Herskovits: At the Heart of Darkness*. The film also explores Herskovits's tenuous connection with U.S. intelligence agencies. Although the film argues that Herskovits was hesitant to get politically involved with intelligence agencies, it does contend that he remained in conversation with these agencies while heading the African Studies Program at Northwestern. Indeed, Herskovits's conversations with U.S. intelligence agencies established a long history of interaction with the Northwestern University African Studies Program. These links between African Studies and U.S. government intelligence agencies would come to a head at the annual meeting of the African Studies Association (ASA) in Montreal. Three months after the appearance of Turner's publication in *Ebony*, he participated in the historic protest that culminated in the formal splitting of ASA and the formation of the African Heritage Studies Association (AHSA). See *Africa Today* 16, nos. 5–6 (October/December 1969); William G. Martin and Michael O. West, "The Ascent, Triumph, and Disintegration of the Africanist Enterprise, USA," in *Out of One, Many Africas: Reconstructing the Meaning of Africa*, ed. William G. Martin and Michael O. West (Urbana: University of Illinois Press 1999), 85–122; Jerry Gershenhorn, "'Not an Academic Affair': African-American Scholars and the Development of African Studies Programs in the United States, 1942–1960," *Journal of African American History* 94, no. 1 (Winter): 44–68; and Horace Campbell, "Low-Intensity Warfare and the Study of Africans at Home and Abroad," in *Out of One, Many Africas: Reconstructing the Meaning of Africa*, ed. William G. Martin and Michael O. West (Urbana: University of Illinois Press 1999), 123–44.

9. James Meriwether, *Proudly We Can Be Africans: Black Americans and Africa, 1935–1961* (Durham: University of North Carolina Press, 2001), 2.

10. James Turner, "Black Studies: A Concept and a Plan," *Cornell Chronicle* 1, no. 2 (1969): 1–8.

11. In 2009 the *Journal of Black Studies* published a special issue entitled "Defining Ourselves: One Name, One Discipline?" It focused on the uses of various names to describe the intellectual enterprise commonly referred to as Black Studies. While several of the contributors supported "Africana Studies" as the most accurate and useful name for the discipline, none of the contributors referred to "Black Studies: A Concept and a Plan" as the document that initiated the use of the phrase in the Black Studies lexicon.

Most of the contributors traced the phrase back to Turner's article "Africana Studies and Epistemology," which appeared in 1984. Instances such as these point to the serious need for an intellectual history of Black/Africana Studies—one that connects the uses of concepts and ideas to temporal realities and a historical timeline. See Patricia Reid-Merritt, guest ed., "Defining Ourselves: One Name, One Discipline" (Special Issue), *Journal of Black Studies* 40, no. 1 (2009).

12. The pictures of Cornell's Afro-American Society exiting Willard Straight Hall are among the most famous images of America's radical 1960s. The images created a media frenzy, appearing on the cover of the May 1969 issue of *Newsweek* and helping photographer Steve Starr capture a Pulitzer Prize. The protest and spectacle had a major impact on universities and colleges across the country, causing many higher-education administrators to support Black Studies programs in an attempt to preempt similar events from occurring on their own campuses. While the Afro-American Society's Edward Whitfield and Eric Evans are featured prominently in the photos, the pictures don't capture the support and participation of members from the Black Ithaca community and Black students from the surrounding colleges. In addition, the photos do not depict the often-forgotten participation of Gloria Joseph, the Assistant Dean for Student Affairs in charge of Cornell's Committee on Special Education Projects (**COSEP**) and the only Black faculty member to participate in the event.

13. Proponents of Black Studies shared a language (and rationale) that was particular to those activist-scholars invested in bringing Black Studies to fruition; but this language (and rationale) was very different than the edict of the university and guardians of the traditional disciplines. So although there was a shared vocabulary among Black Studies proponents, it was unconventional and heretical to the American educational establishment.

14. At the fortieth anniversary of Cornell's **AS&RC**, an audience member asked Turner, "What is one of the biggest regrets you've held about the history and development of the Center?" He replied by saying, "My biggest regret was not working hard enough to develop the urban extension center, and letting the idea fall by the wayside over the years." In 1969 James Turner reached out to Black economist Robert S. Browne to help outline the plan for the Urban Resident Center. Browne was the founding editor of the *Review of Black Political Economy* and founder of the Black Economic Research Center located in Harlem. Browne later helped initiate the Emergency Land Fund for Black farmers in the process of losing their land. See Charles L. Betsey, "A Brief Biography of Robert S. Brown," *Review of Black Political Economy* 35 (2008): 57–60; and John W. Handy, "The Emergence of the Black Econom-

ic Research Center and the Review of Black Political Economy: 1969–1972," *Review of Black Political Economy* 35 (2008): 75–89.

15. When these student activists did not demand an independent Black Studies college, they usually demanded a department and a cultural center or dormitory to complement it. For various examples, see Mark Chiang, *The Cultural Capital of Asian American Studies: Autonomy and Representation in the University* (New York: New York University Press, 2009), 63–64; Joy Ann Williamson, *Black Power on Campus: The University of Illinois, 1965–1975* (Urbana: University of Illinois Press, 2003); Wayne Glasker, *Black Studies in the Ivory Tower: African American Student Activism at the University of Pennsylvania, 1967–1990* (Amherst: University of Massachusetts Press, 2002); Richard P. McCormick, *The Black Student Protest Movement at Rutgers* (New Brunswick, NJ: Rutgers University Press, 1990); and "**BSU** Demands to Leo Cain," Leo Cain Papers (May 25, 1969), California State University Dominguez Hills Archives.

16. James Turner, "Black Studies and a Black Philosophy of Education," *Black Lines* 1, no. 2 (1970): 5–8.

17. W.E.B. Du Bois, *Black Reconstruction in America, 1860–1880* (New York: Free Press, 1992).

18. Ibid., 713.

19. Amilcar Shabazz, *Advancing Democracy: African Americans and the Struggle for Access and Equity in Higher Education in Texas* (Durham: University of North Carolina Press, 2006), 219.

20. Also see James Turner, "Founding Fathers of American Sociology: An Examination of Theories of Race Relations," *Journal of Black Studies* 9, no. 1 (September 1978): 3–14.

21. Michael Thelwell, "Black Studies: A Political Perspective," *Massachusetts Review* (Autumn 1969): 703–12.

22. James Turner, "Black Studies as an Integral Tradition in African-American Intellectual History," *Issues: A Journal of Opinion* 6, nos. 2–3 (1976): 73–78.

23. Lawrence Crouchett, "Early Black Studies Movements," *Journal of Black Studies* 2 (1971): 189–200; Ronald Bailey, "Black Studies in Historical Perspective," *Journal of Social Issues* 29, no. 1 (1973). See also Robert Harris, "The Intellectual and Institutional Development of Africana Studies," in *Three Essays: Black Studies in the United States*, ed. Robert Harris, Darlene Clark Hine, and Nellie McKay (New York: Ford Foundation, 1990).

24. Deborah Gray White, *Too Heavy a Load: Black Women in Defense of Themselves, 1894–1994* (New York: Norton, 1999).

25. The Young Turks of Howard included Ralph Bunche, Abram Harris, and E. Franklin Frazier. For an excellent study of this group of intellectuals, see

Jonathan Holloway, *Confronting the Veil: Abram Harris Jr., E. Franklin Frazier, and Ralph Bunche, 1919–1941* (Durham: University of North Carolina Press, 2002).

26. Many people are already beginning to do work in this area. See Fabio Rojas, *From Black Power to Black Studies: How a Radical Social Movement Became an Academic Discipline* (Baltimore: John Hopkins Press, 2007); Williamson, *Black Power on Campus*; Glasker, *Black Studies in the Ivory Tower*; McCormick, *The Black Student Protest Movement at Rutgers*; and Bradley, *Harlem vs. Columbia*. For the discussion of Black College students and the student movement to start Black Studies, see Robert Malson, "The Black Power Rebellion at Howard University," *Negro Digest*, December 1967, 20–30; and three special issues of *Negro Digest* on "Toward the Black University," March 1968, March 1969, and March 1970.

27. McGann, who was a Cornell graduate student in the Department of Government at the time, would later become the U.S. Ambassador to the Republics of Fiji, Nauru, Kiribati, and the United Kingdom of Tonga and Tuvalu.

28. Manning Marable first used the term "left nationalist" to describe the politics of James Turner, Ronald Daniels, and William Strickland (two of Turner's longtime friends and comrades) in his essay "Through the Prism of Race and Class: Black Nationalism Since the Civil Rights Movement," in *Blackwater: Historical Studies in Race, Class Consciousness and Revolution* (Dayton: Black Praxis Press, 1981). In fact, the book was published during Marable's tenure as an Associate Professor of Political Economy at the Africana Studies and Research Center (AS&RC) at Cornell. Indeed, the AS&RC was not only a precursor to Columbia's Institute for Research in African American Studies, which Marable helped create; it could also be argued that the AS&RC served as an institutional example and model for Marable.

29. James Turner and W. Eric Perkins, "Towards a Critique of Social Science," *Black Scholar* 7, no. 7 (April 1976): 2–11. At the time William Eric Perkins was a professor at SUNY-Purchase. He would later edit *Droppin' Science: Critical Essays on Rap Music and Hip Hop Culture* (Philadelphia: Temple University Press, 1996).

30. See LaTasha Levy, "Remembering Sixth-PAC: Interviews with Sylvia Hill and Judy Claude, Organizers of the Sixth Pan-African Congress," *Black Scholar* 37, no. 4 (Winter 2008): 39–47; Horace Campbell, "The Sixth Pan-African Congress, June 19–27, 1974: An Assessment," in *Pan-Africanism: The Struggle Against Imperialism and Neo-Colonialism, Documents of the Sixth Pan-African Congress* (Toronto: Afro-Carib Publications, 1975), 169–98;

Modibo Kadalie, *Internationalism, Pan-Africanism and the Struggle of Social Classes* (Savannah, GA: One Quest Press, 1975); Walter Rodney, "Towards the Sixth Pan-African Congress: Aspects of the International Class Struggle in Africa, the Caribbean and America," in *Resolutions and Selected Speeches from the Sixth Pan-African Congress* (Dar es Salaam, Tanzania: Tanzania Publishing House, 1976), 21–34; and Marable, *Blackwater*, 93–128; Ronald Walters, *Pan Africanism in the African Diaspora: An Analysis of Modern Afro-centric Movements* (Detroit: Wayne State University Press, 1993); and Fanon Che Wilkins, "'In the Belly of the Beast': Black Power, Anti-Imperialism, and the African Liberation Solidarity Movement, 1968–1975" (PhD diss., New York University, 2001); Cedric Johnson, "From Popular Anti-Imperialism to Sectarianism: The African Liberation Support Committee and Black Power Radicals," *New Political Science* 25, no. 4 (December 2003): 477–507.

31. Haki Madhubuti, "Sixth Pan-Afrikan Congress: What Is Being Done to Save the Black Race," *Black Books Bulletin* 2 (Fall 1974): 44–51; Haki Madhubuti, "The Latest Purge," *Black Scholar* 6, no. 1 (September 1974): 43–56; Amiri Baraka, "Some Questions about the Sixth Pan-African Congress," *Black Scholar* 6, no. 2 (October 1974): 42–46; "Amiri Baraka Interview," *Black Books Bulletin* 2, no. 2 (1974): 33–37, 40–43.

32. In fact, the 1980s saw an explosion of texts that charted ways to "re-Africanize" Black communities and articulate methods to return Black people to the source of their "natural" cultural trajectory, which, as the argument follows, was interrupted by slavery and Western imperialism. Works like these were marketable for independent Black publishing companies in an era that saw the ascent of the New Age movement and a rising American interest in occultism, astrology, esotericism, alternative medicines, holistic health, metaphysics, and natural homeopathic medicines. Some examples include Llaila O. Afrika, *Afrikan Holistic Health* (Brooklyn: A&B Publishers, 1983); Na'im Akbar, *The Community of Self* (Tallahassee: Mind Productions and Associates, 1985); and Wade Nobles, *African Psychology: Towards Its Reclamation, Reascension and Revitalization* (Oakland: Institute for the Advanced Study of Family, Life and Culture, 1986).

33. Daryl Michael Scott, *Contempt and Pity: The Social Policy and the Image of the Damaged Black Psyche, 1880–1996* (Durham: University of North Carolina Press, 1997).

34. James Turner, "Africana Studies and Epistemology," in *The Next Decade: Theoretical and Research Issues in Africana Studies*, ed. James Turner (Ithaca, NY: Africana Studies & Research 1984), v–xxv.

35. See "Transnational Black Studies," *Radical History Review*, no. 87 (Fall 2003).

36. St. Clair Drake, "The Black Diaspora in Pan-African Perspective," *Black Scholar* 7, no. 1 (1975): 2–14; St. Clair Drake, "Diaspora Studies and Pan-Africanism," in *Global Dimensions of the African Diaspora*, ed. Joseph Harris (Washington, DC: Howard University Press, 1982); St. Clair Drake, *Black Folk Here and There*, vol. 1 (Los Angeles: Center for Afro-American Studies at the University California at Los Angeles, 1987); St. Clair Drake, "Black Studies and Global Perspectives: An Essay," *Journal of Negro Education* 53, no. 3 (1984): 226–42; John Henrik Clarke, "Africana Studies: A Decade of Change, Challenge and Conflict," in *The Life and Times of John Henrik Clarke*, ed. James L. Conyers Jr. and Julius E. Thompson (Trenton, NJ: Africa World Press, 2004).

37. Paul Gilroy, *The Black Atlantic: Modernity and Double Consciousness* (Cambridge, MA: Harvard University Press, 1993); Rinaldo Walcott, "Beyond the 'Nation Thing': Black Studies, Cultural Studies and Diaspora Discourse (or the Post-Black Studies Moment)," in *Decolonizing the Academy: African Diaspora Studies*, ed. Carole Boyce Davies, Meredith Gadsby, Charles Peterson, and Henrietta Williams (Trenton, NJ: Africa World Press, 2003); Michael Hanchard, "Identity, Meaning and the African-American," *Social Text* 24 (1990): 31–42.

38. Jonathan Fenderson, "Pan-African Scholarship: W.E.B. Du Bois, Carter G. Woodson and the Encyclopedia Africana," *Journal of African American History* 95, no. 1 (2010): 71–91.

39. James Turner, "Africana Studies and Epistemology: A Discourse in the Sociology of Knowledge," in *The Next Decade: Theoretical and Research Issues in Africana Studies*, ed. James Turner (Ithaca, NY: Africana Studies & Research 1984), viii

40. One could argue that Turner's notion of "Africana" is a fusion of the African focus of the Area Studies project (absent the politically conservative agenda of various U.S. intelligence agencies) and African American Studies (referencing the "Americas"), but his persistent use of terms like "the Black World" and "global black experience" transforms his definition into something more expansive.

41. Jonathan Fenderson, "The Black Studies Tradition and the Mappings of Our Common Intellectual Project," *Western Journal of Black Studies* 33, no. 1 (2009): 46–58.

42. Shihan de S. Jayasuriya and Richard Pankhurst, *The African Diaspora in the Indian Ocean* (Trenton, NJ: Africa World Press, 2003).

43. In recent years, the misuses of the term "Africana" has led Turner to refer to the discipline as "Black/Africana Studies." James Stewart, Maulana Karenga, and Turner agree that the use of the term "Black" (in Black Studies or Black/Africana Studies) denotes a political history and grounding that is often (in)advertently left out when scholars use the phrase "Africana" as a "corrective" to "Black." While I empathize with their critique and understand their concern to be completely valid (and accurate), I also think that part of the problem is that scholars have detached the term "Africana" from its political history (and uses). As a result, I am more inclined to work to unearth the sociopolitical origins of the term and struggle over its uses, instead of inserting "Black" as a caveat. By struggling over the history and meaning of "Africana" and tracing its entrance into the Black Studies lexicon, we also draw attention to the specific movement for Black Studies at Cornell and the important role played by James Turner in Black Studies' intellectual history—this is not necessarily the case when we make the more pragmatic move to place the word "Black" in front of "Africana Studies." In other words, this pragmatic move to place "Black" in front of "Africana Studies" does not force those who misuse the term into a posture where they have to defend their views carefully and with intellectual rigor; instead it forfeits the term (and its history) and lets them off the hook. See Maulana Karenga, "Names and Notions of Black Studies," *Journal of Black Studies* 40, no. 1 (2009): 41–64; Noliwe Rooks, *White Money, Black Power: The Surprising History of African American Studies and the Crisis of Race and Higher Education* (Boston: Beacon Press, 2006).

44. Francis Njubi Nesbitt, *Race for Sanctions: African Americans Against Apartheid, 1946–1994* (Bloomington: Indiana University Press, 2004). See also the forthcoming work of Ronald Williams, "Adversarial Diplomacy: Randall Robinson, the Organization TransAfrica, and the Rise of the African American Foreign Policy Lobby," paper presented at the annual meeting of the 95th Annual Convention, Raleigh, NC, November 11, 2014.

45. Patricia Hill Collins, *Black Feminist Thought: Knowledge, Consciousness and the Politics of Empowerment*, 2nd ed. (New York: Routledge, 2000); Clenora Hudson-Weems, *Africana Womanism: Reclaiming Ourselves* (Troy, MI: Bedford, 1993).

46. It should be noted that Henry Louis Gates Jr. was a professor in the Africana Studies and Research Center while he was teaching at Cornell between 1985 and 1988. It was during this time that he began to accumulate academic cache, acclaim, and capital as a leading scholar in the field of African American literature, publishing *Figures in Black* (1987) and *The Signifying Monkey* (1988). As was the case with Manning Marable, it could be argued that

the Africana Studies and Research Center at Cornell provided Gates with a model for Black Studies, which he appropriated, altered (jettisoning radical politics), and capitalized on (or corporatized) at Harvard. Gates's decision to consolidate the African Studies Program and the African American Studies Program into a single Department of African and African American Studies had institutional precedents at Cornell. Needless to say, Turner's **AS&RC** model at Cornell showed both Marable and Gates that a Black Studies unit could transcend mere departmental or program status, incorporate graduate studies, and contribute to the "respectable" scholarly output on campus, while remaining an independent and productive site of academic research.

47. Originally published in *Ebony* 24, no. 10 (August 1969): 135–40.

48. James Boggs, *Manifesto for a Black Revolutionary Party* (Philadelphia: Pacesetters Publishing House, 1969), 1.

49. Boggs, *Manifesto*, 5.

50. Originally published in the *Cornell Chronicle* 1, no. 2 (1969): 1–8.

51. *Twentieth Century Man: A Black Perspective* (Raleigh, NC: Shaw University, 1968).

52. The script and ideas carried under the headings Africana Studies and Research Center and Basic Program Elements were derived largely from documents developed by scholars and educators at the Institute of the Black World and distributed at a Workshop on Black Studies in which the Center participated.

53. Professor Robert S. Browne has been retained to develop a plan and to do research on the Urban Component under the guidance of and in consultation with the director of the Center. Mr. Browne is director of the Black Economic Research Center in New York City, professor of Economics at Farleigh Dickinson University, and will teach at Rutgers University.

54. Originally published in *Black Lines: A Journal of Black Studies* 1, no. 2 (Winter 1970): 5–8.

55. Originally published (with C. Steven McGann) in the *Journal of Negro Education* 49, no. 1 (1980): 52–59.

56. Sterling Stuckey, "Twilight of Our Past: Reflections on the Origins of Black History," in *Amistad 2*, ed. John A. Williams and Charles F. Harris (New York: Random House, 1971), 261–62.

57. Harold Cruse, *The Crisis of the Negro Intellectual* (New York: Morrow, 1968), 565.

58. Charles Valentine, *Black Studies and Anthropology: Scholarly and Political Interests in Afro-American Culture* (Boston: Addison-Wesley, 1972).

59. W.E.B. Du Bois, *A W.E.B. Du Bois Reader*, ed. H. Aptheker (New York: Macmillan and Company, 1971), 85.

60. Jonathan Grossman, "Black Studies in the Department of Labor, 1897–1907," *Monthly Labor Review* 97, no. 6 (June 1974): 17–27.

61. W.E.B. Du Bois, "The Conservation of Races," in *The Seventh Son: The Thought and Writing of W.E.B. Du Bois*, ed. Julius Lester (New York: Random House, 1971), [1:]176–77 [emphasis added].

62. Arthur H. Schomburg, *Racial Integrity: A Plea for the Establishment of a Chair of Negro History in Our Schools and Colleges* (Yonkers: Negro Society for Historical Research, 1913), 5.

63. Carter G. Woodson, *The A.S.N.L.H.* Leaflet, 1947.

64. Charles V. Roman, "A Plea for Negro History," in *The Black American and Education*, ed. Earle H. West (Columbus: Charles E. Merrill Publishers, 1971), 159.

65. Joseph J. Rhoads, "Proceedings of the 1933 A.S.N.L.H. Meeting," *Journal of Negro History* 19, no. 1 (January 1934).

66. Joseph J. Rhoads, "Teaching the Negro Child," *Journal of Negro History* 19, no. 1 (January 1934): 30.

67. L. D. Reddick, "A New Interpretation of Negro History," *Journal of Negro History* 22, no. 1 (January 1937): 17–18.

68. Ibid., 27–28.

69. Alain Locke, "The New Negro," in *The New Negro*, ed. Alain Locke (New York: Atheneum, 1968), 4.

70. W. T. Fontaine, "An Interpretation of Contemporary Negro Thought from the Standpoint of the Sociology of Knowledge," *Journal of Negro History* 25, no. 1 (January 1940).

71. Originally published (with W. Eric Perkins) in the *Black Scholar* 7, no. 7 (April 1976): 2–11.

72. On this matter, see Harry Haywood, *Negro Liberation* (New York: International Publishers, 1948) and recently reprinted by the October League; W. E. Perkins and John Higginson, "Black Students: Reformists and Revolutionaries," in *The New American Revolution*, ed. Roderick Aya and Norman Miller (New York: Free Press, 1971), 195–222.

73. Herbert Marcus, *Soviet Marxism* (New York: Columbia University Press, 1961).

74. Joel H. Spring, *Education and the Rise of the Corporate State* (Boston: Beacon Press, 1972); Samuel Bowles and Herbert Gintis, *Schooling in Capitalist America* (New York: Basic Books, 1976); and the important book by Mary O. Furner, *Advocacy and Objectivity: A Crisis in the Professionalization of American Social Science, 1865–1906* (Lexington: University Press of Kentucky, 1975).

75. On the model of internal colonialism, see Robert Blauner, *Racial Oppression in America* (New York: Harper & Row, 1972); and Tomas Almagner, "Class, Race, and Chicano Oppression," *Socialist Revolution* 5 (July–September 1975): 71–100.

76. On the oppression of colonial peoples by Western social scientists, see the important essays in Talal Asad, ed., *Anthropology and the Colonial Encounter* (London: Ithaca Press, 1973).

77. Charles Valentine, *Culture and Poverty* (Chicago: University of Chicago Press, 1968).

78. Albert Murray, *The Omni-Americans* (New York: E. P. Dutton, 1970), 38.

79. See Noam Chomsky, *American Power and the New Mandarins* (New York: Pantheon, 1968) and his *For Reasons of State* (New York: Pantheon, 1973), especially the essay "The Function of the University in a Time of Crisis," 318–69; Irving Horowitz, *The Rise and Fall of Project Camelot* (Boston: MIT Press, 1969); on Chile, A. G. Frank, "An Open Letter about Chile to Arnold Harberger and Milton Friedman," *Review of Radical Political Economics* 7 (July 1975): 61–76.

80. On the separation of intellectual and manual work, see Alfred Sohn-Rethel, "Science as Alienated Consciousness," *Radical Science Journal* 2–3 (1975): 65–101, especially 96.

81. Afro-American radicals would do well to become familiar with this journal causing such a stir in the economics profession.

82. Alvin Gouldner, *The Coming Crisis of Western Sociology* (New York: Basic Books, 1970), 483. This is an important book and still undigested by sociologists. Its implications extend far and wide into the ideological nature of contemporary social theory.

83. Perkins and Higginson, "Black Students," 197–98.

84. In much of the poetry and literary criticism, too extensive to interpret here, or as in Kenneth Clark's *Dark Ghetto* (New York: Harper & Row, 1963).

85. On Myrdal, see Ralph Ellison, "An American Dilemma: A Mystical Approach to the Study of Race Relations," *Journal of Negro Education* 14 (1945): 132–48; and on Frazier, see Herbert G. Gutman, "Persistent Myths about the Afro-American Family," *Journal of Interdisciplinary History* 6 (Autumn 1975): 181–210.

86. Karl Marx, "Theses on Feuerbach 3," in *Marx and Engels Basic Writings on Politics and Philosophy*, ed. Lewis Feuer (New York: Doubleday, 1959), 244.

87. Two examples: James Forman, *The Making of Black Revolutionaries* (New York: Macmillan, 1972); and Kirkpatrick Sale, *SDS* (New York: Vintage Books, 1974).

88. The recent debates stirred by the African Liberation Support Committee and the Pan-African Congress, Amiri Baraka's defection to Marxism, and the crumbling of the Portuguese colonial empire leading to the acceleration of liberation in those former colonial territories. For background, see the special edition of *The African World* (July 1974), and for examples of analysis, see Adolph Reed Jr., "Marxism and Nationalism in Afro-America," *Social Theory and Practice* (Fall 1971): 1–39; and Amiri Baraka, *Toward Ideological Clarity* (Newark: Congress of African People, 1974).

89. Lucien Goldman, *The Human Sciences and Philosophy* (London: Cape, 1969), 48. This is an excellent introduction to the practice of a Marxist social science.

90. Karl Marx, "Theses on Feuerbach 11," in *Marx and Engels Basic Writings*, 245.

91. Originally published in *The Next Decade: Theoretical and Research Issues in Africana Studies*, ed. James Turner (Ithaca, NY: Africana Studies and Research Center, 1984). This text was reprinted in 2014 under the title *Theoretical and Research Issues in Africana Studies* by Diasporic Africa Press.

92. John H. Clarke, "Africana Studies: A Decade of Change, Challenge, and Conflict," paper presented at the conference "Consolidating Africana Studies: Bonding African Linkages" on the occasion of the tenth anniversary of the African Studies and Research Center, Cornell University, September 26–28, 1980, 1.

93. A. Wade Boykin, "Black Psychology and the Research Process" (unpublished manuscript), 14.

94. Ibid., 15.

95. Ibid., 16.

96. James B. Stewart, *Toward Operationalization of an "Expansive" Model of Black Studies* (Atlanta: Institute of the Black World, 1983), 1.

97. Ibid., 5.

98. Lorenzo Morris, *Elusive Equality* (Washington, DC: Howard University Press, 1980), 18.

99. Boykin, "Black Psychology and the Research Process," 1.

100. Ibid., 8.

101. Ibid., 7.

102. Sterling Stuckey, comments made during a lecture at a symposium on Black Studies at the Institute of the Black World, Atlanta, 1970.

103. Harold Cruse, comments from a paper presented at a conference sponsored by the University of Michigan on African-American Studies, Ann Arbor, April 1978.

104. Carter G. Woodson, *Mis-education of the Negro* (Washington, DC: Associated Publishers, 1969), 7.

105. Charles Valentine, *Afro-American Studies: An Intellectual Tradition* (New York: Bobbs Merrill Reprint Series, 1980), 9.

106. St. Clair Drake, "Black Studies in Higher Education," *New York University Education Quarterly* 21, no. 3 (1988): 2.

107. Ibid., 4.

108. Ibid., 5.

109. Ibid., 12.

110. Ibid., 13.

111. Richard Goldstein, "The War for America's Mind," *Village Voice*, June 8, 1982.

112. Robert Johnson, "Why Colleges and Students Need Black Studies," *Chronicle of Higher Education*, November 17, 1980, 24.

113. Eleanor Traylor, letter to the director of the National Endowment for the Humanities, Washington, DC, July 1984.

114. Charles Farrell, "Minorities Seen Making No Gains in Campus Jobs," *Chronicle of Higher Education*, June 13, 1984, 1.

115. Anne MacKay-Smith, "Large Shortage of Black Professors in Higher Education Grows Worse," *Wall Street Journal*, July 10, 1984.

116. Farrell, "Minorities," 1.

117. Ibid.

118. Morris, *Elusive Equality*, 18.

119. Laurie R. Hatch and Kent Mommsen, "The Widening Racial Gap in American Higher Education," *Journal of Black Studies* 14, no. 4 (July 1984): 470.

PART IV

1. Jonathan Fenderson and Candace Katungi, "'Committed to Institution Building': James Turner and the History of Africana Studies at Cornell University, an Interview," *Journal of African American Studies* 16 (2012): 127.

2. LaTasha Levy, "Remembering Sixth-PAC: Interviews with Sylvia Hill and Judy Claude, Organizers of the Sixth Pan-African Congress," *Black Scholar* 34, no. 4 (Winter 2008): 46.

3. For a discussion of the founding of the African Heritage Studies Association and the controversial split from the African Studies Association, see Ronald W. Walters, *Pan-Africanism in the African Diaspora: An Analysis of Modern Afrocentric Movements* (Detroit: Wayne State University Press, 1993), 364–72.

4. Fenderson and Catungi, "Committed to Institution Building," 127.

5. For a history of the Sixth Pan-African Congress, see James Garrett, "A Historical Sketch: The Sixth Pan-African Congress," *Black World* 24, no. 5 (March 1975): 6–20; Fanon Che Wilkins, "'A Line of Steel': The Organization of the Sixth Pan-African Congress and the Struggle for International Black Power, 1969–1974," in *The Hidden Seventies: Histories of Radicalism*, ed. Dan Berger (New Brunswick, NJ: Rutgers University Press, 2010), 97–114.

6. For a history of the Fifth Pan-African Congress, see P. Olisanwuche Esedebe, *Pan Africanism: The Idea and Movement, 1776–1991* (Washington, DC: Howard University Press, 1994), 137–64; Imanuel Geiss, *The Pan-African Movement: A History of Pan-Africanism in America, Europe and Africa* (New York: Africana Publishing, 1974), 229–62; George Padmore, ed., *History of the Pan-African Congress: Colonial and Coloured Unity, a Program of Action* (London: Hammersmith Bookshop, 1963); George Padmore, *Pan-Africanism or Communism?: The Coming Struggle for Africa* (London: D. Dobson, 1956); and Penny Von Eschen, *Race Against Empire: Black Americans and Anticolonialism 1937–1957* (Ithaca, NY: Cornell University Press, 1997), 45–54.

7. Julius Nyerere, like Kwame Nkrumah, invited Blacks in the Diaspora to contribute to Tanzania's development. In fact, a number of Black Americans, notably members of the Student Nonviolent Coordinating Committee, comprised a small but significant community of expatriates. Tanzania became a home for African liberation movements, and Nyerere offered political asylum to Black activists who were targets of state aggression in the United States and the Caribbean. With such a vibrant and diverse community, the University of Dar es Salaam was the hub of consciousness-raising and political education for students and activists in Africa and revolutionaries in the Third World. In addition, Nyerere's *Arusha Declaration* and *Education for Self-Reliance*, published in 1967, inspired activists, educators, workers, and others throughout the Black world to maintain a commitment to socialism, self-reliance, and African liberation. Tanzania was therefore an ideal location to host the Sixth Pan-African Congress.

8. Kwame Nkrumah did not live to see the convening of the Sixth Pan-African Congress. He transitioned in 1972.

9. During the initial planning stages of the Six PAC from 1969–71, Bermudan activist Pauulu Kamarakafego coordinated organizational efforts along with Sonia Sanchez, Liz Gant, and James Garrett, among others. When Kamarakafego resigned, Courtland Cox accepted the position as international secretariat general. Cox moved the Six PAC headquarters to the Center for Black Education, an independent Black educational institution dedicat-

ed to training students in science and technology for Africa's development. Other African Americans who joined the organizational efforts included Ka Flewellen, Loretta Hobbs, Geri Augusto, JoAnne Favors, Judy Claude, and Charles Cobb.

10. For reflections on the tensions and contradictions of the Sixth Pan-African Congress, see Horace Campbell, "The Sixth Pan-African Congress, June 19–27, 1974: An Assessment," in *Pan-Africanism: The Struggle Against Imperialism and Neo-Colonialism: Documents of the Sixth Pan-African Congress with Assessment by Horace Campbell* (Toronto: Afro-Carib Publication, 1975), 169–98; Judy Claude, "Some Personal Reflections on the Sixth Pan-African Congress," *Black Scholar* 37, no. 4 (Winter 2008): 48–49; and Walter Rodney, "Towards the Sixth Pan-African Congress: Aspects of the International Class Struggle in Africa," in *Pan-Africanism: The Struggle Against Imperialism and Neo-Colonialism: Documents of the Sixth Pan-African Congress with Assessment by Horace Campbell* (Toronto: Afro-Carib Publication, 1975), 18–41.

11. Lerone Bennett, "Pan Africanism at the Crossroads," *Ebony* 30, no. 2 (September 1974): 159.

12. Sylvia Hill, for instance, returned to Washington, DC, and along with Ka Flewellen, JoAnne Favors, and other women activists founded the Southern Africa News Collective and later the Southern Africa Support Project in 1978. She was also involved in the TransAfrica Forum.

13. For examinations of the anti-apartheid struggle as an extension of Pan-Africanism, see William Minter, Gail Hovey, and Charles Cobb Jr., eds., *No Easy Victories: African Liberation and American Activists over a Half Century, 1950–2000* (Trenton, NJ: Africa World Press, 2008), 157–66; Francis Njubi Nesbitt, *Race for Sanctions: African Americans Against Apartheid, 1946–1994* (Bloomington: Indiana University Press, 2004); Lako Tongun, "Pan-Africanism and Apartheid: African American Influence on US Foreign Policy," in *Imagining Home: Class, Culture, and Nationalism in the African Diaspora*, ed. Sidney Lemelle and Robin D. G. Kelley (London: Verso, 1994), 243–82.

14. It is important to note that Turner's work begins the process of unpacking Pan-African history, but it also falls short of disrupting masculinist narratives, a shortcoming he intently addresses later in his career. Scholarly attention to grassroots struggles and organizations (rather than personalities) uncover the spheres of Black women's influence and contributions, as well as the gendered constraints inherent in Pan-African ideologies. The continual focus on Black male leaders, personalities, and individuals in Pan-African historiography solidifies the invisibility and silences of Black women's Pan-

African theories and praxis—a silencing that is too often reproduced by the critics of Pan-Africanism.

15. Turner's teachings, at their very core, call for pliancy as an integral part of intellectual growth and development. To this end, he consistently pushed his students to engage in *dialectics* as a way to discover one's position, understand opposing views, and work toward synthesis in the pursuit of the truth. Far from dogmatic or essentialist, Turner exhibited progressive Black Nationalist and Pan-African approaches that, at the very least, remained open to engagement and interaction.

16. Originally published (with Rukudzo Murapa) in *Africa Today* 16, nos. 5–6 (1969): 13–14.

17. Originally published in *Black World* 23, no. 5 (March 1974): 11–19.

18. Originally published in the *Western Journal of Black Studies* 3, no. 2 (1979): 80–91.

19. [According to] George M. Houser, executive director of the American Committee on Africa.

20. Less well known is South Africa's importance as a major source of platinum, vanadium, zinc, and various other strategic minerals. For example, southern Africa is the only source (outside of the Soviet Union) for such strategic minerals as: chromium—Rhodesia and South Africa together hold eighty-nine percent of the "free world's" reserve; manganese—one-third of the world reserves; and sizeable deposits of fluorspar, nickel, asbestos, germanium, titanium and lithium.

21. From *Focus*, Bulletin of the International Defense and Aid Fund, London.

22. From a report by managing director of Market Research Africa, W. Tangschmidt, cited in *Johannesburg Star*, August 3, 1974.

23. Ruth Milkman, "Apartheid, Economic Growth and U.S. Foreign Policy in South Africa," *Berkeley Journal of Sociology* 22 (1977–78): 45–100.

24. Tony Roenderman, "Sanctions," in *South African Foundation Briefing Papers*, no. 11, November 1978.

25. Direct investment is used to mean investment of a non-resident (person or corporation) who has a controlling interest in a South African organization. Control means the holding of at least twenty-five percent of the voting or ownership rights by a single person or several affiliated person, ownership of at least fifty percent of the voting rights in a South African organization by various residents in one country. Direct investment is thus distinguished from loans, thought both are sometimes referred to loosely as "investment" or more usually "foreign liabilities."

26. Jennifer Davis, *U.S. Dollars in South Africa: Context and Consequence* (New York: The Africa Fund, 1978).

27. John Burns, "Full Sanctions Awkward: South Africa is Big Business," *New York Times*, November 6, 1977.

28. S. Brand, "The Relation Between Economic Growth and External Balance in South Africa," *South African Journal of Economics* 30 (1962): 302.

29. Sean Gervasi, *Industrialization Foreign Capital and Forced Labor in South Africa* (New York: UN Unit on Apartheid, 1970), 60.

30. Barbara Rogers, *White Wealth and Black Poverty: American Investments in Southern Africa* (Westport, CT: Greenwood Press, 1976), 97.

31. Ibid., 33.

32. Ibid., 127.

33. Donald McHenry, *United States Corporations in South Africa* (Bloomington: Indiana University Press, 1975).

34. Jennifer Davis, *General Motors in South Africa: Secret Contingency Plans* (New York: The Africa Fund, 1978).

35. Ibid.

36. *Racism and Apartheid in Southern Africa* (New York: UNESCO, 1976).

37. In manufacturing the average monthly wage for Whites was $714, for Blacks, $148.40; in mining, $868 vs. $103.60.

38. J. R. Friedman and Diana Ellis, "The Depressed State of the South African Population under Apartheid in the Republic of South Africa" (New York: United Nations, 1976).

39. Clyde Ferguson and William R. Cotter, "South Africa: What Is to Be Done?" *Foreign Affairs* 56, no. 2 (1978).

40. This section is drawn from a position paper of TransAfrica, Washington, DC, 1978, on whose Board of Directors the author serves.

41. Originally published in the *Journal of Black Studies* 2, no. 1 (1971): 3–27.

42. Robert Merton, *Dictionary of American Sociology* (Englewood Cliffs, NJ: Prentice Hall 1967), 294.

43. Theodore W. Schultz, "Capital Formation by Education," *Journal of Political Economy* 68, no. 6 (1960): 571–83.

44. L. Gray Cowan, James O'Connell, and David G. Scanlon, eds., *Education and Nation-Building in Africa* (New York: Frederick A. Praeger, 1965), 5.

45. H. M. Phillips, "Education as a Basic Factor in Economic and Social Development," Final Report of the Conference of African States on the Development of Education in Africa, Paris, UNESCO.

46. Charles E. Merriam, *The Making of Citizens* (Chicago: University of Chicago Press, 1961).

47. Cowan et al., *Education and Nation-Building in Africa*, 6.

48. F. X. Sutton, "Education in Changing Africa," Address at the Eighth National Conference of the U. S. Commission for UNESCO, Boston, MA, October 24, 1961.

49. Remi Clignet and Philip Foster, *The Fortunate Few* (Evanston, IL: Northwestern University Press, 1966).

50. Western Region, House Assembly, 1952: 363–70.

51. David B. Abernathy, "Education and the Politics in a Developing Society: The Southern Nigerian Experience" (PhD diss., Harvard University, 1965), 319.

52. Ibid.

53. Ibid.

54. Eastern Region, Debates (1956) Enugu, Nigeria.

55. Abernathy, "Education," 520–21.

56. J. O'Connell, "Education, Economics, and Politics," in *Education and Nation-Building in Africa*, ed. L. Gray Cowan et al. (New York: Frederick A. Praeger, 1965), 188.

57. Ibid.

58. O. Ogunsheye, "Nigeria," in *Education and Political Development*, ed. James S. Coleman (Princeton, NJ: Princeton University Press, 1965).

59. M. A. Herbert and J. Getzels, "The Social Sciences: Conceptual Framework for Education," *Journal of School Review* 65 (Autumn 1957): 346.

60. B. F. Hoselitz, "Investment in Education and its Political Impact," in *Education and Political Development*, ed. James S. Coleman (Princeton, NJ: Princeton University Press, 1965).

61. James S. Coleman, ed., *Education and Political Development* (Princeton, NJ: Princeton University Press, 1965), 20.

62. Gabriel Almond and James S. Coleman, eds., *The Politics of Developing Areas* (Princeton, NJ: Princeton University Press, 1960), 27.

63. A. W. Lewis, "Education Economic Development," in *Education and Nation-Building in Africa*, ed. L. Gray Cowan et al. (New York: Frederick A. Praeger, 1965), 201.

64. Clignet and Foster, *The Fortunate Few*, 349.

65. Philip J. Foster, "Secondary Schooling and Social Mobility in a West African Nation," *Sociology of Education* 37, no. 2 (Winter 1963).

66. G. McConnell, "The Political Aims of Education in Developing Countries," in *Education and the Development of Nations*, ed. Hobert W. Burns (Syracuse, NY: Syracuse University Press, 1963), 40.

67. F. W. Riggs, "Bureaucrats and Political Development," in *Political Development and Social Change*, ed. Jason Finkel and Richard Gable (New York: John Wiley and Sons, 1966), 413.

68. S. Dube, "The Bureaucracy," in *Political Development and Social Change*, ed. Jason Finkel and Richard Gable (New York: John Wiley and Sons, 1966).

69. A. W. Lewis, "Education Economic Development," 203.

70. Ibid.

71. Adam Curle, *The Role of Education in Developing Societies* (Accra: Ghana University Press, 1961), 7–8.

72. Coleman, *Education and Political Development*, 358.

73. Archibald Callaway, "Underemployment among African School Leaders," *Journal of Modern African Studies* 1, no. 3 (September 1963): 351–71.

74. Coleman, *Education and Political Development*, 29.

75. Callaway, "Underemployment," 351.

76. Margaret J. Field, *Search for Security: An Ethno-Psychiatric Study of Rural Ghana* (London: Faber and Faber, 1962).

77. Coleman, *Education and Political Development*, 73.

PART V

1. Originally published in the *Black Scholar* 1, no. 6 (April 1970): 9–13.

2. The term *African* is used here in keeping with the recent decision made by an international group of Black scholars at the African Studies Association meeting in Montreal of November 1969 that defines all Black people as African peoples and negates the tribalization of African peoples by geographic demarcation based on colonialist spheres of influence.

3. James Boggs, *Manifesto for a Black Revolutionary Party* (Philadelphia: Pacesetters Publishing House, 1969), 1–16.

4. *Jet* 35, no. 13 (Jan. 2, 1969): 30.

5. Boggs, *Manifesto*, 9.

6. Originally published in the *Review of Black Political Economy* 6, no. 2 (1976): 133–44.

7. For a fuller analysis of the divisive forces within classes, see D. F. Dowd, *The Twisted Dream* (Cambridge, MA: Winthrop, 1974), 127. This work provides many historically oriented insights relevant to this paper.

8. For a detailed account of how a neocolonial economy is made to serve the interests of multinational firms and the indigenous comprador class, often with the help of pressure from the government of the former colonial power, see *The Lichauce Paper, Monthly Review*, special edition for July–August 1973. For a theoretical analysis with special reference to Africa, see Samir Amin, "Transitional Phases in Sub-Saharan Africa," *Monthly Review* (October 1973) and the book (by Arrighi and Saul) reviewed by Amin. Insights concerning the ways in which a comprador class, working in part through

the government, may exploit the peasant and working classes will be found in articles on Ivory Coast by Michael A. Cohen, *Journal of Modern African Studies* (1972, 1973).

9. Their writings, available in various paperback editions, offer a good analysis of the weaknesses of the colonial heritage and of the alternatives to neocolonial development.

10. Originally published in the *Black Collegian* 25, no. 2 (February 1995): 123–26.

11. This speech was given on the commemoration of the 50th anniversary of the desegregation of U.S. public education at Cornell University's Africana Studies and Research Center, April 29, 2005. Speakers included Robert L. Harris, Derrick A. Bell, Charles Ogletree, and Kimberlé Crenshaw. A video recording of the event can be found in the Cornell University library: https://newcatalog.library.cornell.edu/catalog/6045630.

INDEX

PAGE NUMBERS IN ITALICS INDICATE
PHOTOGRAPHS.

Bracey, John, 18
Bradley, Stefan, 96
Britain, 224
Brooks, Gwendolyn, *32*
Brown, H. Rap, 86–87
Brown, Scot, 7–8, 307–308
Browne, Robert S., 324–325n14, 330n53
Brown v. The Board of Education, 288, 292–293 *See also* Integration; Segregation
Bruce, John Edward, 80–82, 318n84, 319n88, 319n90
Bukhari, Safiya, 46–47, 49–50
Bunche, Ralph, 150
'Bureaucratic ethos,' 160
Burke, Fred, 202

C

Call to Rebellion (Garnet), 59
Capitalism: Black middle class and Black capitalism, 262–264, 282; fundamental relationships in, 205, 229; influence of, 170; Marxist challenges to, 159; neocolonial ties to, 277–278; racial, 196–197; technology and race in, 264; trade between Africa and capitalists, 219
Caribbean: as Africana member, 106, 122–124, 145, 170, 188; colonization of, 156, 206; color standards in, 76; Great Depression impacting, 204; at Pan-African Congresses, 194, 208, 210–211; study of, 176 *See also* 'Africana' as a theoretical framework
Carlos, John, 119, 303
Carnegie Corporation's study of race relations, 150
Carter, Gwendolyn, 25
Cary, Mary Ann Shad, 78

Castes, 65, 76, 111 *See also* Class; Class consciousness
Césaire, Aimé, 64, 72
Chicago Circle Campus, 113
Chilembwe, John, 206
China, 284
Christian Recorder (periodical), 79
Chronicle of Higher Education, 181–182
Churchville, John, 136
Citizenship, 83
Civil disobedience, 20
Civil Rights, 87, 259, 267, 288
Clark, Dick, 220
Clark, Kenneth, 54–55
Clarke, John Henrik: as ASA dissenter, 25–26, 189; on Black vs. Africana Studies, 168; influence of, 15, 106, 266; teaching at ASRC, *29*; as Turner's mentor, 4
Class: Black middle class, 262–264, 275–280, 285; intra-class hierarchies, 276, 278–279, 281; race and, 269, 298; skin color and, 77–81, 319n89; socioeconomic phenomenon of, 276 *See also* Castes
Class consciousness, 64 *See also* Castes
Clemente, Rosa, 254
Cloward, Richard, 16
Cole, Johnetta, 96
Coleman, James, 157–158
Collective perception, 174
College admission trends, 113
Collier-Thomas, Bettye, 50–51
Collins, Patricia, 109
Colonialism: art of colonization, 138; European, 191, 206–209; Fanon on, 50–51; internal, 56, 156, 261–263, 269–272, 282; modern day, 269–270; protest perspective of revolutionaries, 139; resistance of, 41–43, 193–195,

340n2; results of Nationalist movements against, 235; study of, 97 *See also* Exploitation of Africa; Slavery; White supremacy

Color: class and, 77–81, 86, 319n89; intragroup color consciousness, 75–77, 89, 318n81; literature on, 317n74; as a race, class and gender issue, 81; race designation determined by, 76–79; in social psychology of Blacks, 88

Colorblindness, 72, 258, 267, 305

Colored (nomenclature), 77–78, 79, 84, 85

'Colored Society in Washington,' 319n88

'The Color Line,' 80

Colorphobia, 77, 79, 80–81 *See also* Racism

Combahee River Collective, 48

The Coming Crisis of Western Sociology (Gouldner), 160

'Coming of Age: A Black Revolutionary,' 47

Committee for a Free World, 180

Community networks, 18

The Condition, Elevation, Emigration and Destiny of the Colored People of the United States Politically Considered (Delany), 59

Consciousness, 50–51

Constitutional Law and Minority Issues, 300

Contempt and Pity: The Social Policy and the Image of the Damaged Black Psyche, 1880–1996 (Scott), 105

Conyer, James, 106

Cooper, Anna Julia, 258

CORE, 72–73

Cornell Chronicle, 97–98

Cornell University, 4, 24, 26–27, 38 *See also* Africana Studies and Research Center (AS&RC)

Corson, Dale, 28

Coser, Lewis, 71

Cox, Oliver, 258

Crenshaw, Kimberlé, 292–306

The Crisis of the Negro Intellectual (Cruse), 150

Critical race theory, 292–293, 303–304

Critical Race Theory, 294

Critique of American sociology, 159–160

Crouchett, Lawrence, 102

Crummel, Alexander, 143

Cruse, Harold, 141, 150, 175

Cuffee, Paul, 58

Cultural Nationalism, 149–150

Culture: Black consciousness promoting, 87; dispossession of, 59, 70; Re-Africanization of Black communities, 105, 163–164, 327n32; role of in politics, 55–57

D

Daniels, Ron, 5

Davis, Angela Y., 44

Declaration to the Colonial Workers, Farmers, and Intellectuals, 211

'Defining Ourselves: One Name, One Discipline?', 323–324n11

Delany, Martin, 59, 207

Democracy in economics, 284

Dialectics, Turner encouraging use of, 337n15

Diaspora Studies, 26, 106, 189–191, 197, 307 *See also* African Diaspora

Discipline of Africana Studies, 108, 110

Dispersion, 274

Dollard, John, 315n41

Fred Douglass Book Center, 15, 188
Free African Society, 58
Freedom's Journal, 74
Friedman, Julian, 230

G

Gangs, 16
Garnet, Henry Highland, 59, 206
Garvey, Amy Jacques, 83
Garvey, Marcus, 58, 60–61, 83, 85–86,
    117, 265
Garveyism, 149
Gates, Henry Louis, Jr., 110,
    329–330n46
Gender, 43–44, 81, 108–109
Gender politics of Black Panther Party,
    49–50
General Motors, 221, 225–228, 230
Germany, 208
Gervasi, Sean, 223
Ghana, 278
Gilroy, Paul, 106
Glover, Danny, *293*
Goldmann, Lucien, 165–166
Gonsalves, Anton, 78
Goodwin, Vince (Kalonji Olusegun), 16
Gouldner, Alvin, 159, 160
Gourdine, Meredith, *100*
Gramsci, A., 296–297
Great Depression era, 146, 158, 204
Group Areas Act, 225
Group boundaries, 45, 60, 64, 71

H

'Hamite hypothesis,' 200–201
Hansberry, Leo, 200
Hare, Nathan, 20, 22–23
Harlem, 272, 281

Harris, A.L., 149
Harris, C.R., 319n90
Harris, Luke, 306
Harris, Robert, 8
Harvard, 110, 182, 299–304
Haskins, Jacquelyn L., *31*
Hatch, Laurie, 183
Hayford, Casely, 207
Herskovits: At the Heart of Darkness (film),
    323n8
Hill, Sylvia, 189, 192, 336n12
Historiography of Black Studies, 309n1
History impacting education, 167,
    171–172, 175
Horton, Africanus, 207
Howard University: activism at, 19–23;
    Black graduates of, 182; Studies in
    History series, 145; Studies in the So-
    cial Sciences, 148, 152; Toward a
    Black University conference at, 97;
    Young Turks of, 103, 325–326n25
Hudson-Weems, Clenora, 109
Hughes, Langston, 113–114

I

IBM, 215, 221, 224–225
Iconography, 27
Ideology: in community-building,
    137–139; critique of American sociol-
    ogy, 159–160, 173; defending,
    180–181; in education, 141,
    153–154, 158, 162–163, 179; legal,
    303; non-capitalist, 278–280; in pro-
    motion of social change, 282–283;
    tension in at Six PAC, 194 *See also*
    Pan-Africanism
Ignorance about Blacks, 121
Ikoku, Alvan, 239
Illinois Institute of Technology, 113

Imperialism. *See* Colonialism

'Implications of Class Conflict and Racial Cleavage for the U.S. Black Community,' 263, 275–285 *See also* Racism

Incarceration, 265

'Inequity in the System: Racism in American Society and on College Campuses,' 265

Innis, Roy, 270

Institute of the Black World, 167

Institution-Building. *See* Africana Studies and Research Center (AS&RC)

Integration, 69, 118, 150, 157 *See also Brown v. The Board of Education*

'Integration is Dead,' 50–52

Intellectual history of Black Studies, 102–104, 109, 125, 329n43

Interdisciplinary approach of black studies, 30, 99, 108, 170

Interfaith Center for Corporate Responsibility, 215

Internal contradictions of Black nationalism, 45–50

International Harvester, 228

Introduction to Afro-American Studies, 171, 180

Introduction to Black Studies (Karenga), 180

'Is Ebony Killing the Black Woman?', 66–67

Ithaca: activism in, 33; relationship with AS&RC, 4–5, 32–33, 99, *109, 246*; resident protesters, 27; South Side Community Center's outreach to, 33

J

James, C.L.R., 41–42, 53, 194

John Henrik Clarke Africana Library, 100

Johnson, Robert C., 181

Jones, C. Dalton, *100, 257*

Jones, Faustine, 180

Joseph, Gloria, *46,* 115, 324n12

Journal of Black Studies, 196, 323–324n11

Journal of Negro Education, 104

Journal of Negro History, 145

A Journal of Opinion, 104

K

Kamarakafego, Pauulu, 335n9

Karenga, Maulana, 55, 167, 180

Katungi, Candace, 187–188

Kelley, Robin D. G., 37

Killens, John O., 68–69

Kilson, Martin, 68

Kissinger, Henry, 157, 158

Kitabu Kingdom bookstore, 7

Knowledge: ideological functions of, 159; normative judgements in, 173, 178; politics and, 153, 158, 166; purpose of in teleology of Africana studies, 171; sociology of, 173–174, 297 *See also* 'Africana Studies and Epistemology: a Discourse in the Sociology of Knowledge'

Kofsky, Frank, 71

L

Labor surplus, 271

Lasch, Christopher, 56–57, 118

Law of Personal Presuppositions, 174

League of Nations, 208, 209

'Left nationalists,' 104, 326n28 *See also* Black Nationalism

Lester, Julius, 56

Levy, Latasha, 187–189

Liberation, vision of, 56

Liberator, 320–321n103

CPSIA information can be obtained at www.ICGtesting.com
Printed in the USA
BVOW06s2051120916

461772BV00003B/1/P

9 781937 306212